The Holocaust in Italian Culture, 1944–2010

lat

be re...

The Holocaust in Italian Culture, 1944–2010

Robert S. C. Gordon

Stanford University Press

Stanford, California

Stanford University Press
Stanford, California

©2012 by the Board of Trustees of the Leland Stanford Junior University.
All rights reserved.

No part of this book may be reproduced or transmitted in any form or by
any means, electronic or mechanical, including photocopying and recording, or in any information storage or retrieval system without the prior
written permission of Stanford University Press.

Printed in the United States of America on acid-free, archival-quality paper

Library of Congress Cataloging-in-Publication Data

Gordon, Robert S. C. (Robert Samuel Clive), 1966- author.
  The Holocaust in Italian culture, 1944-2010 / Robert S.C. Gordon.
    pages cm
  Includes bibliographical references and index.
  ISBN 978-0-8047-6345-5 (cloth : alk. paper) — ISBN 978-0-8047-6346-2
(pbk. : alk. paper)
  1. Holocaust, Jewish (1939-1945)—Italy. 2. Nationalism and collective
memory—Italy. 3. Italy—Civilization—1945- I. Title.
  DS135.I8G66 2012
  940.53'180945—dc23

                                   2012002456

Typeset by Bruce Lundquist in 10.9/13 Adobe Garamond

For Barbara, Ben and Leo

Contents

Acknowledgments

I am very pleased to be able to thank some of the institutions and people who have helped me over the years I have been working on this book. The idea for the book grew out of a long period of intense work on one remarkable survivor-writer, Primo Levi. I began to be curious about the world beyond Levi's texts, the cultural field in which he was embedded. A first piece of writing, looking at Levi's contemporaries and their accounts of the concentration camps written in the 1940s, was made possible by the remarkable resources of the archive of the Centro di documentazione ebraica contemporanea in Milan. Further seeds were sown by an invitation from David Forgacs to speak at a seminar on Italian Holocaust cinema in London in 2002. But the hard graft began in earnest only in 2005–6, when I was lucky enough to be offered a Mellon Foundation–John Sawyer Fellowship at the National Humanities Center in North Carolina, USA. The year spent at the NHC was an extraordinary opportunity to immerse myself in the project, drawing on the unparalleled atmosphere and resources of the Center, its community of Fellows, directors, staff and librarians. Thanks go to Geoff Harpham, Kent Mullikin, Lois Whittington and to all the Fellows of 2005–6, especially Theresa Braunschneider, Madeleine Dobie, Martin Jay, Mary Kinzie, Mark Maslan, Alastair Minnis, Ruth Nisse, Silvana Patriarca, Philip Rupprecht and Paul Saint-Amour. The three librarians—Betsy Dain, Jean Houston, Eliza Robertson—provided me with a window onto extraordinary research resources, starting in the Research Triangle and spreading out across the United States, resources almost impossible to replicate in Europe, even for someone working on Italy.

In more mundane periods of university life and work, the project was sustained thanks to the support of the institutions and colleagues in the

University of Cambridge, its Faculty of Modern and Medieval Languages and Department of Italian, the University Library and Gonville and Caius College. The book was brought to completion during a period of leave jointly supported by my university and college, and by the UK Arts and Humanities Research Council's Research Leave scheme.

I am grateful to the administrators and staff of the following libraries and archives in Italy: Centro di documentazione ebraica contemporanea, Milan; Archivio storico Olivetti, Ivrea; Archivio storico Galleria nazionale dell'arte moderna, Rome; Casa della memoria and Biblioteca nazionale, Rome; Centro internazionale di studi Primo Levi, Turin. Salvatore Quasimodo's literary executor and son, Alessandro Quasimodo, kindly gave me permission to reproduce the poem 'Auschwitz' in its entirety. Thanks go also to Emily-Jane Cohen, Sarah Crane Newman, Judith Hibbard, Tom Finnegan and Harvey L. Gable, who have all been enthusiastic supporters of the book and sources of sound and humane long-distance advice at Stanford University Press.

I have tentatively presented work-in-progress on the book to an array of seminar and lecture audiences, in the UK (Anglia Ruskin, Cambridge, Leeds, Reading, Queen Mary, UCL, the Institute for Historical Research), Ireland (NUI Cork), the United States (Boston, Duke, Fordham, Hofstra, NYU, Wellesley, Yale), and Italy (Rome, Turin). Parts of the book have been published in draft form in journals or edited volumes (see Bibliography under 'Gordon'), and I am grateful to editors and publishers for permission to draw on this material, revised and reworked, for this book. My sincere thanks, finally, go to these individuals who generously offered advice, dialogue and help of all kinds: Pierpaolo Antonello, Zyg Baranski, Marco Belpoliti, Ruth Ben-Ghiat, Guido Bonsaver, Richard Bosworth, Ann Caesar, Alberto Cavaglion, Mark Chu, Manuela Consonni, Phil Cooke, Virginia Cox, John Dickie, the late Risa Domb, John Foot, David Forgacs, Nadia Fusini, Nancy Harrowitz, Geoffrey Hartman, Daniela La Penna, Thomas Laqueur, Mary Laven, Adam Ledgeway, Giulio Lepschy, Laura Lepschy, Fabio Levi, Simon Levis Sullam, Stefania Lucamante, Franco Marcoaldi, Penny Marcus, Martin McLaughlin, Alan O'Leary, Sergio Parussa, Emiliano Perra, David Porter, Stan Pugliese, Silvia Ross, Mimmo Scarpa, Jason Scott-Warren, Pauline Small, Risa Sodi, Marla Stone, David Ward, Andrew Webber. The book is dedicated to my family—Barbara, Ben and Leo—for following me to Carrboro, NC, for a year, and for much else besides.

The Holocaust in Italian Culture, 1944–2010

Part I

§1 The Shape of Italy's Holocaust

This book is about the wide field of cultural responses to what we call the Holocaust or the Shoah, as it emerged in Italy over the long postwar era.[1] In recent years, a great deal of research has been devoted to Holocaust legacies, memories and cultures in key national arenas such as Germany, Israel, France and America, and an array of other countries and areas, including, since the fall of the Berlin Wall, the nations of Eastern European and Russia.[2] But relatively little work of either analysis or synopsis has been produced on Italy.[3] Although varying widely in discipline and methodology—from history, to literary or film studies, to sociology, political theory or cultural studies—this body of work dovetails sufficiently well to allow us to shape out a common, cross-border chronological template of phases in the cultural elaboration—what the Germans call 'working through' (*Vergangenheitsbewältigung*)—of knowledge about the Holocaust:

1. *Mid-1940s*: following the camp liberations of spring 1945 and the rapid spread of horrific newsreel and print imagery of the survivors and the dead,[4] there is widespread revulsion at the Nazi crimes, elaborated further at the Nuremberg Trials of 1945–46. Early testimonies appear, but very few gain a wide readership.

2. *Late 1940s to late 1950s*: in a period of reconstruction and Cold War tension, there is a widespread indifference to, even silence surrounding, Nazi crimes against Jews and the camp system. An exception is the spreading international reputation during the 1950s—as book, Broadway play and Hollywood film—of Anne Frank's diary.[5] The establishment of the State of Israel is linked to the Holocaust (as will be the

counternarrative of the *Naqba*, the displacement of Palestinian populations in the war of 1948).

3. *1960s*: the Final Solution begins to emerge as a key historical phenomenon and as a distinct subject for memory and historical understanding. Most accounts point to the Eichmann trial in Jerusalem in 1961 as
a crucial turning point, but also relevant are the generational politics of
the 1960s, with the young challenging the settled narratives of the war
and their parents' complicity; and the 1967 Arab-Israeli Six Day War,
which brought the very survival of the Jews back into vivid play, before
Israel's dramatic victory.

4. *1970s–80s*: awareness of the Holocaust emerges on a wide scale as a
newly central feature in national histories and memory. France 'redis-
covers' from the early 1970s, through books, films and trials, the
extent of Vichy's collaboration and complicity (e.g. Marcel Ophuls'
Le Chagrin et la pitié, 1971). In 1978–79, America, Germany and much
of Europe learn the term 'Holocaust' through the hugely popular television miniseries of that name.[6] France and Germany struggle with
scandals of negationism (the Faurisson affair of 1979 in France) or
revisionism (the *Historikerstreit*, the historians' debate, in Germany in
1986–87).[7]

5. *1990s–2000s*: mass awareness peaks in the 1990s, after the end of the
Cold War, and translates into a pervasive Americanisation of the Holocaust, through the global success of Steven Spielberg's *Schindler's List*
(1993) and the opening of the Washington Holocaust museum in 1993,
among many others.[8] Following the events of 11 September 2001, as
well as accelerated globalisation and multiculturalism, there is a geopolitical shift away from the 'postwar' paradigm, towards a new phase
of war and tensions between Muslims and the West: the Holocaust
remains, however, a powerful shadow over the West and its newly
uncertain role in the world.

With many local variations, this broad-brush 'history of memory' flows
with remarkable consistency across different national contexts, perhaps
especially in the 'Western' sphere (US, Western Europe, Israel). The
story of Eastern Europe and the Soviet Union was tellingly different,
since until the revolutions of 1989 the Soviet vulgate of the war as a
heroic struggle of Communism against Fascism left little room for the
racial aspects of Nazism. A very different account would also be needed

for a history of responses to the Holocaust in the Arab world or beyond. Nevertheless, one of the striking features of the field of Holocaust memory seems to lie in its transnational, deterritorialised dynamics, frequently decoupled from local history.

This macrohistorical picture should not, however, preclude national particularities: on the contrary, as Arjun Appadurai has argued in relation to local-global intersections, the two levels are in constant symbiosis.[9] At the local level, the microhistories of each nation which confronts the Holocaust interweave highly specific national discourses of culture and tradition, history and politics with this emerging transnational phenomenon. The particular mediators and operators within a cultural sphere have a crucial role to play in the timing and nature of local engagement with the Holocaust; and the particular inflections of a national setting determine how talk about it will, in turn, spread back into political and cultural spheres and into the collective cultural memory. Furthermore, elements of particular, national discourses can then emigrate in turn to become global Holocaust artefacts or events in their own right.

∾

The relative neglect of Italy within this field is surprising, not least because it presents compelling instances of continuity and discontinuity with the template above.

Fascist Italy was the model and origin for Hitler's totalitarian racial state and adopted many of the latter's racist laws from the late 1930s onwards, although debate still rages as to how far, and how early, Fascism was (or was not) inherently racist.[10] Fascist Italy was also Nazi Germany's prime European ally as the genocide of the Jews was undertaken and was responsible for administering anti-Slavic and anti-Semitic policy in several occupied regions (e.g. Slovenia), often with ferocious violence, just as it was responsible for horrific colonial crimes in Africa, and just as it had operated forms of racial politics and ethnic cleansing in home border areas, such as Alto Adige, before the war; although important historiographical work has also proposed that Italian officials—up to Mussolini himself—did much to frustrate deportations and massacres of Jews during the early phase of the war.[11] Italy was, then, both part progenitor of and collaborator in genocide, and part uncertain fellow-traveller, even filibusterer. After July 1943, this already complex status was made notably more so as Mussolini fell, and Italy signed an armistice with the Allies and found itself split in two, invaded from the south by the Allies and occupied in the centre and north by Germany (with the help of a restored Mussolini and the diehard Fascists of the Salò Republic), with a civil war or partisan Resistance war raging. The Nazis now started deporting Jews from Italy (mainly to Auschwitz), although the numbers were relatively small, in the thousands;[12] and also approximately 30,000 political prisoners (mostly partisans), deported to Mauthausen, Gusen and nearby; and large numbers—up to 750,000—of Italian soldiers were imprisoned in brutal internment camps.[13] Now Italians were victims of the whole gamut of Nazi violence, although the Salò Republic was also an active perpetrator of deportations and massacres, and the racial bureaucracy of the former Fascist state was still in place to abet the deportation of Jews. Once again, however, alongside this picture of complicity runs an alternative narrative of many individual or local acts of solidarity with the Jewish population, the product of an apparent Italian immunity to racism built into the Italian 'national character'.[14]

This tangled history left Italy with an immense baggage of unresolved questions about itself, its historical responsibilities and its future after the war. It is commonly argued that the entire postwar era in Italy, up to the turn of the 21st century, was spent working through answers to those questions. Initially, as elsewhere, what was later termed the Holocaust did not separate itself out as a discrete event within the mire of the war's and Fascism's history and legacy; but once that distillation process did begin, the Holocaust too would pose deep and troubling questions to the polity and collective identity of Italy and Italians, adding layer upon layer of complexity and daunting challenge.

In response to this history, postwar Italian culture has thrown up striking clusters of writers and filmmakers, artists and architects, historians and intellectuals intent on coming to terms with the phenomenon of the Holocaust. Several of these have taken up prime places in the vast international spectrum of responses to the genocide—authors such as Primo Levi, Giorgio Bassani and Natalia Ginzburg; and directors such as Vittorio De Sica, Lina Wertmüller, Francesco Rosi and Roberto Benigni. Merely for this weight of cultural production, the relative neglect of Italy in accounts of the spectrum of Holocaust culture is surprising.

But the aim of this book is neither to restate the history of Fascist Italy's entanglement with Nazi Germany; nor to collate a canon of the worthiest works about the Holocaust to have come out of Italy. It aims rather to survey and embed those works in the wider field of responses that produced and shaped them, and thereby to trace the progress of the slow, but profoundly illuminating encounter between Italian culture and the Holocaust. The field it draws on includes a wide range of cultural artefacts, agents, works of testimony, events and practices, collectivities and debates. And this field is presented as in turn embedded in a series of other local fields, giving local inflections to the reception and understanding of the Holocaust. So, talk of the Holocaust in Italy is shown persistently to mask questions about Fascism, the anti-Fascist Resistance and its legacies, national character, Cold War politics, the role of the Church, European identity, immigration, multiculturalism and so on.

The book describes the circles of production and reception of this field of knowledge and representation of the Holocaust in Italy, tapping into the work and activism of concentration camp survivors and their associations, the Jewish community and its organs, spreading outwards into the wider culture through culture industries and media, civic commemorations, institutions and all the varied arenas of modern cultural practice. It traces how, by the late 20th century, a vast tranche of Italians—from ageing survivors to young children—came to know something of what was referred to by the terms Holocaust or Shoah, to have some sense of what Norberto Bobbio meant when he described the genocide as '*the monstrous event* in world history'.[15]

As indicated above, the Holocaust can never be wholly contained at the 'national' level, neither in its history of perpetrators, victims and bystanders, of individuals, groups, ethnicities and states; nor in its a posteriori cultural representations. It is and was always a porous, plurilinguistic, transnational phenomenon. This is evinced by the extraordinary, migratory global reach of the pivotal cultural events in our template, from the liberation photographs to Anne Frank's diary, from Eichmann in Jerusalem to *Holocaust* on TV to *Schindler's List* at the movies. This book, then, looks not only at the specifics of Italian responses to Italy's role within experience of the Shoah; but also at the interactions of this field with that larger, transnational phenomenon. In Italy as elsewhere, these two strands—the Holocaust at its broadest and the Italian case at its most local—co-exist and are mutually dependent layers in history and in the production of discourse around it; and the nature of this co-existence is central to the story told here. To give two examples, as Manuela Consonni has shown, Italy had its own responses to the Israeli—and global—media event of the Eichmann trial, even as the Italian press reflected on the extraordinary global attention it was garnering.[16] Conversely, an Italian film such as Benigni's *Life Is Beautiful* (*La vita è bella*, 1997) was a product of deep and largely hidden local and generational histories, masquerading as a Holocaust story (Benigni's father was a military internee);[17] and yet as it was marketed across a global circuit of cinema festivals and mass distribution, filtered through American success, it entered the sphere of transnational Holocaust culture, acquiring new meanings along the way.

This mutual dependence operates wherever the Holocaust establishes itself as a datum of cultural knowledge; but it seems to be charged with particularly interesting dynamics in the Italian case, because of the strange interplay of centrality and marginality in Italy's encounter with the Holocaust. As we have seen, Italy was ostensibly marginal to the mainstream history of the Holocaust (certainly in bald numerical terms) but was also bound to its core through key figures, moments and alliances; similarly the Holocaust has been ostensibly marginal to the mainstream of Italian culture, as has the small Jewish community (hovering for two millennia around 30–40,000 people, or 1/1000th of the modern population), and yet the stories and voices of Italian Jews have at times loomed surprisingly large within the dominant national culture. The web of oblique connections, indirect transmissions, displacements and graftings these telescopic interrelations throw up are at the core of this book's interests.

The same displacements, both within competing fields of national conversation and culture and between national and transnational fields, suggest further that 'memory' is not necessarily the only, nor the best, framing vocabulary for talking about how the Holocaust has taken on cultural form, despite the fact that a language of memory has come to seem *de rigueur* in research in this area. The cultural emphasis in this book is, in part, designed to challenge assumptions about mechanisms of collective memory, seeing instead cultural form as a means to shared knowledge about or awareness of aspects of the past, which become part of a shared cultural conversation (with its own codes and markers), of which 'memory effects' are only one element.[18]

✑

Before setting out the structure of the book, we need to set out the scope of meanings around the term 'Holocaust' itself, in general and as it concerned Italy in particular.[19] Instead of attempting a potted history of events—from Fascist anti-Semitism to war, occupation and deportation, alongside the rise of the Nazis, the Nuremberg laws and the Final Solution[20]—it seems more pertinent to gauge this history and its legacy through some questions of definition. Even this preliminary task is fraught with problems of inclusion and exclusion, echoing issues of 'uniqueness' or comparability in the wider field of Holocaust historiography.[21] We need to know what precisely is being named, and what is stake, when the Holocaust—and cognate terms that cluster around it—is named in Italy and in Italian. In asking this question, it swiftly becomes clear that we are also asking questions of agency, identity and belonging—whose Holocaust is it?—since it can variously be read as an event in Jewish history, German history, also Israeli prehistory, but also Italian history (and many other national histories), Italian-Jewish history, European history, global history, human history, and so forth.

Here are four possible parameters of definition for the Holocaust, each touching on events of the Holocaust in relation to Italy, and each with differing purchase in particular corners and moments within the field of cultural responses this book maps out.

1. The Holocaust has narrowly been taken to refer to the Nazi genocidal project to murder the Jews of Europe (and beyond), the Final Solution to the Jewish Question, particularly as enacted after the Wannsee conference of 20 January 1942. As noted, Italy was a prime ally of Nazi Germany and had already became a 'racial state' in 1938 with the passage of drastic anti-Semitic laws akin to the Nuremberg Laws. As noted also, each phase from 1938 to the early war years to the Salò years produced counternarratives of Italian opposition to the genocide, of moral heroism and resistance. Thus, even under the umbrella of Italy's direct involvement with the tightest definition of the Final Solution, we find in circulation competing narratives and historiographies, each with claims to authenticity. Even simple dating is of consequence here: the backdating of Italy's involvement with the Holocaust to 1938, pushed in the historiography of the 1980s, marks a crucial stage in redefinitions of Fascist complicity and of the definition of the Holocaust itself as viewed from Italy.

2. The term 'Holocaust' has variously taken on stretched or loosened definitions, for more or less coherent historiographical reasons: thus, in much postwar discourse, the place-name Auschwitz came to stand for the entire network of Nazi labour, concentration and extermination camps (often merged together as concentration camps). Under this definition, the Holocaust 'equals' the camps;[22] a slippage which suggests Italian victims might include not only Jews, but also partisan deportees, forced labourers and military internees (and indeed Jewish internees in Fascist camps in Southern Italy up to 1943, or Slovenes in Italian-run camps in

the war, or colonial camp prisoners in Africa). Certainly, in the immediate aftermath of the war, the millions of 'survivors', 'returnees' (*reduci* in Italian), DPs (displaced persons) making their way home across a devastated and chaotic Europe, were something of an indistinguishable mass, alike even in their sheer physical emaciation. Furthermore, if these survivors were visible and mostly similar in appearance, the dead, by contrast—where massive differences in number and degree of suffering lay—were of course invisible.[23]

The consequences of this blurring for Italy, in the postwar months but with shifting balances also for decades thereafter, could hardly be weightier. Around the identity, legacy and moral and ideological valency of those *other* types of 'deportees'—partisans, the conscript army of the Fascist state, forced labourers—traumatic national struggles for memory and identity were played out over the postwar period. This is familiar terrain for historians of modern Italy: the anti-Fascist myth of the Resistance as the founding narrative of postwar Italian democracy; the counter-myth of the 'fall' of Italy in 1943 as 'the death of the nation', the abandonment of the state of its alliances and indeed its legitimacy; and the refraction of each of these through Cold War left-right politics.[24] In other words, talk of the Holocaust—here, deportation to camps of Jews *and others*—circulated at the margins of and in tellingly oblique relation to centrally important, fiercely contested terrains of ideology and memory.

3. A third variant in the definition of the Holocaust points to further blurring between Italian and Holocaust history. A key corrective to the tendency to conceptualise the Holocaust through the site of the concentration camp—the *Lager*, as it has been commonly labelled in Italian—has been to recall the mass, *non*industrialised killing of more than a million people, Jews and others, by shootings, gassings in mobile vans and massacres in the Eastern occupied territories after 1941.[25] These operations, carried out by the *Einsatzgruppen*, constitute a central element of the history of the Holocaust not catered for by the category of 'the camp'. Opening up the term to take in this important history challenges certain stereotypical ideas of the Holocaust as uniquely modernised, systematised, bureaucratically controlled, industrial-scale extermination, and moves towards characterising all extreme Nazi (perhaps especially SS) brutality and mass murder as co-extensive with the Holocaust. In the Italian context, this brings into play a highly contentious set of events: the Nazi massacres of Italian civilians in the years of occupation, Resistance and civil war. These so-called *eccidi* took place in now infamous locations such as

Civitella, Marzabotto, Sant'Anna di Stazzema and the Fosse Ardeatine. As repressed memories of these events returned to the surface, especially in the late 20th century, the tortured legacy, the 'divided memory' of the Resistance loomed very large once again, especially in those cases when the Germans were acting, notionally, in retaliation for partisan attacks.[26] Again, discourse related to the Holocaust coincides with discourse around a central wound in the national collective memory, either through analogy with a particular kind of Nazi violence—the cold-blooded murder of local civilians, in Eastern Europe or Italy—or through an even closer entanglement of histories, as at the Fosse Ardeatine massacre, where 75 of the 335 murdered were Jews.[27]

4. A fourth definition of the Holocaust is already in evidence in this last example, and it goes hand-in-hand with the emergence of the idea of the Holocaust as a universal phenomenon, as something like the essence of Nazism, of modern totalitarianism, or indeed of a dark side of modernity itself.[28] Under this conception, once again, Italy is placed in an ambiguous position, since Italian Fascism stands as the principal precursor and model for Nazism and indeed for all modern totalitarianisms (although some would reject this typological affinity precisely because of the apparent absence of race in its core doctrine).[29] So discussion of the Holocaust in Italy morphs into an indirect discussion of the legacy of a generic Fascism, for Italy and the wider world.[30]

Loaded, local issues of memory and history, then, turn on these shifting definitions of the label 'Holocaust': Italy's complicity and victimhood, the nature and morality of violence in both Fascism and the Resistance, the histories and myths of the Resistance and of the nation-state (embodied in its army), myths and realities of 'national character' and individuals' relation to the state, the general legacy of Fascism. And this list omits other key issues that inflect Holocaust talk in Italy in localised ways, such as the role of the Catholic Church, with its highly controversial relations to both Nazi Germany and the Italian state; and the idea of Italy's Europeanness, in the context of a historical understanding of the war and the Holocaust as somehow a 'founding' event for Europe's postwar polity and institutions.[31] Yet each of these definitions is primarily rooted in the horrific specificities of Nazi violence against the Jews and other ethnicities as it emerged as perhaps the single most significant historical phenomenon of the modern age. The semantic field of the term 'Holocaust' points us to the same field of oblique interactions outlined above that will recur and find multiple form in the events, publications, stories, images, debates, and sites of Holocaust culture in postwar Italy examined in this book.

∾

Part I contains two further chapters. Chapter 2 is dedicated to a single, contemporary and still unresolved case study, the plan for Italy's first national Holocaust museum; its purpose is to suggest how the long-term issues and complexities of Holocaust talk mesh with every single attempt to give it cultural form and engage, from within Italy's cultural field, with the legacy of the Holocaust. If the single case study of Chapter 2 teases out at a micro level several persistent conjunctions in Italian responses to the Holocaust, Chapter 3 takes a macro perspective and attempts to set out a model for the entire field of Holocaust culture in postwar Italy, mapping its various spheres of activity and cultural production, and offering some examples of how these spheres intersect and overlap to give shape and cultural form to Italy's Holocaust.

Having set the parameters from below and above, in Part II the book explores in depth the spectrum of cultural phenomena around which Holocaust responses have clustered or come into focus. Part II is not systematically structured in chronological sequence, but its first and last chapters (4 and 10) frame the rest by focussing on two specific phases, one early and one late, that included defining or watershed moments in the shaping of Holocaust culture and knowledge in Italy. As Chapter 4 shows, the 1940s saw the emergence of the earliest formations of knowledge, images and stories of the genocide, necessarily tentative and incomplete, with an uneven legacy until a first moment of broad cultural dissemination in the late 1950s and early 1960s. In contrast, as Chapter 10 describes, the period stretching from the late 1980s to the early 2000s witnessed an extraordinary late flowering of intense interest in the Holocaust, not only in its own right and for its own sake, but also as a filter for essential debates and doubts about Italy's relationship with its own identity and history.

In between these two framing phases, Chapters 5 through 9 look in turn at a series of orders of cultural phenomena, always with a sense of historical positioning and contextualisation, but focussed as much on the patterns and networks of cultural formation these orders brought with them. So Chapter 5 looks at how a single individual voice of witness—in this case, the Auschwitz survivor and writer Primo Levi—came to shape, or at the very least reflect for a wide tranche of Italians, the warp and weft of Holocaust talk in Italy. Chapter 6 takes a single, but historically and culturally laden, site of events and of postwar commemoration and representation, the city of Rome. Rome was far from the only important site of Holocaust history and culture in Italy, but one where the threads of complexity in the way it intersected with Italy's national history and culture are woven together with telling vividness. Chapter 7 moves onto the terrain of language and looks at a cluster of material, from high literature to popular song, focussing on the 1950s to the 1970s. It shows a certain loosening of the language of Holocaust talk in the period, as it was adopted by a wide panoply of cultural voices, in part to refer to the historical event but also, crucially, as part of a metaphorical and often highly political source of rhetoric referring to modernity and its evils. Metaphors of the Holocaust permeated the youthful, countercultural arenas characteristic of the period. Chapter 8 is concerned with language also, but here in specific relation to Italy's history and historiography of Fascism, anti-Semitism and the war. The chapter looks at two stock phrases, two stereotypes of national character circulating with particular force in the 1980s and after, used to navigate the tricky moral borderlands around Italian complicity, guilt and innocence, in relation to Fascism, war and the Holocaust. Chapter 9, finally, embeds several of the lines of development of Italy's Holocaust culture into fields of transnational cultural exchange, showing how the processing of cultural knowledge and representation of the Holocaust in any single nation is constantly in negotiation with international and transnational cultural lines and networks.

§2 Villa Torlonia

The ancient Roman arterial road, the via Nomentana, heads out north-east from the centre of Rome starting at Porta Pia, one of the monumental gates in Rome's third-century A.D. Aurelian Walls. In 1870, the army of the young Italian state, less than a decade after its formation in 1861, stormed the gates of the city at Porta Pia, overwhelming the forces of the Papal State, leading to the enclosure of the Church as a secular power within the minuscule confines of the Vatican, and to the declaration of Rome as modern Italy's rightful capital. Porta Pia is one of the highest symbols and sites of Italy's Risorgimento patriotic redemption.

Less than a kilometre along the via Nomentana from Porta Pia is an elegant 19th-century estate, the Villa Torlonia, whose neoclassical palace is surrounded by extensive, shady grounds. In 1918, archaeologists discovered here some rare remains of ancient Jewish catacombs from the 2nd and 3rd centuries A.D. From 1925 until 1943, the aristocratic palace at Villa Torlonia served as the Roman residence of Italy's Fascist dictator, Benito Mussolini, and his family. He paid Prince Torlonia a symbolic rent of 1 lira a month. If Palazzo Venezia, beside the Capitoline Hill in central Rome, was the site of Mussolini's official power, containing his grandiose office in the Sala del Mappamondo and his most famous public stage (the small balcony overlooking Piazza Venezia below), then Villa Torlonia was Mussolini's image of home, family, and his role as 'father' of the nation for nearly 20 years.

The Villa was abandoned when Mussolini was deposed in July 1943, with the war going catastrophically wrong for Fascist Italy and with Allied forces already on the ground in Sicily. From September 1943 until June 1944, Rome became an 'Open City', in theory protected and uncontested, but in reality overrun by a Nazi command every bit as fierce as Nazi occupiers elsewhere in Europe. Rome's Jewish community would pay a very heavy price for this 'occupation', when more than 1,000 of its number were rounded up and deported to Auschwitz on 16 October 1943. Sixteen returned. Allied bombings would play their part also. Less than 2 kilometres due south of Villa Torlonia lay the working-class and distinctly anti-Fascist district of San Lorenzo: because it was near the factories and railways around Rome's main train station, Stazione Termini, the area was heavily bombed by Allied planes in July 1943, killing some thousand civilians. In a heralded gesture of solidarity, Pope Pius XII travelled to San Lorenzo immediately after the raid, visiting the ancient basilica of the same name and local bombed-out buildings and blessing the crowd to mass acclaim, as a famous photo records.[1] No papal visit was made to the area of the old Jewish ghetto, however, nor to any other site of the round-up of Rome's Jews of 16 October.[2]

Once Rome had been liberated, in early June 1944, Villa Torlonia was taken over by the Allied High Command in Rome, a role it held until 1947, after which it fell into a period of long, quiet neglect. It opened as a museum in the 1970s and was then restored and restructured in the 1990s as a site of a network of small museums and visitor pathways around the villa, catacombs and park.[3]

In 2005, after much debate at both national and local levels, a corner of the grounds of Villa Torlonia was chosen as the site for Italy's first official and national Museum of the Holocaust or Museo della Shoah.

The lines that converge on Villa Torlonia and the early-21st-century siting of the Museo della Shoah are many and tangled. In their patterning lies the long history this book sets out to explore: the history of how, starting in the weeks and months before the Second World War had even ended and stretching forward to the present day, Italy confronted and gave shape in cultural forms to what we now call the Holocaust or the Shoah. We can use the story of the Villa Torlonia project as a lever for opening up our explorations, as a case study in how cultural lines of response intersect and shape each other, cutting across nodes of history, geography, politics and memory. Four such nodes suggest themselves simply in the planning of a museum of this kind on such a site in contemporary Rome.

First, and most astonishing, is the siting of the museum in the very grounds of Mussolini's home, thereby setting the Shoah—the Nazi genocide and Italy's complicity with it, Italian perpetrators and Italian victims—right at the heart of the legacy of Mussolini and the Fascist dictatorship. Whilst from a distance this may seem unsurprising, in reality Fascist anti-Semitism and its complicity with the Nazi Final Solution was until very late in the 20th century anything but a central feature of historical accounts of Fascism, or even an important one.[4]

Indeed, anti-Semitism was overwhelmingly seen, for decades after the war, by both former proponents and indeed many of its Jewish victims, as an alien, German imposition in 1938 (the date of Mussolini's Racial Laws, modelled, so this story goes, on the Nuremberg Laws as a sop to Hitler). So that, for example, for the most influential of all historians of the Fascist period, Renzo De Felice, anti-Semitism and racial ideology was precisely what distinguished Hitler's regime from Mussolini's.[5] The former was a 'racial state'; the latter was not.[6] The former murdered millions of Jews, whereas the latter, at least until autumn 1943 when it was in effect dismantled, did not deport any Jews to the camps; even after autumn 1943, only ('only') around 7,000 Italian Jews would lose their lives in the genocide.[7] Indeed, for many, as noted in Chapter 1, Italians seemed almost constitutionally, by national character, immune from the disease of racism and possesed of an in-built, 'civilised' decency and distrust of ideology—what Hannah Arendt called 'the almost automatic general humanity of an old and civilized people'.[8] One of the stories this book needs to tell, then, is about Fascism's and Italians' apparent distance from the Holocaust, and about how this notion seems to have been so completely turned on its head by the end of the century. As the Villa Torlonia museum suggests, anti-Semitism and the Holocaust now belong at the very heart and essence of official Italian understanding of Fascism.

The site at Villa Torlonia further connects to a specific characteristic of the history and role of Judaism in Italy, which conditioned the response to and reception of the Holocaust there. As the catacombs there remind us, Jews in Italy, and in Rome specifically, are a small but ancient community, present continuously in the shadow of the Roman Empire and then of the Church for more than two millennia before the Fascist Era. This long history is quite distinct from that of the migratory Ashkenazi diaspora of Germany and Eastern Europe, and indeed from the Sephardic traditions of the Iberian exile and diaspora. Elsewhere in the Italian peninsula, pockets of descendants from both these traditions are strongly present, and part of the Italian-Jewish story and of its experience and memory of genocide; but the line connecting Rome's Jews to ancient Judaea, Rome and the Church allows us to tap into a quite distinct, millennial and highly symbolic dimension to the Italian case in relation to the Holocaust. As always, the temptations of this 'higher', millennial discourse are a source of both historical specificity and myth. This Jewish community of Rome is the one kept close to the heart of the Church over centuries, on which the millennial tradition of Christian anti-Semitism was ritualistically tried out (including the establishment of Rome's own closed ghetto in 1555), which bred in part the Nazi genocide.[9] The Roman question, within the national history of Italy's engagement with the Holocaust, is one to which we will return in Chapter 6.

There is, inevitably also, a set of 'national' and 'state' questions prompted by siting the Museo della Shoah in Rome. Much comment and debate surrounded the construction in the early 1990s of the United States Holocaust Memorial Museum (USHMM) on the Mall in Washington D.C., at the symbolic heart of the culture and history of the nation of the United States and its institutions of state, thousands of miles from the location of the events commemorated there, symptomatic of the fluid globalisation of history, of the powerful role in American public life and culture of its Jewish community and, conversely also for many, of a global 'Americanisation' of the Holocaust.[10] Similar complex national questions, interwoven with the transnational phenomenon of the Holocaust and its remembrance, have characterised debates over museums and memorials in Paris, Berlin and London, and in many other sites and cities.[11] In Rome, the specific urban site of the museum, striking as it is by historical association, is not quite equivalent to Washington's Mall; it is at Villa Torlonia and not Palazzo Venezia, after all. (It is telling enough that more than once since the turn of the millennium the Museo del Risorgimento, or Museum of National Unification, housed in the florid Victor Emmanuel national monument on the Capitoline side of Piazza Venezia, has hosted exhibitions on Fascist anti-Semitism.[12]) It is nevertheless significant that, in 21st-century Europe, there is an imperative, embodied in international conferences and treaties, and in UN resolutions, to provide an official channel of memory of the Holocaust, as if to be a legitimate European democracy now is also to acknowledge and commemorate this 'Event', and where appropriate the nation's role in it. The national, transnational and European elements in Holocaust response in Italy, and the role of official, top-down and state-sponsored initiatives of memory and dissemination, are further running motifs of the story told in this book.

A fourth thread evident in the planning of the Museo della Shoah at Villa Torlonia lies in the apparently minor but, as so often in this field, heavily weighted question of naming and linguistic usage. It is entirely

characteristic of early-21st-century public discourse on the Nazi Final
Solution in Italy—and strikingly different from equivalent discourse in
most other European and American settings—that the museum should
be named Museo della Shoah and not, say, the Museo dell'Olocausto. The
history of the naming of the genocide is a long and complex one, moving
in several distinct waves and trends, from neologisms to metonymies and
euphemisms: the panoply of names runs from the Nazis' own *Endlösung*
to genocide (the term brought into use and defined at Nuremberg), from
Auschwitz to the Lager to the *univers concentrationnaire*, from Holocaust
to *Churban* to Shoah.[13] It has also been commonplace, since the term
'Holocaust' swept all before it following the 1978 US television miniseries,
for many of those closest to its history to lament its deeply inappropriate
connotations (of holy sacrifice) and to call for a change of nomenclature.
Italy is a rare case, however, where a shift in vocabulary seems to have
been concretely effected: in the very late 20th century, *Shoah* overtook
Olocausto as the most prominent term in the media and the public sphere
more generally, as reflected in the name of the museum. This surprising
and unusual shift is further indication of a specific Italian Holocaust response, one that is permeated with anxieties about the foreignness, Jewishness and thereby also the Italianness (or otherwise) of this genocidal
paroxysm. This question of naming is one we will return to in Chapter 9.

   A glimpse at Villa Torlonia, then, offers us at least four nodes of public discourse and cultural expression of the Holocaust in postwar Italy:
its relation to Fascism, to Judaism (and Italian Jewry in particular), to
the Italian nation-state and to language. Further aspects emerge in the
specific, practical details of the conception and planning of the Museo
della Shoah itself, showing how the Holocaust finds itself visually and
architectonically imprinted on the literal and cultural landscape, in ways
we will find echoed and reprised in many other forms of figuration, from
works of literature and historiography to art, film and the rhetoric of
public debate.

   The conception of the museum's building and spaces, as sketched out in
the proposals and mock-up images presented by the architects, has much
to tell us about the state of Holocaust talk in contemporary Italy. The
architects of the museum are Luca Zevi[14] and Giorgio Tamburini. For
several years, starting in 1996, Zevi was involved in an earlier collective
project to build a Museum of Intolerance and Extermination in Rome,
which was planned to include the Holocaust, but with an ambitious brief
to link outwards from the Nazi era to the larger dangers and violence of

the modern era, and the present and future of mankind.[15] Zevi argued that Rome's Jewish community, because of its particular history, was ideally placed to co-sponsor such a distinctively broad conception of a memorial museum; but his project was reined in and turned towards a more conventional Holocaust-centred plan, which resulted in the Villa Torlonia project. It is nevertheless clear that a certain anxiety over the centreing and decentreing of the Holocaust, over the need to record and repeat the hideous historical specificity of the Shoah, alongside the need to build bridges from the Shoah towards our contemporary world—to other genocides, to the moral and historical lessons of the camps—is a permanent feature of contemporary memorialisation and museum pedagogy. Displacements between the Holocaust and contiguous threads of history—through explicit comparison, or loosely resonant metaphorical association—is a process we will encounter again repeatedly (see especially Chapter 7).

In the Zevi-Tamburini project as finally approved, several elements chime with trends set in Washington, Paris, Berlin and elsewhere: in particular, it shows a sculptural conception of architecture that positions the spectator/visitor in emotional relation to the museum space, as well as in educational relation to its multimedia content. Here, the most distinctive and visible feature is the excavation of the main museum and educational spaces in two subterranean floors—in response to space and building restrictions in Rome, but also in a self-conscious echo of the nearby Jewish catacombs—to be topped out by a 10-metre-high, above-ground storey, clad in a massive block of dark granite inscribed with the name of every Italian Jew murdered by the Nazis and Fascists. The image of thousands of names of the dead set in black stone recalls as much the highly influential Vietnam war memorial in Washington as the USHMM or other Holocaust sites, where such a mourning through naming has also become a powerful commonplace.[16]

Zevi and Tamburini further included in their plan a pathway leading up to one entrance named the Avenue of the Just (Percorso dei giusti), echoing Yad Vashem's Righteous Among the Nations, which commemorates all those who risked their lives to save Jews during the Shoah, from Raoul Wallenberg to Oskar Schindler. The Avenue of the Just also picks up on that myth of Italian decency, of the instinctive impulse to help its Jewish neighbours that for many years was claimed as the defining feature of the on-the-ground response to the Holocaust in Italy. In the 1990s, this myth became enmeshed with the complicated legacy of Fascism when the extraordinary case of Giorgio Perlasca—an Italian Fascist who saved

thousands of Jews in occupied Budapest by posing as a Spanish diplomat—emerged in a book and subsequent television dramatisation.[17]

At the level of spaces and content, Zevi and Tamburini, aided by Holocaust historian Marcello Pezzetti[18] and others, set out a museum that
finely balanced the Shoah of European Jews, the genocidal campaigns
against other groups (Rom, homosexuals, the disabled, political oppo-
nents, Slavic populations and so on), Italian Fascist anti-Semitism and
a specifically Roman history of persecution and complicity. As a frame
and introduction to this content, they planned an entrance hallway dedicated to Primo Levi, confirming his central and iconic role in Italy as
the prime mediator of Holocaust awareness and the embodiment of the
dignified figure of the survivor capable of stitching together all the competing threads of memory, history, analogy and interpretation placed before the visitor (see Chapter 5). It is worth noting also, as evidence of the
internationalisation or Americanisation of the Holocaust, as well as of a
multimedia conception of memory, the input to the Rome museum of
the influential Steven Spielberg Shoah Foundation, with its vast video-
testimony archives.

There is also, finally, a story to tell of the public, community and party
politics behind the museum at Villa Torlonia. Although already the product of extensive discussion among the Jewish community, the architects
and various intellectual and political groupings, the plan for the museum
was by no means settled in 2005. The sequence that followed between
2005 and 2010 (and beyond—building the museum has not yet begun, at
the time of writing) allows us to add at least two further, crucial dimensions to this case study, which once again provide us with key coordinates
for our exploration of Italy's postwar imagining of the Holocaust.

The first of these dimensions is party political. When it was approved
by the Rome city council in Summer 2005, the Museo della Shoah was a
project sponsored by the then-ruling party of the city, that of its mayor
and prominent national leader Walter Veltroni: the Democratici di Sinistra (Left Democrats, DS). The DS was one of several post-Cold-War
reinventions of the historic Italian Communist Party (PCI), which had
been one of the great mass parties of postwar Italian Republican politics.
The values of the PCI were rooted in the politics of the anti-Fascist Resistance of 1943–1945 and the democratic Constitution of 1947–48 that
grew out of the Resistance.[19] It thus seemed natural and coherent for the
DS to associate itself, as an ethical and political statement, with a museum commemorating the Fascist or Nazi-Fascist horrors of the Holo-

caust (although, as we shall see in Chapter 9, the relationship between the Left and Jewish communities was much complicated by the geopolitics of Israel, especially after the Six Day War of 1967 and again the Lebanese invasion of 1982).

The Rome council vote of August 2005 to approve the museum project was unanimous, but bureaucratic complications, and planning protests from local residents over the size of the building and the loss of green space delayed the project until after Veltroni lost office in 2008. The new mayor, Gianni Alemanno, was a member of Silvio Berlusconi's rightist Popolo della Libertà (People of Liberty, PdL), now the national governing party; but his past was rooted deeply in one of the constituent parties that merged into the PdL, that is Alleanza nazionale (National Alliance, AN), previously the Movimento Sociale Italiano (Italian Social Movement, MSI), the principal postwar extreme-right, neo-Fascist party in Italy. Alemanno was a (former) Fascist. He did not treat the museum as a priority, and some of his less reformed colleagues on the ex-Fascist right began to militate against it. Veltroni resigned in protest from the board of the museum only months after leaving office, when Alemanno commented that whereas the Racial Laws were a form of 'absolute evil', Fascism as a whole should not be tarred with this same label. Nevertheless, AN had joined the unanimous vote of 2005, although only on condition that mention was made in the museum project of the innocent victims of the infamous Titoist Communists killings on the Italo-Yugoslav border during the war, in the so-called *foibe* or gullies in Istria.[20] For the right, commemorating the victims of Nazism called for a parallel acknowledgment of the victims of Communism to 'balance out' the horrors of 20th-century totalitarian murder. This principle had been writ large on a national scale in the institution of a national Holocaust day of memory on 27 January 2001, soon followed by the establishment of a parallel day of memory for victims of the foibe (and of the postwar exodus from Istria and Dalmatia of ethnic Italians and anti-Communists) on 10 February 2005. Alemanno then held to this line, and it was his city council that approved the final project and the start of building works, notionally in early 2010, although this was set back. That an ex- or post-Fascist such as Alemanno should push through and approve, in collaboration with Rome's Jewish community, the Museo della Shoah, tells us something powerful and confusing about postmodern or post-ideological politics; but it is perhaps not as surprising as all that, since just as the left had historically positioned itself since the 1960s as pro-Palestinian, so the right, and especially the former Fascist right led by its national figurehead Gianfranco Fini, had strategically moved into a strongly pro-Israeli position and had made a point of using this and a sober observance of Shoah remembrance to legitimise itself as a party of government in Italy and to distance itself systematically from its Nazi, Fascist, antidemocratic and racist forebears.

Party politics and ideology, or rather the ghostly remnants of 20th-century ideologies that haunt 21st-century cultural politics, have had a crucial role to play in shaping public discourse and cultural activity around the Holocaust. But there is another, characteristically Italian, dividing line to consider also, not between left and right, or Jewish and Italian, but among highly diverse regional cultures, identities and histories within Italy. Once again, the story of Villa Torlonia offers us a neat illustration. The Rome project had a problem to deal with, in the form of an already extant national law, number 91/2003, approved by Parliament in April 2003, under the rubric 'Establishment of a National Museum of the Shoah'.[21] The law was voted by both left and right, naming as official collaborators in this museum the Ministry of Culture, national and local Jewish bodies, a Milan Jewish history archive and, finally, the regional and local government of Emilia-Romagna. Why Emilia-Romagna? Because this prior legislative approval for a national museum of the Shoah in 2003 was not for anywhere in Rome, but rather for a site in a former prison on the edge of the central-northern Italian town of Ferrara.

Ferrara, like many regional centres and former city states throughout the Italian peninsula, has a rich and densely localised Jewish history. In Ferrara, it stretches back to at least the 13th century, and onwards through the legacy of the d'Este ruling family and later centuries of papal rule. In Italian Holocaust culture in particular, Ferrara has loomed especially large because of an extraordinary cycle of novels published from the 1950s into the 1970s, set mostly in Ferrara of the thirties and forties, by the local writer Giorgio Bassani, collated under the general title *Il romanzo di Ferrara* (*The Novel of Ferrara*). At the heart of this six-volume cycle lies the 1962 novel *Il giardino dei Finzi-Contini* (*The Garden of the Finzi-Continis*), set amongst the doomed adolescents of Ferrara's Jewish community in the 1930s.[22] The location of the museum in Ferrara perhaps owed as much to that semi-imaginary literary space—Bassani was the first storyteller of Italian-Jewish life and the Shoah to penetrate widely across the national culture—and to its central geographical position as to any historical primacy in the experience of the Shoah. As it turned out, however, this sensitivity to regional variety and to the provincial multiplicity of Italian-Jewish life was a weakness when the national and international cultural capital being accrued to the Shoah was expanding. When the rival Roman project emerged—supported by external money, the institutional centre of the Jewish community and the glamorous support of the Spielberg Shoah Foundation—the national government, in the shape of the centre-left Minister for Culture Francesco Rutelli (an ex-mayor of Rome himself and former leader of the national centre-left coalition), looked for and eventually found a compromise. Rome would have the Museo della Shoah, to set alongside the capital-city museums of Berlin, Paris, Washington and Jerusalem; Ferrara would have its own museum also (and 15 million euros to fund it), renamed, in a clause tacked onto the national finance bill of December 2006, the National Museum of Italian Judaism and the Shoah.[23] Ferrara's museum would share in and contribute to a project stretching across the national territory to memorialise and officially tell the story of the Shoah; but it would do so explicitly as an endpoint to that millennial Jewish-Italian history noted above, with all its multiple centres and distinct histories of prosperity and persecution, of emigration and immigration, of expansion and destruction over many centuries.

The Milan Jewish archive and research institution or CDEC (see Chapter 3) has collaborated with and continues to contribute its expertise to both the Rome and the Ferrara projects. Indeed, it has presented in its recent work a particularly interesting and articulated conception of a single, transversal and complementary national museum network for the Shoah made up of four distinct elements, which crystallise the plural geographies but also the multimedia and multiform dimensions of a culture of Holocaust history and remembrance in 21st-century Italy. As Michele Sarfatti, historian and archive director, explained in a 2007 article, the four spaces to be conceived as a single 'space' will be the Rome Museo della Shoah; the Ferrara museum; a memorial and study centre constructed around Platform 21 at Milan's Stazione Centrale (from where 15 train convoys of Jews and other prisoners departed during 1943–1945); and finally, a permanent, online, digital exhibition and 'museum' space on the persecution of Jews in Italy, 1938–1945.[24]

This regional variety of Italian and Italian-Jewish history, culture and politics, and the tensions amongst national, regional and local sets of responses to the Shoah—and within that already complicated spectrum, the further complication of Rome's status as a local case and also a symbolic 'national' centre—are all layers of geopolitical complication that we will need to be alert to as we look for an Italian shape to historical responses to the Holocaust in this book.

Given all the complex factors and delicate negotiations and investments that have gone into the project for a national Holocaust museum in Italy, it is perhaps not surprising the project has yet to come to fruition. Indeed, its very incompleteness stands as a useful indicator of the ongoing vitality and uncertainty of Italy's response to the Holocaust. This book sets out to probe further and explores some of the faultlines and filters of cultural history, memory and knowledge that this single case study has signalled.

Subject to the successful negotiation of further bureaucratic or political obstacles, and to the awkward business of guaranteeing funding, building was to start on the Museo della Shoah during 2011, the 150th anniversary year of the unification of modern Italy; but work on the site has not begun at the time of writing. Latest estimates of its unveiling in 2013 look optimistic, at best.

§3 The Field

How is it that awareness, knowledge, stories, images and forms of understanding of a discrete historical event spread through a national culture, and how do these cultural forms wax and wane and change shape over decades and generations? One of the things this book sets out to argue, and to show happening in practice, is that such a process is rooted in a complex microfield of cultural production and transmission around that historical event, a field we can map and explore and use to situate the myriad single works of art, the events, monuments and public debates, and more, which address that event. This final chapter of Part I sets out the contours of the field of cultural production around the Holocaust in postwar Italy.[1]

By its very nature, the field of Holocaust culture is eclectic and in dense intersection with several other, equally or more elaborately complicated fields of cultural production in Italy (and beyond). Every corner of our field also has coordinates as part of several other, distinct fields: thus, a novel about the Holocaust is, necessarily, both part of a Holocaust culture and part of the history of the Italian novel, its shape determined by the latter just as its response to the Holocaust must be defined in relation to the former. Thus, Primo Levi's 1947 Holocaust memoir *Se questo è un uomo* (*If This Is a Man*)[2]—although not quite a novel—fits in part with the tendency towards reportage and nonprofessional writing in neorealist literature of the 1940s. Furthermore, the lines of condition and definition also cut back and forth across the boundaries between the two fields: thus, Levi's memoir is shaped as a work of literature and makes a distinctive contribution to the history of the novel *also* because it was forced to confront problems specific to the Holocaust (how to represent genocidal violence; how to avoid stereotypes and clichés; how to show respect for victims etc.), leading it towards unusual stylistic and formal solutions. In formulating his powerful strictures on the limits of representation and of language in *If This Is a Man*, for example, Levi pushed some of the mimetic assumptions of neorealism to breaking point, *because of* the extremes of horror he had witnessed and now tried to convey. Conversely, a certain kind of narrative, certain modes of storytelling (in tune with or in contrast to other kinds of contemporary literature; documentaristic or experimental; character- or plot-centred or focussed on ethics or politics, etc.) contribute to the emerging threads and patterns in the way the Holocaust is discussed and interpreted at a given time. So, in the taboo-breaking subcultures of the 1970s, intellectually informed by psychoanalysis and psychosexual analyses of history and ideology from Wilhelm Reich to Herbert Marcuse, a newly turbid, sexualised idiom for depicting Nazism and its apoplectic extreme in the camps emerged with force in Italian theatre, film and historiography (see Chapter 7).

Even this two-way, or rather four-way, movement of the vectors shaping a narrative about the Holocaust is simplified and schematic: in reality, there are always many other threads of connection and definition, each interacting with the others in a multiplicitous complexity having no clear certainty about source or cause and effect. Thus the author of a novel about the Holocaust may be, say, a Holocaust survivor; she may be part of an active group of Holocaust survivors, with a particular political allegiance; the book may have been published in a particular year or moment alongside other key Holocaust artefacts, works or events; it may be published by a publisher with a definite location, perhaps the author's home city, with a defined cultural or political project, into which a work on the Holocaust or *this* work on the Holocaust fits for various and quite particular reasons; and the book may be reviewed and discussed, positively or negatively, in certain media, and marketed and read by certain kinds of readers (e.g. school children, students, intellectuals, academics); and it might stay with or return to public attention years later through republication or adaptations for a television drama. And so on. In other words, also at play here are overlapping micro- or macrofields relating to individual biography, the workings of group agency and associationism, the tenor of a particular year or moment of cultural production, the history and specificity of a city in a wider national history, the history of a publisher, of a field of media response, of reader reception and of commerce and marketing: all fields with their own elaborate internal dynamics, which intersect momentarily in this one instance—and then by extension in uneven clusters—with our small corner of cultural production, out of and about the Holocaust.

Whilst this spiralling complexity may be something of a truism in the multiple and loose causality behind cultural production of any kind (and not necessarily in and of itself a revelatory one: there is no guarantee that 'subatomic' details get us closer to the truth of origin), it nevertheless does seems especially pertinent when, as here, the function that interests us is a single historical referent—that is, a particular event in history and how it has passed into language, representation, cultural figuration, and thus also collective knowledge and understanding. A field held together and emanating outwards from one single point of reference—an event, *the Event*—will inevitably be centrifugal and centripetal, and multidirectional in its dynamics.

There is a key point in terms of method, here: national Holocaust talk, Holocaust knowledge and awareness, Holocaust memory or memory effects are all produced through a buzz of hugely varied and often uncoordinated cultural activity, out of which individual moments, works and individuals, as well as connections, formulae, stereotypes and categories (including, paradoxically, the core category of 'the Holocaust' itself) emerge as significant in highly unpredictable ways. And this is to suspend for now the further complicating factor of how this field strongly pushes against single 'national' maps of fields of Holocaust talk: as mooted in Chapter 1, Holocaust culture has constantly cut across national borders and national cultural coordinates, leading to local inflections and local appropriations, misreadings and distortions, so that any one national Holocaust culture is also in significant part a distorted mirror of a notional 'higher', supranational Holocaust culture (which cannot exist in pure supranational form anywhere).

The remainder of this chapter offers a prospectus of the general order of phenomena that come together to form the cultural field of Holocaust talk in postwar Italy. There are four principal, overlapping spheres of cultural activity that populate the field and determine its shape and the agents at work within it.

~

1. The first is what we might call the *associationist* or *institutional* sphere. Although none of these spheres necessarily has priority over the others, whether in chronology (who was the first to speak of these things?) or in

influence (whose voice was most listened to?), it is undoubtedly the case that the first semipublic channels of activity and expression for those Italians who experienced the Holocaust first-hand came by way of groupings and societies set up in part for the purpose of marking those events and supporting its victims. Serge Barcellini and Annette Wieviorka call these groups of victims' families, associations and civic authorities 'actors' or 'agents' of memory.[3] The only category of cultural agent to precede or accompany such early group activity was the lone, individual survivor, writing or telling his or her story of survival upon return, for visceral reasons of trauma and catharsis, or to mourn and pay tribute to those who did not return. For mutual support and to gain a voice in public, survivors and victims' families came together to form associations, even before the war had ended, and further collective initiatives continued to be shaped in new associations or grafted onto larger groups over the course of the postwar era.

Three associations are worth mentioning as particularly influential examples, active in their own ways over different phases of the postwar era, often in collaboration with one another or with other associations from related spheres: ANED, UCII (later UCEI) and CDEC.

ANED is the Associazione nazionale degli ex-deportati politici, the National Association of Ex-Political Deportees. ANED held its first national congress in 1957 and was recognised by the state as an nonprofit organisation (*ente morale*) in a presidential decree of 5 November 1968, but it was already active in more than one city, helping and serving the interests of returnees or the families of those who had not returned, as early as September 1945. A founding statute for ANED in Turin exists dated 6 September 1945, and already by 1946 it had undertaken a range of practical, welfare and also memorial activities.[4] Throughout the postwar period, ANED would support a vast range of initiatives, sponsoring monuments and memorials across Italy and in the camps themselves (at Mauthausen and Auschwitz, for example), collating archives and creating exhibitions, arranging conferences and camp visits, school visits and book publications, oral history and memory projects, and much more besides.[5] Many of the most activist and high-profile concentration camps survivors—including Primo Levi, but also Piero Caleffi, Bruno Vasari, Gianfranco Maris, Italo Tibaldi, Teo Ducci, Lidia Beccaria Rolfi and others—were also longstanding, committed ANED members.

It is also the case, as in so much of the field we are exploring, that ANED was originally and centrally focussed *not* on the Jewish genocide but on the figure of the 'political' deportee, that is, the partisan, anti-Fascist deportee, as its full title if not the acronym indicates. This has been a constant source of ambiguity and tension in the field of Holocaust talk in Italy; it has often seemed, and this is a case in point, as though the Jewish experience was subordinate to and to be understood in terms of the Resistance and its dominant ideologies and values. ANED, although politically unaffiliated, nevertheless clearly emerged from the leftist spheres of Resistance activism, and its activities intersected regularly with larger Resistance associations such as the national partisan association ANPI, and other splinter and competing Resistance groups, as well as associations of former military internees. Despite the apparently muted focus on the Jewish genocide, many Jewish participants in ANED embraced its 'nationalising' and 'combatant' mode of commemoration and discussion, at least initially. As the Jewish genocide grew first in group consciousness and then in wider public awareness, however, a certain formal recognition of its distinct importance emerged: ANED's full title shifted in a 1968 statute to a more embracing, if awkwardly reformulated remit: 'A national association made up of ex-political and racial deportees to Nazi concentration camps, the KZ, and families of the fallen, known by the title National Association of Ex-Political Deportees to Nazi Camps (ANED)'.[6]

UCEI is the Union of Italian Jewish Communities, the official body of Italian Jewry, founded in 1930 by the Fascist regime shortly after the latter's 1929 settlement with the Catholic Church (until 1987 it had the slightly different official title of UCII, Union of Italian Israelite Communities). UCII/UCEI has consistently played a rather more low-key role in the construction of Holocaust awareness in Italy compared to the public, didactic and in a sense campaigning project of ANED. But UCII/UCEI has nevertheless been at the heart of the discussion and collaborative organisation of events and memorials, claiming a voice for the Jewish victims of Nazi violence, whilst always balancing this purpose against its own communal politics and general interests, and the especially delicate task of its relations to Israel, the Zionist project and its prime role as overseer of contemporary Jewish-Italian life.[7] It too has sponsored and supported activities of fundamental influence: one telling and powerful example of how behind-the-scenes interventions of associations lay the groundwork for public work that goes on to shape and define aspects of the larger field is the history, little known until recently, of UCII's sponsorship and commissioning of the research that led to the publication by Einaudi in 1961 of one of the first and still most influential historical accounts of Fascist anti-Semitism, Renzo De Felice's *History of Italian Jews Under Fascism*.[8]

Also from within the ambit of the official organisations of Italian-Jewish life, but in some respects born in opposition to UCII's somewhat staid, or for some overly Zionist, positions, came the founding in the mid-1950s of CDEC, the Centro di documentazione ebraica contemporanea (Centre for Contemporary Jewish Research). CDEC was first set up in a room in Venice, by the Italian Jewish Youth Federation (the generational element is significant), modelled on the pioneering French institute, the Centre de documentation juive contemporaine, set up in Paris in 1943 through the heroic efforts of Isaac Schneerson and others. CDEC took over the work of Colonel Massimo Adolfo Vitale, who had single-handedly run CRDE (Comitato ricerche deportati ebrei, Search Committee for Jewish Deportees), starting in late 1944, with the aim of finding, identifying, returning and helping Jewish survivors.[9] The historical archive built up by CDEC, and the crucial work of historiography emerging from it from the 1960s onwards—including expert evidence to war crimes trials—was to make it the primary academic institution of Jewish Holocaust memory in Italy in the postwar era. For example, it spent more than five years gathering material for sessions held in Italy of the trial of Friedrich Bosshammer, who was sentenced in West Berlin in April 1972 for the murder of more than 3,000 Italian Jews. Perhaps its contribution is best encapsulated in the monumental achievement of one book, *The Book of Memory*, modelled on European examples themselves rooted in a Jewish tradition of memory books, which names and documents every single victim of the genocide from Italy.[10]

Associations and organisations—an interest group such as ANED, an official communal representative body such UCII/UCEI, a scholarly archive and centre such as CDEC—are not necessarily the most high-profile actors in the broad cultural field around the Holocaust in Italy, but they are fundamental and often-determining presences, creating, sustaining and disseminating through their activism an array of public events and cultural artefacts in the field. They also tend to be the locus of early activities, the first agents in the field, setting parameters and patterns from the very first months and years, long before other sectors of the wider culture became aware of them. They are also connected in important ways to other public bodies and institutions which have a determining influence on how the Holocaust is received and discussed in civil society more broadly. Thus, circling around entities such as ANED, UCEI and CDEC, we might situate a series of public and state institutions: Parliament and the presidency of the Republic and the occasional (in two senses) but key role of legislation or decrees regarding public memory and education (e.g. legislation on history teaching in schools, on memorial days, or indeed validating associations themselves); judicial process, such as war crimes trials, some of which become intensely important public events, such as the trials of SS officer Erich Priebke in early 1990s Rome (see Chapter 6); schools and universities as publicly governed institutions, responsible for the first education of young generations in historical legacy and understanding, governed by legislation but very often influenced by and collaborating with voluntary associations and educational projects shared between private and public spheres; political parties, with their own roles in national and local law and policy, but also—and especially in the era of the mass party politics of the PCI and the DC—working as cultural associations in their own right, sponsoring their own initiatives about the Holocaust and supporting associations (such as the Resistance associations linked to PCI); and, finally, in a related ambit, the Church as a vast institution and network of associations in its own right, with an ongoing influence on (and anxious interest in and object of controversy about) the portrayal of the local and wider history of the Holocaust. This first sphere, then, of activist associationism is subtended—as indeed the entire field necessarily is—by the widest and highest forms of state, national and public institutions, each intersecting with the Holocaust in patchy but powerful ways.

2. The second sphere, like the first, is relatively hidden to the outside observer and the wider culture but is formative in shaping the field of Holocaust culture and settled understandings of it that dominate at any one time. We can label it the *academic* sphere. It takes in the field of academic research, scholarship on aspects of the Holocaust, published in books, journals and latterly online, but also and increasingly, as a distinct field of academic expertise is established—given the title 'Holocaust Studies' in the English-speaking world—it includes a cross-over element in which scholarship is used as a seedbed for other people's work and for more open cultural initiatives concerning the Holocaust. So the academic sphere, at times directly coinciding with the associationist sphere (as is the case with CDEC), takes on a kind of consultancy role to the wider culture and provides a stamp of authority and a guarantor of historical, and thus by extension also ethical, validity for

all sorts of other activities (exhibitions, school education, films, television discussions, etc.). Academic historiography is also the sphere where, crucially, new ideas, newly discovered documents and controversial interpretations or revisions tend to be first tested out: the more controversial they are, the more likely they are to 'go public' quickly, and here we can include as a sort of 'para-academic' event the characteristically Italian notion of the public controversy or 'affair'—the *caso*—in which a spate of contrasting and polemical views, usually laid out by academic and intellectual voices of authority, follow rapid-fire over a few days of media coverage, often triggered by scholarly articles in journals (or by a speech, a book, a film, etc.). It is symptomatic both of the difficult Fascist legacy in Italy and also of widespread suspicions of the postwar state and the consequent flourishing of conspiratorial readings of contemporary history that controversies frequently flared around (re)discoveries of hidden or repressed complicity with Fascism. Examples abound, from the early 1960s when Renzo De Felice's history of Jews under Fascism, mentioned above, caused almost by accident the collapse of a political party, the Radical Party, by naming its secretary, Leopoldo Piccardi, as a participant in the Fascist racial campaigns of the 1930s; through to the early 21st century, when the former Communist and moral beacon of anti-Fascism Ignazio Silone was accused of being a long-term spy and informer for a Fascist police official.[11]

As with the associations, academic work and the debate it creates were often highly politicised and political culture was often highly intellectualised in postwar Italy. Apparently arcane academic debate, on the Holocaust as on many other matters, swiftly found channels to enter a wider public sphere and to shape and reshape public assumptions and lines of knowledge, often along politically polarised lines. In the Holocaust field, the key case once again was De Felice, suspected on the left of a form of rightist revisionism or even veiled apologia in his massive historiographical project on Mussolini and the larger history of Fascism.

One further feature of the academic sphere related to these forms of political-intellectual engagement needs underlining, as it is particularly pertinent to work on the Holocaust, and indeed to the gamut of work on 20th-century history amongst postwar generations of historians, and is perhaps one of the long-term factors beyond ideology that rendered this historiography so prone to passionate polarisation. This is the strong tendency for the historians to have intense first-hand investment in the events they are writing about. The phenomenon of the survivor-witness-historian was a decisive feature of early international historiography on the Holocaust. It started with many of the first great interpreters of the concentration camps, from Léon Poliakov to Eugen Kogon, Hermann Langbein and Hans Marsalek.[12] This is a pattern that ties in the academic sphere to the associationist: more often than not (and unlike the young De Felice in the late 1950s), it was the survivors themselves who began the work of historiography, alongside the work of testimony, and indeed often these two merged and blurred together with less anxiety over disciplinary boundaries and forms of transmission than we may have now.

~

3. The third sphere of cultural production around the Holocaust is perhaps the central focus of attention for a book of this kind, since it is where the activism of the associations, the research and debates amongst academics and intellectuals, and also the stories and voices of individuals, spread out into the wider culture. This is the *cultural* sphere, in the narrow sense of that term, although one with almost endless possible microvariations in form and kind. This is where we find all those works, sites, artefacts and events in which representations, stories and images give cultural form to the Holocaust. A significant tranche of this sphere is taken up with written material. As with the associations, the history of stories about the concentration camps loosely begins with the first-hand testimonies of survivors and victims and then develops, layered on top of those early textual forms, to take in complex variants on forms of semifictional, fictionalised or other hybrid writings that are commonly labelled Holocaust literature.[13] Such a literature, across the spectrum from testimony to fiction, also extends to include minor threads of lyric poetry and drama. And this sphere of written accounts or representations of the Lager is always interwoven with translations of works from other languages, which circulate and have an impact within the Italian field in locally inflected ways.

Other forms of narrative art run parallel to written forms: there is a discrete history of Holocaust film (fictional and later also documentary) coming out of Italy, from early in the postwar period, accelerating especially after 1959 (and, as with literature, inextricably linked with foreign cinema); just as there is an increasingly important phase of television production around the Holocaust, especially from the 1980s onwards, including both factual programming and historical drama.[14] Other aural and visual arts also come into play here, from painting and drawing to musical composition, at times included within or inspired by book publications, sculpture and architecture. Much important close textual or formal analysis of such Holocaust cultural artefacts has concentrated on the private histories and traumas behind them and on their complex reflections on ethical and mimetic aporia; but it is rather how they are positioned within their field of production and transmission, how they are projected into the public sphere and translated into forms of knowledge and awareness, that interests us here.

The cultural sphere perhaps finds its epitome as a public-oriented channel of transmission in sites and spaces of public display, whether permanent (museums, monuments and memorials to the history of the Holocaust) or temporary (gallery and museum exhibitions, with their catalogues and accompanying cultural events, conferences and press conferences). In the conception, planning and sponsoring of, and in the cultural and aesthetic shape given to, such public sites of commemoration and history, we can see the densest confluence of the complex of factors and agents feeding into the representation of the Holocaust at a given cultural moment. It is no coincidence that Villa Torlonia and the Museo della Shoah in Rome, explored in Chapter 2, offered such a rich source and catalyst for the study of the entire field.

Finally, we need to include in the cultural sphere also public and cultural events, as well as spaces and sites. Events can interact with other cultural and institutional actors in differing ways. Exhibitions and performances, and book launches themselves, constitute local events around which talk and debate and public participation proliferate. (The same could be said for the controversies mentioned above, as part of an event pattern in the academic and media spheres.) More weighty and planned are the formal, public and on occasion state-sponsored events of commemoration, national or local anniversaries, within which the Holocaust or the anti-Semitic and racist aspects of Fascism occupy a more or less central place. These can be annual calendar events of national or transnational origin (e.g. 25 April for the national Liberation of Italy, the Resistance and the end of the war; 16 October for the round-up of Rome's Jews; 23 March for the Fosse Ardeatine; 27 January for the liberation of Auschwitz and subsequently for the international commemoration of the Holocaust) or decennial anniversaries (1938, 1943, 1945), which lead to a concentration on certain events across certain calendar years. It is, for example, widely acknowledged that serious historiographical attention to Fascist anti-Semitism was given a striking boost by the 50th anniversary

of the Racial Laws in 1988 (see Chapter 10); and that the earliest efforts to
create a specific awareness of the camps and of the genocide came in the
wake of the larger 10th anniversary of the Liberation and commemorations of the Resistance of 1955.[15]

෴

4. The fourth and final sphere within the field—following the associationist, the academic and the cultural—is of a transverse and somewhat looser and framing nature, containing the major conduits for the
widest dissemination, reception and even distortion of the figures and
ideas, the people, artefacts and initiatives thrown up by the other three.
This is the sphere of the *culture and information industries*, and the media.
Newspapers and popular magazines, television, radio and, more recently,
the internet have all had crucial roles to play in transmitting knowledge,
awareness, effects of shared memory and culture around the Holocaust to
a broad, non-expert and semi-participatory public, and in giving the latter
tools to interpret and understand it.[16] Mediatisation of Holocaust awareness can take many forms, circulating through the other spheres in different ways: from publicity for events or publications and reviews of them
(spiralling into controversies on occasion) to interviews and discussion
fora around events or openings; from information about developments
outside Italy in the press or on television to an apparatus of interpretation
of an informative, pedagogical or civic kind around films or anniversary
events (such as television discussions following screenings of particular
films).[17] It is important to note the specifically superficial, but capillary,
spread produced by these forms of mediatised knowledge—a form of acknowledgment, more than deep knowledge of the Holocaust—that is entirely characteristic of modern informational flow and of much awareness
of the Holocaust beyond the groups of closely engaged 'gatekeepers' and
knowledge producers.

Just as the associationist sphere has, in an ideal chronology, an especially prominent role to play in the early, private or semiprivate phases
of the history of Holocaust knowledge, so, broadly speaking, the intense
mediatisation of the Holocaust, and thus its spread across the wider culture in images channelled into mass cultural form, is more prominent
in later phases, beginning with the general expansion in modern mass
cultural forms, from a popular print media and a mass publishing mar-
ket to the launch of television and its growth in the 1950s–1960s and
deregulation in the 1980s, through to the globalised and multichannel,

hypertechnologised media of the 1990s and beyond. But, this chronology—from private trauma and memory to group articulation, to wider
public formulation, and on to dissemination as mass-mediatised noise—
is declaredly schematic; and it is crucial to acknowledge the extent to
which it is falsely so. As we have seen, associations such as ANED continue to be intensely active into the new millennium; and also the media,
in the form, say, of the photographs and newsreels of the concentration
camp liberations of 1945, famously played a crucial role from the very
start in establishing the sheer, hideous extremes of Nazi persecution in
a vast worldwide public consciousness, in a very real sense preceding the
entire history of long cultural elaboration we are tracing here.

Particularly worthy of attention, and situated in certain senses within
this fourth sphere, but also directly implicated within all the others, is the
area of book publishing. We will see at several stages how trends and clusters within the publishing industry, how individual publishers and how
the genesis of certain key publishing initiatives offer powerful evidence of
the interplay of multiple agents in the general cultural field around the
Holocaust. The historical catalogues of key publishers contain a wealth of
indicators of the cultural conception and work done with the Holocaust
at various moments in postwar Italian cultural history. De Felice's *History*
can once again serve as an illustration, this time for the role of its publisher, Einaudi. Einaudi's contribution to a new focus on the Holocaust
and related events in a crucial period going from the mid-to-late 1950s
to the early 1960s, is marked and striking evidence of a moment when
the intellectual prospectus of a certain left-leaning and anti-Fascist, high
intelligentsia, such as the group around Giulio Einaudi in Turin, came to
include as *de rigueur*—for a combination of historical, political and ethical reasons, including a sensitivity to international intellectual and publishing trends—due attention to the Nazi genocide. Between 1958 and
1963, Einaudi published more than a dozen books that directly addressed
or indirectly touched on the genocide or the history of the camps, works
of scholarly and popular history, original research and translations from
English and French, works of first-hand testimony and autobiographical
narrative and works of contemporary documentation, such as from the
Eichmann trial of 1961. This cluster of work included, but was far from
limited to, the second edition of Primo Levi's *If This Is a Man* of 1958 (a
book Einaudi had turned down in 1946–47) and the first edition of his
next book, *The Truce* in 1963, the two books that established Levi as a
major voice in Italy.

~

It is against the background of a model of an eclectic, interactive and highly dynamic field of cultural production that an analysis of the role and meanings of the Holocaust in postwar Italy needs to be carried out. It has been something of a limitation of certain studies of Holocaust culture that single events and images, texts, moments and monuments, and also single sectors or genres (Holocaust literature, Holocaust cinema), have been analysed, often with great depth and subtlety, but not necessarily then read back into the thick and heavily determining, articulated field of the kind just described. Even in setting out the model in descriptive outline as we have done here, certain key dynamics and axes of interpretation emerge, and these and others will run through the chapters that follow like hidden seams. So, for example, the sheer variety of cultural material and directions of circulation come through strongly. Dissemination of Holocaust culture occurred certainly from private to public, from first-hand to second-hand out to wider communities, from older to younger generations, from intellectual elites and from the central networks and institutions of cultural authority outwards. But the picture is more complicated than what these conventional high-low vectors suggest: the Holocaust has also been the site of marginal knowledge, of hidden narratives struggling to be heard; it has at times circulated in low-level capillary networks, and migrated to centres in displaced or distorted forms, working also as code for other more 'central' concerns of the nation and its civic spheres. There are both narrow and 'thick' forms of knowledge of the Holocaust in circulation, as well as wide and 'thin' forms of awareness, and these strands have distinct if intersecting histories. Take, for example, the low-level pedagogical work of the reading of Anne Frank or Primo Levi in the classroom by generations of schoolchildren in Italy, especially from the 1960s onwards, or the growing trend from the 1990s onwards for class trips to concentration-camp sites. For many children, the impact of this first contact is never forgotten, even if it never develops further, remaining at the level of a diffuse and affective consciousness, which informs their general understanding of the world, of history, of their nation and identity thereafter. It is further clear that there are different, on occasion competing, layers of causation and agency in the building of Holocaust awareness, whether individual or collective, participatory or general, commercial or intellectual, political or religious, all intervening to shape networks of representation and to settle the conventions at work within the field. Single individuals, such as Primo Levi, can emerge to give powerful idiosyncratic shape to local perspectives on the Holocaust (Chapter 5); just as long-term, behind-the-scenes group effort, as with ANED, can perform a shaping role (and indeed, there are often dynamic symbioses between the two, as there were between Levi and ANED).

These and many other recurrent threads and nodes, each with its own rhythm of development and interaction, together give shape to the field of Holocaust culture. The chapters of Part II set out to describe and probe the field from six complementary perspectives.

Part II

§4 New Knowledge

1. Commemoration and Return

Milan's Monumental Cemetery resembles many of the great civic cemeteries of Europe's cities of the 19th century: a vast terrain dominated by imposing stone mausoleums and monuments to the great and the good, the well-to-do families of a newly modernised and prosperous country. The vast chapel and entrance function also as a so-called *famedio*, where the proudest and most famed of citizens of Milan are commemorated. Beyond the famedio, the park of the cemetery opens out behind a small gravel cross-roads. Here, in 1946, a new monument was unveiled, dedicated 'To the Fallen in the Nazi Extermination Camps'. This was one of the very first public monuments in Italy specifically dedicated to the victims of the camps, and in its planning and form we find crystallised several features of cultural responses to the Holocaust in the immediate postwar months and years in Italy, which this chapter sets out to sample.

The monument was planned and sponsored in 1945 by one of several associations of camp survivors to have emerged in the postwar months, ANPPIA (the National Association of Italian Antifascist Political Victims). It was designed by the BBPR architectural studio, specifically by one of its partners, Enrico Peressuti. Following work on this monument, the BBPR studio became the most influential designers of Holocaust and deportation memorials over the entire postwar era in Italy.[1] They were responsible for a 1965 Italian memorial at Gusen concentration camp near Mauthausen; a 1973 monument and museum to the deportee at Carpi, the central town near the holding camp at Fossoli from where deportations to Auschwitz and elsewhere took place from early 1944; a 1980

Italian memorial pavilion at Auschwitz; a 1982 memorial at Ravensbrück; and a 1998 Monument for the Deported in Milan's Parco Nord. At Carpi, for example, they created a space synthesising historical record and commemoration, made up of vaulted rooms filled with names of deportees and engravings by the artists Corrado Cagli (a camp survivor), Renato Guttuso, Picasso and others.[2] The principal reason for this intense and quite exceptional engagement was personal: of the four partners of the BBPR acronym, Gian Luigi Banfi had died at Gusen-Mauthausen after fighting in the Resistance; Lodovico Belgiojoso had followed the same path but survived the camps; and Ernesto Rogers had fled to Switzerland to avoid racial persecution (his father died in Auschwitz).

Peressuti's design for the 1945–46 monument followed the rationalist style that the young architects had adhered to during the Fascist era but turned it to historical and anti-Fascist memorial purposes: earth from Mauthausen was encased in a glass cube, crossed by a simple geometric metal lattice, the whole circled by barbed wire. The work is powerfully abstract and universal alike, rejecting in its original conception the named plaques of traditional remembrance and even the solemn figuration of the Unknown Soldier, evoking instead the earth and air of some total reality, in a space marked by symbolic enclosure or imprisonment. The specifics of place (Mauthausen) are present but opaque, evocative of a mood rather than a chronicle of history. In this, it captured a powerful impulse to universal reflection as a response to war, loss and the horrific extremes of Nazi violence, prevalent in the postwar moment. There were echoes also of a geometric reduction of a Christian cross (at the base of the cube), of an urn (the earth enclosed) and of the barbed wire as both prison but also crown of thorns. Although not a work of traditional representation, then, it nevertheless chimed with elements of traditional ritual and with certain contemporary 'neorealist' tendencies, in its antirhetorical simplicity and in its symbolic poetry of the contemporary. As Bruno Zevi has pointed out, the work was poised between architecture and sculpture, between an evocation of intimate internal space and experience, and external public space.[3] All of these aspects, and their tensions, permeate the larger field we are exploring here.

The tensions come to the fore in the history of the monument after 1946. The families of the victims and ANPPIA were less than satisfied with the lack of names and so of the possibility of private mourning: after 1947 they began to add their own improvised nameplates and photos of loved ones. The monument was already run down by the late 1940s, with signs of rust and disrepair. Reconstruction led to the addition of seven emblematic, formal name plates, until a third version in 1955 simplified the design once more. There was, in other words, already a telling difficulty in encompassing private and public mourning and in capturing the symbols and affect that would satisfy different constituencies. And yet, the monument was a striking success in other ways, fixed in a place of remarkable public prominence, and visually and conceptually highly resonant. Its aim was to commemorate a deliberately unspecified category of the Fallen, without distinguishing between grades of Lager or between reasons for deportation; even so, it built a quite tightly specific symbolism around the archetypal site of the camp itself (a Nazi phenomenon, not Italian, it is implied) as a sort of essence of what had been visited upon the monument's designers, the city and the nation. The delicate balancing act in this early memorial—between the sponsors and the cultural interpreters; and between different experiences for commemoration—was entirely characteristic of the uncertain positioning of the camps in the memorial landscape of the postwar era, partly within and partly occluding what we now call the Holocaust. In what follows, we will first fill in the confused, fluid context of awareness and early response to the Holocaust, from the late war years to return and recovery; and then look forward to the first emergence of a prominent and articulated field of Holocaust culture, beginning in the mid-1950s and gathering strength rapidly in the period of the late 1950s and early 1960s.

In hindsight, it is extremely difficult to recapture first awareness of the Nazi genocide and insert the first glimmerings of information and response into the vast and fast-moving panorama of news about the endgame of the global war in 1944–45. Already in the early years of the war in Italy, fragments of information had filtered through. Primo Levi, in his autobiography *The Periodic Table*, notes how he and his friends both grasped and chose to ignore hints about what was happening to Europe's Jews, as they carried on in a state of 'self-imposed blindness'.[4] When in 1971 he came to write a deposition, via CDEC, for the trial of Friedrich Bosshammer (Eichmann's representative in Italy), he pinned down specifically five sources of information circulating in northern Italy before his own deportation: Swiss newspapers (*Gazette de Lausanne*); clandestine allied radio (Radio London); the British White Paper on German atrocities (which Levi translated for himself); Italian soldiers returning from Russia,

Croatia and Greece, who had seen Jews killed and deported; and Jewish refugees from Croatia and Poland.[5]

Levi's testimony of an eclectic and patchy, but ominous, gathering of information holds not only for the years before but also in a sense for the years immediately after the end of the war. As a wealth of new historical work has shown, Europe's war spilled over into its dramatic 'postwar' with, at times, only the symbolic caesura and euphoria of war's end.[6] Even in early 1945, in the continent's press coverage, the rapid turnover of news meant that concentration camp liberations, including images of hideous piles of corpses and skeletal survivors that in retrospect have haunted our post-Holocaust world, were surrounded and succeeded in quick order by news from the Eastern fronts, the final battles in Berlin, surrenders and victories. The liberation of Auschwitz on 27 January 1945—now a solemn international date of remembrance—was a detail compared to news of the Yalta conference days later; Hitler and Goebbels committed suicide the day after Dachau was liberated on 29 April.

This revised perspective takes on specific further complications in the Italian case, where the entire period from 1943 to 1948 constituted at many levels a single phase of transition from Fascism to civil war, occupation and Salò, to democracy and a new Republic (the first postwar elections were held on 18 April 1948).[7] The nation, the state and the very idea of Italy were in tumult, and the national print media was no exception: it was hardly on its feet as the war ended—*Corriere della sera*, for example, was closed down by the liberation forces in 1945—and where it was, it was closely focussed on the fight for the nation's survival from one side or another. In April and early May 1945, then, when Europe's press, radio and newsreels were briefly transfixed by appalling images from Bergen-Belsen, Buchenwald and other sites, Italy was living through the death throes of its own war, with the liberation of Milan and the North declared on 25 April, and the execution and infamous public display of Mussolini on 28 April, diverting almost all attention from those far-off camps and their atrocious remains.

There were exceptions, certainly, in particular in the organs of militant anti-Fascism that had been active during the Resistance struggle. The socialist paper *Avanti!* published several articles in late April and May 1945 on Italian holding and pre-deportation camps at Bolzano and Fossoli, and on Mauthausen, the principal destination for Italian Resistance deportees. In late May, a cortege in Milan commemorated victims of the 68 'martyrs' from Fossoli—who had been executed by the Nazis in the camp on 12 July 1944—and lists of some 1,500 Italian Mauthausen victims were published in series in *Avanti!* leading to a headline on 27 May that read:

Mauthausen: Name of Everlasting Infamy
The 'Concentration Camps'—Killed with Gas, Petrol and with Torture—Half a Million Men Burned in the Ovens[8]

A handful of articles included photographs, as in the Communist paper *L'Unità* on 30 May 1945. But most of the Italian press had to wait until late 1945, with the start of the Nuremberg trials, for a concerted acknowledgment of what was beginning to be called genocide, war crimes or crimes against humanity (although even at Nuremberg, other agendas and narratives were to the fore in the international prosecution). On 14–15 December 1945, *L'Unità* published articles and photographs under the titles 'Talk of Death Camps' and 'Six Million Dead—But Himmler Wanted More'. Despite this delay of only a matter of months, convincing accounts of the history of imagery of the Holocaust—the tropes of corpses and survivors, shamed SS troops, barbed wire and train tracks, barracks, ovens and ditches—have traced the origin of these shared visual horrors to those very first press, radio and film accounts in spring 1945; and it is therefore not insignificant that the Italian public for the most part missed out on this moment of shared revulsion.[9]

There were also reflections, if not always of the most lucid kind, in intellectual arenas on the 'Jewish question'. Benedetto Croce, for example—something of a liberal hero for his detached anti-Fascism over the preceding decades—became embroiled in a defence of an unpleasantly anti-Semitic set of essays by the politician and future president of Italy's Senate, Cesare Merzagora. Merzagora's 1946 book *The Fearful* included several broadsides against those Jews fortunate enough to return, exhorting them not to expect to return also to the jobs they had lost after 1938, not to make trouble, and not to forget that there was much to commend Fascist anti-Semitism.[10] Croce's preface to the book, whilst (like Merzagora) rejecting persecution per se, nevertheless struck similar notes, against the ostentation of Jewish particularity and difference, insisting that returning Jews not expect 'privileges or preferences' for their suffering and that they do all they can to merge with other Italians instead of clinging onto traces of a 'barbaric and primitive religious culture'.[11]

Croce and Merzagora were anxious about religion, but also about return. There were nearly two million Italian prisoners of war, held in Axis or Allied prisons, to join the mass of displaced persons of all nationalities

in the postwar months traversing countries and continents on journeys
of return and difficult reintegration.[12] These floods of hungry, weak and
traumatised DPs were not easily split into distinct groups or categories
(Jews, political prisoners, forced labourers, military prisoners of war,
enemy alien internees, defeated armies, and so on), with particular stories
to tell of their experiences.[13] Italian prisoners of all kinds took longer than
others to return home, in part for political reasons: Italy was caught between its earlier Axis status and its fragile post-armistice alliances, and its
displaced populations suffered delays as a result.

In 1945–46, then, getting home, finding relatives or news of their death,
or militating for practical support and reintegration were complicated
and troubling tasks. This was the core impulse behind what little press
coverage there was; the lists from Mauthausen in *Avanti!* were part of an
effort to identify, find and bring home survivors. Similarly, this is what
led to formation of the early associations, such as ANED and ANPPIA,
and to the activity in this postwar phase of Massimo Vitale's CRDE or
DELASEM, a Jewish refugee organisation that worked to reunite families
and aid emigration to Palestine.[14]

In all this flow of activity, coverage, comment and movement of peo-
ples in the months after the war ended, the contours of what would later
be labelled the Holocaust were nevertheless present. As in several other
Western European countries, the mid-1940s saw an uneven, largely private or group awareness of the genocide, but one with surprisingly rich
and varied public manifestations and forms of representation, spotted
with patchy moments of wider acknowledgment of the sheer horror of
what the Nazis had achieved. Memorials such as BBPR's at the Milan
cemetery show how early cultural forms of commemoration and mourning, but also reflections on the meanings of the war and Nazi horrors,
ran alongside the practicalities and processes of return. And we can see
something analogous if we turn to the first written accounts of the camps.

2. Literature, History, Testimony, 1944–1947

The variety and complexity of the postwar moment is well reflected in
the spectrum of early written accounts of the concentration camps beyond daily journalism, a rich if small-scale field ranging from literature
(prose, theatre and poetry) to historiography, to first-person testimony.

Perhaps surprisingly, the first significant attempts in Italian to give written form to the genocide came not from the survivor-writers but from the

markedly contrasting pens of two high-literary intellectuals, Giacomo Debenedetti and Curzio Malaparte. Debenedetti's *16 October 1943* was written in late 1944.[15] It is a short, restrained, but also vividly human and on occasion hard-edged 'on-the-ground' chronicle of the night of 15–16 October 1943, in the former ghetto area of Rome, when more than a thousand Jews were rounded up by the Nazis and deported by train to Auschwitz. Interlaced with this diary of deportation, Debenedetti, himself Jewish, looks back to September 1943 and the remarkable, tragicomic episode of the 'tribute' of 50 kilogrammes of gold demanded from the Jewish community in Rome by the newly arrived Nazi authorities. Briefly, this extends also to the Fosse Ardeatine massacre of March; and the aftermath of this event would loom still larger in Debenedetti's companion piece *Eight Jews*,[16] which begins with the courtroom testimony of policeman Raffaele Alianello claiming mitigation for having removed the names of the eponymous eight Jews from the preparatory lists of victims destined for the Fosse. Looking at what he calls this 'fiendishly [*canagliesca*] ambiguous'[17] plea from a Fascist official from a declaredly Jewish perspective (itself unusually bold in 1944), Debenedetti's reflections are acidly focussed—as were Croce and Merzagora—on the problem of Jewish difference, in both Fascism and the new democracy. Debenedetti too calls for an end to the Jewish 'privilege', of being 'chosen' as either victim or saved. In a much quoted phrase, he calls for Jewish victims to be treated no differently from other victims, 'lined up alongside all the dead of this war [...] soldiers just like them [...] *Soldier Coen . . . Soldier Levi . . . Soldier Abramovic . . . Soldier Chaim Blumenthal, age five years* [...]'.[18] *Eight Jews* is in complex relation with Croce's calls for the abolition of difference (as was Debenedetti with Croce himself), acutely aware of the public aspect of Jewish identity, beyond private mourning, and claiming also a national Italian (and human) identity for Jewish victims of war. It also tellingly reflects upon the partial and inadequate judicial processes, such as the trial of the Fascist police chief at which Alianello was a witness.

Eight Jews and *16 October 1943* work as something like Ur-texts for several lines of both Holocaust literature and testimony in Italy. *16 October 1943* in particular was crucial as a model for the early postwar decades, in its reportage and chronicle, linked like several deportation testimonies to the neorealist moment, in its engagement with justice, national identity and collective responsibility, in its hints at the ambivalent role of the bishop of Rome (an issue that would explode into international controversy and scandal from the mid-1960s), all filtered through the ter-

rible sequence of events suffered by the Jews of Rome (see Chapter 6).
In literary terms, Debenedetti's text established an influential model for
Holocaust writing of the bystander-writer (neither 'survivor' nor entirely
disinterested observer): sober, respectful chronicle with elements of narrative invention, 'second-hand' listening and transmission and tentative
enquiry into complex moral and psychological problems.

Debenedetti was in Rome during and after September and October
1943, and he spoke to victims and protagonists of the events he relates.
His work was, in other words, also a kind of reportage. In this (but in little else), *16 October 1943* resembles Curzio Malaparte's *Kaputt*, a vast work
of high literary performance and artifice, based on Malaparte's extensive
reportage as a war journalist across Axis (and Axis-occupied) Europe.[19]
In his travels around the military postings and dining tables of the old
and new aristocracies of the Nazi imperium, Malaparte dwells on several
occasions on the Jewish Question and its ongoing 'Final Solution' taking
place just a short distance from those bibulous diners. He sees, apparently
first-hand, the massacre at Iași in Romania, and he strolls, accompanied
by a guard, through hideous scenes of the Warsaw ghetto. His tone is of
weary sorrow, of cynical detachment from his Nazi hosts, much as when
he wittily relates dining with Otto Frank, waiting to meet Ante Pavelić,
or encountering Himmler in an elevator. Nevertheless, for all his narcissistic flaws, Malaparte deploys considerable literary resource in capturing
the physical degradation, the grotesque scenery of Nazi Europe and the
horrors of war and genocide as they happened.[20]

Debenedetti and Malaparte—writing before the end of the war, before the phase of return and before the establishment of either a neorealist orthodoxy in Italy or any model for witness writing about the
camps—represent contrasting models for the field of Holocaust literature in Italy: semidetached chronicle on the one hand, melodramatic
and narcissistic elaboration on the other; Italian or European; from
below or from above; from within and about the Jewish community
or from within the Nazi-Fascist elite. Both, however, are knowingly literary elaborations, as is also the case with a third early literary work
worth mentioning for its already eccentric but incisive feel and its self-
conscious literary-philosophical reflections from a Jewish perspective:
Umberto Saba's *Shortcuts and Short-stories*.[21] Saba's epigrams, annota-
tions and anecdotes circle around and return repeatedly to Majdanek
and to images of the camps, to Hitler and Mussolini. They are fragments of sense and nonsense from the maelstrom of this early moment,

torn between relief at the end of the nightmare and an intuition of a profound caesura 'after Maidaneck' (sic).[22]

Alongside these very early literary responses, although for the most part unnoticed, there were also clusters of first-person testimonies by returnees, appearing in numbers within months of the war's end. Some were too traumatised or simply unable to convey the horrors of what they had seen, whereas others felt the urge to write down what they had lived through, though they often found audiences—and publishers—unable or unwilling to listen.[23] Primo Levi was turned down by Einaudi (on the advice of Natalia Ginzburg and Cesare Pavese), as well as other Italian and indeed American publishers, before finding a local, ex-Resistance intellectual, Franco Antonicelli, whose small De Silva house took the work on. As Levi later reflected:

> At that time, people had other things to get on with: building houses, looking for jobs. There was still rationing, cities were in ruins, the Allies were still occupying Italy. People didn't want to hear [about the camps], they wanted other things, to dance, to party, to bring children into the world. A book like mine and many others that came after were almost like a discourtesy, like spoiling a party.[24]

Levi was far from alone. Ettore Siegrist, author of a memoir of Dachau, complains in his preface that he was turned down by all the major publishers.[25] Indeed, the figure of the returnee and the difficulties he faced, the vision of the devastated homeland he found, reflecting his own depletion but also cutting him off from it, was one of the defining shared stories of the moment. One work of literature that proved extraordinarily powerful and resonant in capturing the national psyche at that moment was Edoardo De Filippo's play *Napoli milionaria!* (1945), built around the forlorn figure of ex-soldier Gennaro Jovine, a traumatised returnee to Naples from internment and labour in a Nazi camp.

Many survivors, finding little interest from publishers, left their works to gather dust in drawers, sometimes for decades; others, like Levi and Siegrist, found small, local outlets for their work and even had some minor successes (Levi was well reviewed in Turin; Siegrist's book went into a second edition). These muted beginnings, the unread corpus of early memoirs, were laying the groundwork for an important recurrent pattern in the field of Holocaust culture over the long postwar era: that of the layered periodic reprise of Holocaust documentation, especially first-person testimony, through the (re)discovery and late (re)publication, on occasion posthumous, of manuscripts or small books from the early after-math of the war. This is one of the many ways in which the field defies linear chronicling of its progress, since waves of writing about the camps have appeared in clusters of publication and republication—telling indicators of moments of a surge in interest in the subject (Chapter 5).

For all the problems of publication and audience, however, the mid-1940s nevertheless did produce a significant body of testimonial writing and accounts of the camps, a powerful corpus of first figuration of deportation and the Holocaust. Works of instant history included Giancarlo Ottani's *A People Weeps* and Eucardio Momigliano's *Tragic and Grotesque History of Italian Racism*.[26] Ottani was a journalist; *Un popolo piange* quotes extensively from primary and secondary sources, from press, anecdotes, histories of Jews and other reportage. It is an anthology, written in what he declares as a 'rapid, summary, journalistic style' (p. 5), although it is not without its passionate rhetoric. Its accuracy can be judged by Ottani's final estimate of Jews killed in Europe—5.5 million—and indeed it is a much more efficient account than his near-contemporary novel based on the same material, *The Death Camps*,[27] which is full of ciphers and set-piece speeches on Zionism, the war and Nazi massacres. If anything, *The Death Camps* demonstrates the steep difficulty of capturing this history in narrative form. Momigliano's work, although largely neglected until recently in favour of the 'first' Italian histories of Fascist anti-Semitism such as De Felice's, has been given its due recently for the early formulation of the Italian-Jewish history of persecution, and more problematically for its presentation of what was already emerging as a key trope of explanation of Italy's Holocaust: the figure of a kindly, natively nonracist Italian, waylaid by the ideological racism of Nazism or Nazi-Fascism. Here is one such formulation from Momigliano:

> Italy has never known anti-Semitism. A tradition of millennial civilization had always infused in its governments and people a broad, benevolent tolerance towards the Jews; and even when, spurred by the religious intolerance of a sovereign or a pope, their freedom was constrained and their lives regulated, at times harshly, the application of these laws was always in practice indulgent, consisting most often of taxes and tributes.[28]

As we will see in Chapter 8, the assumption on show here of the decency and tolerance of the Italian character was a tool even in the political diplomacy of the postwar moment—shoring up an account of Italians as 'innocent' of the crimes of the Fascist state—as well as a pervasive feature of early explanations of Italian responses to anti-Semitism.

Another kind of factual reportage from the concentration camps appeared in the shape of a medical report on the hygienic and health conditions of the camp at Monowitz-Auschwitz III. The report was coauthored by a Turinese Jewish doctor who was a survivor of Monowitz, Leonardo De Benedetti, and was published in the respected medical journal *Minerva medica* in 1946.[29] It describes in sober, painstaking and technical detail the common medical conditions that afflicted the prisoners, their diet and sanitary conditions, and the basic workings of the camp. The report is important evidence of the variety of low-level forms in which information was circulating in this period, and it would no doubt have been forgotten entirely (indeed was forgotten for many years) were it not for De Benedetti's coauthor, Primo Levi.[30]

Beside these occasionally awkward first attempts at historiography or other forms of factual reportage or analysis, first-person accounts appeared in quite large numbers, published in journals, often Resistance journals, or printed by local publishing houses. Fifty-five were published in book or pamphlet form between 1945 and 1947, by Jewish, military and political deportees, or by journalists and novelists.[31] Of these, forty-seven were published in 1945 and 1946, and only eight in 1947 (although three of these were published by Mondadori, a major Milanese publishing house, and thus enjoyed substantially greater readership than the others).[32] Not a single text of this kind was published in 1948 and two or fewer in each subsequent year until 1959 (excluding translations and republications). Twelve of the 1945–1947 texts were by or primarily about Jewish deportees, and six of these were by or about women; nineteen are by or primarily about political deportees, and eleven are by or about military internees. Eight were translations.

Across this uneven and varied corpus, certain threads and tropes emerge in the style, rhetoric and self-presentation of these often urgent, traumatised and improvised testimonies, threads that will resonate in later periods of response to the Holocaust: these include the intersection of deportation and Resistance, affinities with contemporary neorealist literature and recourse to a mix of traditional literary culture and newly disturbed formulations for capturing the horrific reality of the camps.

Throughout the corpus, we find an uneasy parallelism between armed Resistance (where most of the deportees' stories begin) and deportation. The same two strands were blurred in the BBPR project and across much of the landscape of postwar return. For many, deportation is experienced as resistance, or literally the Resistance, truncated or continued, and the camp inmates shape their identity and strategy for survival, and their dignity on return, by clinging to an identity as partisans or soldiers, both of which figure as patriots, so that the discourse also becomes one of re-claimed national identity. One example of many, from Francesco Uliv-elli, who was held in Bolzano camp: 'We felt the scent of victory as we marched in the concentration camps, just as our partisans felt it as they marched and gathered around the bivouac fires'.[33]

Modes of deportation writing also echo certain modes of Resistance writing, itself the principal source of the postwar cultural explosion in Italy known as neorealism (present also in the BBPR monument). The elemental and collective storytelling impulse in neorealism is echoed in Levi's episodic storytelling, which he compares to 'the stories of a new bible'.[34] Similarly, in Gaetano De Martino's *1945*, inmates awaiting de-portation in Milan's San Vittore prison exchange stories of how they were caught: 'everyone had their own story to tell'.[35]

The texts also display the oral qualities—unliterary, clipped, driven by dialogue—typical of neorealism (and of its American models). Here are two examples of the hard-boiled, semipoetic realism of Enzo Rava's 1945 testimony *Martyrdom*:

> The police station; a filthy cell; they beat me so hard I don't know what's go-ing on any more; I collapse. [...] An awful night.
> [...]
> Showers. The usual drill. The usual fierce attack. They look at our mouths; do they think there's some gold still left? . . . Naked in the shower. They give us some rags; a treat.[36]

Beyond neorealist modes, however, the early deportation texts also have recourse to long-standing traditions of writing and rituals of death, mourning and suffering. The old models that were evoked range from the great literary canon to formal, internal conventions of genre. For many Italians, Dante's *Inferno* is a familiar and recurrent reference point: Levi drew extensively and subtly on Dante, but many others also evoke Dante's Gates of Hell, the Malebolge, the Germans as Hell's demons and more.[37] Other traditions tapped include classical or Romantic literary models of lament, or indeed prayer. Two examples from epigraphs: classical funerary poetry is evoked by Alba Valech Capozzi in the epigraph to her 1946 work *A24029*; and Levi famously adapts the Hebrew prayer the *Shema*, in his epigraph to *If This Is a Man*.

At times, however, these traditional tropes are shown to be strained to the breaking point, as if to intuit the dimension of some new experience, some aporia at the heart of the horrors of deportation. An example is the constant anxiety over the collapse in the camps of conventional wartime virtues of action, honour and heroism, or Christian and/or socialist virtues of altruism or solidarity, since only the selfish survive there.[38] Ultimately this anxiety entails an interrogation of the very nature of man, as a category, a species, a bearer of value, as Levi's title 'If This Is a Man' evokes so eloquently. Interrogating this 'humanist'—and partly Christianising—topos of Man as part of a response to the Holocaust is a telling feature of this postwar moment more widely (Chapter 7).

Although it is not knowingly used in a gender-specific sense, the evocation of soldierly virtues and their failure, and the use of the term *uomo* also alerts us to issues of gender and to the work by women in this early corpus. They frequently show different emphases in their accounts of the camps—on friendships, communities and intimate bonds created in the camps, and also on a range of distinct sufferings of the female body—and thus provide rich counterpoints to some of the harder, realist foci. Gender in Holocaust writing is already at this early stage a defining terrain of distinction, and it will become more so in line with trends in feminism, women's history and oral history in the 1970s.[39] For concrete historical reasons (because Jewish men, women, children and the old were all deported, not just fighting—and largely male—partisans, labourers or soldiers), as noted above, the key women's voices of the mid-1940s were Jewish deportees. The testimonies by Liana Millu, Frida Misul, Luciana Nissim, Giuliana Tedeschi and Alba Valech Capozzi are already acutely aware of the specifics of women's experience of the camps as well as of the continuities of shared suffering; and intuitively aware also of the challenge to all traditional forms and values offered by the genocide.[40] Two of these works in particular—by Millu and Tedeschi—in later republications and reelaborations will become crucial entries in the canon of Italian Holocaust literature.[41]

In form and language too, a cluster of early accounts are tellingly troubled and complex, unable to render in clear realistic terms their traumatic weight of experience. Charles Cohen's 1945 *A Buchenwald Notebook*[42] uses the old literary conceit of the found manuscript—in this case a camp diary left behind by an errant survivor after the war—to uncanny effect, posing newly intense problems of identity and its dissolution, memory, first- and second-hand testimony and self-knowledge. In works such as this, the corpus comes closest to adumbrating conceptions of the Holocaust as a deep ontological fracture or loss, an idea that becomes a philosophical commonplace later in the century.

Loss is reflected variously in crises of selfhood, language and meaning, and ultimately of being. Loss of self is conveyed, in *A Buchenwald Notebook*, in imagery of the absence of mirrors in the camps, and therefore literally and metaphorically of self-recognition: 'If I touch my face I feel I am touching death [...] no-one would recognize me, not even myself. My looks have changed, crumbled from within, like a grand old palace that has become a tomb' (p. 11).

Compare Enzo Rava: 'The word "I", "me", is so strange. It feels strange somehow. I am not conscious any more; I don't think any more, I don't think' (Rava, p. 69).

There are comparable points in *If This Is a Man*: 'Already my body is no longer mine [...] when we haven't seen each other for three or four days, we struggle to recognize each other'; or, as he catches his reflection, 'we look ridiculous and repugnant'.[43]

A crisis in language is noted by many of the survivors. Levi, again, dwells with great acuity on the damage done to language in the camps:

> Our way of being cold has need of a new word. We say 'hunger', we say 'tiredness', 'fear', 'pain', we say 'winter' and they are different things. They are free words created and used by free men living in comfort and suffering in their homes.[44]

But he is not alone. Here is Enea Fergnani, writing about Mauthausen: 'Work, hunger, cold, illness, death. They aren't the same words for us as they were before coming to Germany. Here work, hunger, cold, illness, death mean torture, massacre, torment; or worse, hatred, cruelty, violence'.[45]

Finally, Aldo Bizzarri's 1946 *Mauthausen Hermetic City* delineates not only the failure of language but a more essential fracture in the chain of meaning and being itself:

> What sense is there to this story? [...] The reply is no sense, no reason. That goes for everything at Mauthausen, it is absurd to search for a thread of connection, for a logic [...] The only fixed point in the landscape, behind the constantly changing absurdities of each day, is death. [...] Indeed, as author my task was not so much to show how one might have survived it as to recall that everyone was there to die.[46]

Bizzarri, in two works of 1946–47, creates a variety of hybrid solutions in form and genre to the 'problem' already emerging of how to write about the Holocaust. Like Ottani, Bizzarri wrote both factual and narrative accounts of his deportation. *Mauthausen Hermetic City* is an acute sociological analysis of the camp 'system', combining analytical reserve and cathartic emotion. His 1947 work of narrative fiction, *Living Not Permitted*, sets narrative itself at the heart of his representation of the camps: eight prisoners gather on successive Sundays to tell each other stories and poems (with echoes of Boccaccio). The stories they tell are apparently of the outside world, but they cannot help echoing and interrogating the meaning of their present predicament in the Nazi camp. Each meeting is precarious and poignant, and as the novel proceeds fewer are present each week, as they are either moved on to other camps or are killed.

The struggle to find a form and a tone both to contain the facts of the camp experience and also to complement them with the sense of its enormity is the catalyst for the formal variety of these texts. Many of them declaredly but disingenuously eschew all forms of literariness in favour of 'fact' only: these are not professional writers or literary intellectuals, after all. But many note also that the documentary evidence was already established in the photography, images and newsreels (although as we have seen, these had patchy circulation). Several texts include images from these sources, as if to say that writing must do more than document:

> From the very first days when documents arrived films, newsreels, radio, official accounts, rumours it was clear that no human word could speak the horror of the Nazi camps. No number. [...] Hence the need to get away from the strictly documentary [...].[47]

And Levi too in the Preface to *If This Is a Man*:

> Thus my book adds nothing in terms of ghastly details to what readers all over the world already know by now on the disturbing subject of the death camps [*campi di distruzione*]. [...] It is rather intended to provide evidence for a calm examination of certain aspects of the human mind.[48]

Where Levi moves into ethical reflection, others move towards fictionalisation (Bizzarri), semifictionalisation (Rava's book is all historical fact, aside crucially from its fictional protagonist), irony and sarcasm (Misul), drawings (Brunello, Gregori), poetry (Meneghetti).[49] Often the root of this formal experimentation lies in self-disavowal, in the crises of selfhood, language and being noted earlier: the struggle for form is a struggle for a voice for a now-unrecognisable self. This is perhaps clearest of all in Paolo Liggeri's odd but illuminating preface to his 1946 memoir, *Red Triangle*:

> These are the memories of a friend, a very dear friend whom I love as myself and who—strange coincidence!—is called Paolo like me, was arrested with

me and stuck with me throughout our imprisonment and return. A brotherly love, cemented by our common suffering, has bound our souls so close that even I, rereading these pages, feel I am reading my own words. [...] Some of you will smile and think this is a literary device. I shall not even try to convince you otherwise.[50]

Far from eschewing literary form, the movements or even games with form obliquely evoke problematics of writing down the experience of deportation and return. Literary narrative and literary form if anything preceded and intermingled from the outset with the emergence of the semiprivate corpus of testimonial writing we have been describing, as in the case of Ottani and Bizzarri or in the literary or mimetic struggles of the first-person accounts, or indeed in the literary elaborations of Debenedetti, Malaparte and Saba. The confusions of the early postwar years are reflected in the complex variety of early written formulations of Holocaust response and representation, in the tensions evident in their textual patterns and turns of phrase, as indeed they were in the problems of form and naming in the Milan Cemetery monument.

3. 1958–1963: The New Field

The years from the late 1940s to the late 1950s are often seen as years of silence and neglect of the genocide, in Italy and in Europe more generally, years of reconstruction and Cold War retrenchment in which the voices of Jewish survivors fell quiet and in which little interest was shown in listening to survivors' tales where they were told. The picture is largely confirmed by Bravo and Jalla's catalogue of testimonial writings on the concentration camps, which registers an almost complete collapse following 1948.[51] From within the Jewish community, there was a wish to move beyond the trauma of war, to rebuild communities, to look towards the new state of Israel after 1948 rather than recall the storm of persecution.[52] The silence was by no means universal, however; the mid-1950s saw a string of important events, interventions and initiatives on the camps, deportation and memory, in particular after the tenth anniversary of the Liberation in 1955. It is nevertheless the case that the late 1950s and early 1960s saw something of a step-change in attention to the Holocaust, in quantity and quality, a shift in what Samuel Moyn has called the 'regime of memory'.[53] To give a sense of this shift, we can sample four overlapping areas of cultural output—nonfiction book publishing, fiction books and films, media events and other forms of public response, Jewish response—concentrating especially on the period 1958–1963, with forays backwards to the mid-1950s.

Between 1958 and 1963, a varied range of important testimonial and historiographical material on deportation (anti-Fascist or Jewish) and the concentration camps appeared. There had already been significant publications since 1954, such as the highly successful Mauthausen memoir *It's Easy to Say Hunger* by the socialist ex-partisan Piero Caleffi;[54] or the recovered testimony of a Triestine Jewish victim who died shortly after returning home in 1945, Bruno Piazza's *Because Others Forget*.[55] A cluster of new first-hand accounts were published during 1959–60, for example Mario Bonfantini's *A Leap in the Dark*, telling of the writer's escape from a deportation train that left from Fossoli; and Emilio Jani's *My Voice Saved Me*, of the author's singing in Auschwitz.[56] Perhaps the most significant debut work of testimony was Edith Bruck's 1958 *Who Loves You Like This*, a strikingly intense memoir of Bruck's deportation to Auschwitz as a young girl from Hungary, her survival, emigration to Israel and 'escape' to Italy.[57] Bruck's extensive work as a survivor-writer, still continuing with vigour in 2012, would develop into the richest contribution in Italian after Primo Levi's.

Two further strands of publishing were symptomatic of a growing interest in Holocaust-related material: republications of earlier works of testimony and translations (both often picking up work from the 1940s). Republication is, of course, best illustrated by the 1958 Einaudi edition of Levi's *If This Is a Man*. But other important accounts of both Jewish and partisan deportation confirm the trend: Debenedetti's *16 October 1943* was reissued by Il Saggiatore in 1959;[58] and a much admired 1946 account by Piero Chiodi of his time as a partisan and camp prisoner, *Bandits*, was reissued in 1961.[59]

Translations, following the mid-1950s success of Anne Frank's diary and French political deportee Robert Antelme's *L'Espèce humaine* (The Human Race),[60] proliferated in 1958–1963. Two Holocaust diaries recovered from the rubble of the Warsaw ghetto, by David Rubinowicz and Emanuel Ringelblum, appeared with major Italian publishers in 1960 and 1962 respectively.[61] And the autobiography and apologia by the first SS commandant of Auschwitz, Rudolf Höss, written from his prison cell before execution in 1947, was translated by Einaudi in 1962.[62]

Höss's autobiography came with a preface by the British military jurist and official at Nuremberg, Edward, Lord Russell of Liverpool.[63] Russell was the author of the most widely read account of Nazi crimes at that time, *The Scourge of the Swastika*. This and several other important foreign works of history were also translated at this time, appearing alongside the beginnings of a corpus of original historiography in Italian. Russell's book was published in 1955 by Feltrinelli, the newly established Marxist-oriented publishing house, which went on also to publish Piazza and Bonfantini. Russell's book was a marked success, going into four editions in two years.[64] In the same year, Léon Poliakov's *Bréviaire de la Haine* (Harvest of Hate), the first discrete, documented history of the genocide, was translated also.[65] 1962 saw two further highly significant translations: Gerald Reitlinger's *Final Solution*; and American journalist and historian W. L. Shirer's general history of Nazism, *Rise and Fall of the Third Reich*.[66]

Finally, Holocaust historiography in Italian also began to appear. Alberto Nirenstajn collated a powerful history of the Warsaw ghetto in *Remember What Amalek Did to You* in 1958.[67] Caleffi, now a Socialist senator, followed up *It's Easy to Say Hunger* in 1960 with *Think, People!* a collaborative work of popular history of Nazism and the Final Solution, with 120 pages of photographs, put together with graphic designer and former Communist Resistance fighter Albe Steiner.[68]

By far the most significant work of original research was De Felice's *History*, not only because it marked this historian's first foray into the field of the historiography of Fascism, where he would come to be the preeminent voice in subsequent decades; nor only because it marked a sea change in attention paid to the specifically Italian history of Fascist anti-Semitism; but also, as explored in Chapter 3, for the collaboration between Einaudi and the Jewish community that produced it, and for the political storm it caused.[69]

In fiction, this period saw a shift into a more narratively inventive, literary attention to the Holocaust, as illustrated again by Levi in the marked shift in style and technique between *If This Is a Man* and *The Truce*, the latter as much a picaresque tragicomedy as a work of sober witness; but also in a parallel development in Edith Bruck's first work to her second book, the collection of stories *We Will Go to the City*, which included a child's-eye fantasy of salvation.[70]

Around Levi's and Bruck's second books, a flow of new autobiographical, semifictional or fictional literature on the Holocaust appeared, again both by Italians and from abroad, works centred on Italy as well as on the wider European genocide. *The Truce* appeared with Einaudi in 1963, as did Natalia Ginzburg's family memoir *Family Sayings*,[71] which, whilst not centrally a work of Holocaust literature, was nevertheless evocative of the world of the Jewish, anti-Fascist intelligentsia of Turin. In the muted but powerful figure of her husband, Leone Ginzburg, tortured and murdered by the Nazis, or in her feckless but principled brothers, Ginzburg built Jewish figures of iconic anti-Fascist victimhood and heroism, figures of a sort of displaced Holocaust. A few months earlier, in 1962, a third major text had paved the way for this exceptional moment for Italian-Jewish narratives of anti-Semitism, shadowed by the Holocaust: Giorgio Bassani's *Garden of the Finzi-Continis* was the peak achievement of his cycle of stories about Ferrara, begun with *Five Ferrarese Stories* and *The Gold-Rimmed Spectacles*.[72] These books marked the emergence of a sophisticated poetics of Holocaust memory and mourning, with origins in Proust and Freud, and also of a grand Italian literary model for the genre of the historical novel, Alessandro Manzoni's *The Betrothed*.[73]

The trio of works by Levi, Bassani and Ginzburg offer powerful evidence for a general opening of mainstream literature towards representation of the Holocaust, although all of them approach the genocide from an oblique or even implicit angle, telling local stories, following premonitory moments or aftereffects, exploiting the looming shadow of the genocide in readers' minds.

If we turn to the field of translated fiction, we find two examples of powerful international successes translated into Italian in 1959–60. The Israeli survivor-writer known as Ka-Tzetnik 135633 (the pseudonym was his concentration camp number) published the international bestseller *House of Dolls* in 1953; translated by Mondadori in 1959, it went into seven editions in nine months.[74] Set in a camp brothel, *House of Dolls* was one of the first controversial Holocaust fictions, one of the first major works to establish a trend that would peak in the 1970s, for the 'sexualisation' of the Holocaust. André Schwarz-Bart's Prix-Goncourt-winning novel *The Last of the Just* (1959) was a grand meditation on and intense depiction of the camps—ending in the gas chambers—recast (once again not without controversy) into a millennial Jewish history through the Talmudic legend of the thirty-six Just Men. It was published in Italy by Feltrinelli in 1960 and was into its tenth edition by 1963.[75]

In cinema, as Millicent Marcus has penetratingly shown, this same period saw the first major, if somewhat disconnected (what Marcus calls 'diaphanous') cluster of Holocaust filmmaking in Italy.[76] As with written narratives, films show evidence of attention both to the Holocaust as an international phenomenon and to specific local, Italian aspects of this history, including its oblique relations with national legacies such as the Resistance. Three examples: 1959 saw the release of Gillo Ponte-corvo's second full-length fiction film, *Kapò*, a Lager film which has noth-ing direct to say about Italy but which was nevertheless deeply influenced by the conflation of Pontecorvo's Resistance experience, his Jewish fam-ily and the persecution it suffered, and his reading of Primo Levi.[77] Also in 1959, Roberto Rossellini's film *General della Rovere*, starring Vittorio De Sica, told an affecting tale of partisans in prison, whose climax drew in the story of persecuted Jews.[78] And in 1961, Carlo Lizzani released *The Gold of Rome*, a reconstruction of the persecution of Rome's Jewish com-munity by the Nazis and Fascist in 1943. The young hero of the film chooses to assert himself as both Jew and Italian, by heading into the countryside to join the Resistance. Both Lizzani and Rossellini (and in-deed De Sica) draw a very direct line of connection in film history back to neorealism, suggesting that aspects of the Holocaust were now posing ethical and aesthetic questions, to do with what stories 'civic' or commit-ted or 'national-popular' films should be telling. Documentary work from the same period suggests a similar thrust: Liliana Cavani was working in television, making for RAI 2 a documentary *History of the Third Reich* (1961–62), in which the genocide played a rare prominent role.[79]

Several of the books noted here had a popularising or educational form or agenda, an aim to reach out to a wider public; and cinema and televi-sion documentaries drew large audiences. There is further evidence else-where of large-scale dissemination of Holocaust awareness in this period, in the form of mediatised events and new public fora for response.

One epoch-making media event of the early 1960s dominates all ac-counts of global awareness of the Holocaust: the Eichmann capture, trial and execution between 1960 and 1962. Italy was no exception;[80] although only one Italian witness spoke at the trial (Hulda Cassuto) and one ses-sion was devoted to Italy (on 11 May 1961), Italian newspapers such as *Corriere della sera*, *La stampa* and *Il giorno* ran regular dispatches from the court.[81] As many as eight 'instant' books were published on Eichmann in Italian between 1961 and 1963, several going into multiple editions; and that is to exclude the first Italian edition, in 1964, of the most resonant document to emerge from the trial, Hannah Arendt's hugely controversial *Eichmann in Jerusalem*. The chief prosecutor, Gideon Hausner, published his opening address in several languages, prefaced in Italy by the jurist and anti-Fascist Alessandro Galante Garrone.[82]

As part of the media event surrounding Eichmann, popular magazines ran features accompanying the trial. *Storia illustrata* held a roundtable on the trial, with Primo Levi, philosopher Remo Cantoni, psychoanalyst Cesare Musatti and jurist Francesco Carnelutti. The same issue ran an article by Gerald Reitlinger, as his *Final Solution* was being prepared for Italian publication on the back of the trial.[83] *L'espresso* also ran features on Eichmann, including an account by a court correspondent and author of one of the instant books, Sergio Minerbi, and a tie-in to the upcoming release of Lizzani's *Gold of Rome*.[84]

Although this concerted media interest was a relatively new phenomenon, there had been coverage of a more sporadic and sensationalist kind in magazines in preceding years, typically focussed on the grotesque criminals and monsters of the Nazi era and the war. *Storia illustrata*, which began publishing only in 1957, had already run several articles on individual Fascists and Nazis, on military aspects of the war, on Nuremberg and on Hitler (including a July 1959 piece on why he hated the Jews), and in amongst this a single article, in March 1960, on the genocide. *L'espresso* ran a lurid enquiry in April 1960 into the so-called Black Panther, a notorious Roman-Jewish Nazi informant.[85]

Media events commingled with other public events, of a more local, collective kind: commemorations, public discourses, exhibitions, conferences. There were varied programmes reflecting on Italy's sense of its own past, from 1955, the tenth anniversary of the Liberation, when an exhibition on the camps opened in Carpi, to 1960–61, which saw the dual markers of the fifteenth anniversary of the Liberation in 1960 and the centenary of the unification of Italy in 1961.[86] Cycles of public lectures were held in major cities, notably Turin, Milan, Rome and Bologna, drawing large, intergenerational crowds. On occasion, space was allotted to the history of anti-Semitism and genocide: Caleffi spoke on the topic in the Milan cycle in 1961; Norberto Bobbio gave a public lecture at the Turin synagogue in January 1960; and Primo Levi and Giorgio Bassani shared a platform, for perhaps the only time, during the Bologna lectures.[87]

Exhibitions also began to proliferate. The Carpi exhibition toured in 10 major cities (including Rome and then Turin in 1959, where Levi's public speaking career began), expanding its material as it travelled; and it spawned separate local initiatives in more than 30 smaller towns. ANED was centrally involved in the initial exhibition, along with several other associations and groupings; as a result, ANED would begin to construct its own standing body of display material.[88] In Rome in 1959, the Galleria nazionale d'arte moderna hosted an exhibition on the international architectural competition to design a monument for the site at Auschwitz

(Chapter 9). Exhibitions spaces at the national and local levels were clearly attuned to a newly heightened profile of the Holocaust in Italian public culture.

It is important, finally, to look also at the communities of victims and survivors, the 'actors of memory', at this moment of paradigm shift. Within the Jewish community, there is evidence of a reactive and at times anxious response, as well as a proactive influencing of the new Holocaust awareness.

The proactive mode is evident in the sponsorship of De Felice's *History* by UCII; and also in at least two other important projects addressing Fascist anti-Semitism in the period 1961, appearing under the aegis of key Jewish institutions: the recently formed CDEC published a series of historical papers in three volumes on Jews under Fascism;[89] and the authoritative Zionist journal *Rassegna mensile di Israel* published a series of densely researched articles on the same topic by Israeli historian Meir Michaelis.[90]

This opening out towards and sponsorship of concerted historiographical work was, however, not without its anxieties, evident in the way some corners of the Jewish community reacted to the proliferation of Holocaust material. There were, for example, mixed responses in the pages of the *Rassegna mensile* (whose dual focus on Italy and Israel sat uneasily with a secularising or Holocaust-centred vision of Jewish identity). Whilst there was striking growth in reviews and articles on the Holocaust in the journal, not infrequently worries were expressed about the attitudes on display or the possible excess of interest. To give examples by three leading contributors to *Rassegna*: Giorgio Romano criticised Giacomo Debenedetti for his depiction of the victims of persecution as 'lay' or lapsed Jews; Dante Lattes carried on an intense polemic with Salvatore Quasimodo some apparently anti-Semitic comments by the latter; and G. L. Luzzatto reviewed Bassani's *Garden* with some hostility for its risky mix of history and fiction.[91]

A final review from *Rassegna* serves also to recall a wider socio-religious dimension to this anxiety: in 1962, a group of South American Jesuits, writing under the pseudonym Maurice Pinay, published a fierce anti-Semitic tract, entitled *Plot Against the Church*, describing a vast Jewish conspiracy to destroy the Church, perversely discerning a Jewish hand even behind the Holocaust. The book was written specifically to challenge the liberalisation of Church attitudes to the Jews on the part of the Second Vatican Council and John XXIII (whose papacy coincided with the period

1958–1963). The book was reviewed with rigorous hostility by De Felice in *Rassegna*,[92] but its presence points to a delicate moment in the history of the Church and the role of Jewish identity in Italy, and the Holocaust in relation to that; one that was about to explode into international scandal in 1963 with the controversy over the accusation of Pius XII's neglect of the Jews in the 1940s, in Rolf Hochhuth's play *The Deputy*.

∼

An eclectic wave of output and activity relating to the Holocaust emerged in Italy around the years 1958–1963. This wave rode upon various other, highly important changes in the wider culture. With the war now 15 years past, the time was ripe for a general, detached reassessment of aspects of its history, including the genocide. Crucially, this shift coincided with a moment of expansion and diversification in the publishing industries, so that scholarly, educational and broadly popular (high-, middle-, and low-brow) material all found space for covering this new angle on the recent past, and international networks of dissemination and translation were strengthening also. Certain publishers engaged seriously and extensively, but also commercially, with this new, cosmopolitan and contemporary topic, in particular 'politicised' houses such as Feltrinelli and Einaudi.[93] Distance also meant that a 'memory' culture, *strictu senso*, emerged strongly for the first time (Bassani, Ginzburg), alongside documented historiography; and this dual development complemented a tendency to shift away from interest in the evils of Nazi leaders to the experience of victims. Such changes in media and in attitude also reflected wider changes commonly associated with the years 1958–1963 in Italy—that is, the socio-cultural and economic changes known as the 'boom'—which contributed to a loosening of cultural mores (including in the Church), to diversification, to the start of a generational shift. The new cultural elaborations in this period did not so much make up the first phase in which the Holocaust was addressed in Italy—private and smaller-scale work, often by survivors and their associationist networks such as ANED, had been produced ever since the war, as we saw in Chapters 3 and earlier in this chapter—but rather the first time the Holocaust entered the general public sphere and public discourse, the first time the media saw it as a discrete event capable of attracting audiences, and the first time writers used the vocabulary of genocide as an element of shared cultural and public knowledge.

§5 Primo Levi

The particular inflections that shape the cultural forms given to the Holocaust in a single national arena, the received wisdom and common knowledge that circulate around it, the symbols and icons that come to express it emerge through elaborate processes of mediation. Chapter 4 looked at the mediation of a specific moment, the maelstrom of the immediate postwar years, and its conjunction of historical transition with cultural practice and production. Mediation comes in many other modes also: a collective mood or affective dimension can tinge Holocaust response—a more or less worked-out guilt, in the case of Germany, say; or a mood of mourning and patriotic defiance in the case of Israel.[1] It can work through the particularity of other local histories quite apart from the Holocaust: for example, American memory of the Holocaust has been read in part as a displaced engagement with its own 'genocidal' pre-history, from the destruction of the Native American populations to the dark history of slavery;[2] or recent work by Michael Rothberg has suggested a powerful link between the early glimmerings around 1961 of French disinterring of repressed histories of the Jewish victims of Vichy and the contemporary late-colonial war in Algeria.[3]

These are complex and deep patterns of mediation. But local inflections of larger cultural and memorial discourse can also be determined by the agency and accidental influence of single voices in a given cultural field. Peter Novick, for example, dwells compellingly on the figure of Elie Wiesel and his extraordinary moral authority over a series of American presidents, Washington elites and a wider American public, directly shaping how the Holocaust has been memorialised there as a result.[4] This was far from predictable for a Transylvanian-born survivor, with a Kabbalistic formation, whose first work was published in Yiddish in Buenos Aires and who became a Francophone intellectual before relocating to the United States. And yet, clearly, something in his voice and position resonated with and adapted to contemporary American cultural currents and modes of thinking, including political interests: Novick locates the root of this adaptability in an affinity between Wiesel's mystic Judaism and the Christian constituency in American public life, with a view of the Holocaust as a form or 'sacred mystery'.[5] The telling unpredictability of Wiesel's rise to prominence in Holocaust talk in America—as well as a certain impatience with his rhetoric—leads Novick to formulate this question: 'What would talk of the Holocaust be like in America if a skeptical rationalist like Primo Levi, rather than a religious mystic like Wiesel, had been its principal interpreter?'[6]

The question begs another: What was talk of the Holocaust like in Italy, where Primo Levi was indeed its principal interpreter over many decades? Levi's profile in postwar Italy gradually achieved a remarkable pitch of admiration and authority, continuing well after his death and spreading from Italy out into the wider world, to make him a figure almost to rival Wiesel as the epitome of the writer-survivor-witness. But the ways in which an individual, even one as admired as Levi, interacts with, is shaped by and shapes the field of Holocaust talk around him is by no means straightforward. This chapter attempts to gauge some of the complexity of Levi's particular role and influence within the local Holocaust culture of postwar Italy.

1. Levi's Cultural Profile

At a certain point in the history we are tracing, the figure of the Holocaust survivor in Italy, and certainly that of the survivor-writer, became overwhelmingly identified with Primo Levi. As fellow survivor-writer Giuliana Tedeschi put it, rather tetchily, reflecting on the decades between her first testimonial work, *This Poor Body* (1946), and her second, *There Is a Place on Earth* (1988), 'In any case, Primo Levi's books had taken up all the space available'.[7] But Levi's cultural profile had its own particular history—and limitations—within the Italian cultural sphere.

Levi's entry into the public cultural sphere can be dated to the late 1950s and early 1960s. Although his first book, *If This Is a Man* was reviewed and admired in its first edition of 1947 within narrow circles in Turin and within Resistance networks beyond, it was not until republication in a second edition in 1958, following a contract with Einaudi in 1955, that his second 'career' as a public witness and writer could begin. In 1959, he appeared in a public forum for the first time, at a conference connected to a Turin exhibition about the camps; and he wrote a review of an exhibition on Auschwitz in Rome for *La stampa*. In 1961, he gave his first published interview, about Eichmann, in the popular history magazine, *Storia illustrata*, and he also wrote on Eichmann for the liberal-left journal *Il ponte*.[8] He began to work on his second, more 'writerly' work, *The Truce*, which would win the Campiello Prize in 1963 and launch him on a literary career of some note, alongside his 'career' as a Holocaust survivor, which grew as invitations to speak in schools flooded in. From this point on, Levi began to take on many of the activities typical of an Italian intellectual of the day. He wrote articles, reviews, essays and stories for newspapers, at first sporadically for organs such as *Il giorno, Il mondo, Corriere della sera* and *La stampa* and then, from the mid-1970s, as a regular columnist for *La stampa*.[9] He gave interviews to the press, radio and television, but also to a large number of students and researchers; attended conferences and gave public lectures, as a Holocaust survivor, to promote a particular book or event and, occasionally in later years, as an opinion maker on broader issues, such as the morals of science or Israeli politics. He published varied books, on Holocaust and non-Holocaust themes, won prizes regularly (always a sign of profile and patronage). He penned prefaces for his own publisher, Einaudi, but also for a long list other publishers, large and small. These were prefaces to novels, works of history or catalogues of exhibitions, for the most part related to Judaism or the Holocaust. He himself translated Holocaust literature (most notably the Dutch writer and historian Jacob Presser's 1957 novella *The Night of the Girondins*), works of anthropology (by Claude Lévi-Strauss and Mary Douglas) and literary works (including Kafka's *The Trial*).[10] Behind the scenes at Einaudi, he became an occasional consultant, writing a number of in-house reports, suggesting works for translation, exchanging ideas and advice with writer and Einaudi editor Italo Calvino.

In the mid-1980s, Levi's profile took a further leap forward with the international, and especially American, lionisation of his work, and subsequently his enhanced international reputation was reimported back into Italy. His activity was intense in this period; between 1981 and 1986 he published no fewer than seven books of stories, essays, poetry and fiction. If anything, though, his posthumous profile and reputation following his suicide in 1987 reached an even higher pitch, in Italy as well as abroad, coinciding with a widespread contemporary fascination with all things Holocaust-related (and Americanised mouldings of it).

This portrait of a proactive public intellectual and writer, with all the tools in place to shape and influence his principal sphere of interest, the Holocaust (much as Wiesel has done within the American context), requires careful qualification, however. Levi's cultural activism was, in reality, relatively restricted in quantity (he was, after all, in full-time employment at a paint factory until retirement in the mid-1970s), range and authority, compared to the typical 'professional' literary intellectual of his day. His position was relatively marginal to the core centres of intellectual activity of the time. He was close to Einaudi, but only as an occasional friendly interlocutor. He became one of their most consistently best-selling authors, but this in itself suggested he was not at the cutting edge of their most innovative projects:[11] indeed, many of those sales (as will be discussed below) came through schools editions of his works. He was a liberal socialist in politics, not connected to the party, fellow-travelling or ex-communist intellectuals who shaped so much of postwar Italian culture. Indeed, as we shall see, his links to a certain moral politics associated in the 1940s with the Action Party, whose partisan formation he had joined in 1943, are an important prism for reading his perspective on the Holocaust. He was a scientist, not a humanist intellectual, in a still overwhelmingly humanist culture, and he wore his amateur and eclectic curiosity for things cultural, linguistic and literary very much on his sleeve. He formed friendships with other contemporary writers who were decidedly marginal figures, such as Mario Rigoni Stern and Nuto Revelli, sharing interests, attitudes and experiences rather than high intellectual projects. Literary critics—who remained surprisingly powerful figures in the cultural establishment in Italy—tended to neglect his work, at least until the 1990s, treating it as worthy but hardly of great literary merit.[12]

In sum, Levi's cultural capital and potential to shape Holocaust talk in Italy was of a quite specific kind. Over the period from the 1960s until his death (and afterwards), he grew into a hugely respected figure, a moral model, well known as a name to a very large number of Italians, and the essential point of reference in the 'niche' area of the Holocaust, but not a dominant voice at the established centre of the culture. His status was both vaguely defined and capillary. If his occasional writings and public works focussed on the Holocaust, his written

work—at least between 1963 and the early 1980s, in science fiction, autobiography, industrial and chemistry work narratives, essays—was often
in only oblique relation to the concentration camps. The real sphere
of his activist influence was at more subterranean and localised levels
than, say, Wiesel's dialogues with presidents, his Nobel prize and his
globally televised speeches. Levi's activities at the local level included his
longstanding commitment to giving talks at schools, close collaboration
with ANED in Turin, promotion of work with publishers, and other
paraliterary activity (translations, interviews, reviews). Perhaps most important of all for his capillary presence in the field, though, was the
experience of reading Levi at school, often at middle school, shared by a
large number of Italian children from the early 1960s onwards.

To get a sense of Levi's particular configuration of the Holocaust,
as transmitted in schools and other public arenas, we need to set aside
the nuanced detail and compelling power of his own testimonial writings per se and concentrate instead on his occasional and pedagogical
writings. It is here that he most self-consciously and openly engages
with the large field of response to the Holocaust, makes choices and
recommendations, sees affinities, rejects certain positions and promotes
certain others; all whilst never writing as a professional historian or
intellectual.[13]

What follows is a reading of this low-level, 'public' Levi, at work in
the cultural sphere, charting his particular map of the Holocaust. It
builds on the wider emergence in the 1950s of a new field of Holocaust
culture, as traced in Chapter 4, of which Levi was a regular vessel and
symptom. It then looks at strands in Levi's career concentrated in the
1970s and 1980s—his phase of most intense public cultural activity and
influence—as he shaped and transmitted his particular vision and understanding of the Holocaust phenomenon: first, a pedagogical snapshot
from 1973 of Levi's 'ideal' library of Holocaust reading, followed by a
survey of his work of 'patronage' of other writers on the Holocaust; then,
aspects of the contexts and comparisons he posits for the Holocaust and
his naming strategy for the Holocaust, including a particular instance
from 1980 of his rhetoric of public commemoration. What emerges is
a calibrated, if not always consistent, profile of the Holocaust filtered
through the values of a single individual, balanced between national
(local, cultural, political) experience and politics—including his own
political vision—and universal questions of history and morality.

2. Levi's Holocaust Library

Levi's library has not yet been made available to researchers, although we know him to have been a broad and eclectic reader throughout his life. The epitome of this is his 1981 anthology *The Search for Roots*, a self-portrait made up of extracts from the books that shaped him.[14] The section of Levi's library on Nazism and the Holocaust represented something of an exception to his normal reading patterns governed by eclectic curiosity, since it seems to have been close to comprehensive, covering several language areas and conscientiously maintained. As he said to an interviewer at his home in late 1986: 'If you look over at that side of the bookshelves, you will see it is made up only of books on Nazism and the persecution of the Jews, and so on. This house is saturated with persecution'.[15] Stuart Woolf, a historian and translator of Levi's first work, notes that, whilst Levi did not read academic history journals, he nevertheless

> read widely and deeply into the historical literature. He followed new pub-
> lications (for the most part as they appeared in Italy) on the Second World
> War and especially on Nazism and the persecution of the Jews [...] Levi's
> readings, in short, seem to me to have been similar, and sometimes identical,
> to those of that broad, cultured reading public curious and passionate about
> contemporary history.[16]

From this substantial, but tellingly middle-brow, library, what did Levi principally rely on for his own work on the Holocaust? What can this tell us about his own understanding of the event, as his voice became ever more influential in Holocaust talk in Italy, and in its formation within the cultural field behind the scenes? We can begin to gauge this by looking at a 1973 republication of *If This Is a Man*. This edition was the first of the book to appear in Einaudi's 'Readings for Middle School' series, a crucial means, as was suggested above, for the capillary dissemination of his voice on the Holocaust to a broad readership.[17] The founding of the series, and the presence of Levi's work within it, reflects significant shifts in educa-tion in the 1960s, in particular the updating of the history curriculum to include, at least in theory, the 20th century. In general, the period saw an increase, in both Italian and history teaching, of sensitivity to and willing-ness to tackle contemporary issues in school, for an expanded and newly socially aware young generation.[18] The role of a generation of war and

Holocaust witnesses, often marshalled by associations such as ANED, in
visiting schools and events across Italy, was crucial in transmitting this
knowledge to young (often very young) students. Levi was a committed
participant in this project. His appendix to *If This Is a Man*—added in
1976 and now considered an integral part of that work, as well as a key
source for *The Drowned and the Saved*—distilled from dozens of school
visits and student encounters the questions he had been asked repeatedly
over many years. He was not alone in this: many who wrote testimony
also spoke to the young. Edith Bruck published in 1999 a memoir and reflection on her existence as a public witness and educator, entitled *Signora
Auschwitz*. The book is a forceful meditation on the conflicts between
private trauma and public pedagogy.[19]

Through the 1973 edition, Levi 'visited' hundreds of schools he could
not attend in person. Unusually for the series, he became his own editor:
he wrote a new introduction, provided explanatory notes and two maps
and, crucially, included also a short bibliography of further reading. It is
worth reproducing in the form it is given there:[20]

> *General works on national socialism and the Jewish question:*
> G. Hausner, *Sei milioni di accusatori*, Einaudi, Torino 1961.
> L. Poliakov, *Il nazismo e lo sterminio degli ebrei*, Einaudi, Torino 1955.
> ———, *Auschwitz*, Veutro, Roma 1968.
> Lord Russel [sic] of Liverpool, *Il flagello della svastica*, Feltrinelli, Milano 1955.
> W. L. Shirer, *Storia del Terzo Reich*, Einaudi, Torino 1962.
> *Dall'antifascismo alla Resistenza. Trent'anni di storia italiana (1915–1945)*,
>   Einaudi, Torino 1961.
>
> *Testimonies and documents:*
> R. Antelme, *La specie umana*, Einaudi, Torino 1954.
> P. Caleffi, *Si fa presto a dire fame*, ed. Avanti! Milano 1954.
> G. De Benedetti [sic], *16 ottobre 1943* (brief history of the capture and
>   deportation of the Jews of Rome), Il Saggiatore, Milano 1959.
> Anna [sic] Frank, *Diario*, Einaudi, Torino 1954.
> J. Hersey, *Il muro di Varsavia* (history, reconstructed with documents, of the
>   Warsaw ghetto and its uprising), Mondadori, Verona 1951.
> R. Hoess, *Comandante ad Auschwitz* (autobiography of the Nazi
>   commandant of the Auschwitz Lager), Einaudi, Torino 1960.
> P. Levi, *La tregua* (followed by *Se questo è un uomo*), Einaudi, Torino 1965.
> S. Wiesenthal, *Il Girasole*, Garzanti, Milano 1970.

There are several aspects of the bibliography that are worthy of comment. First of all, it is striking how much of this material is rooted in the late 1950s–1960s period. There is a clear prevalence of Einaudi books (eight of fourteen), in part no doubt due to 'in-house' loyalty, but in part also a reflection of a particular commitment of Einaudi to publishing work on the Holocaust (at least from the mid-1950s; they had, of course, rejected Levi in 1946).[21] The list is also notably cosmopolitan, with Italian work (Caleffi, Giacomo Debenedetti, *Dall'antifascismo alla Resistenza* [From Antifascism to the Resistance]) alongside a broad, complex European history and historiography (six of the eight Einaudi items and ten of fourteen overall are translations, from French, English, German, Dutch and Hebrew).[22]

The group at Einaudi also brings with it a communal dimension to Levi's Holocaust work, which is crucial for understanding his operations in this field and the networks and exchanges on which the field itself was built. Thus not only does he stick to his publishers; he also had direct or indirect connections to several of the texts. He wrote a preface to Poliakov's *Auschwitz*, as he did to a 1985 edition of Höss; and he contributed to Wiesenthal's *Sunflower*.[23] He knew Piero Caleffi and several of the contributors to *From Antifascism* (one of those public lecture cycles from 1960–61), including its animator Franco Antonicelli, who had published *If This Is a Man* in 1947, and Alessandro Galante Garrone, the Turinese jurist who wrote a preface to Hausner. There is a straightforward biographical dimension to this 'networked' bibliography: Levi was a man of close private and loyal friendships. But there is also a cultural politics on display, even a politics *tout court*: Levi's Holocaust is sourced to a Turinese, leftist, cosmopolitan milieu, with strong links to the Resistance formation he had briefly joined in 1943, Justice and Freedom, which later briefly became the Action Party.[24] 'Actionist' values are central to any understanding of Levi's self-positioning as a Holocaust writer and to the picture of the Holocaust he passed on in his work and his public activities.

There is also in the list an implicit conception of evidence and history, issues that are intensely contested in the field of Holocaust historiography.[25] As the division into two sections indicates, Levi attempts to strike a balance between historiography per se and first-hand accounts by protagonists, between historical record and testimony. But it is striking how the immediacy of the event is of central importance, the rooting of history in first-hand experience, whether written by protagonists or based on first-hand documentation, trial depositions or conversations. Caleffi, Antelme, Frank, Levi himself and Wiesenthal were all victims, former deportees; Poliakov was an escapee from German prison, a 'résistant' and a pioneer historian; Höss and Eichmann (present via Hausner) were, of course, prime perpetrators on the other side of the Final Solution. Others are 'second-hand' witnesses, but still closely engaged on a personal level. Debenedetti, Hersey, Russell and Shirer all declare the debt their work owes to contact 'on the ground' with protagonists or to trial witnesses from Nuremberg and elsewhere.[26] This not only confirms Woolf's point that Levi was no academic historian but instead more attuned to a middle-brow form of history designed for a broad readership (here, children and their teachers); it also points to Levi's affinity with the figure of the 'witness'—that is, first- or second-hand testimony—as the key form of historical framing for the Holocaust, perhaps, as has been argued, of the entire era of post-Holocaust history. Accounts of the emergence of this figure point to the Eichmann trial, of which Hausner's book is a document, as the moment the figure and paradigm of the witness established itself, through Hausner's deliberate strategy of staging the trial as a procession of heart-wrenching depositions by survivors.[27] And yet, Levi balances this witness-oriented view with a certain kind of historiography, typical of the 1950s, characterised by documentary, trial-based accounts, covering an articulated range of spheres of interest, including Nazism in general, the deportation of Italian Jews from Rome, the Italian Resistance, the Final Solution's victims and perpetrators.

On the side of the witness, there is a powerful cluster of work from 1954 (at least in their Italian editions): Antelme, Caleffi, Frank. Each represents a pioneering milestone in one or another form of European testimonial writing (Italian, French, Dutch; Resistance and Jewish deportation; survivor writing and the recovered voices of the dead). The close coincidence of their publication and their success in Italy undoubtedly helped open up the field for witness writing in mainstream publishing, a field into which *If This Is a Man* would shortly be inserted by Einaudi.[28] Levi had already noted as much in 1966, when reflecting on what had changed in the years between the two editions of his first book:

> Ten years passed: the public read Vercors' *The Arms of the Night*, Russell's *Scourge of the Swastika*, Rousset's two books, *It's Easy to Say Hunger* by Caleffi, *The Human Race* by Antelme, *The Forest of the Dead* by Wiechert. People began to talk about the concentration camps again.[29]

Between Antelme, Caleffi, Frank and Levi, there is another common thread, characteristic of reflections on the war and the Holocaust in the 1940s: 'humanist' discourse on the Holocaust of the postwar years, in the sense of moral reflections on the values and limits of 'the human being' (Chapter 7). This is self-evident in the titles of Levi's and Antelme's books and is also behind the universal resonance of Anne Frank's diary. Comparable evidence comes in Levi's choice of Wiesenthal's *Sunflower* rather than his better known, 'Nazi-hunting' memoir *The Murderers Are Among Us* (published in Italian in 1967).[30] *The Sunflower* is a work of testimony-as-moral-thought-experiment, as the subtitle and wrap of the English edition suggest:

> *The Sunflower. On the Possibilities and Limits of Forgiveness*
> You are a prisoner in a concentration camp. A dying Nazi soldier asks for your forgiveness. What would you do?[31]

The range of the histories and the balance of these with witness reports covered in Levi's bibliography brings us to a final, central issue: the question of 'which Holocaust' Levi is presenting here. First, it is worth noting that Levi is consistently interested in the Holocaust as a Nazi or 'German' phenomenon. He shows it residing with the victims, through their testimonies, but also, perhaps principally, with the perpetrators and the regime behind them. Hausner, Poliakov, Shirer, Russell, Höss and to a degree Wiesenthal all offer investigations of Nazi Germany and/or Nazis, as much as of the victims.[32] He is also consistently open to aligning his experience with that of political or Resistance fighters and deportees, as well as Jewish victims (he was both himself, of course): *From Antifascism* is a product of ex-partisans, and Antelme and Caleffi were political deportees. Jewish victims, including Jewish-Italian victims (in his own work and Giacomo Debenedetti's), are given strong prominence also. In this regard, it is interesting to note Levi—a secular and non-Zionist Jew—echoing official Israeli modes of Holocaust remembrance; that is, an emphasis not only on victimhood but also on redemptive and strong images of Jews as resisters. Hersey's *The Wall*, for example, is about the Warsaw ghetto uprising, which became *the* central redemptive, heroic event in Israeli 'nationalist' conceptions of the Holocaust, to balance out the negative stereotype of Jews going to their deaths 'like lambs to the slaughter'. By extension, the capture and trial of Eichmann became a mythical signal of the power of the Israeli state to redeem and reverse Jewish victimhood.[33] This position of Levi's was particular to 1973, no doubt, in a phase between the Six Day and Yom Kippur wars when the majority of the Jewish diaspora warmed to Israel's survival against the odds. Later, in 1982, Levi would polemically reject Israeli policy in Lebanon, in a series of rare public political interventions.[34] He would also dedicate a major work at that time, *If Not Now, When?* to Jewish resistance in Eastern Europe during the war, with a socialist-Zionist tinge.[35]

This one brief bibliography, designed for young readers at a specific point in Levi's career, should not be overburdened with significance. Nevertheless, it serves as a useful and symptomatic snapshot of the particular vision and understanding of the Holocaust Levi embodied and expressed in his public role: it indicates his affinity with the Turinese, liberal-socialist Actionist intelligentsia, and its engaged, cosmopolitan view of history; it indicates as well his preference for first-hand documents and witness voices from both sides, supplemented by early on-the-ground historiography; for a 'moral' or 'humanist' enquiry into the Holocaust; and for an ecumenical embrace in his conception of what the Holocaust takes in, of Nazism and the Resistance, alongside a due emphasis on the Jewish experience of persecution. These lines can be followed through, confirmed and qualified by looking across the wider range of his work as a cultural activist, in his occasional writings and promotional work.

Levi's paraliterary work in the 1970s and 1980s was marked by engagement with a wide range of writing on Nazism and the Holocaust. A handful of authors and books became his prime working interlocutors: Austrian-born Auschwitz survivor Jean Améry's *At the Mind's Limits*;[36] German historian Hermann Langbein's *Human Beings in Auschwitz*;[37] and Gitta Sereny's *Into That Darkness*, an enquiry into the mind of the notorious commandant of Treblinka (and the Risiera di San Sabba camp outside Trieste), Franz Stangl.[38]

Améry was the subject of an essay in *The Drowned and the Saved* and indeed of an extensive, tense dialogue from a distance with Levi, on a range of moral issues, from forgiveness to the role of culture and the intellectual to suicide.[39] Langbein was a survivor of Auschwitz and a witness at the 1963–1965 Auschwitz trial, as well as a historian, all of which fits the pattern of Levi's preference for witness evidence and first-hand knowledge. He was an anti-Nazi and political, not a Jewish deportee; but as Levi points out, this 'privileged' status gave him key insights into the entire hierarchy of the camp inconceivable for the Jews.[40] So Levi's ecumenical conception of the Holocaust, system-centred and drawing in several categories of victims, is maintained and confirmed in his admiration for Langbein. Furthermore, the title *Human Beings in Auschwitz* extends the moral-humanist thread of Holocaust reflection noted above. Sereny's work also chimes with Levi's moral explorations, here of the minds of the Nazi perpetrators or German bystanders, and it does so in a way that echoes Levi's preferred method of enquiry in its reliance on human, face-to-face encounter. Sereny's portrait of Stangl was a key stimulus to Levi's reflections on the core moral concept of his later work, the 'grey zone' (Chapter 8).

If Améry, Langbein and Sereny were privileged interlocutors within Levi's principal writings, they and others belong also to Levi's public work of promotion. Between 1966 and 1987, Levi reviewed, presented, translated and wrote prefaces for a striking range of Holocaust-related writing, of which these are the principal examples:[41]

1. Yitzhak Katzenelson, *Il canto del popolo ebraico massacrato* [Song of the Murdered Jewish People] (Turin: Amici di Beit Lohamei Haghetaot, 1966)
2. Léon Poliakov, *Auschwitz* (Rome: Veutro, 1968)
3. Joel König, *Sfuggito alle reti del nazismo* [Escaped from the Nazi Net] (Milan: Mursia, 1973)
4. Edith Bruck, *Due stanze vuote* [Two Empty Rooms] (Venice: Marsilio, 1974)
5. Jacob Presser, *La notte dei girondini* [The Night of the Girondins] (Milan: Adelphi, 1976)
6. Lidia Beccaria Rolfi and Anna Maria Bruzzone, *Le donne di Ravensbruck* [Women of Ravensbrück] (Turin: Einaudi, 1978)
7. Ferruccio Fölkel, *La Risiera di san Sabba* (Milan: Mondadori, 1979)
8. *Le immagini di* Olocausto [Images of 'Holocaust'] (Rome: ERI, 1979)
9. Liana Millu, *Il fumo di Birkenau* [Smoke over Birkenau] (Florence: Tip. Giuntina, 1979)
10. Walter Laqueur, *Il terribile segreto* [The Terrible Secret] (Florence: La Giuntina, 1984)
11. Hermann Langbein, *Uomini ad Auschwitz* [Human Beings in Auschwitz] (Milan: Mursia, 1984)
12. Marco Herman, *Da Leopoli a Torino* [From Lvov to Turin] (Cuneo: L'Arciere, 1984)
13. *Ebrei a Torino* [Jews in Turin] (Turin: Allemandi, 1984)
14. Vittorio Segre, *Storia di un ebreo fortunato* [History of a Fortunate Jew] (Milan: Bompiani, 1985)
15. Rudolf Höss, *Comandante ad Auschwitz* [Commandant at Auschwitz] (Turin: Einaudi, 1985)

16. *Gli ebrei dell'europa orientale dall'utopia alla rivolta* [The Jews of Eastern Europe from Utopia to Revolt] (Milan: Edizioni di Comunità, 1986)
17. Anna Bravo and Daniele Jalla, eds., *La vita offesa* [Life Offended] (Milan: Franco Angeli/ANED, 1986)
18. *Storia vissuta* [Living History] (Milan: Franco Angeli/ANED, 1988)
19. Lidia Beccaria Rolfi and Bruno Maida, *Il futuro spezzato. I bambini nei lager nazisti* [Broken Future: Children in the Nazi Camps] (Florence: La Giuntina, 1997; preface dated 1980)

This varied list both confirms and adds new elements to the picture we are building of the shape of Levi's Holocaust culture. It confirms his propensity for networks, suggesting also the networks and groups that subtend the entire field of cultural production on the Holocaust (items 4, 6, 9, 14, 16, 17, 18, 19). For example, ANED published 17 and 18,[42] and CDEC 1, meshing together political and racial dimensions of deportation work. It is striking to note Levi opening up new specialist approaches in Holocaust research *through* these personal, communal and associationist connections: thus, items 6 and 9 give space to what was then the relatively understudied question of women in the concentration camps; item 19 to the experience of children; items 17 and 18 to the uses of oral history. All these topics would become strongly influential in the field over the following years, passing from academic fields to a wider public dissemination in narratives, films and documentaries, partly through Levi's patronage and imprimatur.

The list also confirms, and takes in new directions, Levi's engagement with Judaism. This engagement works at three distinct levels: in items 1, 12 and 16 we see Levi's new interest in the Ashkenazi, Yiddish culture of Eastern Europe, which he had encountered for the first time at its moment of demise, in Auschwitz.[43] This largely book-learned culture would feed directly into *If Not Now, When?* It is interesting to note that the same period (late 1960s to 1980s) coincided—and Levi was, again, part cause and part symptom—with a revival of interest amongst Italian literary intellectuals in Jewish Mitteleuropean literature, overshadowed by the legacy of the Holocaust.[44] In 3, 4, 12 and 14, by contrast, there is further evidence of the persistent, if muted role played by Israel. Thirdly, local Jewish identity also emerges as a focus of interest: in item 13 (as in 'Argon', the first chapter of his 1975 work *The Periodic Table*) Levi investigates the particular local history of Turinese or Piedmontese Jewish culture and language.[45] And more broadly, items 3, 5 and 12 show Levi balancing out his newly acquired Eastern fascinations with a focus on *Western* Judaism, with its own history and experiences of the Holocaust. As he notes of Presser's novel (item 5):

> This brief work is one of the few of literary merit that depict Western European Jewry. Whilst there is a rich and glorious literature of Eastern, Ashkenazi, Yiddish Judaism, the Western branch, deeply assimilated into bourgeois German, French, Dutch, Italian cultures, has contributed greatly to those cultures, but has rarely depicted itself [*Opere*, I, p. 1208].

Item 12, by Marco Herman, moves from East to West to another East altogether—from Poland, to Italy (the Resistance near Cuneo), to Israel (a kibbutz and the army in 1948)—and Levi's preface makes a virtue of the story's capacity to draw threads of connection between cultures, places and extraordinarily diverse, epoch-making events.

Several of Levi's prefaces address specifically Italian histories and specifically Italian issues in relation to the Holocaust. The ANED-sponsored material belongs under this heading, as do the narratives of Italian camp survivors. Of particular note, though, for its subject matter and its timing, is his article on Ferruccio Fölkel's book (item 7), one of the first to open up the history of the camp at the Risiera di San Sabba near Trieste, the only Italian (and indeed Western European) concentration camp to have a working gas chamber and crematorium.[46] The Trieste area continued to be a complicated and disputed site for many aspects of Italian history, and national and ethnic identity, well into the 1970s and beyond, for the problems of Slavic identity within Italy and Yugoslavia, as well as the problem of both Fascist and Communist ideologies and racial violence in the region. The site of the Risiera was emerging as a powerful presence in this field. It was recognised as a national monument in 1965, by presidential decree, and turned into a looming monument and museum site by architect Romano Boico, who designed a series of hard, high stone structures meshed in with the remains of the old brickwork factory, unveiled in 1975. It was also the centre of a difficult and highly problematic and contested trial in 1976, leading to the condemnation *in absentia* of the last commandant of the camp, Josef Oberhauser. The confluence of these events, made possible in part by isolated work such as Fölkel's (and Levi's sponsorship of it), began a long process of confronting the tensions in Italy's borders in geography, ethnicity and also complicity with the Nazis.[47]

The issue of Italy's co-responsibility for the Holocaust is a recurrent concern for Levi, even as he tended to subscribe to the view that Italians were less 'infected' with racism than Germans or the Fascist state.

In his comments on Walter Laqueur's *The Terrible Secret* (item 10),[48] he describes a complex spectrum of shared responsibility, including Italy's: 'For the massacre of the Jews almost every European nation carries some part of shared responsibility [*una quota di corresponsabilità*], from open complicity, in the case of Fascist Italy, to aiding and abetting to omission of aid' (*Opere*, II, p. 1230).[49]

Finally, item 8, a preface to a magazine article on the TV drama *Holocaust*, is worth mentioning separately as it indicates a certain attention to popular or mass cultural dissemination of Holocaust awareness, an area which has become ever more central and controversial in late-20th-century discussions of Holocaust memory, with repeated battles over the propriety or otherwise of such phenomena.[50] Levi expresses certain reservations of taste concerning *Holocaust* but defends its essential accuracy and veracity, and its positive consciousness-raising among a wide public. In a similar vein, Levi made a telling contribution to the 1975 episode on genocide of the popular British television history *World at War*.[51] It is worth contrasting this openness to formulaic, but effective, mass cultural forms of representation with his decided hostility to the intellectual pretensions and corrupt morals, as he saw it, of the 1970s cinema vogue for eroticised imagery of Nazis, epitomised by Liliana Cavani's 1974 film *Night Porter*.[52] The contrast gives us a rare instance of Levi actively 'policing' and positioning, through his commentator's authority, prevalent cultural forms of representation of the Holocaust circulating in the national cultural arena. Implicitly, though, the full gamut of his public and occasional interventions perform something of the same function.

3. Naming and Rhetoric

Levi's notional Holocaust library, sampled here, represents only one of several possible ways of testing the terrain of his historiographical and cultural vision of the Holocaust, and so the kind of filter he placed on his influential projections of an image of the Holocaust. We can touch briefly on three complementary strands of enquiry to fill out our map of the terrain.

A first useful area is Levi's engagement with discourses contiguous to or intersecting with Holocaust talk, such as racism, the 'bomb' and the Gulag. Central to Levi's discussions of racism was an investment in an *ethological* understanding of the term as an animal instinct, before it was ever an historical phenomenon. Such a conception is already present in the preface to *If This Is a Man*, where he talks of the universal human impulse to believe that "'every stranger is an enemy'" (*Opere*, I, p. 5). Through the influence of Konrad Lorenz, ethology also shapes his most extended general discussion of racism, the 1979 lecture 'Racial Intolerance' (*Opere*, I, pp. 1293–1311). Levi's talk of the threat of nuclear destruction, which so permeated the general culture of anxiety of the Cold War of the 1950s to 1970s, was also extensive, if not quite apocalyptic. His science gave him crucial parallel insights into the twin threats of modernity—Auschwitz and Hiroshima—and what they tell us about technology; about the public morality of science, with its balance of risk and responsibility; and about the very rationalism and scientific empiricism which formed him.[53] Finally, in his late years in particular, Levi was increasingly drawn to the comparison between the Nazi camps and the Soviet Gulag (and indeed other genocides), as a means to teasing out the specific features of the former, whilst rejecting facile claims of equivalence.[54]

There are also analogies and vocabularies for the Holocaust that Levi tellingly omits or rejects. We saw earlier his hostility to the psycho-sexualised Nazism of Cavani and others of the 1970s vogue. This can be extended to wholesale discomfort with psychoanalytical readings of Nazism and the camps, evident in particular in a series of hostile responses to the work of Bruno Bettelheim.[55] This stands in interesting relation to his individual-centred analysis of the Holocaust; for Levi, this leads to sociological, ethological or anthropological understandings, rather than to hidden layers of the psyche. Even when he describes Gitta Sereny's intense encounters with Stangl, his interest is in Treblinka and the mechanisms of the mind which allow certain actions and omissions, not in drives, emotions or desires.

There are key omissions also in Levi's historiography. We have seen his affinities with early histories, symptomatic of a Resistance-centred (and to a degree less specifically Jewish) perspective. But even within these constraints, it is striking to notice the absence of Raul Hilberg's 1961 work, *The Destruction of the European Jews*, perhaps the single most important history of the Holocaust.[56] Hilberg has drawn criticism, however, for his adamant refusal to draw on testimony or in general on victims' evidence, and this clashes strongly with Levi's individual-centred, testimonial and moral dimensions, although not necessarily with some of his other historiographical choices (e.g. Poliakov).[57]

A further line of enquiry regards Levi's strategies for 'naming' the Holocaust. The importance of this area is hardly exclusive to Levi: issues of language and naming have been central to several areas of Holocaust

research, from work on the distortions of the German language operated by the Nazis, including the devastating euphemism *Die Endlösung*,
the Final Solution;[58] to the coining of the word 'genocide' during the
Nuremberg process, to the intense debates about the term 'Holocaust'
itself.[59] Of all survivor-writers, Levi perhaps displayed the most acute and
sustained interest in language, sign systems and naming. The terms he
uses for the 'event' now known as the Holocaust are telling. His very first
published work—the 1946 medical report on Auschwitz, coauthored with
Leonardo De Benedetti—already talks of 'the annihilation of Europe's
Jews' (*Opere*, I, p. 1339), a striking phrase for 1946, when the specificity
of the violence against Jews was struggling to emerge from within the
more generalised sense of Nazi barbarity. The dominant naming strategy
during the 1940s and 1950s came from phrases such as Rousset's *univers
concentrationnaire*, which implied a closed, articulated hierarchy of camps
and violence, the Jewish element one among others. Indeed, Levi himself,
as we have seen, shared some of this conception, whilst always noting the
exceptional position of the Jews within that 'universe'.

If we jump forward to his very last writings on the Holocaust, in pieces
from early 1987, we see the struggle for naming is still ongoing: in an
article on the German Historians' Debate, the last in a long series of responses by Levi to negationists and revisionists dating back to 1979, he
uses terms such as 'Hitler's massacre of the Jewish people', 'Auschwitz' (but
in inverted commas and quoting a comparison with the Soviet 'Gulag' of
which he is critical), 'hell', 'black hole' and 'Lager' (*Opere*, II, pp. 1321–24).
He seems to avoid standard and loaded terms—although elsewhere he
resigns himself to the prevalent word 'Holocaust'—to push attention towards careful historical distinctions which require extended elaboration,
reflecting the need for calm dissection of the revisionists' positions. In another late piece, the preface to *Life Offended* (item 17 above), we find terms
which suggest the community of survivor-deportees, Jewish and political,
with a shared, broadly similar memory of suffering: 'mass political deportation' (including his own), 'this modern return to barbarity', 'Lager, *KZ*',
'returnee' and, mostly blunt and all-embracing of all, '*there*' ('*laggiù*').

The single most significant and distinctive entry in Levi's Holocaust
lexicon, however, was the term *Lager*, which he used substantially more
than any other writer and which has, as a result, entered common usage in
Italy.[60] It is a term which aims for neutrality but which, like all the others,
has weighty and often ambivalent connotations. First, it takes us back to
early postwar frameworks for understanding Nazism and the Holocaust,

echoing Rousset's univers concentrationnaire in suggesting a notion of 'the camp'—by metonymy the vast camp network and the metaphorical world of suffering it stands for—as a specific, enclosed site or space, with its own laws and history (see Chapter 7). It avoids privileging a single place or name, and thus 'sacralising' specific sites, which has been a strong thrust in the rhetorical use of place names such as 'Auschwitz' or, to use an example vividly present in Italian political deportation culture, the quarry at Mauthausen. It allows the full spectrum of differing camps—labour, concentration, extermination—to be taken in under one term, and it has nothing specifically Jewish about it. If it has any strong specificity, it is on the side of the perpetrators, evoking the foreignness and the Germanness of the Holocaust, in both language and culture, all consistent elements of Levi's presentation.

Levi's rhetorical deployment of a language for 'public' Holocaust rhetoric is at its most concerted in the short text he wrote for a monument to Italian victims at Auschwitz, only the last part of which was then used within the monument block itself in 1980 ('To the Visitor', *Opere*, I, pp. 1335–36). The text walks a political tightrope, one not without its slips and imbalances. The monument was sponsored by ANED, and Levi adopts the collective voice of ANED's constituency of political ex-deportees, whilst also making clear the Jewish identity of the overwhelming number of Auschwitz's victims. He also takes pains to comment on the Italian dimension to this history, since this is a national monument on the site of Auschwitz (itself a loaded idea: see Chapter 9); but he carefully addresses the general visitor to Auschwitz ('from whatever country you hail') and thus the universal message and warning that Auschwitz represents, above and beyond national histories.

He begins by merging several lines of history, through the figure of fire:

> The history of Deportation and extermination camps, the history of this place cannot be separated from the history of Europe's Fascist tyrannies: from the first fires at Union buildings in Italy in 1921, to the book burnings in Germany's squares in 1933, to the wicked flame of the crematoria at Birkenau, there is an unbroken thread. It is ancient wisdom, as Heine, a German and a Jew, warned long ago, that whoever burns books ends up burning men, that violence is a seed that never dies.

Several of Levi's characteristic inflections of the Holocaust are linked together here. The generalised phenomenon of 'deportation' (ANED's constituency) is set alongside (as distinct from, but of the same order as) extermination camps; both are incarnated in this camp, Auschwitz ('this place'); and all are given a genealogy which moves in causal steps from Fascist Italy to Nazi Germany to the Holocaust. The continuity is clinched with a figure of German and Jewish culture (Heine) and comes to a climax on an essential ethical issue for Levi, violence.

The piece continues with two paragraphs, one about Fascist Italy, one about anti-Fascism and the foundation of the postwar Republic on anti-Fascist ideals. Levi is tapping into those 'Actionist' and other leftist Resistance legacies within Italian political identity; he links Turin factory workers in 1923 to Resistance martyrs of 1943 to Italian victims at Auschwitz, all integral to Holocaust memorialisation. The balancing act is clear: Levi uses the camp to set out a 'good' Italy (and good Italians; later he notes the benevolence of the Italian people even after 1938) and a 'bad' Italy, giving a (Crocean) image of Fascism as a parenthesis in the history of 'a country that has been civilized and returned to civilization after the night of Fascism'. Elsewhere, Levi saw the civilised world as permeated with intimations of the Lager: the strain between the two positions is good evidence of the delicate rhetorical demands of this monument, where Levi's public role both constrains him and allows him to shape public awareness.

The next paragraph complicates the national side to the monument further still, by describing Italian military victims, dying for the Fascist state as 'unconscious victims' of Fascism. Predating and anticipating highly charged public debates of the 1990s over the equivalence of 'red' and 'black' allegiances in Italy's history and the recovery of 'lost' stories of the internees and civilian labourers, Levi's text pushes as far as possible the effort to render Auschwitz integral to a shared national history and national trauma.[61]

The text then returns to the partisans before two paragraphs which home in on the depths of the fate of the Jews. Levi again stresses inclusiveness, noting that Jewish victims were Italian and foreign, rich and poor, men and women, elderly and children, healthy and sick, yet all destined to die. In another contradictory impulse, he plays down Jewish identity or difference, just as he emphasises and speaks through the victim's Jewishness: 'We children of Christians and Jews (but we dislike such distinctions)'.

In stressing the terrible arbitrariness and indifference of the killing and the scale of numbers, he comes to assert a kind of uniqueness: 'Never, not even in the darkest eras, had human beings been killed in their millions, like harmful insects, babies and the dying put to death.' As in his rejection of the equivalence of the Gulag and the Lager, here Levi picks out a particular redundancy or excess of Nazi violence (the killing of infants and the old), what he will call in *The Drowned and the Saved* 'useless violence'. This is not a uniqueness based on genocide per se, nor on the systematic modernity of the process (although he does underscore the scale of numbers); it is rather a unique form of moral blindness and totalising excess, the end product, as his texts set out, of a concrete historical process.

Primo Levi was not just a great writer and chronicler of Auschwitz. He was also, for a large number of Italians over several decades, from schoolchildren to the wider reading public, the prime mediator of Holocaust knowledge. In looking at how he read the Holocaust, what he read and promoted, his naming and public rhetoric, this chapter has been searching for a rather elusive object of enquiry: the influence of one individual in reflecting and shaping a field of Holocaust culture. What has emerged is a picture of what we might call a 'weak agent' of transmission. Rather than pushing a programmatic line, Levi moves between competing foci, checking and balancing, addressing different issues, levels of understanding and constituencies. Nevertheless, certain 'strong' emphases and inflections are also evident, in particular in the balance amongst the three core configurations of the Holocaust in history and culture: as universal, national, or Jewish.

Levi's Holocaust is, above all, rooted in universalising conceptions of a kind crystallised in the immediate aftermath of the war. Although overlaid with four decades of reflection, reading and writing, his work maintains throughout powerful affinities with approaches characteristic of the late 1940s and early 1950s, with Rousset, Kogon and Antelme supplemented later by Langbein, Sereny and others; that is, with the 'humanist' and analytical, moral and social dissection of the concentration camp network and hierarchy as a site of collective and individual dissolution. In a sense, this merely reiterates, but with due contextualisation in intellectual history, Alberto Cavaglion's influential notion that Levi's entire oeuvre represents a sustained glossing of *If This Is a Man*,[62] where we find an integrated picture of the *univers concentrationnaire* as he saw it.[63] He also shares a focus on Nazis and Nazi Germany—on the perpetrator—which was characteristic of a time before the 'Holocaust' crystallised as a phenomenon in its own right, just as the nature of Nazism was the central moral-historical problem for Russell and Shirer, not yet the meaning of genocide or the trauma of the victim.

This 'humanist', universalist dimension also pushes Levi in loosely politicising directions, such as in talk of the possible return of 'fascism' (*Opere*, I, p. 1187), or in his moral-political campaigns on nuclear weapons and science, or against revisionism and negationism. And Levi's highly complex ethical discourse has its roots in this early postwar paradigm also, since it founded his early notion of the camps as a 'vast scientific experiment' and of his own work as a study of certain 'aspects of the human mind'. All these political and ethical impulses suggest Levi's influence on (or resonance with) a general sense of 'futurity' in Italian Holocaust talk: the Holocaust is used in public discourse as a warning against future lapses and dangers for democracy.

Further, Levi's implicit Holocaust historiography is one of agency more than structure. He presents the Holocaust through individuals (and small groups and networks, up to and including the nation, each with its national characters); and in particular in narratives of individuals not as psychoanalytically conceived subjects of unconscious impulses but rather as archetypes of historical realities; as victim, witness, perpetrator, bystander, and all the gradations of the 'grey zone' in between (*Opere*, II, pp. 1017–44).

On the national level, Levi's Holocaust is strongly rooted in the Italian politics of postwar anti-Fascism. His anti-Fascism, his interest in individual and group resistance, reflects an Italian 'Resistance' paradigm, and in particular an 'Actionist', moral vision of resistance. A great deal of his writing is collective and rooted in the narrow but intellectually influential circle of Turinese, ex-(Actionist) partisans, ex-deportees, many of them Jewish. His involvement with ANED consistently underscores the collectivity and cultural-political characteristics of his Holocaust. This also afforded Levi, and through him the Holocaust within Italy, a distance from the polarities of Italian ideological wars (DC versus PCI), much as the dissolution of the Action Party in 1947 left its legacy in a substratum of Italian political culture, which reemerged as a moral-political force at particular moments, such as the 1990s.[64]

Finally, Levi's shifting and tentative engagement with the Jewish dimension of the Holocaust sits somewhat uneasily with these first two elements but is undoubtedly also persistently present. He always insisted on the Jewish specificity of the Final Solution and on Jewish resistance (along with other resistances), and he did much to learn and transmit the lost

Jewish culture of the victims, especially after the late 1960s. But it can be argued that neither his Judaism nor the Jewishness of the victims provided him with his core interpretative categories of the event—such as 'resistance' or 'Fascism'--in the way that both the universal and the national dimensions undoubtedly did. In this, Levi was once again both symptom and cause of the shape of national conversation about the Holocaust in postwar Italy.

§6 Rome

Italy's history as a 'nation', both before and after the 19th-century Risorgimento, has always been variegated and fragmented, and its 'national' culture richly diverse and decentralised. Unlike France or Britain, with their all-controlling metropolitan capitals and centralised institutions of power, Italy has been characterised by regional splits, panoplies of small city-states and principalities, wars, rivalries and fierce local independence of power, language and culture. Unification in 1861, and the addition of Rome as capital in 1870, did little to tame and harmonise these teeming tensions.

Fascism's hysterical nationalism was a concerted attempt to counter this 'weak' nationhood, centred, particularly from the 1930s onwards, on a renewed myth of Rome.[1] It is at least a historical irony, then, that during the war, and especially in the months following Mussolini's fall in July 1943, Italy's destiny seemed to be determined almost anywhere but in Rome. The Allies were advancing from the south; the Germans were installed in the centre-north, where, in the countryside, small towns and mountains, the histories and myths of the anti-Fascist Resistance were being created. There was certainly an urban Resistance in Rome (the GAP), as we will see, but it was of a distinctly different order from the bands, incursions and networks in the centre-north, where its core history was written and where its legacy would penetrate the deepest. Furthermore, the king and Mussolini's successor, Marshal Badoglio, literally abandoned Rome and ignominiously fled for Puglia, at dawn on 9 September 1943, leaving a token force and some heroic Resistance fighters to make a brief stand against the Nazis. Nevertheless, perhaps precisely because of the crisis of legitimacy created by this voiding of

Rome as the nation's literal and symbolic centre of nationhood and state power, there is an anxious resonance to the events of Rome in 1943–44, in a search for what is left of Italy.

A similar picture emerges of the spread of Nazi violence in Italy during the long tail of the war in 1943–1945, including the enactment on Italian soil of the Final Solution, of massacres, deportations and desperate flight, of holding and concentration camps, gas chambers and train convoys. The geography of this Holocaust seems principally centred on a patchwork of towns and landscapes of the centre-north, from the hills above Turin to the Swiss border, from the San Vittore prison in Milan to the Risiera di San Sabba on the periphery of Nazi-administered Trieste, to the holding camp near Fossoli in Emilia-Romagna. All these sites have very particular, difficult and crucially important histories within the field of Holocaust culture, and its construction of civic engagement and memory effects, in the postwar era. And yet, in ways both historic and symbolic, Rome has returned again and again as a (perhaps *the*) prime site of Holocaust stories and images in postwar Italy.

Certain of the reasons for this Rome-centred perspective are not hard to guess. The city's delicate strategic, diplomatic and geopolitical position, as well as its millennial pull as the imaginary centre of Italian, Christian and European civilisation (including that of the Nazis), all played their part.[2] So too did the added visibility that accrues to capital cities— even of a decentralised nation like Italy—and all the more so, as over the postwar era dominant strands of the culture industries—the press, cinema, television, literary elites—were based in Rome and used the city as a production site and a source of stories.[3]

But there is more to it than this: something in the very tangled and complex stories of Rome in 1943 and 1944 contains a strange fascination and emblematic power, something of the shape and resonance of myth, which gives shape to large collective experiences and legacies of the entire era, and the myth and legacies are poised between Italian and Holocaust histories.

The strange bond between Rome and the Holocaust—the source of what we might call the 'Roman question' in Italy's Holocaust culture—has its origin in a series of interconnected events in the city between late summer 1943 and spring 1944. For reasons both concrete and imaginary, these events brought into combustible conjunction at least four of the dominant axes of Italy's modern history and identity, each one at a moment of terrible instability or crisis, and each in some way intersecting with the city's

Jewish population and with the Holocaust: Italy as a nation, Fascism and its symbols, the Resistance, and the Church. Through this conjunction, played out both at the time and since in postwar culture and memory, the 'Roman question' within the larger cultural history traced in this book becomes a fundamental indicator of where the Holocaust stands within Italian culture and within that culture's sense of what 'Italy' and 'Italian' might mean, in history and in the present. This chapter first follows the sequence of events of 1943–44 in Rome and traces their larger connotations, before exploring some of the ways in which they have returned and gained cultural traction, through sites, memorialisations, trials, and representations in historiography, fiction and film, from the 1940s to the present.

1. Rome 1943–44. A Chronicle

Events between July 1943 and June 1944 transformed Rome from the proud capital of an imperialist and totalitarian regime into an exhausted, bombed, divided and institutionally suspended state of confusion.

19–25 July 1943. San Lorenzo. On 19 July, the American air force drops more than 4,000 bombs on Rome, striking especially at railway and airport depots. The civilian toll is 951 killed, mainly around the working-class district of San Lorenzo. On 20 July, Pope Pius XII, in a rare wartime excursion beyond the Vatican, visits the area and the damaged basilica of San Lorenzo, blessing the crowd with his arms outstretched before them. The direct attack on Rome is an important factor in prompting the dramatic removal of Mussolini from power by the Fascist Grand Council on 25 July.

8–10 September 1943. Occupation. After a tense period of euphoria and hiatus following Mussolini's fall and arrest, a pre-planned Armistice announcement between Italy and the Allies is made on 8 September. The government leader Badoglio and the king leave Rome on 9 September. The German army enters and de facto occupies the 'open city' of Rome on 10 September, after brief resistance at Porta San Paolo.

26–28 September 1943. Gold. Leaders of Rome's Jewish community are summoned by Rome's Gestapo commander Herbert Kappler, who demands a 'tribute' of 50 kilogrammes of gold, to be paid within 36 hours. He threatens to deport 200 Jews if the gold is not forthcoming. After a frantic struggle to gather donations from the community, with help from non-Jews and a promise of support from the Vatican, the gold is presented to the Nazi authorities. In the following days, the collection of rare books and scrolls in Rome's synagogue is looted, destroyed or transported to Germany.

16 October 1943. Round-up. Starting at dawn, 1,259 Jews are rounded up from the former ghetto area and from various locations throughout the city. The operation is carried out by an SS division, aided by the Italian police; it is the largest single round-up operation of the war in Italy. After two days of detention, 1,023 victims are deported on a train convoy from Tiburtina Station on 18 October, reaching Auschwitz four days later. Only 17 would return. Over the following months a further thousand Roman Jews are arrested, tortured, killed or deported.

23–24 March 1944. Via Rasella—Fosse Ardeatine. On 23 March, a column of northern Italian, German-speaking SS soldiers are attacked and bombed as they march along a central Roman street, via Rasella, by a group of Roman GAP partisans, killing 32 (another died shortly afterwards). Following communications from Berlin (including Hitler's direct *diktat*) a 10-for-1 reprisal is ordered within 24 hours. A list of 335 victims is drawn up (five more than the 'correct' number, apparently due to clerical 'error'). Victims are arrested or taken from those already held in Regina Coeli prison, the Gestapo headquarters on via Tasso and elsewhere, and include young and old, civilian bystanders, criminals, anti-Fascists, and 75 Jews. They are taken in lorries to the Fosse Ardeatine quarry and catacombs on the Appian Way at the edge of the city and shot in the head in groups of five. The operation is led by SS officer Erich Priebke, among others. The site is sealed by dynamiting rocks, and an announcement of the reprisals is then made, stating 'the order has been carried out' (with no indication of where or how). The site will be discovered and opened shortly after Liberation on *4 June 1944*.

2. A Tangled Web

This dramatic cluster of events—bombings, occupation, resistance, persecution and deportation, reprisal and massacre—has been revisited, reconfigured and reinvented time and again in the cultural and public spaces of the postwar era. Already within the chronicle above, a complicated set of connotations is apparent, connecting them to axes of European and Italian history and culture that converge on Rome, and to varied aspects of the Holocaust.

The events of 1943–44 tap uncannily into the millennial history of Rome noted earlier—of Empire, Church, Western civilisation, Italy and the anti-Semitisms of all of these—in a dense semiotic web of symbols and reso-nances. So, for example, beneath the perverse, almost burlesque demand of the gold tribute by Kappler—as though he is toying with Rome's Jews, as annihilation hovers in the background—we hear echoes of an age-old his-tory of tributes and taxes, to ancient emperors and to the Church, includ-ing those demanded of the Jews of Rome by the papacy in the 16th century to pay for conversion of Jews to Christianity. The Nazis were knowingly playing at being Caesars—'Render therefore unto Caesar the things which are Caesar's' (Matt. 22:21)—a game evident in the very terminology of the Third *Reich*, as in the Fascist cult of *Romanità*—and the Vatican, once itself in the role of emperor and tributee, in 1943 plays the role of behind-the-scenes guarantor for the supplicant community, in a gesture that is caught between generosity and half-hearted compromise.

The sense of a knowing revisiting, replaying and reconfiguring of an-cient history is created also in the uses of the geography and sites of the city of Rome, for example in the choice for the Nazi reprisals of a site of early Christian burial, evocative of Roman persecution of Christians, now inverted and perverted into a site of Nazi persecution of Jews (with the Church ambiguously on the sidelines). There is a comparable coin-cidence of millennial history and geography, in this instance of Church anti-Semitism, in the streets of Rome's ex-ghetto, the low-lying area by the Tiber where Jews have lived since Empire and where the Nazis took hun-dreds of the local community on the morning of 16 October 1943. These streets, the ghetto (created by Paul IV in 1555), were also the site and sign of the presence of Jews 'under the very windows' of the Roman Church and the papacy, a deliberate reminder to Christendom of the sin of the Jews in not following, indeed in murdering, Christ.[4] The lines of fracture and controversy around the Church's role in the Holocaust, in conjunc-tion with its long history of anti-Semitism, are already signalled here, in the Vatican's ambivalent, or diplomatically quiet, role in the face of de facto Nazi occupation of the city. This applied not only to its half-promise to guarantee the gold tribute in September 1943 but also to the large num-ber of priests, monks, nuns, or individual Christians who sheltered Jews during these months, and the fraught question of whether or not Pius XII approved—perhaps even ordered—Christians to help or rather ac-tively discouraged this or kept silent. Here, as in many other respects, rela-tions of the Bishop of Rome with the Roman Jewish community reflect in microcosm the actions of the papacy across Europe. Beyond Church politics and Christian-Jewish relations, there is also embedded in this powerfully archetypal story the weighty moral issue that sets individual responsibility (to help Jews) against 'higher' institutional (party, Church or state) orders or duties.

Between the 1960s and 1970s, the Church question would explode into academic debate, but also into larger cultural controversy, through works of serious theatre, starting with Hochhuth's *The Deputy*, to Hollywood movies such as *Massacre in Rome* (George Pan Cosmatos, 1973), which pitted Richard Burton's Nazi officer against Marcello Mastroianni's lone priest trying to prevent the Fosse Ardeatine massacre.[5] It is telling, however, that both *The Deputy* and *Massacre in Rome* ran into legal difficulties in Rome, through the direct intervention of the Church or the indirect censorship fed by a political deference to the Church. An attempt in 1965 to stage the first Italian performances of *The Deputy*, by a group around leading actor Gian Maria Volontè, was crushed by a massive police raid, a siege of the small private theatre club where it was held, and arrests, based first on a technicality on access to the building and later on the Fascist-era Concordat with the Church, with rules for the protection of the image of the Church in the city of Rome.[6] *Massacre in Rome* meanwhile led to a prosecution of writer Robert Katz, director Cosmatos and producer Carlo Ponti, set in motion by the niece of Pius XII: all three were convicted although later amnestied.[7]

In simply 'staging' this history in these places, then, the Nazis were tapping into and almost taking up roles within age-old histories of the Roman Empire, the Church (with its own history of anti-Semitism) and Fascism's own extended attempts to appropriate these very same multiple, millennial histories. Such ironies of historical geography continue to the present day, as we saw in Chapter 2, with the siting of Mussolini's villa, and soon also the Museo della Shoah in Rome, next to the site of Jewish catacombs at Villa Torlonia.

Alongside these macrohistorical echoes and ironies, and with equally powerful resonances of their own, is a series of more recent and concretely historical, specifically national dilemmas, echoed and restaged by the events of 1943–44 in Rome, which only add to their cultural resonance. First, there is the direct question they raise of the collapse and survival of the Italian state and nation, posed by the dismissal of Mussolini, the Armistice and the evacuation of Rome by king and government. In the late 1990s, a historiographical debate—a *caso*—exploded on precisely

these questions, prompted by historian Ernesto Galli della Loggia's book
La morte della patria, which suggested that 8 September 1943 marked the
abandonment of the people by the state, just as the king and Badoglio
had abandoned Rome.[8] Galli della Loggia was heavily criticised for, in
effect, legitimating the Fascist regime, since the *patria* that died was the
Fascist totalitarian state.[9] The national question thrown up by events in
Rome is also, in other words, a question of Fascism and its relation to
Italian history, the state and its people; and only a step away from what
has been perhaps the most significant debate in the historiography of Fascism in the postwar era, the so-called consensus debate, shaped by Renzo
De Felice, and also cultural historians such as Philip Cannistraro, over
how far and quite why the majority of the Italian population under Fascism accepted totalitarian rule with more or less passive assent.[10] Finally,
the papacy is relevant here too, with all its troubled relations with and
hostility to the new 19th-century nation-state of Italy, followed by its reconciliation with Fascist Italy in the 1929 Concordat. Pius XII's visit to his
basilica at San Lorenzo also looks like an event in that history, the pope
as a *national*, public figure of authority, consoling Rome and Italy as his
flock, against the Allies' bombs, just as Mussolini falls.

   A flood of questions was triggered by the Armistice, in Rome and
throughout Italy and Axis Europe, where as many as a million Italians
were under arms: Who now fought for Italy? Should Italian soldiers fight
or disband? Conversely, for whom did or should Italian soldiers now
fight: the king, the Allies, the Axis, the Resistance, or indeed no-one?
What was a patriot, a 'good Italian' to do? The questions were political
and juridical, but also intensely personal and moral; and they were to become further politicised late in the 20th century, when an argument was
made for a sort of ideological-moral equivalence between the choices of
1943: to join the Resistance, to join the Salò army, to stay at home. This
was a way of reclaiming moral justification for those who just happened
to end up on the wrong side of the divide (the 'boys of Salò', they would
be labelled, the childish term underlining their lack of responsibility).[11]
In Rome, as we have seen, the futile skirmish at Porta San Paolo held up
a fragile image of a rump army fighting with an improvised Resistance as
all that was left of a national military defence. The same Resistance, of
course, would carry out and claim legitimacy for the via Rasella attack
as an act of war and of national Liberation, staking a claim as the 'army'
of a new Italy. In the months following, by contrast, the Nazis were aided
by Italian Fascist police, more or less reluctantly facilitating the round-

ups of both 16 October 1943 and 23–24 March 1944. The official forces of the Fascist state did not, in other words, simply disappear; one of the most violent and intense public explosions of anger against the Fascists was to come in September 1944 in Rome, on the occasion of the trial of the Fascist police chief Pietro Caruso for his role in the Fosse Ardeatine massacre, during which the former director of the Regina Coeli prison was lynched.[12]

Conversely, as Alessandro Portelli has explored in his magisterial oral history of conflicting memories surrounding via Rasella and the Fosse Ardeatine, the choice to fight with the Resistance was in fact, long before revisionist debates of the 1990s, far from a universally admired one.[13] As in many other cases of what has been called the 'divided memory' of the Resistance that has run like a seam beneath Italy's postwar history,[14] popular and often false beliefs and rumours became established in sectors of the Roman population which laid the blame for the horrors of the Fosse Ardeatine firmly at the door not of the Nazis but of the partisans at via Rasella.[15] If they had given themselves up, the false legend had it, the reprisals would not have taken place: the action was futile, the price was too high, the reprisal avoidable and so too the GAP partisans were cowards for not owning up to it. The falsity of this 'urban myth' is alluded to in Portelli's title, taken from the Nazis' declaration that the reprisal order had 'already been carried out'. There was, in other words, no possibility for the partisans to take action to prevent the reprisals. As with the soldiers and their impossible choice of loyalties, so too the precarious state of national and moral identity, the obfuscation of how a 'good' Italian should act at this moment—collaborate, resist, wait?[16]—left deep divisions that have not been fully reconciled over the entire postwar era.

The controversy over the responsibility of the partisans for the Fosse Ardeatine massacre is one troubled way in which that event or set of events has come to stand for deep dilemmas in Italy's postwar coming to terms with Fascism and the war. The Jewish dimension of the massacre—more than one in five of its victims were Jewish—only adds to this fraught complexity. As noted in Chapter 1, a line of affinity connects Nazi massacres of civilians across occupied Europe to the European Holocaust as a whole, and specific national disasters such as the Fosse Ardeatine form part of this chain, as do the civilian massacres at Marzabotto, Sant'Anna di Stazzema and dozens more acts of mass murder, with several hundred victims, which peppered the Nazi occupation of the centre and north of Italy, but which had a difficult and often neglected or conflicted memorialisation in the postwar era.[17] The scale, the Jewish presence and the methods (shooting hundreds dead and burying piles of corpses in mass graves) of the murders at the Fosse Ardeatine evoke with particular force the Einsatzgruppen massacres in Eastern European and so the early phases of the Jewish Holocaust and other Nazi programmes of racial mass murder.

The Jewish dimension of the Fosse Ardeatine massacre has grown ever more significant in linking Italian history to the Holocaust (indeed, to excess: Portelli quotes schoolchildren who believe all the victims of the Fosse Ardeatine were Jewish);[18] but also, conversely, in attempts to link Jewish-Italian history and memory to Italian history, memory and identity. The taxonomy of victims—itself a mode of remembrance that has become a dominant trope in Holocaust and other postwar memorialisations and memory cultures, from the Washington Vietnam memorial to the Bologna train station memorial—has increasingly come to seem like a cross-section of Italy itself: because of the almost random, hurried, patchwork way the list of victims was actually compiled, deliberately made up of civilians, young and old, as well as those notionally suspected of anti-Fascism and others held for concrete acts of Resistance, or simply for being Jewish; and because it was bureaucratically recorded. So, as at the memorial site itself, the Jewish victims are part and parcel of this nationalised memorial site and memory, the Jews an integral part of Roman and Italian shared historical suffering; and that side of Italian collective memory which points up its role as victim of Nazism is concomitantly enhanced. Put simply, the Fosse Ardeatine massacre was simultaneously the most 'national' of Nazi massacres in Italy and the most 'Jewish'.

Complex questions over the nation, the Church, Fascism and anti-Fascism raised by the events in Rome were made more charged still by the presence and role of Rome's Jews within them. In a strange inversion, as the contours of the Holocaust become more clearly defined over the latter years of the 20th century and the legacy of anti-Fascism ever more blurred, the Jewish aspect of these questions began to look something like a litmus test case for addressing them. This worked its way not only through a set of questions about Italian national identity—the Jews as victims or as neighbours to be hidden from harm, as a test of national citizenship and of national character (Chapter 8), for *both* the Jews and the non-Jews—but also through a set of parallel, Christian or universal moral questions (the duty to protect the weak and persecuted, tested out by how the Jews were treated). At each of these levels, for Jews and non-

Jews, this was played out as a challenge both to individual conscience and to collective communal or institutional responsibility. Again and again, in cultural probings of these Roman events, this anxiously patrolled borderline is crucial: the individual and her or his decency or guilty neglect of the neighbour, set alongside the macrohistorical actions of states, authorities, institutions, armies and collectivities to save or harm the Jews, for their own sake, and to redeem the nation (or indeed humanity). The neighbour question, as we will see below, returns with insistence in postwar narratives of Rome's Holocaust.

Finally in this tangled web of historical and symbolic connections, it is also worth noting the strange role of Rome in an international spectrum of postwar Holocaust culture. If we invert the telescope, the events of 1943–44 become not only an oblique metonymy for Roman or Italian history but also an anomalous, though somehow also analogous, test case for the European Holocaust. The Nazi genocide, and postwar efforts to record it, have overwhelmingly centred on Eastern European centres of deportations and exterminations between 1942 and 1945. We saw in the previous chapter how Primo Levi, among others, turned his attention to another, Western European set of Holocaust experiences and stories, just as in France, Holland, Italy and elsewhere a repressed history of Western collaboration and complicity with the Nazi genocide began to be confronted.[19] The case of Rome resonated along this geographical and historical faultline, seeming to show many of the typical ambivalences of Western European histories, but also certain attributes that linked it, strangely, to the Eastern story. In particular, the site of the old ghetto and the round-up, deportations and massacres in Rome echoed, as if in hypervisible form, the horrific and in some ways hidden histories of the Eastern Nazi ghettoes, their massacres and liquidations. As a result, some of the dilemmas of response and responsibility thrown up by the latter recurred in Rome too, as became clear in late-1960s controversies that were picked up again in the 1990s.

The starkest example was the question of collaboration, which, in relation to Rome, was pushed into public debate by the polemical work of an American leftist freelance writer and historian, Robert Katz.[20] His 1967 work *Death in Rome*, recounting the events leading to the Fosse Ardeatine, stoked the fires of the Church debate by claiming to have uncovered documentary evidence that Pius XII had knowledge of the upcoming massacre many hours before it happened.[21] In Katz's next book, *Black Sabbath*,[22] he proved equally fierce in his condemnation of the Roman

Jewish community leaders for their decision to take on the demand for the gold tribute in September 1943, hoping to buy the safety of the community from the Nazis. Katz, in other words, set up Rome's Holocaust story as close, comparable, even identical to that of the Jewish Councils or *Judenräte*, the community leaders of the Eastern European Nazi ghettoes who in many cases agreed to act as proxies and organisers on behalf of the Nazi torturers and murderers of their people, in the almost always forlorn hope of softening the treatment, delaying deportations and saving lives.[23] Katz's account is clearly influenced by the immense controversy unleashed over this question by Hannah Arendt's *Eichmann in Jerusalem*, which deplored in devastating fashion the humiliations and useless compromises of the Judenräte, making this issue a permanent quandary in moral and political responses to the Holocaust.[24] Over the course of the 1970s and 1980s, Primo Levi repeatedly returned to this question, probing the moral ambiguity, but also intense human complexity, of Chaim Rumkowski, the power-crazed leader of the Lodz Judenrat.[25] Quite apart from the concrete similarity of the decisions and dilemmas of the Rome community leaders compared to those of the Judenräte, it is more than anything the symbolic weight—of the gold tribute, of the site of Rome, of this most ancient of Jewish communities—that lends some substance to Katz's parallels, for all his occasional ideological tendentiousness (typical of the era). Rome's specific power, this place of all places, under the very windows of Western Christendom, rubs up against and resonates with the most troubling stories and choices the Holocaust has left us.

3. Events, Monuments, Stories

The web of highly complex issues thrown up by the events of 1943–44 in Rome—on Italy, Europe and the war, the Church, the nation and the regime, the Jews, the Romans and the Italians, the Fascists, the Nazis and the Holocaust, morality, justice and responsibility, history and memory—builds persistently, in varied form and shape, in public spaces, in collective events and in stories, throughout the postwar era. We can take samples from each of these arenas to gauge and give a sense of particular Roman presences and inflections in the field of Italian Holocaust culture.

First, it is worth flagging up not so much an event as a non-event. In the late 1990s, journalist Furio Colombo and others began arguing for the establishment in Italy of a national Holocaust memorial day. The choice of date was a heavily loaded one, and one that split even those arguing in favour of the idea. For those intent on aligning Italy with a shared European or global memorialisation of the Shoah, a harmonised and internationally significant date was to be preferred. Even here, however, the varying contours and definitions of the Holocaust that have run throughout the postwar era—the Holocaust as an event in human history, in Jewish history, in German history, in European history and so on—meant that choosing a date was not easy. In the end, the internationalist solution was embraced in Italy and in most other European countries following an international conference in 2000. The day chosen was 27 January, the date of the Soviet liberation of Auschwitz, the camp that had come, by the end of the century, to embody and epitomise in its very name the horrors of the Final Solution. Colombo argued instead that Italy's national memorial day should emphasise that the Holocaust was—also—an event in *Italian* and *Italian-Jewish* history, and so he proposed instead 16 October. The round-up in Rome on that date in 1943, he proposed, literally brought the Final Solution to the very centre of the city and the nation, in the form of both Nazi persecution and the collaboration of Fascist institutions and individuals.[26]

By the 1990s, then, at least for Colombo, Jewish victims could and should stand as emblems of Italian victimhood of Nazi violence (and the Fascist police as emblems of Italian complicity). In the 1940s, immediately after the Liberation, commemorations at Fosse Ardeatine show a very different picture. The Fosse quickly became a site of pilgrimage and shared mourning: Patrizia Dogliani describes a march by tens of thousands of former partisans in Rome in December 1947, from the central Roman Forum and Capitoline Hill out to the Fosse Ardeatine, linking the massacre to the centre of national history and power.[27] Plans for a memorial monument were quickly put in place, with a government-sponsored competition for the design launched as early as 1944, and the venue was soon established as a central national site of mourning for all those who fell in the liberation of Italy, not only for the victims of this single massacre.[28] As Rebecca Clifford has shown, however, the Jewish dimension was hardly acknowledged at all in the conception and construction of the monument.

The competition—the first public architectural competition after the war—came with official approval and the support of the association of the victims' families, ANFIM: a remarkable fact given the complete absence of national, official monuments to the Resistance elsewhere in Italy.[29] The architectonic and sculptural ensemble which won the compe-

tition was inaugurated on 24 March 1949. It was designed by a group including architects Giuseppe Perugini and Mario Fiorentino, and sculptors
Mirko Basaldella, who designed the dramatic gates onto the monument
complex, and Francesco Coccia, whose sculpture 'The Three Ages' portrayed a boy, a man and an old man, all victims of the Nazis. The core of
the project were 335 regular tombstones joined by one extra tomb, a sort
of 'unknown soldier' for all those who fell in the Resistance, the whole
covered over by a looming, low, vast canopy, a final conjoined tombstone
bringing together all the victims. Clifford shows that the varied identity
of the victims helped seal this national, inclusive status, as did Coccia's
sculpture.[30] This unified, nationalising rhetoric of the monument paid
little or no attention to the Jewish victims, and this is confirmed by the
stone inscription welcoming visitors and pilgrims, which actually uses the
term 'Holocaust' but with no connotation of the term as used today and
no separate reference to the Jewish victims:

> Travellers thirsty for liberty
> we were rounded up without reason
> from streets and from prison
> in reprisal
> hurled together
> slaughtered entombed in these caves
> Italians do not curse
> mothers, wives, do not weep
> sons, carry with pride
> the memory
> of your fathers' holocaust [*olocausto*]
> Let the execution visited upon us
> serve beyond revenge
> to consecrate the right to human existence
> against the crime of the assassin

This was in stark contrast to the role the monument and the memory of
the Fosse Ardeatine had taken up by the 1990s, when, Clifford shows, the
Jewish dimension threatened to swamp (and even aid in the forgetting of)
the shared national legacy of anti-Fascism and liberation. This inverted
focus emerged especially in the context of the uneven history of legal
prosecution of the perpetrators of this crime.

The trials of Nazi perpetrators—from Nuremberg in 1945 to Jerusalem in 1961 to Frankfurt in 1963, to the dozens of more or less minor
trials held throughout the postwar era—have crystallised and at times

shifted public conceptions of the Holocaust and of the legacies of Nazism and the war in different countries. In Italy, a combination of institutional chaos after the war, continuity with the Fascist era, violent reprisals, and the political expediency that led the Communist Party leader and then Justice Minister Palmiro Togliatti to support a large-scale amnesty for former Fascists in 1946 meant that there was no coordinated programme of trials, nor any systematic judicial response to the crimes of Fascism. As one historian has called it, this was Italy's 'missing Nuremberg'.[31] Nevertheless, in an uneven patchwork over the decades from the 1940s to the 1990s, the events in Rome of 1943–44 surfaced in the courtroom also, with flashpoints of controversy in the 1950s and 1970s.

During the period 1944–1947, several Nazi and Fascist officers and officials were tried in Italy for the reprisals at the Fosse Ardeatine. British Military Courts prosecuted the three most senior Nazi commanders responsible for German forces in Italy, focussing specifically on the Ardeatine reprisals: Generals von Mackensen and Maelzer were sentenced to death in Rome in November 1945 and Field Marshal Albert Kesselring was likewise first sentenced to death in a court in Venice in May 1947.[32] Kesselring's sentence was commuted and he was eventually released on grounds of ill health in 1952, to great controversy, and he remained a staunch defender of German 'military operations' in Italy. The Allies allowed the new Italian government to put on trial some Italian Fascists. As chronicled by Giacomo Debenedetti, one of the first of these was the Fascist police chief of Rome Pietro Caruso, tried in September 1944, for his role in helping select and provide the Ardeatine victims: during the trial prison chief Donato Carretta—a witness at the trial—was strung up and lynched by a mob of 7,000.[33] Caruso was found guilty and executed on 22 September. An Italian military tribunal also tried and imprisoned the SS officer directly responsible for the massacre, Herbert Kappler, who had previously attempted to escape from Italy with the help of the Vatican. Thirty years later, a sick Kappler escaped from prison in Gaeta in August 1977, apparently carried out in a suitcase by his wife. Despite a clamorous reaction in Italy, including two contemptuous articles by Primo Levi calling for ministerial resignations and lambasting the blind eye turned to the escape by both Italian authorities and German public opinion,[34] Kappler remained in West Germany until his death a few months later.

By the 1990s, as Clifford and Portelli noted, the Holocaust dimension of the Ardeatine killings loomed very large. This was to be confirmed in the remarkable sequence of events of the late extradition and three trials during 1996–1998 of Erich Priebke, the SS captain in charge of the actual shootings. The Priebke case echoed the Eichmann case in the early 1960s, but unlike the Jerusalem trial it failed in several respects to work through the Italian or Roman legacy of the Holocaust or even to give voice to the victims. Priebke was living in Argentina when found by a television crew, extradited and put on trial (anomalously) in a military court. Press and public interest was intense, but the trial fizzled out in technical evidence and led to a verdict of guilty but with the crime held to be beyond the statute of limitations. The crowd in court was appalled and erupted into loud protest (the violence a dim echo of the Caruso trial); there were marches to both the nearby ghetto area of Rome and the monument at the Fosse. The government intervened and found a way of rerunning the trial: Priebke was found guilty again, sentenced to 15 years and then life imprisonment, but was held under light custody, later commuted to house arrest. He was still living comfortably in Rome in 2010 at the age of 97.[35]

∾

From this confusing network of trials, little legal, historical or moral clarity emerges. But the cultural processing they evince shows how the events and the sites of Rome in 1943–44, from the ghetto to the catacombs and its monument, continued to resonate in public culture, with an ever stronger presence of the Holocaust and all its associations. A similar pattern can be seen in narrative responses to the Roman question.

There is a rich and evolving strand of book and film narratives about Rome in 1943–44, exploring the history and legacy of the tangled web of associations with Rome described above. A small, but heavily significant, corpus of work, this has stretched forward from the very earliest months after the liberation of Rome in mid-1944 to the early 21st century, cutting across from the highest literary achievements of the era to middle-brow fiction writing and filmmaking to popular genre works; and in each of these modes it has mixed and remixed elements of the Rome question as laid out here. To gauge some of this fluid range of topic and tone, we can pick out three representative pairings of texts or stories, sketching in the first two, before looking in closer detail at the third as a particularly useful case study.

The first pairing has a clear point of origin in two works of 1944 which we already encountered in Chapter 4: Giacomo Debenedetti's diptych of literary reportage and reflection, *16 October 1943* and *Eight Jews*. These apparently rather artless texts have only come to grow in importance, for their tone and style, for their formulation of a kind of second-hand but intimately felt chronicle narrative, and for their tying together for the first time in a loose sequence the events of the gold tribute, the ghetto round-up, the Fosse Ardeatine and indeed the early postwar trials. Debenedetti's patchwork touches on many, if not all, of the questions that we have suggested permeate the entire postwar era of reflections on Rome: questions of the Jewish community and responsibility, the 'neighbour' question—that is, the non-Jewish Romans who did or did not save Jews—the national question of identity, patriotism and the extent to which victims of the Holocaust or of Nazi civilian massacres had in some sense also died for the nation; and even, although only in passing, the Church's complicated role of resistance and neglect. Debenedetti's fundamental contribution can be paired with a novel of the 1974, Elsa Morante's literary bestseller and *cause célèbre*, *History*. Morante picked up intensely on the events depicted in *16 October 1943*, expanding upon it to a massive degree and projecting onto it, and onto its setting in occupied Rome and the period around the 16 October round-up and deportations, something like a vision of history itself as the universal scandal of the suffering of women, children and the weak.[36] As Risa Sodi has shown, *La storia* intersects with and borrows at several stages in its ambitious canvas from the history of Italian Holocaust writing (including from Debenedetti and Bruno Piazza).[37] The protagonist, Ida Ramundo, is half-Jewish but has concealed the fact from those around her. She is raped by a German, symbolically a citizen of Dachau. She and her son, Useppe, witness the Rome round-up and deportations of 16 October 1943 (they are drawn in one convulsive sequence to the wailing voices from inside a cattle truck), and Useppe later happens upon and is stunned by magazine images of the camp liberations. A key figure for the compelling, but confused, philosophy of history behind the book is revealed to be Davide Segre, a troubled Jewish anarchist and escapee from a deportation train. Morante's vast canvas of the 'scandal' of History uses the figure of the Jews, the aura of the Holocaust and an allegorical analogy between the '*umili*' (the meek) and the victims of genocide.

A second pairing, a book and a film, takes us forward to the late 1990s, the phase of most intense cultural activity around the Holocaust since the 1940s. It also takes us to the heart of a crucial retrospective or 'back-dating' thrust in the shape of Italy's understanding of the Holocaust in this period, in historiography but also fiction and film narrative. Increasingly, from the late 1980s onwards, Italy's Holocaust is perceived as beginning not in 1943 but rather with the Fascist Racial Laws of 1938. As if to underscore this move, the Holocaust also increasingly comes to be portrayed as 'close to home', its victims ordinary people, the lives destroyed just like ours. This is the strongest form taken by what we might call the 'neighbour' paradigm. Both Rosetta Loy's 1997 book *First Words* and Ettora Scola's 2001 film *Unfair Competition* share these features, although the former is a subtle literary memoir and piece of personal and historical research (in particular on the Church's role) and the latter a piece of genre comedy in the idiom of the old *commedia all'italiana*, with popular stars Diego Abatantuono and Sergio Castellitto.[38] Both pivot around the Racial Laws, the exclusion from rights and citizenship of Italy's Jews, and both experience them from the point of view of the non-Jewish neighbour: Loy herself as a girl in *First Words*, watching with what she remembers now guiltily as indifference, as a neighbouring Jewish family withdraw and disappear from her life; and the two warring shopkeepers in *Unfair Competition*, one Jewish, one not, always comically bickering, but movingly bound in a friendship that is allowed expression only when the Jew is persecuted and taken away.

Finally, we can look at a pairing of films that both turn around the dramatic events in the streets and communities of Rome's ghetto area in September and October 1943. It is worth dwelling a little longer on this final pair, made more than two generations and more than forty years apart, because they neatly illustrate, in their distance and diverse modes of cultural processing, how the same set of Roman events can be reprised, with tellingly different emphases and balances, reflecting contrasting periods in postwar Italian political and cultural history, modes of negotiation of the legacies of Fascism, war and Resistance and the Holocaust, as well as moments in the history of 'engaged' filmmaking.

In 1961, Carlo Lizzani was already a veteran film director who had worked at the heart of the 1940s neorealist movement and was established in a long career moving between committed political and popular filmmaking. Lizzani's *The Gold of Rome* resembles a late but conventional entry in the neorealist, documentarist canon, in that it faithfully and 'from below' chronicles a real sequence of events—the 36-hour debate in the Jewish community and the scramble triggered by Kappler's demands for his 50 kilogrammes of gold. But the film is also theatrical, even formally tragic or melodramatic in its mode of handling the drama: the unities of place and time are heavily marked, creating powerful, if heavy-handed, effects of intensity and suspense. Shots of clocks ticking punctuate the film, along with frantic efforts to cover ground searching for help out in the city (urban negotiations being another archetypal neorealist trope), followed by anxious returns to the central site of the drama, the synagogue in the heart of the ghetto, and, inside the synagogue, the scales weighing the gold. The shooting style is communal, choral, with an emphasis on crowds scenes, congregations, groups and families, complemented by elements of city filming, with street scenes and documentary-style footage of the synagogue, the Nazi headquarters, the Vatican. These choral, documentary and heavily neorealist elements are complemented by more unusual aspects of Lizzani's style here, which touch on some of our core concerns in the history of Holocaust responses.

Foremost amongst these is a strong element of anthropological observation, even of the recently formulated practice of *vérité* filmmaking,[39] in the way Lizzani establishes the sheer Jewishness of this story, this place and this community. The production was made in collaboration with the Jewish community and synagogue authorities in Rome (just as in the same period De Felice was being sponsored by UCII to research and write his *History of Italian Jews Under Fascism*—as we saw in Chapter 5, this was a period of renewed commitment by the Jewish community to get the story of Italy's Holocaust told); and nowhere is this clearer than in the opening sequence of the film. Behind the credits, we see, and indeed feel, a shot of ancient walls and stones in the Roman ghetto, followed after the credits by an extraordinary, documentary-anthropological sequence in which a handheld camera witnesses and observes at length from within the great synagogue a communal service in progress, with the songs and Hebrew prayers left powerfully unexplained to the 'lay' audience. The film is taking risks here, entering what is an 'alien' world for most of its spectators in order then to penetrate it through the narrative, and to live its tragedy from within, in an operation of quite complicated cultural-anthropological repositioning. Nothing like this had been attempted before 1961 in Italy, and it is all the more remarkable coming in a film which also, as we will see below, tells this Jewish tragedy as a story of national citizenship, of Italian as much as Jewish tragedy and redemption. The dynamic project of making Jewish-Italian history over into Italian history finds one of its first and most powerful instances here.

The communal, collective and urban elements of *The Gold of Rome* not only form the basis of a hybrid style between neorealism and anthropological observation. They also act as structural props, calling forth and providing an on-screen audience and stage for the film's moments of set-piece historical didacticism, speeches and dialogue through which Lizzani articulates with emblematic clarity the communal tragedy of Rome's Jews and the moral quandaries it brings. Most of these moments are provided by characters in the interconnected triangles of conflict, love and sacrifice that form the narrative heart of the film. In this thread of melodrama, the film touches on several of the facets of the events of September and October 1943 that have been noted above as persistently resonant for Italy's contemplation of its Holocaust.[40]

Two triangles form the melodramatic geometry of *The Gold of Rome*, allowing it to tie together its historical and moral, Jewish and Italian dimensions. Both triangles feature the film's young hero Davide, played with James-Dean-like (and so anachronistic) intensity by French actor Gérard Blain. The first triangle is a love triangle across the Jewish-Christian racial divide; it centres on Davide and Giulia, his Jewish friend and former schoolmate (Anna-Maria Ferrero), and her Christian fiancé, Massimo (Jean Sorel). As the drama of the gold tribute unfolds, and the tragic end that it promises and then delivers hovers in the background, Giulia is offered through her family the chance of conversion, and so perhaps escape. She seems to accept the chance, and so to reject her hidden love for Davide in the process; but in a grand gesture of her own at the end of the film, she will choose her Jewish identity and destiny (and so deportation and death) over her escape route, thereby staying faithful to Davide in some way. Davide, meanwhile, argues that Jews must reject all the demands of the Nazis and fight, leading him to a form of redemptive and heroic sacrifice at the end of the film, by heading for the countryside to join the Resistance, binding his Jewish identity and fate to the struggle for Italy. (The same rhetoric of sacrifice informs the ending of Rossellini's *General della Rovere*, where it is also briefly linked to Jewish victimhood.) Davide and Giulia's love is itself unfulfilled, but it drives them towards forms of moral authenticity and sacrifice. (A minor character is shown to commit suicide in the sight of German soldiers in one climatic sequence of the film, a prefiguration of the central role played by sacrifice in the climax of the film.) The rhetoric of these impulses looks back strongly to the 1940s—and is part of a general surge in Resistance idealism in the early 1960s—but it is powerfully linked also to shared emblems of Jewish and Italian identity. The Roman resistance and the fate of Rome's Jews are tied here to the same history: in their different ways, both Davide and Giulia become 'good Italians' as they learn to become 'good Jews' at one and at the same time, both through gestures of principled sacrifice.[41]

Davide gets to argue his cause and his conviction that the Jews should fight and not accommodate the Nazi demands via the other 'triangle' of the film, which pits him as the rebel voice against the elderly community leader, the president of the Jewish community (Filippo Scelzo), in front of the gathered crowds of members of that community, the film's chorus. If Davide is clearly the hero of the film and in the right, the president is nevertheless shown to be well meaning, and also in his way heroically proactive in leading and successfully galvanising the community into action. It is also the role of the president to take the film out into the streets of Rome and, crucially, into the high institutions of the city, those very institutions that will be the focus of enquiry in postwar historiography: to raise the gold, he visits the Vatican, Roman city officials, Italian Fascists, bankers (in the film, his brother is a bank official who has rejected his Jewish origin) as well as dealing with the Nazis and his own Jewish community and authorities at the synagogue.

Through this second triangle, the film moves in at least two crucial directions anticipating movements in Holocaust memory and representation characteristic of the rest of the 1960s and beyond: first, the Holocaust is probed through generational conflict between an old establishment (the president) and youthful rebellion (Davide). The young student rejects his elder's compromises with and passivity in the face of Fascism. Blain's anachronistic leather jacket is telling here, since this contest feels as much like the generational conflicts—already staged in films such as *Rebel Without a Cause* (1955)—destined to dominate 1960s culture, including the culture of response to the Holocaust (see Chapter 7), as it does a documentary reality of the 1940s. Secondly, the very terms of the debate here are of immense importance for both Italian memories of war and Holocaust memories. In Italy, this is the De Felice question of consensus; in the context of the Holocaust more broadly, it is the Robert Katz/ Hannah Arendt question of the Judenrat. In the film, the answer is clear: for both Italy and the Jewish community, Resistance is the right response, although the older generation's position is far from venal or corrupt. But even by posing the question in these terms, as the film does with acute intensity, and certainly by staging the Jewish and the Italian questions as one and the same quandary, *The Gold of Rome* represents an extraordinarily important moment in postwar responses to the Holocaust.

The film ends, fulfilling the tragic aura of inevitable catastrophe that has permeated it throughout, in a flash forward from September to October, to the dawn of 16 October, in a sequence that moves from the noise and blind panic of the arrival of the Nazi troops to a final sequence of silent shots of the deserted streets around the synagogue, the ghetto and the Teatro di Marcello.

Jumping forward four decades to Ferzan Ozpetek's 2003 film *Facing Windows*, and into an idiom of filmmaking acutely attuned to the multiculturalism, identity politics and aesthetics of postmodern contemporaneity, it is surprising to find elements of the Roman story of 1943 replayed in ways not entirely disconnected from their telling in *The Gold of Rome*. The film centres on a contemporary woman, Giovanna (Giovanna Mezzogiorno), whose marriage is in trouble, whose work is unfulfilling and who becomes drawn to a stranger she sees in an apartment opposite hers (Lorenzo, played by Raoul Bova). In the midst of this string of typical contemporary troubles (a disaffected 21st-century take on Lizzani's melodramatic love triangle), on the Ponte Sisto bridge in central Rome by the old ghetto area Giovanna encounters an old man, lost and amnesiac (Massimo Girotti, in his last role). The mystery of the man's identity, and Giovanna's role in solving it for him and for us, and the (quite trite) life lessons it teaches her, will form the central substance of the film (the equivalent of Davide, the president and the community, the second triangle of *The Gold of Rome*). The man, his identity confused between two names, Davide and Simone (one his real name, one the name of his dead lover), is, we will learn, both Jewish and gay, a survivor of the 16 October round-up and of deportation to Auschwitz (where his lover died).

Facing Windows, like *The Gold of Rome*, mixes private lives and love-stories with the historical drama and tragedy of the Holocaust, and specifically with the fateful events of 16 October 1943 in the homes and streets of the Roman ghetto. In their different ways, the films are both partly didactic exercises, teaching the audience a history they may not have known and life lessons to be derived from it—Lizzani through direct chronicle, Ozpetek through the emotional journey taken by Giovanna. In fact, Ozpetek's film is quite sketchy on specific details of its 1943 setting: on the experience of being gay and/or Jewish in a period of persecution, on the round-up, on the Nazis and Fascists or indeed the Jewish community, on how Davide was eventually arrested and how he survived, and so on. But the film goes to extensive and significant trouble to transmit through Giovanna's experiences a newly acquired awareness of history, trauma and the lessons of suffering, however loosely documented: not least through a long-held close-up of Giovanna's eyes staring out at us the audience under the closing credits, stirring music in the background, as if to say 'you too now know this' (echoes of Levi's injunction 'Meditate that this has been'). The narrative and stylistic modes of the two films are entirely different, of course: where Lizzani's was documentaristic, with a vein of anthropology, even *vérité* thrown in, Ozpetek's is built on fluid interchanges of present and past, on structural patterings and overlaying of fantasy and reality, governed by mysterious processes of memory. Indeed, memory is a crucial dimension that is quite absent from *L'oro*. In *Facing Windows*, the events around 16 October open the film and pepper the plot in flashback, but the audience cannot disentangle them or interpret them until they are revealed in stages to Giovanna and to us by Davide/Simone's returning memory: the bulk of the film is instead set in contemporary Rome, where the dim echoes of the Holocaust are all but drowned out and ignored in the mess of contemporary living that the narrative follows. The central underlying quandary now is not whether to act, to resist in a time of terrible crisis (although this dimension does emerge, both literally and metaphorically, as the film's central mystery is solved); it is rather how to relate to the past, to histories which are ours or which we have inherited but never quite known or understood, as we live through ordinary tribulations of ordinary modern lives. Tighter analogies are hinted at in those tribulations: typically for Ozpetek, motifs of multiculturalism and immigrant communities form a natural but tense backdrop to Giovanna's life, with her Turkish friend Emine, African neighbours and Chinese workmates (the chicken factory Giovanna works in is compared to a Lager at one point). The Holocaust is not, in and of itself, the central problem here but rather what is left of it in the early 21st century, how it relates to our own moral choices, and what happens when it erupts unexpectedly into our lives.

Despite these differences, there remains something in the use and power of the Rome setting of *Facing Windows* that confirms, even in a work where it is almost an incidental, the continuing resonance of the return to these streets and the events of Rome's Holocaust. We can see this, above all, in the use of the stones and walls of the ghetto, shown precisely as in *The Gold of Rome* as a frame to the film in shots at the very start. *Facing Windows* opens with a flashback sequence set in 1943. The young Davide fights with a co-worker in a bakery and escapes, running off into the dark. The sequence ends on a dramatic shot of Davide's bloodied handprint on a wall, at a fork in the ghetto backstreets. We later learn that this is the night of 15–16 October and the fork marked Davide's terrible moment of choice amongst individual, affective and collective loyalties: turn one way to warn and save his lover Simone; turn the other to alert his family and community. At this defining moment, the handprint of the opening sequence fades before our eyes into the merest of traces, as the shot dissolves from 1943 to the present day at the same spot on the same ghetto stone wall. The message is powerfully clear: the history of Rome's Jews, of Rome's Holocaust, remains written in faint traces of blood in its very stones and streets, a new archaeological stratum in this most ancient and stratified of cities (as Freud described it in *Civilization and Its Discontents*). It is reiterated in various ways throughout the film: as the confused, elderly Davide/Simone sees people from 1943 before his and our very present-day eyes; or as Davide's unsent letter and messages to Simone, at the fountain near the Teatro di Marcello, become messages to Giovanna and today's audience; or as Davide's tattooed number on his arm is revealed as the first (and, of course, immediately recognisable, even clichéd) sign of the solution to the mystery of his identity. The seepage of the past of the web of historical events and the difficult legacy of Rome's Holocaust into an oblivious, unaware present is rooted in the millennial stones of Rome and the fragile bodies of its survivors.

§7 Shared Knowledge

One of the overarching trajectories traced in this book is the uneven spread of knowledge of the Holocaust in Italy, moving outwards from the victims, their families, and their associations towards the wider culture and society. This movement from first-hand to second-hand knowledge, from those who saw to those who can only imagine, is one of the fundamental—and continually renewed—dynamics within the field of Holocaust culture over several postwar generations. And along the pathways of this history of dynamic transfer, the meanings, forms and uses of Holocaust talk undergo profound change.

The periodisation of this turn outwards, part transmission and part transformation, is hard to pin down. Some of the very earliest monuments and testimonies were already intent on forcing public attention onto Nazi violence, deportation and the camps, although undoubtedly a more invisible mode of introverted, individual and group mourning and memorialisation was more characteristic of the early postwar phase. Didactic and disseminatory impulses gathered strength again in the mid-1950s. As we saw with the Carpi exhibition of 1955, mentioned in Chapter 4, for example,[1] the first-hand witnesses and their associations were intent on producing and guiding early forms of knowledge and representation of the camps, gatekeeping but also strongly encouraging the passage from private to public knowledge, from first-hand to second-hand and soon also from the war generation to a new, young generation.

This was by no means the only cultural dynamic at work in the early phases of transmission, however. There was also material, talk and imagery of the camps circulating 'ungated', as it were, out in the general culture, from the very earliest postwar weeks and months. The dissemination of images from newsreels and photo reportage of Allied camp liberations, followed by accounts of the Nuremberg trials months later, already established in 1945 a set of powerful visual tropes which, although not at the time strongly linked to the genocide of the Jews but rather more emblematic of Nazi depravity and the just cause of the Allies' war, persisted in the global cultural imaginary and became widely recognised. Piles of skeletal dead bodies; ranks of skeletal survivors, shaven-headed in striped uniforms with red, yellow or other coloured stars; piles of shaven hair, shoes, suitcases; barbed wire fences; prison blocks. Although disrupted in their transmission in Italy, these and others were already common knowledge by 1947, according to Primo Levi's preface to *If This Is a Man*, where he talks of 'hideous details' that are already well known the world over;[2] and they would become even better known through pioneering work such as Alain Resnais's 1955 documentary *Night and Fog*.[3] Indeed, from work such as his, new and equally persistent images become attached to the Holocaust (although Resnais does not identify the vast majority of camp victims as Jews),[4] shorthand for the entire appalling history, its message and meanings: the train tracks and cattle-truck convoys; the gate with the sign *'Arbeit macht frei'*; the gas chambers and the crematorium ovens; tattooed numbers.

Whether through the concerted efforts of survivors, their communities and groups, or through the separate and looser circulation of imagery and tropes of the Nazi camps, or more likely a fluid combination of both and other factors also, at some point in the later 1950s, and with striking energy from the 1960s and 1970s onwards, a step change occurred in the quality as well as the quantity of talk about the Holocaust. Put simply, everyone began to have at least some idea of what was being talked about when the Holocaust or the camps were mentioned. As Jeffrey Shandler puts it, writing of the American case, at a certain point (after 1979, for Shandler) the Holocaust becomes a 'household word'.[5] Similarly, if perhaps some years earlier, awareness of the Holocaust became a given across the Italian cultural sphere, part of the standard cultural baggage of everyone from intellectuals to schoolchildren.

This new range of awareness brought with it new cultural uses and displacements. A vocabulary for talking about the Holocaust—literally, in the form of certain strange lexical neologisms and importations (genocide, Lager, Auschwitz, Holocaust)—entered the mainstream of intellectual discourse and the cultural field generally, first as direct markers of those historical events and sites, but also, crucially, as flexible and highly recognisable metaphors. The same period also saw the rise of so-called Holocaust fiction, in which fictional narratives—by both survivor-writers and authors quite unrelated, autobiographically, to the experience of deportation or persecution—used the aura of the Holocaust as background, as a setting for good stories, as a source of drama and suspense. Public discourse could also now draw on evocations of the camps and specifically the Jewish genocide as part of its rhetorical armoury, a powerful emblem not only for history but also for its legacy and for contemporary reality. As part of this same process of loose cultural dissemination, in some contexts the Holocaust soon also became a cliché, a lazy trope, a dead metaphor, one increasingly in distorted relation to the history it denoted. Over the same post-1960s period, the tropes of Holocaust commonplaces appear in anti-Semitic graffiti, desecrations or racist sporting chants, as well as in the strangely obsessive negationist subcultures that appear in Italy as in other countries in this phase.[6]

For many of the gatekeepers of Holocaust knowledge, those bound traumatically to the events themselves, this initially much-hoped-for spread of awareness, which turned in the 1980s and 1990s into something like an avalanche of attention, turned sour, breeding cynical or lazy exploitation of their traumas, and (variously) stereotypical, Americanised, or sentimentalised distortions of history.[7] Like the proverbial rippling from the stone in the pond, the further away from the central event all this cultural talk became, the weaker the substance of the connection from talk to historical event often seemed. Widespread but often superficial or misshapen awareness of a few simple dates, place names and images from history tended to replace depth of knowledge of the historical reality behind them. This is what Tim Cole has called the 'saturation' of our culture with the Holocaust, an easy ubiquity, an obligatory lip service that takes the place of true understanding.[8] The bind is inescapable and has been replayed in furious debates every time the tools of mass culture are deployed to tell Holocaust stories (*The Diary of Anne Frank*, *Holocaust*, *Schindler's List*, *Life Is Beautiful*), when those closest to the experience and the events cry foul for all the simplification and cliché, easy tears and redemptions that the forms of mass culture offer to grab the attention of vast audiences.

And yet, the story of this step change in the scale, subjects and objects of Holocaust talk is central to any understanding of the emerging cultural role of the Holocaust in Italy, as anywhere else. This is not only a story of misuse and abuse but also a story of how the Holocaust became integrated into something like a worldview or set of postwar worldviews, a plural framework of postwar public understanding of history and of our contemporary world. This chapter searches out evidence in Italian culture of this looser, second-hand, displaced Holocaust talk, its deployment as code and metaphor for talking about all manner of other things. It opens with a section on the vocabulary of the 1940s but moves on to concentrate especially on the period from the late 1950s and early 1960s to the 1970s, as one of particularly intense change, in cultural terms, in sociopolitical terms and in generational terms, creating a fertile atmosphere for new uses of language and history, including those of the Holocaust. It looks at a sample of key cultural works across the spectrum of cultural expression at the time—from lyric poetry to popular song, from public debate to film and theatre—all of which in some way use Holocaust vocabulary and imagery in newly public, metaphorical ways.

1. Uomo, deportato, ebreo

As we saw in Chapter 4, in the immediate aftermath of World War Two the genocide of European Jews had only blurred contours in public awareness and was, if present at all, subsumed within the appalled contemplation of horrific extremes of violence thrown up by this 'total' war. Even where the genocide did find space and expression, the suffering of Jews was frequently contained and constrained within the terms, within the very language of talk about other extremes. For Italian Jews, survivors and families of both survivors and the dead, their accounts of deportation to the concentration camps or of hiding, exile, fighting and persecution blurred and merged into thousands of other ostensibly comparable Italian stories—of Resistance followers deported to Nazi labour and concentration camps; of Italian soldiers interned in Nazi camps and civilian forced labourers; of victims of brutal Nazi and Fascist violence, in particular the civilian massacres carried out across central and northern Italy between 1943 and 1945. Conversely, Fascist 'genocidal' violence—against Slavic populations, against colonial subjects in Africa—was covered in almost complete silence. From these linked experiences, further circles of experience, history and memory pulled in different, but overlapping and communally shared, directions: for the Jews, behind their stories lay a Europe-wide, appalling and initially only half-acknowledged or half-understood phenomenon, the genocide. For the Resistance deportees, their 'fight' to survive in, say, the quarry at Mauthausen was lived and narrated as an extension of the partisan fight in the hills of Piedmont or Romagna, part of the redemptive struggle of the Resistance for liberation and for a future Italy. For the soldiers interned (including some guilty of their own campaigns of ethnic violence), their impossible fate and their choices challenged the very status and legitimacy of the nation, the state and its rulers. And for many thousands of these soldiers and deported workers too, their Italian 'national' stories were played out on foreign soil and in dense interaction with other national and international histories. The sheer sweep of this total war—both the myth and reality, the vast shared shock of the World War—meant that any and every war story or experience seemed for a time part of an all-but-undifferentiated mass of extreme experience, at once individual, collective, national, international, universal, even transcendental. Reflections upon them veered from the historical to the political, to the moral and philosophical; and cultural responses too tended towards the macrocosmic, portentous and vague, leaving little space for clinical distinction and historical specificity. Primo Levi later described the landscape of Eastern Europe in the months after war's end as a 'primeval Chaos',[9] and this quality was replicated in the cultural arena and helps explain a crucial blurring of categories and vocabularies in the war's immediate aftermath, a blurring that left residues for many years to come, even as more distilled versions of this history were analysed out.

Put simply, large questions were posed by the war experience, and large answers—dystopian memories, utopian dreams—were called for; and the language to talk about them often came in simple, universal archetypes and catch-all, but intensely powerful, vocabularies. This section looks at some of those archetypes as they were deployed in Italy, in relation to what was later labelled the Holocaust. They are important not only in their own right as markers of how the genocide was processed early on but also as a first stage in a longer process, which will develop dramatically once the Holocaust enters wider cultural currency from the 1960s, of the metaphorisation and so a sort of 'metabolisation' of the phenomenon in cultural terms. Three keywords or archetypes typical of the early postwar moment stand out: *uomo, deportato* and *ebreo* ('man' or 'human being', 'deportee', and 'Jew').

Postwar Europe was awash with anxious contemplation of what World War had done to the very notion of 'Mankind' and the values of 'humanism' that had subtended centuries of European civilisation. The horrors of the concentration camps were a limit case for these now frail categories. Robert Antelme's *Human Race* was the subtlest of many expositions of the

problem: for Antelme, the category of the human survived the concentra-
tions camps, but only as a thinned-out residue.[10] Antelme had extensive
contact in this period with Elio Vittorini, whose novels *Men and Not Men*
and *Conversation in Sicily* had probed the category of the human and the
problem of what remained of it, not only in the suffering man but also
in the executioner and torturer.[11] Levi, like many of his generation, read
Vittorini, and the influence shows in the questioning of the human limits
spelled out in the title and substance of *If This Is a Man.*[12]

Two Italian contributions to this 'humanist' wave come from writers of
Jewish origin and strong anti-Fascist pedigree, both victims of Fascist dis-
crimination and violence: Alberto Moravia and Natalia Ginzburg. Both
write essays in 1946 that use the idiom and archetypal figure of 'man' as
code for their contemplation of war, history and, as a veiled figure within
this, the genocide.

Ginzburg's piece was published in *L'Unità* under the title 'The Son
of Man'.[13] She had spent the war years in the Abruzzi, Turin and Rome,
with her Russian husband, the Jewish intellectual and anti-Fascist Leone
Ginzburg, who was tortured to death in Rome in 1944. Her essay is a
stunned and eloquently simple expression of a sense of absolute fracture.
Fascism and the war have turned her generation into 'a generation of
men/human beings' (p. 71) for whom there is no respite from a sense
of violence, threat and persecution. There is no return: she uses the figure of home, and the impossibility of returning home, as a sustained
metaphor for the break that had occurred. Her refrain is simple: 'There
is no peace for the son of man [...] he has nowhere to rest his head'
(p. 71). Despite her persecution as a Jew and anti-Fascist, and despite
her husband's murder, Ginzburg does not mention anything specifically
historical, including the camps, but her simple generic terms—of home,
the impossibility of return, the deep psychological and existential 'abyss'
(p. 72)—centred on the title image are enough to evoke the full panoply
of the history that lies beneath the surface. This allusive and universalising mode of talk is a key thread in oblique emanations of Holocaust talk.

Alberto Moravia's essay 'Man as End' was written in 1946.[14] He had
spent the years after 1938 struggling with the Fascist anti-Semitic legislation, which led to his inclusion on a list of banned Jewish authors.[15]
After September 1943, he escaped capture by hiding in the Ciociaria hills
south of Rome with Elsa Morante, who was then his wife. 'Man as End',
written in the fervour of the postwar months in Rome and in a period
of extraordinary literary productivity for Moravia, was his fullest moral,

historical and philosophical reflection on the war and his maturity. It
is important for the history of Italian intellectual culture because of its
ambition and its programmatic form, as well as for its evident echoes
of and parallels with European existentialism, Christian humanism and
strains of Marxist philosophy (including Adorno and Horkheimer). It
was precisely this eclectic mix of strains of thought, and the grand sweep
of macrohistory he attempts, that characterised this early mode of general reflection on the war and the Holocaust, through the imponderable
question of what the horrors of Nazism meant for our understanding
of history and of humanity itself. 'Man as End' offers a powerful early
example of the direct use of the concentration camp and Nazi 'extermination' as a key figure and encapsulation of the threshold that Nazism
had crossed, of the essence of its historical and moral meaning. The core
argument is that man must be 'an end', not 'a means' for states to im-
pose from above a rationalist, quantitative and rigid model of utilitarian
functions. Rationalist states are violent and functional; men as means are
like men turned into bricks, soap, or ashes.[16] As these images suggest,
the camps hover around the centre of Moravia's argument: 'The German
concentration camps of the Second World War are merely the novels
of De Sade, translated and lived out in reality' (p. 96). Chiming with
both Vittorini and Antelme, Moravia finds the essence of the human in
what is left over, the residue and the suffering, when man is used as pure
'means' rather than 'end'.[17] The camps were the perfect illustration of this
perverse or 'absurd' form of modernity: a perfectly rational and inhuman
end, pursued through the 'means' of millions of men, with extreme violence and pure reason producing immense suffering and thereby, paradoxically, vast reserves of residual humanity.[18]

Ginzburg, Moravia and all the archetypal figuring of the suffering of
man as a response to war and the camps carry with them, often explicitly,
echoes of Christian vocabulary and iconography. Ginzburg's title, 'Son
of Man', could hardly make this clearer. And Levi's title *If This Is a Man*
is not the only one to evoke the *Ecce homo* tradition; take, for example,
Gino Gregori's testimony of 1946 *Ecce homo Mauthausen*.[19] In visual art
also, the figure of Christ's suffering as a symbol of the victims of war generally, but also the victims of persecution and genocide more specifically,
was widespread. This applied to Christian artists, such as the sculptor
Giacomo Manzù, who used the life of Christ throughout the 1940s in a
series of bas-relief works, including a 1947 'Christ with General' in which
a strung-up Christ, a figure for human suffering in war, is looked over

by a pot-bellied helmeted soldier;[20] and also to the Communist Renato Guttuso, in his powerful sequence of Picasso-inspired works of the 1940s, 'Flight from Etna', 'Crucifixion' and 'The Massacre'.[21] Guttuso went on in 1944 to create a compelling series of ink drawings marking the Fosse Ardeatine massacre, with the German title '*Gott mitt uns*'.

When used generically, and certainly when used in a Christian idiom, the universal figure of 'man' or 'mankind' clearly cannot also be a figure for specifically Jewish genocide, 'the Jew'. Indeed, the universalising paradigm has been read by some as a way of occluding the Jewish specificity of the Holocaust in this early period of response.[22] Where we do find the figure of the Jew in this phase, it is symptomatically often in uncomfortable or incomplete form. We have already encountered in Chapter 4 the deeply awkward disquisitions of Benedetto Croce on the question of Jewish reintegration after Fascism and the persecution. A similar tension is evident in probably the earliest film to tackle the Holocaust in Italy, *The Wandering Jew*, directed by the former leading director of the Fascist period, Goffredo Alessandrini in 1948. The film retells the ancient myth of the Wandering Jew, following the history into the concentration camps, retaining an apparent nobility in the hero Matteo Blumenthal, but also an extensive baggage of anti-Semitic tropes, from the legendary curse against the Jews itself to the hero's redemption in Christ in the Lager.[23]

Even within the Jewish community, there are signs that the figure of the Jew only awkwardly finds a place alongside other, stronger figures in this period, whether universal ('mankind') or national and political. When the journal *Rassegna mensile di Israel* began publishing again in April 1948 after nearly ten years' interruption, its opening editorial is nervously defensive about the need to turn once again to a cultivation of Jewish learning after 'the dark and painful era of persecutions, massacres and horrific war'.[24] In keeping with most responses from within the Jewish community, the focus on the genocide is muted and emphasis is rather on rebuilding.

Something of the same reserve is on display, finally, in early monuments specifically dedicated to Jewish victims. In Chapter 4, we encountered BBPR's 1945–46 glass-cube Monument to the Fallen near the entrance to Milan's cemetery. If we follow a path round to the right of this monument, we enter a quiet, walled-off corner of the cemetery that contains the Jewish section. Here, on 13 July 1947, another monument was unveiled, a Monument to Jewish Sacrifice. Sponsored by Raffaele Cantoni, a highly proactive president of UCII, and by the Milan community, it was designed by architect Manfredo D'Urbino.[25] The monument centred on a large stone sculpture of a menorah with flame, flanked by twelve tomb-stones encased in marble. It contained ash taken from Dachau, just as the BBPR monument used earth from Mauthausen. The 12 Jewish victims commemorated in the monument, echoing the 12 tribes of Israel, repre-sented the range of Jewish suffering as the community wished to present it both to itself and to a wider public, in its own space alongside the civic cemetery. Each tombstone briefly evokes the victim's death. The range is very telling: all 12 died on Italian soil, suggesting a powerful impulse to present their sacrifice—and the Jewish sacrifice in general—in a national, patriotic framework.

The wider European persecution through deportation shadows several of the 12: one (Dora Pisetzky Luzzatti) was killed in the holding/concen-tration camp at Bolzano, a threshold for deportation to central European camps for many Italians; another (Odoardo Segrè) escaped from a depor-tation train to return to fight for liberation; and a third (Wilhelm Wein-berg) committed suicide in Milan's prison to avoid deportation. Four fought as partisans in the liberation struggle (Viviano Borcioni, Angelo Finzi, Giacomo Mendes, Segrè), and one volunteered to fight with the Allies (Gilberto Coen). The manner of their deaths is also interesting, presenting a sort of anthology of Nazi violence in Italy, as it intersected with the Holocaust as well as the national struggle. Only one, Segrè, died of natural causes, having lived to witness the final Liberation of Milan and Italy. Borcioni was shot by Germans; Salo Rath was killed in prison; Israel Epstein, Finzi, Mendes, and Coen were killed fighting for partisans or armies; Weinberg killed himself. One of the 12, crucially for a specifi-cally Jewish history of 'sacrifice', was a victim at the Fosse Ardeatine (Edo-ardo Della Torre). Another (Ester Botton Mosseri) was one of 16 killed in the first of all the Nazi massacres of Jews on Italian territory, at Meina on Lake Maggiore on 22 September 1943 (49 were killed in towns near the lake around that date).[26] The final victim commemorated, Araf Lazzes, was killed inside the Milan synagogue. Jewish experience is briefly evoked also in the cases of Coen, who was in exile and returned to volunteer; and Epstein, described as an 'activist in the Jewish Risorgimento in Eretz Israel' who was killed in Rome (but note how even this is 'nationalised' or 'Italianised' by the use of the word 'Risorgimento' linked to Zionist nationalism).

The 12 victims of the Monument to Jewish Sacrifice point us to the historical and memorial shape given to the figure of the 'Jew' and to Jewish sacrifice, but also to its links with the third archetypal term, the 'deportee'. As has been noted, it was the Resistance that provided the pivotal national narrative for the new Italy after the war; and within that model, this most commonly used word for partisans who ended up in concentration camps was able to function as a flexible catch-all term. ANED was not for nothing the most successful of the camp-victim and indeed Holocaust-victim associations in Italy: its identification of the category of 'ex-deportee' proved powerfully evocative and open to links both to the armed and civil Resistance, on the one hand, and on the other, in time as they came to the fore, to the racial persecution and 'deportations', military, civilian and others. The first public exhibition on the camps, the 1955 Carpi event, was variously named as the National Exhibition of Nazi Lagers, Celebration of Resistance in the Concentration Camps, Exhibition of Deportees in the Nazi Camps and so on.[27] The nexus Resistance-'deportees'-Lager was a defining container category for the first 10 to 15 years of talk about the camps. Already, however, behind the scenes, the groundwork for a new, specific vocabulary of the Holocaust per se was being laid, even in the 1940s.

2. Auschwitz in Lyric Poetry. Salvatore Quasimodo

In August 1948, the Sicilian poet Salvatore Quasimodo, previously famed for his 'hermetic', classicising poetic idiom, but like many of his generation now in a more engaged phase of writing, attended the World Congress of Intellectuals for Peace in Wroclaw, Poland, alongside figures such as Pablo Picasso, Bertolt Brecht, Paul Eluard, Giorgio Caproni and a large number of other pro-Communist or fellow-traveller writers and artists. The delegates visited the site of the Auschwitz complex of camps and were deeply marked by the experience.[28] The poem Quasimodo wrote after the visit, entitled simply 'Auschwitz', was published in his 1956 collection *False and True Green*, one of a short sequence of four poems that includes powerful evocations of the Resistance and some its most famous martyrs (for example, the 15 partisans murdered and put on public display in Piazzale Loreto, Milan in August 1944; and the seven Cervi brothers shot in Reggio Emilia in December 1943).[29] Written in 1948, as the first wave of chronicle and testimony, of immediate response, was coming to a close, and published eight years later (just as new testimonial and public waves were beginning), Quasimodo's 'Auschwitz' represents something of a watershed: it is perhaps the first major instance of a work in Italian of

detached, high-literary, nontestimonial figuration of the Holocaust, with
the site of Auschwitz as its emblem and the Jews as its central victims.
The poem is as striking for its genuine lyric power, as for its multiple use
of the tropes of an incipient Holocaust imaginary, of Holocaust literature
per se, that would take shape in the wider culture in the following two
decades. It is worth quoting in full in Italian and English:

Laggiù, ad Auschwitz, lontano dalla Vistola,   1
amore, lungo la pianura nordica,
in un campo di morte: fredda, funebre,
la pioggia sulla ruggine dei pali
e i grovigli di ferro dei recinti: 5
e non albero o uccelli nell'aria grigia,
o su dal nostro pensiero, ma inerzia
e dolore che la memoria lascia
al suo silenzio senza ironia o ira.

Tu non vuoi elegie, idilli: solo   10
ragioni della nostra sorte, qui,
tu, tenera ai contrasti della mente,
incerta a una presenza
chiara della vita. E la vita è qui,
in ogni no che pare una certezza: 15
qui udremo piangere l'angelo il mostro
le nostre ore future
battere l'al di là, che è qui, in eterno
e in movimento, non in un'immagine
di sogni, di possibile pietà.   20
E qui le metamorfosi, qui i miti.
Senza nome di simboli o d'un dio,
sono cronaca, luoghi della terra,
sono Auschwitz, amore. Come subito
si mutò in fumo d'ombra   25
il caro corpo di Alfeo e d'Aretusa!

Da quell'inferno aperto da una scritta
bianca: 'Il lavoro vi renderà liberi'
uscì continuo il fumo
di migliaia di donne spinte fuori   30
all'alba dai canili contro il muro
del tiro a segno o soffocate urlando
misericordia all'acqua con la bocca
di scheletro sotto le docce a gas.

Le troverai tu, soldato, nella tua   35
storia in forme di fiumi, d'animali,
o sei tu pure cenere d'Auschwitz,
medaglia di silenzio?
Restano lunghe trecce chiuse in urne
di vetro ancora strette da amuleti   40
e ombre infinite di piccole scarpe
e di sciarpe d'ebrei: sono reliquie
d'un tempo di saggezza, di sapienza
dell'uomo che si fa misura d'armi,
sono i miti, le nostre metamorfosi.   45

Sulle distese dove amore e pianto
marcirono e pietà, sotto la pioggia,
laggiù, batteva un no dentro di noi,
un no alla morte, morta ad Auschwitz,
per non ripetere, da quella buca   50
di cenere, la morte.

(Down there, at Auschwitz, far from the Vistula, / my love, along the northern plain, / in a death camp: cold, funereal, / rain on rusting poles / and knots
of iron in fences: / and no tree or birds in the grey air, or in our thoughts,
just the inertia / and pain left by memory / in its silence empty of irony or
anger. // You do not want elegies, idylls: only / reasons for our fate, here, /
you, tender to the contrasts in our minds, / uncertain before the clear / presence of
life. And there is life here, / in every No that feels certain: / here we'll hear the
crying of the angel the monster / our future hours / the beat of the afterworld,
which is here, forever / and moving, not in an image / of dreams, of possible pity. / And here are the metamorphoses, here the myths. / No names of
symbols or gods, / these are chronicles, places on earth, / these are Auschwitz,
my love. Just as in an instant / the dear flesh of Alpheus and Arethusa / was
changed into a shadowy smoke! // From that hell opened by a white / phrase:
'Work Will Set You Free' / poured forth the smoke / of thousands of women
thrust out / at dawn from their kennels up against the shooting / wall or suf-
focated screaming / for mercy at the water with their skeletal / mouths beneath
the gas showers. / You'll find them, soldier, in your / history in the shape of
rivers, animals, / or have you too become ash of Auschwitz, / medal of silence? / Long braids of hair remain in glass / urns still tied in rings / and endless shades of small shoes / and scarves of Jews: they are relics / of a time of
wisdom, of knowledge / of man measured out in arms, / they are our myths,
our metamorphoses. // Across the expanses where love and tears / rotted and

pity, beneath the rain, down there, a No beat inside us, / a No to death, killed at Auschwitz, / not to let death, from within that void / of ash, come again.)

The poem is tellingly poised between a series of familiar literary topoi and echoes—the address to a lover-companion (l. 2), echoes of myth and literature (Ovid's *Metamorphoses*, but also Montale), elegies and idylls—and an awareness of the inadequacy of these in the face of this place ('Down there', l. 1) and this name, 'Auschwitz'. The allusions to Dante and to other Christian and classical landscapes of the afterlife and rituals of death—angels, monsters, the beyond, hell (ll. 16, 18, 27)—all commonplace from the very first accounts of the camps as we saw in Chapter 4, are there also, but these are not enough.

Balancing out and soon overwhelming the topoi of the literary tradition are new tropes and new phrases for a new imaginary-literary field. Several of them chime with the visual tropes present in the emerging post-1945 image bank, already both hauntingly familiar, generic, horrifically strange: the barbed wire (l. 5), the gate at Auschwitz-Birkenau with its epigram *Arbeit macht frei* (l. 28), the skeletal victims and the gas chambers with their showers (l. 34), the smoke and ash from the crematoria (ll. 25, 29, 51), and the piles of objects of the dead, the hair, the shoes, the scarves (ll. 39–42). Even the phrase 'death camp' (l. 3) was one of the earliest of epithets applied to the Nazi Lager, and Quasimodo is alert to the phrase and indeed frames the entire poem around the simple term '*morte*' that the phrase gives him.[30] The list is an extraordinary one, extensive and yet subtly integrated into a lyric whole, which also sets the poet himself, the eye of the beholder—a figure with no direct role in this place and this history, a visitor—near the centre, but also obliquely to one side.

There is little pathos in the evocation of place and sight. Indeed, the lyric resources seem to be slightly muffled: the syntax is relatively simple and lucid, if loosened in places, the lexicon mostly general and generic. Almost the only exception is the proper noun *Auschwitz* itself, as though all the rest were simply a gloss on this one name. This promotion of the place name itself as a metonymy for an entire catastrophe of history is highly prescient on Quasimodo's part.[31] And the indeterminate feel to much of the poem's vocabulary becomes itself a resource in the new language of Holocaust writing—much as Levi had laid emphasis on the new meaning of banal, everyday words when transposed to the Lager, in influential passages of *If This Is a Man*—from the generic features of the landscape (cold, rain, rust, iron, trees, birds) to the blandly nonspecific terminology of response (inertia, pain, memory, silence).

The link with Levi—whether self-conscious or not[32]—is telling. The story of transmission from the first-hand witnesses and survivors out into the wider culture, in this case into the upper echelons of literary creation and the literary establishment (Quasimodo was awarded the Nobel Prize for Literature in 1959), is here played out even at the level of transmission of tone and style. The indeterminate sobriety in this poem is similar to that found in many early testimonies, a tone of mourning and incantation almost, a sort of antipoetry: in this sense, perhaps the key lines of Quasimodo's poem are ll. 22–24: 'No names of symbols or gods, / these are chronicles, places on earth, / these are Auschwitz'. The resources of literary recreation, of symbols and myth hesitate here. Instead we have the events, the place and the name of that place. These are the terms and the sights that will spread into looser, wider cultural consciousness over the following decades.

Quasimodo's 'Auschwitz' intuitively sets out some of the most powerful channels for the transmission into literary culture of both the fact of the Holocaust and the language in which to talk about it. It is also exceptional, for the time, in its direct and simple acknowledgement of the genocide, of Auschwitz as a predominantly Jewish history, of relics of the dead as Jewish relics (l. 42).[33] Which fact makes it doubly interesting to note that Quasimodo was by no means always a voice for, or even friend to, the Jews: in 1960–61 he was involved in a nasty polemical spat with one of the leading Jewish and Zionist intellectuals of the day, Dante Lattes, who accused him of a none-too-veiled anti-Semitism in an article the poet had written in December 1960 in which he spoke of Jewish financial power and of the inability of Jews to feel any sense of patriotic duty or loyalty. Lattes's reply, in the journal he edited, *Rassegna mensile di Israel,* entitled 'Tu quoque Quasimodo?', expressed high rhetorical outrage at this perceived betrayal.[34]

That forms of unthinking, low-grade anti-Semitism persisted in Italy after the war and the Holocaust, even amongst the sophisticated anti-Fascist elite of which Quasimodo was part, should not come as any surprise, as we saw with the case of Croce. Indeed, Lattes had taken Croce to task in 1948, just as he vigorously attacked Quasimodo in 1961.[35] What is interesting to note, however, is how Quasimodo could be both guilty of a lazy anti-Semitism and the author of a poem closely attuned to the emergence of the Holocaust, and its Jewish dimension, as a central event in history, as an obligatory staging post in the development of modern lyric literature and a modern consciousness; and, finally, also of an Italian national, anti-Fascist consciousness, as attested to by the place of the poem 'Auschwitz' alongside a powerful poetry of the Resistance in *False and True Green.*

3. Auschwitz in Popular Song. Francesco Guccini

If Quasimodo's poem captured, in its chronicle of a visit to the site of Auschwitz and in its parading of an anthology of new archetypes (names, objects, states of mind), a new metaphorical energy emerging around the Holocaust, in the mid-1960s an even more schematic and if anything more powerful version of Auschwitz as metaphor was captured for the newly alternative, youth-centred 'poetry' of popular song. In 1965, Francesco Guccini, born in Modena in 1940, was near the beginning of a long career as a *cantautore*, a term coined in the late 1950s for Italian singer-songwriters who are often politically or socially engaged and tell the story in song of the values and feelings of a certain region or generation.[36] The first cantautori were heavily influenced by the French tradition, but Guccini and others in the mid-1960s began to look also to American voices, especially the Beat poets and the extraordinary recent emergence of Bob Dylan, in particular his second studio album *The Freewheelin' Bob Dylan* (1963), with anthems of protest ('Blowin' in the Wind') and apocalyptic vision ('Masters of War', 'A Hard Rain's A-Gonna Fall'). Like Dylan in this period, the predominant musical mode for Guccini was modern folk, with guitar and voice laying heavy emphasis on simple lyric power, and stories of poverty and protest. Guccini released his own first album only in 1967, with the Dylanesque title *Folk Beat N.1* (1967), but for several years before then his songs circulated and were sung by groups close to him; one was even banned by RAI for blasphemy (its title was 'God Is Dead').[37]

In 1964–65, Guccini came across the first edition of one of the most powerful and widely read and reprinted works of testimony about Mauthausen, by ex-partisan and political deportee Vincenzo Pappalettera, *You Will Pass Through the Chimney.*[38] Guccini had also read Levi, seen an iconic photograph of a child in the Warsaw ghetto, heard his father's experience as a military internee.[39] Combining all these striking memories and new knowledge with the influence of Dylan, Guccini wrote a song that was to become one of the best-known cantautore works of the 1960s, an emblem of protest song.[40] Like Quasimodo's poem it was entitled simply 'Auschwitz', with the alternative title 'Song of the Child in the Wind'. It speaks in the voice of a dead child, turned to ash in the crematorium and now 'here in the wind'.

The song's lyrics echo both Pappalettera's book and Dylan's 'Blowin' in the Wind', the former in the line 'I died . . . I passed through the chimney' and the latter in a diffuse series of echoes, starting with the part-apocalyptic, part-fantastic image of the wind in the title and the refrain. The two songs share a series of simple, universal words and images that place them in the same semantic field of association: these include the cannons of war ('how many times must the cannon balls fly / Before they're forever banned?' Dylan; 'Still the cannon thunders [...]' Guccini); sound and silence ('how many ears must one man have / Before he can hear people cry?' Dylan; 'At Auschwitz so many people / but only a single great silence' Guccini); and death and killing ('how many deaths will it take till he knows / That too many people have died?' Dylan; 'when will it be / that man can learn / to live without killing' Guccini). Indeed, the songs also share a general style and structure, both built around simple sequences of elemental evocations of man, violence and suffering. It is within this universalising, folk-simple, Biblical, at times apocalyptic idiom that Guccini's direct evocation of Auschwitz and of the voice of the dead child finds its place and resonance in the history of the assimilation of the Holocaust into the wider Italian culture. Some of these elements are shared by Quasimodo's poem: despite the latter's origin in a high classical and hermetic tradition of lyric poetry, both evoke at several points similar imagery of cold, snow or rain, wind, smoke, silence and death. And, quite unlike Dylan's archetypal protest lament which does nothing to evoke the Holocaust directly, Guccini shares with Quasimodo the searing centrality of the name itself, the place, 'Auschwitz'; although it is strikingly symptomatic and important for this discussion how powerfully Auschwitz seems to sit beneath the surface of Dylan's anthology of questions, for anyone inclined to find it there.[41]

Guccini's song is tightly woven around simple repeated motifs, rhymes and assonances. It splits into two sections, the first focussed directly on Auschwitz, the second projected outwards into the present and future realities of mankind. In the first part, and indeed in the first words and founding conceit ('I died with one hundred others'), the song is at its boldest, taking on and speaking in the voice of the dead child victim of the genocide. In doing so, Guccini connects to his own generation and to the pathos of child's-eye point of view. But the step into fantasy, the imaginary voice of a dead child, a ghostly presence floating in the wind (haunted, like Quasimodo, by the literal smoke of burnt bodies from the crematorium chimneys), is a powerful step away from the values of chronicle and testimony that in different ways governed most of the first-hand accounts of the 1940s. The Holocaust is now literally an act of the imagination, voiced by this ghostly innocent, the child who cannot smile.

Numbers also contribute here. The figure of six million dead, for example, has its own complicated history, quickly emerging after 1945 and establishing itself over the postwar era as one of the most familiar topoi of global Holocaust talk, as if the number itself were enough to connote the entire Final Solution. (Toni Morrison needed only to allude to it in the most oblique way in the epigraph of her novel of slavery, *Beloved*, which simply read 'Sixty million and more'[42]). Without using the figure of six million, Guccini's song nevertheless draws on the aura of numbers, in its crescendo from the one voice to the 'hundred' who died with him to the 'millions / in dust here in the wind' along with him. And the numbers are something of a prelude and accompaniment to the overarching and governing trope of the composition—one familiar from Levi's *If This Is a Man* and the whole panoply of postwar humanist rhetoric discussed above—of 'man' and 'mankind', of human values, solidarity and species identity, to which the small voice of the dead child appeals, and through which the song makes its transition from the first to the second part, from the Holocaust to present and future reality, from Auschwitz to the world.

In the second part, the song addresses mankind as a whole, to ask how man can still kill, how a man can 'kill his brother' (with an obvious Biblical allusion to Cain and Abel), to lament that the 'human beast' is still killing today ('still' marks the quiet shift to the present), that wars are still raging. Without any concrete historical allusion, it is clear that Guccini is hooking the Holocaust lament onto a generalised lament for wars in Vietnam, Algeria and the rest of Africa, and the gamut of upheavals that inspired and convulsed the 1960s youth movements. In other words, in this period of heightened political consciousness and heightened generational consciousness, coupled with a much broader awareness of the phenomenon of the concentration camps, with books such as Pappalettera's and Levi's, read with a heightened sense of history, ideology and emotion, a song such as Guccini's marks the entry of the Holocaust four-square into the cultural politics of the 1960s.

The Holocaust is now in the mix of popular youth culture, an ingredient in a vague but heady cocktail of what is wrong with the world and how the young will change it. If anything, this mix is even more apparent in Guccini's 1967 generational anthem 'God Is Dead', mentioned above for being banned by RAI (although it was played and praised by Radio Vaticana): here the Holocaust, the extermination camps, are mentioned once in a litany of evidence for the metaphorical 'death of God', for the decadence of a 'tired' civilisation, alongside corrupt politics, consumerism, racism and hypocrisy:

> I've seen
> people of my age go away
> along roads that never lead anywhere
> [...]
> refusing to swallow our weary civilization
> and a god that is dead
> on the edges of the road god is dead
> in cars on hire-purchase god is dead
> in myths of summer god is dead
> [...]
> in the extermination camps god is dead
> with the myths of race god is dead
> with party hatreds god is dead.[43]

4. Auschwitz and Hiroshima. Two Holocausts

On Guccini's album *Folk Beat N.1*, the song that immediately preceded 'Auschwitz' was called 'The Chinese Atom Bomb', describing the devastating spread over the skies of China of a 'death cloud', a nuclear explosion annihilating all the nature and the ancient civilisation beneath it. The first song of the album was another postapocalyptic vision called 'We Will Not Be There'. For long periods of the era following the 1945 bombings of Hiroshima and Nagasaki, and especially in the darkest phases of the Cold War through the 1960s and 1970s, the threat of a nuclear 'Holocaust', the uneasy tension of global 'mutually assured destruction', and the apocalyptic imaginary brought on by man's newly acquired catastrophic capacity to destroy the world, ran alongside and in strange consonance with the new broad awareness of the Holocaust and the Nazi genocide of the 1940s. There were, of course, other analogies tried out at different times—other genocides to be compared to the Nazi project (Armenia,

Cambodia, Rwanda, ex-Yugoslavia, not to mention the Gulag), or indeed renewed attention to *other* Nazi genocidal projects (against Rom and Sinti, homosexuals, the Slavic 'races', including Italian complicity in the latter)—just as there would be other apocalyptic threats, most potently the late-20th-century emergence of climate change fears. But for the larger part of the postwar era, the twin peaks of this modern apocalyptic anxiety of destruction, and the key sites of the mutually reinforcing aesthetics and rhetoric of crisis that went with it, were undoubtedly Auschwitz and Hiroshima.[44] They became dominant metaphors to capture a new form of modern, civilised, technologised, total violence, which for many seemed to embody the very essence of modernity itself. The Bomb and the Camp were entwined with each other to such as a degree that it is all but impossible to trace the cultural shape and relevance of the Holocaust over the postwar era, without looking at patterns of symbiosis with contemporary cultures of nuclear war.

The dominant metaphorical field in which nuclear and genocidal Holocausts intersected was that of science. Both historical events—the application of technical-industrial methods to mass murder in the annihilation camps; and the unleashing of the power of the split atom by the researchers at the Manhattan Project (more than one of them, of course, Jewish refugees from Fascism and Nazism, including Enrico Fermi)—demonstrated for postwar generations the appalling possible risks of perversions and disproportionate violence in the pure application of reason and the scientific method.[45]

This critique of science through these two historical singularities came to have particular resonance in Italy's cultural field of Holocaust awareness for the simple reason that the most prominent of Holocaust witnesses and writers in Italy, Primo Levi, was also a professional scientist and intensely devoted to giving voice to his field of chemistry and to science in general in his writing, to combatting what the Cambridge writer and scientist C. P. Snow lamented in a famous 1959 lecture as the abyss between the 'two cultures'.[46] Levi's writing throughout the 1960s and 1970s and into the 1980s—the phase coinciding with what we are describing as the 'metaphorisation' of the Holocaust—was permeated by an exploration of the conscience and morality of the scientist as well as of the social and political consequences of scientific modernity. In both his quirky science-fiction stories and his short essays for *La stampa* and other publications, he touched on these matters frequently; and at each step along the way, this dimension of his work found deep connections to his reflections on the Holocaust and permeated out into the wider field of Holocaust culture we are tracing. For example, Levi figured the scientist frequently as a modern Prometheus (or Ulysses, or Faust, or Adam, or Frankenstein), dangerously interested in the sheer fascination of knowledge and human creation itself, untempered by limit or danger. On the one hand he could be the inventor character in several short stories, Gilberto:

> a dangerous man, a small harmful Prometheus: clever and irresponsible, proud and foolish. He is a child of the century, as I said, even a symbol for our century. I've always thought that he'd be capable, if necessary, of building an atom bomb and dropping it on Milan 'just to see what happened'.[47]

On the other hand, there is the diabolical figure of the Nazi experimental scientist, Professor Leeb, in the story 'Angelic Butterfly', whose obscene attempts at genetic modification of humans—in order to turn them into angels—echoes Nazi eugenics or the horrific experiments of Josef Mengele and all the 'Nazi doctors'.[48] Utopian aspirations and disastrous dystopian realisations on the part of research scientists, once again cast as Frankenstein, recur as Levi uses both 'Holocausts' as figures for a warning against the arrogance of scientific man. In his essays on the responsibility of the scientist, Levi is more sober and less apocalyptic than in his fiction, promoting a pragmatic vigilance and social awareness on the part of practising scientists.[49] But even here his language on occasion encourages resonant historical parallels: in an essay in *Other People's Trades'*, he warns:

> The whole of humanity today [is] condemned to live in a world in which everything seems stable, but it is not, in which terrifying forces (and I am not only thinking here of nuclear arsenals) are in a restless slumber [*Opere*, II, p. 781].

Here, the characteristic ironic and simple parenthesis is enough to evoke in the reader all the other terrible forms of violence that threaten mankind, or with which man threatens the world, energies of persecution and war, ideology and genocide included.

Perhaps the two key points in Levi's work where the nexus of Auschwitz and Hiroshima is figured most powerfully, and with a clearest eye on the external realities of the contemporary world and of history, come at the end of his 1982 novel *If Not Now, When?* and in a 1978 poem called 'The Girl of Pompei'. Both make use of the imagery of children—a typical device for creating a universalising aura, as we saw with Guccini's song—and both play at running strands of history parallel to each other, seeing recurrent patterns and ironies between events continents or millennia apart in human history. *If Not Now, When?* ends its epic group tale of a band of Eastern Europe Jewish partisan fighters in the war with the birth on 7 August 1945 of a baby boy to two of the survivors of the band, who have made it to Italy. Between Russia, the struggle to survive hunted by the Nazis, the journey to safety in Italy, where they are helped by the DELASEM organisation, as the group awaits a boat to Palestine, the boy is born on the same day as news arrives of the first atom bomb at Hiroshima (*Opere* II, pp. 481–510). Past, present and future, human death and human life, the two Holocausts, combine in a single moment of hiatus, and Levi leaves the novel and all these threads of history hanging there, deliberately unresolved.

In 'The Girl of Pompei' (*Opere*, II, p. 549), three child victims of catastrophes both manmade and natural are set alongside each other: the eponymous girl from Pompeii, incinerated but preserved and now excavated for visitors to relive her fear and anguish; a 'girl from Holland', i.e. Anne Frank; and a 'schoolgirl from Hiroshima'. All three stand for innocence destroyed, burned out of existence; but Anne Frank and the Hiroshima victim are specifically bound together as they are without tomb or resting place, no trace of their body or life remaining, except perhaps ash (ash preserved the girl from Pompeii; Anne Frank is nothing but ash 'in the wind', to echo Guccini); and, we might add, as both victims of man's ingenious technologies of murder. Levi ends with a plea to politicians to pause before destroying the world in a nuclear Holocaust, in imperative terms that echo the epigraph to *If This Is a Man*: 'Before you press the button, pause and consider'. The appeal is to a consciousness of history and to a recognition of the humanity of the individual and the individuality of the human being, even in her exemplarity. And its force is built on the metaphorical bond that unites Auschwitz and Hiroshima.

As Pierpaolo Antonello has shown, this pairing of the two Holocausts, genocidal and nuclear, was not unusual in this period.[50] The anthropologist Ernesto De Martino, in *The End of the World*, a study of cultures of the apocalypse from early societies to the modern-day bourgeois West, contemplated the same scenario as Levi's poem, as he evoked the possibility of the world ending at the push of a button:

> When you are tempted to press the button [...] when you are victim of this
> temptation remember not the two hundred thousand at Hiroshima or the six

million Jews, but just one human face in pain, the concrete faces of people
you have loved and seen suffer, some girl hurt and weeping that you've encountered along the way.[51]

Alongside Levi and De Martino, we can turn again to Elsa Morante, who
as we have seen was intensely engaged in the 1960s and 1970s with a vi-
sionary account of history, with the Holocaust close to its centre, during
the gestation of *History*. Morante's most successful, if highly eccentric,
work of essayistic prose was her 1965 lecture (published posthumously),
'For or Against the Atom Bomb'. In this grand-scale, antirationalist, an-
tiscientific screed, the bomb is for Morante what Antonello describes as
'the ultimate image of the process of falsification and inauthenticity produced by advanced capitalist society'.[52] And in this, it is all of a piece with
the extermination camps:

> Our bomb is the flower, or the natural expression of our contemporary soci-
> ety, just as Plato's dialogues are for Greek civilization [...] and the extermina-
> tion camps were for the petit bourgeois bureaucratic culture that was already
> infected with an atomic suicidal rage.[53]

Auschwitz and Hiroshima come together under the rubric of the modern
apocalypse, each illuminating and complicating the other in ways historical and metaphorical. They shadow each other, so that when a writer with
a strong apocalyptic vein such as Giorgio Manganelli talks of a present
day consciousness of 'living on a planet that is, *morally more than physi-
cally*, uninhabitable' (emphasis added),[54] we can see in that moral dimension a shadow of the camps and what they tell us about man's modern
depravity, just as the physical degradation of the planet talks to images of
radiation or today's ecological disaster.

Twentieth-century Italian culture has long had a powerful apocalyptic
dimension, in the persistently dark visions of the modern genre of science fiction, or, at the higher end of the intellectual spectrum, in the
ending of Italo Svevo's 1923 novel *Zeno's Conscience* through to Pier Paolo
Pasolini's railing against the demolition of millennial popular cultures by
consumerist modernity in the 1970s.[55] As we will see in the final section
of the chapter, apart from the specific twinning of Auschwitz and Hiroshima, in the culture of the 1960s and 1970s, the Holocaust takes up a key
metaphorical role also in a far wider political discourse of critique, often
apocalyptic critique.

5. Auschwitz and Ideology. Lager, Genocide, Fascism, Jew

As talk of the Holocaust spread beyond the sphere of the survivor, it acquired an ever stronger and ever more macroscopic metaphorical energy or 'aura'. From the 1960s onwards, this coincided with, was reinforced by and itself helped reinforce the generational politics of the time and its investment in a totalising critique of society and history. These were years of radical generational change, in which the 'sons and daughters' of Fascist and Resistance 'fathers and mothers' came to maturity and were educated in newly modernised, mass-participation schools and universities, and themselves became highly politicised, in part by coming to terms with and violently challenging the ideology of Fascism itself and their fathers' and mothers' passive acquiescence in it. This led to an intensely ideological, often violent contestation of one generation and its institutions by the next (coupled with forms of violent reactionary response), and in several nations across Europe, including Italy, the terrain and vocabulary of this contestation often relied heavily on the history and the metaphorical lexicon of the 1930s and 1940s, of Fascism, Nazism and the Lager. The Holocaust became a metaphor for power, ideology and violence; for oppression, Fascism, capitalism and the bourgeoisie; and with it emerged a new version of the archetype of the 'Jew' as victim and simultaneously as the emblematic figure of modernity.[56]

In Italian intellectual culture of this period, no figure embraced with more metaphysical intensity this new role for the Jew and for the figure of the Lager than poet, film director and maverick intellectual Pier Paolo Pasolini, probing it in his pseudo-Pauline poetry, and in his allegorical experiments that drew on a cocktail of Frankfurt School philosophy, Dante and the New Testament. Showing his typical, magpie instinct for feeding on the deepest anxieties of the present, Pasolini's verse, drama and film of the 1960s and 1970s are filled with images of Israel, the Lager, and the figure of 'The Jew'. Perhaps the earliest significant rehearsal of these tropes came in a 1962 poem, 'Monologue on the Jews', built around an extended meditation on photos of Jewish survivors at Buchenwald; and continued in a series of other poems from the early 1960s that would feed into his 1964 collection *Poems in the Shape of a Rose*.[57] In part, this engagement was stimulated by Pasolini's journey to Israel in search of locations for his 1964 film *The Gospel According to Matthew*.[58] The journey led to a series of meditations on the Jews of Israel, on their complex and conflicted relationship with the Europe they left behind—haunted by the trauma of the Holocaust, exile and nostalgia—and with the Palestinians around them. (Pasolini, in his typically voracious, often erotic impulses, identified simultaneously with the Jews and the Arabs, as with the poor, blacks, prisoners, and so on: in short, what he called 'all banished humanity'.) The Jew of Israel was also, for Pasolini, caught between the First and Third World—in Pasolinian terms, between neocapitalist bourgeoisie and the lumpenproletariat.

Pasolini's identification with the figure of the Jew (describing himself as 'a Jew by culture and by choice') and his extraordinary vocation for 'theological' scandal came together in his several lyrical assaults on Pius XII, from a 1959 epigram marking his death ('To a Pope') to the acid poem 'The Enigma of Pius XII' in his 1971 collection *Transhumanize and Organize*, an imagined inner monologue by the pope dated 1944, in which Pasolini imagines Pius's deep affinity with Hitler, sharing a vision of the state as transcendent, and a hostility to the Jews as somehow the source of all secularism and rationalism.[59] Although the specifics of the growing controversy over Pius's actions and knowledge regarding the genocide are not explicitly evoked in these pieces, nevertheless the larger 'scandal' of history and the Church's role within it taps into the same source of historical critique.

Once established in the early 1960s, the topos of the Jew and tropes derived from the Holocaust grow ever more persistent in Pasolini's convulsively creative late phase of work, stretching from the late 1960s until his violent murder in 1975. His 1966 verse tragedy *Calderòn* culminates in its final sequence with the protagonist Rosaura's vision of a Lager.[60] His 1969 film *Pigsty* is centred on two German industrialists and father figures (living with a thin veneer of respectability), who made their money exploiting the Nazi death camps. But the autonomy and power of this thread of imagery and vocabulary reached a peak in his final two years of work, in forms that would be immensely influential in the wider culture in Italy, in both journalism and film. Much of the rhetoric of Pasolini's frenetic late campaigns of these years against the cultural devastations of the new consumer society was couched in terms derived from Fascism and the camps: consumerism was the 'new Fascism' and its effect on the 'authentic' cultures it engulfed was, literally, 'genocidal'.[61] And in his final terrible allegory, staged in the mannered, hideous torture of the film *Salò or the 120 Days of Sodom* (1975), the villa where the horrors of the film are set is a distorted (because elegant and refined) figure for the grotesque space of the Lager, and the four dignitaries who rule over it are Sadean allegories of Nazi and bourgeois capitalist power. The link to the camps and to the Holocaust in *Salò* is oblique, allegorical, but patent nevertheless: the film begins with a conference of dignitaries at a lakeside meeting near Salò (Salò for Wannsee); it then moves to a round-up of victims and shootings (one frame shows a road sign pointing to Marzabotto), with the selected prisoner-victims enclosed in the isolated villa where they are systematically tortured, degraded and finally executed.

This crescendo of references in Pasolini's oeuvre represents the most elaborate, riskiest, at times highly schematic, distorted and historically suspect, and yet also immensely powerful parade of elements of the Holocaust, transformed into metaphor or allegory for the purposes of his rampant ideological critique. But Pasolini was far from alone. With variations in tone and pitch, there is a vast spectrum of deployments of Holocaust vocabulary in the intellectual and literary culture of the period and in wider popular culture also, in the service of any and every ideological contestation of the moment.

Of particular importance for the culture of the Holocaust in the late 1960s and 1970s was a wave of European art house (and also genre) cinema—with a notable concentration in Italy—which took the sexual permissiveness and psychoanalytically informed thought of the youth movements and new intellectual currents of the moment, merged them with a new psycho-historiography of Nazism, and produced an arc of sexualised or eroticised, indeed frequently pornographic, film allegories of Fascism and genocide.[62] Pasolini's *Salò* was the most extreme and disturbing exemplar of this trend, drawing on De Sade's work to depict an enclosed world of Fascistic sadomasochistic sexual domination and violence to stand, literally and allegorically, for the essence of Fascism and also the essence of fascistic 'neocapitalist' consumerism.

The trend had begun in Italian, and indeed European, cinema with Luchino Visconti's 1969 historical melodrama *The Damned*, which narrates the rise of Nazism through the prism of the sexual proclivities of the scion of a great industrialist family recruited to the Nazi cause.[63] The trend reached a peak, and also took a direct turn towards the emblematic site of the concentration camp and the Holocaust, in 1974–75, with *Salò*, but also Liliana Cavani's *Night Porter* (1974) and Lina Wertmüller's *Seven Beauties* (1975). Cavani, working in an idiom a long way from her television history documentaries of the early 1960s, drew the contempt of many of those closest to the experience of the Holocaust (including Levi) with her staging of the erotic complicity of a former concentration-camp guard

(Dirk Bogarde) and a former inmate (Charlotte Rampling). Wertmüller's film told the story, in a mixture of bawdy grotesque and comic caricature of a Neapolitan low-life (Giancarlo Giannini) and his adventures, sexual and criminal, in Naples and in the camps. As we will see in Chapter 9, besides the risqué sexual dimension Wertmüller had interesting things to say (and ways of saying it) about stereotypes and national character as a mode of reading history.[64]

In reality, the psychosexual readings of the Lager were only one in a panoply of metaphorical deployments of the figures of the camp and the victim at the heart of the cultures and subcultures of the 1960s and 1970s. Another, overlapping instance was in the sphere of institutions. The Lager hovers in the background, a sort of extreme or founding paradigm, for a whole range of institutions of coercion and social control, which became a prime focus for both politically committed literature and social protests of the time. Part of a sort of Foucauldian intellectual and cultural moment, 'carceral' institutions such as prisons, factories, asylums, hospitals, even schools and universities were all frequently—explicitly or implicitly, at times lazily, at times aptly—compared to concentration camps.[65] The very term 'Lager' itself, one made prevalent as we saw in Chapter 5 by Primo Levi's adoption of it, became a catch-all for this vast array of institutions of coercion.

Significant works of fiction of the period tap into this analogy, including for example Italo Calvino's *The Watcher* (1963), set on the day of an election in the eerie Cottolengo hospital and asylum in Turin, which in loose ways seems at times to take on the characteristics of a Lager; and the same could be said for the alienating factory setting in Paolo Volponi's near-contemporary expressionist novel *Memorandum* (1962).[66]

A powerful example of social movements tapping into something similar was the antipsychiatry movement led in Italy by Franco Basaglia, a movement which culminated in one of the most significant countercultural successes of the 1970s, Law n. 180 of 1978, which ordered the closure of the asylums and the integration of their patients or inmates into society.[67] Within the anti-asylum movement, the Lager analogy was commonplace, found in everything from graffiti to pamphlets to works of serious intellectual substance, such as Angelo Del Boca's 1966 investigation entitled simply *Asylums as Lagers*.[68] A further example was Giuliana Morandini's 1977 collection of interviews with women inmates of asylums, *And So They Locked Me Up*: in the introduction to the book, the analogy is writ large, the asylum is 'the metamorphosis of the Lager, but the Lager has not disappeared' and this is sustained through the testimonies.[69]

Morandini, like many feminists, is interested also in a genealogy of the oppression of women: her 'imprisonment' through institutions such as the family, through antiabortion and antidivorce politics, patriarchy and prejudice, prostitution and so on. Thus she notes the link from women's oppression in asylums to the Lager back towards the torture, imprisonment and murder of witches. And this analogy sets up a final thread of connection that fits the Lager into genealogies of Italian intellectual culture of the period, linked to a concern with law, justice and oppression, and its state-sponsored transgressions. Witchcraft, heresy, the inquisition and the practice of torture are related sources of fascination and of historiographic and literary enquiry in a cluster of writers again starting in the late 1960s, such as Carlo Ginzburg and Leonardo Sciascia. A key locus in Sciascia's immersion in this field of neo-Enlightenment enquiry is his 1981 essay on Alessandro Manzoni's early-19th-century fragmentary historical essay, *History of the Column of Infamy*, which dissects the iniquities of the torture and execution of two 'plague spreaders' in 17th-century Milan.[70] Sciascia's recovery of Manzoni's text brings into focus the functioning of official, bureaucratic process; its power to silence and distort victims leading to hideous suffering; and its application by 'ordinary', upstanding citizens, who as individuals allow themselves to torture, corrupt and execute innocents, in some sense knowingly. Sciascia reaches, as do so many others, for an analogy with the camps: 'The rightness of Manzoni's vision can be judged if we set up an analogy between the Nazi extermination camps and the trials of the spreaders, their torture and death'.[71]

He is reminded of a (now largely forgotten) French novel of the 1950s on the Nazi camps, Charles Rohmer's *The Other Man*,[72] which he describes as 'the most awful part of what has remained in our mind and conscience of all the literature on the Nazi horrors'.[73] Rohmer's novel was published in Italian in 1954 in the highly influential Einaudi book series for new writing called 'Tokens' (*I gettoni*), edited by Vittorini. As we saw, Vittorini had been close to Antelme in the 1940s and was responsible for publishing the translation of the latter's *Human Race* in Italy, also in 1954. It is to Vittorini's own cover notes for Rohmer's book that Sciascia turns to clinch his argument, one which in 1954 seems to anticipate the 1960s debate over Arendt's phrase the 'banality of evil' and the role of bureaucracy in the genocide. It is worth quoting at length, for its acute comments on precisely the process we have been tracing in this chapter, that is, the shift in status of the Holocaust and the camps from subject of first-person testimony to a flexible analogy, a tool and a test case for any understanding we might aspire to of history and of the present:

> The experience of the concentration camps produced in the immediate post-war years a large number of documents, testimonies, chronicles and diaries of exceptional interest; but perhaps only now can we say it is beginning to be understood in its essence as a limit-case, an absolute point of comparison.
>
> After Antelme's *Human Race*, still personal and pregnant with the indignation of the survivor, this novel by Rohmer, so calm and mathematical, perhaps marks a new direction for 'concentrationary' literature. Rohmer does not give us personal experience: the protagonist of his story does not even have a name, he is 'a man': a mere object who enters the house of his persecutioners, a tool for cutting wood, sweeping, lighting fires, utterly 'denied', invisible. Through the eyes of this passive witness, this stranger, this 'other man', we see the world and life of the executioners from top to bottom: a world—and this is the key of the book—that is monstrously similar to our own, with space for the subtlest tenderness, the most delicate feelings; a life in no way sinister or distorted, but made up of private pleasures and pain, of careful actions, full of banal, domestic warmth, flowing without upheaval, alongside the flash of the crematorium ovens and the immense anonymity of the extermination camp.
>
> There is no explicit condemnation here, but rather *a demonstration by reduction to the absurd, in which it is precisely the element of humanity still present within the bureaucrats of Evil, their ability to feel and act like each one of us, that gives the exact measure of their negativity.*[74]

This chapter has looked at fragments and threads of the literary, intellectual and popular culture of a period stretching from the 1950s to the 1970s, drawing on a cluster of key terms already running through early Holocaust talk of the 1940s, but with its centre on the subcultures and literary and radical intellectual rhetoric of the 1960s. At some point during this period, a vocabulary for talking about the Holocaust—including the very terms *genocide, Lager, Auschwitz,* and a whole range of stereotypical tropes and images for the Holocaust—entered mainstream intellectual discourse, as both literal markers of an historical event and flexible and highly recognisable analogies or metaphors. These metaphors emerged from both the contemplation of the perpetrators—the Nazis and their genocidal system and institutions of violence as figures for a sort of species or class violence within modernity—and of the victims—with the dead victim or the 'Jew' as a figure for the overwhelmed and oppressed, subject to power. All this allusive vocabulary often had its origin in a specific learning process, in the transmission of knowledge from first-hand witnesses to second-hand reimagining and redeployment: thus Guccini writes his song after reading Pappalettera and Levi, just as Gillo Pontecorvo was deeply marked by his reading of Levi before making *Kapò* in 1959. This new level of presence of the Holocaust in cultural conversation and imagination, however, also brought a distorting willingness to stretch its historical specificity for any and every current purpose. Analogy is a double-edged sword, and it is no coincidence that the same period saw also intense debate on the so-called uniqueness or otherwise of the Holocaust as an event in human history, a highly charged point of principle for many of the 'gatekeepers' of Holocaust history and memory, and one that would go on to be at the centre of revisionist debates of the 1980s, when a group of German historians argued for a series of similarities and lines of precedence between the Soviet Gulag and the Lager.

The analogies and metaphors have kept on coming well beyond the 1970s, in both intellectual and mass culture. We can end with two indicative examples from the early 21st century, taken from opposite poles of the cultural spectrum: television and political philosophy. Already Elsa Morante, in 'For or Against the Atomic Bomb', had in her decidedly apocalyptic vein compared television to the concentration camps as parallel and monstrous epitomes of petty bourgeois culture.[75] In 2000, when the Italian version of the international reality television show *Big Brother* was launched, several of the more cynical commentators saw in the set-up (an enclosed place, a prison where inmates were under surveillance 24 hours a day, put through humiliating and often absurd trials and then gradually 'eliminated') analogies not only with the totalitarian state evoked jokingly in the Orwellian title, but also, stretching the point, with the Lager and with Nazi medical experiments. This, for example, was the comment of novelist Sebastiano Vassalli:

> *Big Brother* is, in my opinion, one of the most instructive programmes in the history of television, and it is so instructive because it is a scientific experiment dressed up as a television programme. What is more, it is a scientific experiment that might well have been conceived by the scientists of the Third Reich (the Mengeles, Claubergs, Ding-Schulers, etc) if Hitler had won the war.[76]

More seriously, perhaps the single most internationally influential political philosopher writing in 21st-century Italy is Giorgio Agamben. Agamben has written extensively on the Holocaust (drawing heavily on Levi), in particular in his important work *Remnants of Auschwitz*.[77] But his most influential wider work, on contemporary crises in the state, has been significantly centred on the figure or metaphor of the concentration camp as a norm or *nomos* of modern life, as a space for exclusion and for the enactment of what he calls 'states of exception', where the subject-hood and citizenship of victims, their status as subjects of law and rights, simply collapses into what he calls 'bare life'.[78] In a sense, Agamben is turning back here to the Foucauldian analogies raised by Sciascia, to the workings of power that establish torture as a norm, from 17th-century Milan to Guantanamo and Abu Ghraib by way of Auschwitz.[79] Among a huge spectrum of philosophical, but also political, work to draw on Agamben and apply his dense political theory to contemporary social problems is a 2006 book by journalist Marco Rovelli, on the treatment of illegal immigrants in contemporary Italy as they are blocked and imprisoned in holding camps, suspended without status as subjects or citizens, for all intents and purposes invisible to the state and stateless. The issue of globalisation, and its underside in the desperate movements of populations of economic and political migrants, is a defining problem for the new century. Rovelli's book, however, is framed in several ways to link it back to the Holocaust and to the darkest history of the previous century. Rovelli's own appendix draws on Agamben and Arendt; Erri De Luca, a young radical writer immersed in Yiddish and Biblical Hebrew, provides a preface in which he calls Rovelli's chronicle of the immigrants' predicament a modern *History of the Column of Infamy*; a postface on racism and antiracism is included by Moni Ovadia, a Jewish Italian performer of Bulgarian origin who has become the most popular public face in contemporary Italy of a revival of Ashkenazi, Yiddish culture and humour, including songs and plays about the Shoah.[80] Finally, though, and most tellingly of all for the conjunction of the Holocaust with contemporary social and political critique, through a dynamic of loose metaphor and analogy, there is simply the title of Rovelli's book: it is called *Lager italiani*.[81]

§8 Grey Zones and Good Italians

Across Part II, we are exploring a spectrum of structuring presences within a single national field of Holocaust culture. Thus far, we have seen how particular moments—such as the immediate aftermath of war and first impressions of the 1940s (Chapter 4)—can shape forms of knowledge and awareness of the Holocaust; how a powerful single voice and presence, such as Primo Levi's, can act as a conduit and filter for the broader cultural field (Chapter 5); how the history and stories of war and genocide told about a single place, such as Rome, can give shape to the national culture and its Holocaust representations (Chapter 6); and how words and images, vocabularies and metaphors can emanate outwards from the specifics of the Holocaust, to permeate a generic modern vocabulary of war and violence, politics and protest (Chapter 7). This chapter, like Chapter 7, is also concerned with forms of knowledge shaped by language, but it tackles the movement of language, the circulation of stereotypes, stock phrases and keywords, in a significantly different way.

The focus of this chapter is on national questions, on Italian processes of working through, in language and culture, traumatic shared problems of history, ideology and morality, of Fascism, the war and the anti-Fascist Resistance. As has been argued throughout, there is a constant and uneven two-step in the second half of the 20th century between, on the one hand, these core national historical problems for Italy and, on the other, the patchwork of memories and cultural figurations of the history and experience of the Holocaust. At certain moments, these two fields intersect, mutually shaping each other. And whilst it is inevitably the case, as we have repeatedly seen, that most often the dominant national history shapes talk of the apparently 'marginal' history of the Holocaust within it—so, for example, the vocabulary of the Resistance coloured, for decades after the war, images and vocabularies of the camps and of genocide—there are also moments when the reverse has been the case, when Holocaust talk has filtered through, from the margins, somehow to shape central conversations about national history and memory. One of the key mechanisms through which this surprising reversal has taken place—a mechanism that, tellingly, operates as powerfully within 'higher' academic discourse as it does out in a much broader spectrum of public culture—has been through the transmission of certain keywords or phrases from one side to the other, from Holocaust talk to national conversation; in particular phrases and ideas rooted in the highly suspect, loose and yet remarkably pervasive notion of 'national character'.

Silvana Patriarca's illuminating book *Italian Vices* tackles the question of 'national character' not so much as a concept in its own right but as a metaconcept, in other words as an historical and cultural tool that has been used in a vast gamut of public discourse and debate to help appropriate, fix and define nationalism, the nation and senses of national identity in Italy, from the Enlightenment to the Risorgimento through Fascist attempts to forge a 'new Italian', to the postwar era.[1] Indeed, according to Patriarca, the category of national character becomes activated as a driver of cultural formation at the moment of 'passage into nationhood', during the formation of the modern nation-state, a long process under way across the Risorgimento and long post-Risorgimento period, up to and including the present.[2] Patriarca points to a persistent tendency to denigrate, rather than celebrate, national character in Italy, a form of antipatriotism—in widely perceived Italian vices such as laziness, effeminacy, cunning, corruption, opportunism and so on—as evidence of Italy's particularly difficult emergence into modernity and nationhood. In the aftermath of moments of fragility and near dissolution of the nation-state, then, of vacillation in a collective idea of what it is to be 'Italian'— epitomised here by the moment of impossible choice after 8 September 1943—it is perhaps not surprising that both the language and the affect of national character return with considerable power. And since, as we have seen, that moment coincided with and has increasingly come to be read, in the later 20th century, in terms linked to the Holocaust, as well as in exclusively national terms, we can begin to see how the terminology of national character might translate from one sphere to the other.

This chapter focusses in particular on two keywords or stock phrases, which have, in often overlapping usages, shown a remarkable capacity to pose difficult general historical questions through tropes of national character. They have gained especially wide currency since the 1980s but have origins stretching back as far as the 1940s. They both contain within them powerful and flawed stereotypes, myths, narrative tropes and explanatory tools for dealing with the collective past; and they both pose a cluster of difficult questions concerning both the Holocaust and Fascism, questions of individual and collective complicity, guilt, responsibility and the tricky moral, political and legal distinction between commission and omission in historical action. Both, as we will see, found their origin and primary contemporary uses within Holocaust talk. The first is the problem of the 'grey zone' (*zona grigia*); the second, the myth of 'good Italians' (*italiani brava gente*).

1. Grey Zones

The journey of the phrase the 'grey zone' from the ambit of the Holocaust to the centre of debates on Fascism and anti-Fascism in 1980s and 1990s Italy was a remarkable and tellingly awkward one. It began in a crucial, delicately argued and highly influential chapter in Primo Levi's final set of reflections on the Holocaust, the 1986 book *The Drowned and the Saved*. The chapter is entitled, precisely, 'The Grey Zone'.[3]

Levi's intention in 'The Grey Zone' is one of moral nuance and careful complication, recognising that at the heart of the profound difficulty of historicising and understanding the Holocaust lay a limit to the black-and-white instinct that we all share as human beings. As he had done as far back as the 1947 preface to *If This Is a Man*, Levi recognises this universal tendency in what he calls the 'man-animal' to divide the good from the bad, the friend from the enemy, the master from the slave, and he embraces the useful clarity of this simple model, whilst noting its inevitable reductiveness. 'The Grey Zone' explains that the reality of the Lager—and not only the Lager—was built on deliberate creation of confusions, of indecipherable areas of ambiguity in between the innocent victims and the guilty perpetrators. Victims were degraded by the system, and perpetrators were shielded from the effects of their actions, creating a vast grey area of complicity, moral compromise and mitigation which defy in many cases our easy moral (or indeed, judicial) judgements. The essay goes on to illustrate the point with a series of powerful test cases, mostly focussed on victims. It sets out the everyday tricks, acts of collaboration and so-called privileges needed to have any hope of survival. As

Levi points out, the 'privileged'—himself included—were a tiny minority of prisoners, but a vast majority amongst survivors. He considers the myriad roles taken up by that minority, each bringing with it a dose of power, relief from suffering, but also responsibility and complicity: from the Kapos and other minor functionaries to the Sonderkommandos; to the case of the ghetto leader of Lodz, Chaim Rumkowski.

Throughout the essay, Levi proposes a series of careful distinctions, engaging intensely with the moral difficulty of his topic. The chapter is peppered with typically Levian incisions and asides, linking the terrible moral compromises, small and large, forced by the system and the overwhelming workings of totalitarian power onto the prisoners and the guards, to general truths about human society and power. The category of the grey zone is laid bare as an appalling miasma in the Lager, but offered up also as a tool for moral analysis of all human action. Levi also makes a tricky argument for, on the one hand, absolute rejection of banal relativism (all were guilty of compromise, so none were especially guilty) or specious psychologism (we all contain within us phantasms of the persecutor and the persecuted), in the face of the grey zone's existence; and, on the other hand, recognition that, given the nature of the system of genocide in the camps a humility in *our* moral judgements, leading perhaps to a suspension of judgement, is essential: 'the condition of the victim [*offeso*] does not rule out guilt—indeed often victims were, objectively, gravely at fault—but I know of no human court we might trust to judge them' (*Opere*, II, p. 1023).

Of all the essays in *The Drowned and the Saved*—and the book stands as one of the most influential and cited in all Holocaust writing—it is perhaps this one that has had the profoundest influence and resonance in discussions of the Holocaust in Italy and beyond. Its impact has clearly derived in part from the combined narrative and conceptual power of Levi's writing, from its troubled but lucid disentangling of deeply difficult moral and historical quandaries, from its uncertainties and even inconsistencies, and from its careful migration between the specifics of the Lager and the general transferability of its eponymous moral concept. Its success derives also no doubt from the sheer resonance and quotability—between cliché and revived metaphor—of the phrase the 'grey zone' itself. In a way entirely predicted by Levi's comments on simplification and stereotype in this essay and elsewhere in *The Drowned and the Saved*, the quotability of this stock phrase also explains its capacity to be appropriated and slightly, but significantly, reshaped or misused. And this is vividly in evidence in the history of its usage as it migrated in public discourse and historiographical debate in Italy after the publication of *The Drowned and the Saved*.

Alberto Cavaglion has chronicled perhaps the first instance in the appropriation and distortion of Levi's grey zone, its first translation into the public arena and into the field of general history of the Nazi and Fascist era, the moment it threw a spotlight on the shadows of Italy's unresolved response to its own complicities with Fascism.[4] It is symptomatic of the strange ambiguities of such migrations that this instance moved from Levi's work and his phrase 'the grey zone' first of all to Austrian history and politics before rebounding back towards Italian complicities.

In the weeks around the publication of *The Drowned and the Saved* in spring 1986, an international political and diplomatic scandal was in full flow: Austria was in the process of electing a new president, the former Secretary General of the UN, Kurt Waldheim. During the campaign, gaps and inconsistencies in Waldheim's autobiography emerged regarding his wartime activity in the Nazi army, provoking fierce international and national controversy, in a country that had notoriously failed to address its deep complicity with Nazism, from Hitler's origins to its own enthusiastic anti-Semitism. Austria had built its own powerfully self-serving myth of national innocence around the notion of the country as Nazism's 'first victim', rather than its welcoming collaborator.[5] More than one commission of historians and the Austrian Nazi hunter Simon Wiesenthal looked at the Waldheim case and concluded separately that he had not taken part in atrocities, nor could he have intervened to prevent them, but that he must have known of their existence; and in any case, his silences and attempts to falsify his record during 1938–1945 were culpable. Serious diplomatic embarrassment ensued, along with a period of troubled self-contemplation in Austria.

Waldheim suddenly came to embody, at the highest levels of state and global diplomacy, the weighty historical, political and moral problem of how to judge, especially how to judge forty years on—Levi's problem of which 'human court' can decide—those caught up in, more or less willingly, the Nazi or Fascist system on the side of the perpetrators. Levi's category of the grey zone, although forged as a tool to disentangle the moral labyrinth of Auschwitz or the Judenräte, seemed well suited to the case in hand; Waldheim was guilty of cowardice, of having grown up in and been absorbed into a general Austrian complicity with Nazism, but he was no war criminal. The leading Italian journalist Giorgio Bocca, whom we saw

earlier reporting on the Eichmann trial in 1961, picked up on the connection in an opinion piece published in *La repubblica* on 12 June 1986.
Bocca placed Waldheim firmly in Levi's grey area, citing his book and
concluding, on balance, that no one should be deprived of forgiveness or
understanding for a youthful error, for

> a single black mark in his life and, we should note, a black mark that in
> bureaucratic dossiers is cut off from its personal and social context [...]
> weighing in the balance as much as and more than a whole life, all the hun-
> dreds or thousands of right, upstanding actions that came afterwards.[6]

Cavaglion recalls Levi's horror at a presentation event for *The Drowned
and the Saved* in Milan on 12 June, when confronted with Bocca's use
of his terms to whitewash Waldheim.[7] Levi's old friend, the jurist Alessandro Galante Garrone, replied indirectly on Levi's behalf in *La stampa*,
in a short piece given the title 'Waldheim the Grey'.[8] He warned that,
for all the necessity of a certain amount of forgetting of the past, and of
mitigations in grey, 'Levi knows perfectly well, and has never hidden it,
what was black and what was white in the *univers concentrationnaire*.
Waldheim's grey, as he puts it, contained at the very best some 'rather
dark shadows'.

Galante Garrone also warned of the necessities as well as the dangers of
comparing Austria to Italy. Both lost tens of thousands in the anti-Fascist
Resistance (Bocca, Galante Garrone and Levi had all fought for Justice
and Freedom in the Resistance). And both nations had failed to find a
satisfactory collective resolution to their Nazi or Fascist pasts. It was too
convenient, then—too 'opportunistic'—to choose a generic version of
that grey zone to flatten out history.

The migration of the concept of the grey zone into Italian history is
already under way here, in the explicitly uncomfortable clash between
Bocca and Galante Garrone, but also, half-hidden, in the personal history of Giorgio Bocca himself, and what it represents more widely. Before
Bocca's heroic participation in the Resistance, he had—like many of his
generation—adhered to the Fascist regime and its youth movements. He
had even, for a time, enthusiastically embraced the anti-Semitism of the
Racial Laws, writing as late as 1942 as a young journalist in Cuneo in
praise of the *Protocols of the Elders of Zion*, describing the war as 'an Aryan
rebellion against Jewish efforts to place Europe in a state of slavery'.[9] Was
Bocca's plea for the forgiveness of Waldheim for a single misjudgement of
youth, for a 'black mark' to be set alongside the thousands of good deeds

thereafter, a plea for personal redemption, and by extension an appropriation of the idea of the grey zone as a way of easing the consciences of a
generation of Italians caught between Fascism and anti- or non-Fascism,
in that period of impossible historical and moral chaos from the late
1930s to 1945?

The migrations from Levi's concept to this tricky local territory are
already manifold: from victims to perpetrators or their allies, from the
Holocaust to the terrain of the war, from transversal or even universal
moral questions to the local specificities of Austria and Italy, and the analogies between them. And across them all, the loosening image of 'grey-
ness' proves both compelling and malleable. Levi had, for the most part,
focussed in his essay on the complex universe of the prisoners, the victims
and their privileges and complicities. He was equally interested elsewhere
in the perpetrators and their margins for resistance and rejection of the
'system'; as we saw in Chapter 5, he was fiercely against forgiveness as
some Christianising gesture, preferring instead to recognise human complexity but also to judge the perpetrators as firmly responsible for their
actions. The debate around Waldheim, and from there to analogies with
Italian Fascism, inverted the argument and shifted the historical terrain. It
is no coincidence that, precisely in the years around 1986, a central thrust
of new historiography of the Resistance and the legacies of Fascism and
anti-Fascism converged on similar terrain, on the problem of the middle
ground, of the bulk of the Italian population as it stood in the war years
between two extremes and two military forces. The image of the grey
zone was to find great purchase here too.

In the local context of Italian Resistance historiography, and the politics
and mythology of a culturally powerful, leftist Resistance memory that
stretched over the entire postwar era, the equivalent of Levi's black-and-
white, the categories of historical wrong and historical right, were clearly
to be found in the split between Fascism and anti-Fascism, between Right
and Left, Black and Red. After 1989 and the collapse of the First Republic, those old Cold-War polarities would themselves fray and dissolve, and
the Holocaust would in some sense fill the vacuum left behind (see Chapter 10); but even before that watershed, the middle ground between the
poles of Fascism and anti-Fascism had been thickening. Renzo De Felice's
work on the broad popular acceptance or support of the Italian population for the Fascist regime, especially between 1929 and 1936, his so-called
years of consensus, was the cause of intense debate and controversy in the
1970s, an academic controversy that became a massive public and media

event—another *caso*—through the success of his bestselling book-length interview, *Interview on Fascism*, of 1975.[10]

De Felice emphasised several fundamental distinctions in his interview, in an effort to define the phenomenon and the specificity of Fascism. He drew a clear line between Italian Fascism and German Nazism—including his insistent claim (although he would adjust his view later, to take colonialism into account) that Fascist racism was an extrinsic import from Nazi Germany. He attempted to separate the Fascist movement from the Fascist regime and, in his periodisation of the regime's history and its relation with the larger populace, he traced a movement from consensus in the early 1930s to fracture in the late 1930s, with the passage of the Racial Laws in 1938 marking a crucial moment of 'divorce' between regime and people. Although not yet expressed in these terms, the movement from consensus to detached divorce was akin to a movement between shades of grey.

De Felice was clearly operating in a 'revisionist' mode, intent on reclaiming from the taboos of a postwar anti-Fascist intellectual consensus a more nuanced and in some ways also—much to the fury of the left—less unrelentingly dark picture of the Fascist phenomenon. This was evident also, for example, in his thesis that Fascism was, among other things, a force of modernisation. But on the other side of the political-historiographical spectrum, stretching and 'greying' were under way also: the narrow, fighting Resistance of a few tens of thousands at most was enlarged in the 1980s by work on the new category of 'civil resistance' (extending 1970s work on women partisans, support networks and women deportees), introduced by the French historian Jacques Sémelin in 1989.[11] Claudio Pavone's hugely influential *A Civil War* of 1991 also stretched and added nuance to understandings of the nature and scale of the Resistance as a war, as a site of collective action and as a political and moral historical phenomenon.[12] And De Felice would return with force to the question of the Resistance, adapting his consensus model to focus his attention once again on the vast centre ground of the nation's shared experience of 1943–1945. As had happened 20 years earlier, his principal public statement came in a book-length interview, issued in 1995, at the height of post-Cold-War public debates over history and its public uses. The title of the book was *Red and Black*.[13] Beside the tens of thousands of active Resisters and the hundreds of thousands of Salò soldiers or indeed prisoners of war, De Felice set the millions of ordinary Italians who, as he put it, waited out the war, waiting until the Allies made their way to victory, neither on one side nor the other, indeed at times helping both sides for the sake of self-protection, looking simply to make it through and to protect their families. This was the phenomenon of '*attesismo*' or '*attendismo*', or 'wait-and-see-ism', that allowed De Felice to refute, indeed to ridicule the myth of a mass uprising against Fascism in the form of an armed Resistance, what he called the 'Resistance vulgate'. The chapter in which De Felice clinically sets out his case for attendismo is entitled 'A Large Grey Zone'.[14]

In the chapter, De Felice describes the 'substantial detachment' of the mass of Italians from both the Salò Republic and the Resistance, let alone from the occupying Germans. This led to a 'survival strategy', especially in rural areas, of being 'a friend to everyone without helping anyone', largely sympathetic to an anti-Fascist outcome but fearful of provoking violence if any action is taken in that cause. This vast band of the population was the 'grey zone of civil *attesismo*' (an ironic echo of the 'civil Resistance'), where choices were avoided wherever possible. The myth of ethical and political choice, as defining of the Resistance epos, is contrasted by De Felice with the trauma of those few choices that the mass could not avoid, especially the conscript call-ups of 1943–44. Otherwise, their predominant choice was not to choose. The same passivity characterised significant parts of Italy's intellectual caste, captured by Cesare Pavese in his postwar autobiographical novel *The House on the Hill*, whose title image, of the refuge where the teacher-hero guiltily waits out the war, became a parallel metaphor to that of the grey zone.[15]

In Levi, as in Pavone, and in different senses in Bocca and De Felice also, the success of the grey zone as a formulation reflected a shift from ideology—at least from Cold War ideological rigidities—towards morality; and with that shift came a concomitant focus on the individual or family and their choices—or nonchoices—in the face of history, rather than on groups, collectivities and systems. And with the focus on the individual came nuanced moral judgements, liberal acknowledgements of contradiction and tension in the story of every individual, family, group and nation, Bocca's weighing the balance of good points and bad points. Messy aspects such as national character intrude here, as when in *Red and Black* De Felice describes Fascist means for blocking Jewish deportations: 'Italian-style tricks, which, although morally squalid, nevertheless... would save thousands of lives'.[16] Although in his original formulation in *The Drowned and the Saved* Levi had explicitly rejected this calculus of good versus bad deeds and although there was still much emphasis in his essay on the moral complexity of, precisely, an individual constrained and robbed of moral autonomy by a system of persecution, torture, hunger and confusion—and thus on a tension between political and moral dimensions—the notion of the grey zone was picked up most often as a way of opening up local, momentary choices of individuals, intimate concerns, instincts for self-preservation and for hiding away from danger and so on. The Holocaust was now less powerfully resonant as a system, an extreme totalitarian politics—as it had been in Rousset; or as it had been in Robert Katz's caustic critique of the Judenräte of Rome (Chapter 6)—but much more so as a crucible for the ultimate test of individual morality, one that by analogy could be applied to the millions of Italians faced with the collapse of systems and structures of the state or nation in 1943. Through the individual and his or her morality, qualities of character, national character, also accrued to the '*attendisti*', citizens of the grey zone. In this formulation, detached from Levi's careful reflections but borrowing much of its power and suggestiveness, the grey zone has become a nearly ubiquitous, drifting category. As Pavone notes, the historical usefulness and precision of the notion risks being lost in the drift:

> the grey zone has found itself at the centre of a debate that goes well beyond its own terms, as it aims to attain the level of a global judgement on Italian history and on the character of Italians, in short on the very national identity of Italy.[17]

2. Good Italians

As Patriarca demonstrates, national vices, persistent stereotypical notions of flaws and failings in national character that somehow need to be corrected, have long been used as the levers for the creation and imposition of a 'good' national identity from above, fed by patriotic laments for the nation's weaknesses. The process is intrinsic to modern nationalism, but it has perhaps been particularly pronounced in Italy's modern history. The passive, detached, self-serving and introverted 'amoral familism', as one anthropologist famously described the value system in Italy's south,[18] seems perfectly reflected in the attesismo of the civil war period. At the same time, another stereotype, this time a positive one, a stereotype of national virtue, competes with and complements the national vice of the grey zone, with its emollient equidistance from and indifference to the strong positions of active Fascism and anti-Fascism. Viewed through the rosy lenses of virtue, Italians' 'natural' scepticism of authority, of the tyranny of the state and of the rule of law, combined with a naturally humane empathy for fellow human beings—for neighbours, as discussed in Chapter 6—led to a native resistance to the worst of Fascist persecution, including racism, to an instinctive impulse to resist or ignore dogma, simply to get on and to get by without being polluted even by 20 years of totalitarianism. In this view, consensus becomes a form of surreptitious preservation of autonomy, a sign of simple, native decency resisting Fascist rhetoric and bluster. This is the root of the myth of the 'good Italian', the homely notion of Italians as '*brava gente*' (good folk). Once again, as with the grey zone, throughout the long history of this myth of national character as a convenient and compelling lens through which to see Italy's wartime history, the Holocaust has hovered strangely close to its core.

Origins of stereotypes of national character are difficult to locate, but recent important research by Filippo Focardi and others has shown how the modern expression of this idea of the good Italian had its origin in a very particular diplomatic strategy of the 1940s within the nascent Italian republic.[19] Driven by its nervous desire to be accepted as an ally of the Western democracies, as a member of the new United Nations and other institutions and international programmes, including the Marshall Plan, the Italian government undertook a sustained diplomatic strategy to distance Italian Fascism from German Nazism, to talk up individual acts of Italian courage, including aid to and rescue of Jews and others, even before the fall of Mussolini's regime (as well as Italy's anti-Nazi role after 1943). The fundamentally decent Italian people, in other words, were presented as having been traduced by the evil of the regime that governed and oppressed them. Michele Sarfatti has noted similar, parallel internal processes, in the months following the war, of omission and distortion in the public record and the official memory, which amount to the very first steps in the repression of active Italian responsibility for persecution of Jews and Fascist violence (part of the playing down of the need for purges of the Fascist state infrastructure).[20] Actively set in contrast to the image of the good Italian was a counterimage of national character, of the irredeemably 'bad German'; as Focardi explains, these two were a mutually defining pair of stereotypical images, one relying on the other to perform the task of historical, moral and thus political distinction.[21]

The pattern of De Felice's historiographical line of interpretation is echoed here: the people are to be treated separately as agents from the state, and judged separately accordingly. And just as in the case of the grey zone, the character trait of the good Italian makes for an individual-

centred, and narratively forceful, frame for bringing history into view and
shared understanding. As public attention to the Holocaust in the 1980s
proliferated, in several contrasting directions—the period saw a surge in
publication of both new and old testimonies, a rise in local and international negationism and revisionism and a new wave of historiography
both of the Holocaust itself and also of Fascism with a greater focus on
anti-Semitism—the narrative and consolatory power of stories of good
Italians meant that the myth became a prominent feature in the expanding and multidirectional cultural field.

A key media product that set itself up squarely as a promoter of this
part-historical, part-mythical narrative of the good Italian, using it as
the core explanation of Italy's and Italians' role in the Holocaust, was the
TV documentary, *The Courage and the Pity*, made by Nicola Caracciolo
and broadcast on RAI 2 in November 1986.[22] Already the title, in its self-
conscious contrast with Ophuls's groundbreaking 1971 documentary *The
Sorrow and the Pity*, which cracked open the repressed history of Vichy
France's complicity with the Holocaust, declares its aim: where venal collaborators elsewhere colluded to deport Jews, by contrast Italians, whether
neighbours, friends, priests or nuns, or indeed Fascist officials, diplomats,
or soldiers, did all they could, in private and behind the scenes, to save
'their' Jews. Interviewing an extraordinarily rich range of more than 60
Jewish survivors and refugees as well as observers and rescuers, the programme deliberately set out, as Perra notes, to turn negative stereotypes
into positives, for example praising the labyrinths of Italian bureaucracy
as a means to slow and prevent (German) persecution and deportation.[23]

Caracciolo declared his work as deliberately tendentious, setting out to
prove a hypothesis, as he puts it in the introduction to the book of the
documentary, 'that in the war years, Italians stayed immune to that awful
"psychological epidemic", as Reich might have called it, of anti-Semitism,
at least in its murderous Nazi variant'.[24] The rest of Caracciolo's introduction is a relentlessly optimistic rendition of Italians' role in saving Jews—
the Fascist government was the 'protector' of Jews; no part of the Italian
army participated in the horrors of genocide; ordinary people, the clergy
and an 'infinite series' of simple acts of friendship added up to a 'humani-
tarian conspiracy' to save the Jews.[25] Where he attempts an explanation
for the kindness, Caracciolo comes awkwardly close to a veiled anti-Semitism, noting the difference of assimilated, ordinary-looking Jews of Italy,
compared to the exotic foreign aspect of Eastern European Jews.[26] In this
he is the heir to a 19th-century, and later Crocean, form of assimilationist

antiracism: the Jews are to be embraced, even saved, so long as they do not look or act too Jewish.

Renzo De Felice and Daniele Carpi are credited as Caracciolo's main historical consultants, and De Felice's preface to the book that accompanied the transmission, whilst far more coherent and lucid than Caracciolo's, nevertheless pithily summarises the 'good news' story of the Italian rescue of Jews. He lists eight bullet point assertions, each detaching Fascism and the Italian people from the anti-Semitic impulse: so, for example, Italian racism was unknown; Italian Fascism was not anti-Semitic and the Racial Laws were externally dictated; the Racial Laws were softer than their Nazi equivalents and in any case poorly received.[27] De Felice goes on to to talk about an inbuilt sense of decency and solidarity, especially a 'peasant solidarity', combined with a shadow of attendismo—the good Italian thus explicitly merging with the grey zone—that led many in the countryside to look kindly on Jewish refugees.

Although a much wider range of views and stories is on show in the documentary, through the range and quality of interviewees, the framing of *The Courage and the Pity* is clear, almost embarrassingly so: this is the myth of the good Italian writ large, using the Holocaust (with, in Caracciolo's case, an inadvertent dose of anti-Semitism) as its clinching evidence. It is perhaps not a coincidence, however, that the period which produced Caracciolo's apologia and the relentless imposition of De Felice's idea of Fascism also produced the beginning of a strong backlash against the simplicities of the myth and the stereotype of the good Italian, as well as a series of influential stories that continued the dual process we saw in the case of the grey zone: of complication and inversion of the categories of historical morality and national character, all bound up with the recovery of myriad individual stories, at a moment when overarching master narratives, of Fascism as of the Holocaust, were cracking.

The backlash in historiographical terms began in the new wave of work on Fascist anti-Semitism after 1988 (see Chapter 10), in which a questioning of the myth of the good Italian came to be a central part, as a much cited essay by David Bidussa exemplified.[28] This questioning ran parallel in contiguous fields also: for example, in work on the Italian occupation of the Balkans by Davide Rodogno; or in the rediscovery of Italian concentration camps in Calabria following pioneering work by Carlo Spartaco Capogreco in the late 1980s; or—of increasingly central importance over the 1990s and after—in the field of the history of Italian colonialism, such as in the newly influential work of Angelo Del Boca, which underscored with astonishment the almost complete neglect of the atrocities carried out by the 'decent men' of Mussolini's army in Africa.[29]

Returning to the Holocaust specifically, for those in the 1980s and after who were closest to the role of gatekeepers and those, typically on the left, who were hostile to De Felice's positions, the imperative now was to consider the historical and moral specificity of Italian guilt and persecution, to rescue the genuinely horrific nature of Fascist racial persecution from disappearing under the sheer scale of the Nazi equivalent. Symptomatic of this has been the success of the categories of Italian continuity proposed by historian Michele Sarfatti—in clear contrast to De Felice's account of ruptures and fractures—which directly connected the 'persecution of rights' of Italian Jews of 1938–1943 to the 'persecution of lives' of 1943–1945 (and indeed, also onwards to a hypothetical future extension of Italy's own genocidal plans, plans only accidentally truncated by the end of the war, as Sarfatti notes).[30] Intersecting with the question of the grey zone once again, the two models of De Felice and Sarfatti set radically different store by the choice to rescue or aid the Jews. For one, it shows a certain decency of character, but also a distance from any Fascistised ideology (or any ideology at all) and a localist instinct to huddle together and sit out the violence of the war; for the other, now, the 'choice' to help Jews is as potent and 'active' a choice as the existentially and politically defining 'choice' of the old Resistance myth, the choice to fight the Nazi-Fascists, whether in the armed struggle or the civil one.

The contested terrain between good Italians and grey zones was most vividly and resonantly on display in this late-20th-century moment in another recovered story of rescue, that of Giorgio Perlasca. Perlasca, born in 1910 and formerly a convinced Fascist soldier, was by wartime living in Budapest and was less than enthusiastic about the anti-Semitic turn in the regime. After 1943, he declared himself a monarchist and, seeing the mass deportations of Hungarian Jews in 1944, set about saving as many as he could, posing as a Spanish diplomat and issuing false documents. He aided the survival of more than 5,000 Jews. Perlasca was a forgotten figure until 1988, when he was named by Yad Vashem as one of the 'Righteous Among the Nations'. Following this, his story was picked up first by a neo-Fascist newspaper, then in 1990 by a popular RAI television programme (*Mixer*), then in 1991 in a best-selling book by the left-wing campaigning journalist (who had worked for *Mixer*) Enrico Deaglio, who would later edit the magazine *Diario*, which was highly active in the Holocaust memory politics of the early 2000s.[31] The book was followed in 2002 by a critically and popularly acclaimed television drama for the main public channel RAI 1, *Perlasca: An Italian Hero*.[32]

Perlasca's story and success, his emergence at what Perra has called 'the centre of Holocaust memory in Italy' (p. 223), as precisely 'an Italian hero', is compelling. Put simply, he was both good and grey, and he embodied in his heroism, ambiguity and uncertainty many of the issues of morality, national identity and national character that were circulating around the stereotypes of the grey zone and the good Italian in the 1980s and 1990s. He had been a committed Fascist, but not an anti-Semite, indeed was instinctively hostile to Nazi and Fascist anti-Semitism; he was a patriot, and heroic in his risk taking and sacrifice, but also 'typically Italian' in his trickery, fakery and posing. He was also, crucially, not charismatic—this was a vessel for ordinary heroism—and Deaglio (echoing Caracciolo's trick) signalled this by playing on and inverting for this Italian case a key document of international Holocaust remembrance: where Caracciolo turned *The Sorrow and the Pity* into *The Courage and the Pity*, Deaglio turned Arendt's phrase 'the Banality of Evil', into his title *The Banality of Good*. And the circle is completed by the subtitle of the television drama: Perlasca is finally Italian *because* of his muddled, but ultimately humane, sense of what is right. His is an individual story which, because of his Fascist formation, detaches this history of Italy's Holocaust from ideology, presenting an axis of lived lives and moral choices as transcending collective categories and politics. The Holocaust here stands as a test of the resilience of a certain ambiguous but benign Italianness, as much as a critique of Italy's compromised and complicit history.

In retrospect, the confluence of features of national character that hover around Perlasca are present repeatedly in earlier narratives that come into contact more or less incidentally with the Holocaust. A certain idea of national character—of the muddling, distracted, dishonest, cowardly or morally ambiguous, but ultimately 'good', ordinary Italian (man)—is, in other words, one of those structuring presences in Italian Holocaust culture, a filter through which both national character and the Holocaust are commonly seen in Italy. In the ambit of cinema alone, we can find a cluster of examples in three films starring major Italian comic actors from three distinct generations, each in their way commonly embraced as images of a certain Italianness, in character and attitude, and each here in roles that confront more or less obliquely the horrors of the Holocaust. The films are *Generale della Rovere* (Roberto Rossellini, 1959), *Everybody Home* (Luigi Comencini, 1960) and *Seven Beauties* (1975); the actors, respectively, are Vittorio De Sica, Alberto Sordi and Giancarlo Giannini. *Il Generale della Rovere* brought together two great icons of neorealism in Rossellini, the director, and De Sica, reprising his career as an actor. Here, he plays Bardone, a seasoned con man who is offered during the war the chance by the Germans to save his own life by posing in prison as a Resistance hero—the eponymous General della Rovere—in order to trick the other prisoners into revealing details of the Resistance network. Confronted with this ultimate con, the fake general embraces the role and chooses instead to die a hero's death, with the Resistance prisoners, joined at the last—as if to clinch the moral and historical righteousness of the choice and his own 'goodness' (and Italianness)—by a group of praying Jewish prisoners.[33] In *Everybody Home*, Sordi—who, as Patriarca argues, perhaps more than anyone else has embodied the affectionately flawed vices of the contemporary Italian male[34]—plays one of a group of Italian soldiers after 8 September 1943 and the Armistice, heading for home to wait out the war, a classic band of Italian *attesisti*; but in making their journey across war-torn Italy the group begin to understand the world around them, the need to fight, the meaning of the war. One key episode of the film sees the soldiers meet a Jewish girl, a victim of persecution, and help her escape, with tragic consequences. Sordi's character is called Alberto Innocenzi—as if his movement from innocence to awareness is an allegory for the nation's history—and the encounter with the Holocaust is one stage in a profound arc of adaptation to a new vision of what is right (for Italy). Finally, the murkier and more complex case of *Seven Beauties*, in which Giannini plays the criminal, incompetent and grotesque Neapolitan stereotype Pasqualino, stages its shocking and ironically harsh portrayal of a concentration camp and the horrors of torture, violence and sexual degradation that go on there, by constantly intercutting its scenes set in the war and the Lager with a tawdry and garish parade of Neapolitan scenes of murder and sex. If it is hard to represent Pasqualino as a good character—indeed, he ends up being forced to 'choose' to shoot his friend in the camp, in contrast to the noble Spanish anti-Fascist Pedro—he is nevertheless a signal of that corrupt but vitally alive Italian/Neapolitan character, a vitality he is entirely drained of by the Lager experience.[35]

∾

The twin stereotypes of the grey zone and the good Italian come together in a surprising cultural confluence of morality, national identity and national character. Pavone suggests a direct, linear, almost causal link between the two as historical categories: 'It is from the grey zone that the most heartfelt champions of the myth of "Italian goodness" emerge', as though former cynical bystanders of the war later played up the good Italian motif for self-serving reasons.[36] But this sequencing seems reductive in the face of the pervasive and complicated intersections and mutual reinforcements between the two described here, in their validity as historiographical tools and their penetration as stock phrases or clichés. From the academic to the mass cultural end of the spectrum, from right to left, from home to abroad, the phrases and stories associated with them have circulated around and probed an elaborate set of difficult questions in history. Although ostensibly opposite—the grey zone contains the vice, the good Italian the virtue—they are in fact bound up closely with each other, and what is more, they seem to come into constant and highly revealing contact, even at their origin, with stories of the Holocaust.

There is an interplay of simplicity and complexity on display here, which is crucially symptomatic of the larger phenomenon we are studying: how a complex historical set of events is given a certain cultural shape—and therefore also simplified and categorised—within a given national culture, in different ways at different times. These two stock phrases become, in the 1990s especially, instances of how history is often seen as determined at the level of individual experience and personal attributes of character, which in turn reflect a shared national character, rather than large ideological or structural categories, in movements of states, institutions, parties or churches. At one level, this is a contrast between popular history, interested in individual stories, and academic historiography, with its analyses of structure and complex causality. At another level, there is a substantial and widespread analytical position here: ordinary individuals acted with their own complex motivations, quite distinct from systems and structures. This corrective paradigm has held in several arenas: thus, ordinary Christians—monks, nuns and priests—protected and saved hundred of Jews, even if the higher Church and papacy were for many inadequate in their response; or ordinary Italians helped their neighbours and worked around the Racial Laws, even as the state, the regime, the party and the Parliament shamefully became enthusiastic racists. The category of quotidian agency confounds assumptions of structure through a simple, paradoxical inversion. Perlasca's fascination as a 'good Fascist' in the face of the Hungarian Holocaust is a case in point. Around the same period as the rediscovery of Perlasca's story, the great oral historian and soldier, Resistance fighter and chronicler of the peasant

classes Nuto Revelli was writing *The Lost Soldier of Marburg*, a strange
and fascinating book in which Revelli becomes obsessed with finding
the identity of a particular German soldier killed by Resistance fighters
in Piedmont.[37] Revelli's fascination is with the notion—something that
seems to strike him as conceivable for the first time since the 1940s—that
this might have been a 'good German'. Like all this field of stereotype and
national character, Revelli's search and the book that recounts it make
for shaky history, but for remarkably powerful storytelling and cultural
reprocessing of historical received opinions and settled assumptions.

Revelli's good German, Perlasca the unassuming procurement officer,
the young 'boys of Salò', Sordi's conscript soldier Alberto Innocenzi: all
these have in common, finally, an ordinariness, and it is perhaps this that
is the key to the combined power of the grey zone and the myth of the
good Italian. Even the first work to use *Italiani brava gente* as its title, a
film of 1964 directed by Giuseppe De Santis, told the story of, again,
a group of ordinary Italian soldiers, here on the Russian front. Attention
to ordinariness is shared by the sophisticated methods of history-from-
below and by the instant affect of saccharine popular stories, with simple
individualistic morals, that place us in a position of empathy with the
past. And the Holocaust, within this spectrum of ordinariness, represents
the weightiest and most morally compelling of stories *against* which to
tell this history, the best testing ground of national character.

§9 Transnational Lines

This book is a study in the shape and substance of a particular field of Holocaust culture within one European nation, with its local history of complicity with and suffering from the Nazi genocide, and with its local set of responses to both its own role and the wider historical phenomenon of the Holocaust. It belongs in a well-established field, as noted in Chapter 1, of studies of single national histories of responses to the Holocaust. Taken together, this field of work gives us a patchwork panorama of the supranational phenomenon of the Holocaust's aftermath, how it had an impact upon and played out in an array of national settings and how, with variations and parallels, over the long postwar era it worked its way into a global, cultural consciousness. Within this wide perspective, certain figures, events, images and moments from one or other single country might be said to have 'turned global', to have become pivotal in that globally circulating supranational cultural field, transmitted through mass media and absorbed by millions across many countries. Instances of such pivotal cultural phenomena were used to build up the stock chronology of Holocaust response offered at the start of Chapter 1 (the camp liberation photos and newsreels, Anne Frank's diary, Eichmann's trial, *Holocaust, Schindler's List*, etc.). The list might be supplemented by other lists of less vastly penetrating but more 'prestigious', intellectually influential, elite cultural phenomena, again each produced within a single national context, and taken up and spread into the supranational. To this 'high' list might belong Claude Lanzmann's *Shoah*, Arendt's *Eichmann in Jerusalem*, and the canon of survivor-writers, including Elie Wiesel, Paul Celan, Tadeusz Borowksi, Etty Hillesum, Primo Levi, Imre Kertesz, and others. Such figures are imported into local, national fields, just as, conversely, local presences filter out into the supranational field. In the Italian case, Primo Levi, Benigni's film *Life Is Beautiful*, Bassani's *Garden of the Finzi-Continis* and De Sica's film of it, Wertmüller's *Seven Beauties* and others add up to a perhaps surprising contribution from a country where, numerically at least, the impact of the Holocaust on the ground was relatively small.

To proceed in this taxonomic way is reductive, but it undoubtedly reflects a real dynamic that is perhaps peculiar to vast-scale historical events, to events which are enacted across national borders as they happen—here, millions of victims deported across national borders, targeted by ethnicity, in some sense irrespective of national origin and identity—and which become 'world historical' as they are related, narrated and historicised thereafter. From this global purview comes also the capacity for events such as the Holocaust to operate not only supranationally, in historical and cultural terms, but also as universal phenomena, with lessons to impart about, say, the nature of mankind, the human mind and the human body, about the workings of violence, guilt, morality and responsibility (and so on), an array of questions which, as we have seen, has occupied a great deal of important reflection on this Event, and which has little specifically to do with the national origin of whoever might ponder such weighty questions.

There is, however, a space in between the national and the supranational, a space that is less compartmentalised than these two and that, traced in its own historical workings, might explain how those other two come into contact and interact on the ground of cultural production and dissemination. We can call this space 'transnational', a term which tells of the fluid and migratory ways that the Holocaust and the language and imagery surrounding it have constantly crossed national cultural borders, been inflected and absorbed in peculiar ways in each local setting, have forged and shaped new representations and responses which have themselves in different, unpredictable arenas and forms migrated out into other cultures. Transnational lines within Holocaust culture have always been deeply formative of both the singly national and the supranational-cum-universal layers of that culture, creating webs of connection and intersection, of reception, transmission and translation (literally and geographically understood) across boundaries of nation and culture. Less attention has been paid to this crucial dimension at work within and across all the single national case studies, because its modes are many and varied, because it is hard to pin down, and because it renders fuzzy the defining terms of our case studies. And yet it is an essential element in any account of the culture of the Holocaust to notice and to probe both the immigrations and the emigrations that question the limit shape and definition of what it is we are studying when we study a national response to the Holocaust.

This chapter examines a series of variant samples of the network of transnational lines of transmission of Holocaust talk in and out of Italy over the postwar era. It is deliberately eclectic in the corners of the field that it taps into and in the other cultures it chooses to show interacting with Italy's. It looks first at three other cultures, perhaps the three key arenas of Holocaust history and memory—Israel, America and Europe—and offers vignettes of how Italian responses to the Holocaust are shaped by, and on occasion also shape, parallel responses there. It then looks at dynamics of transnational exchange in language, through the impact of translation and of translingualism on the spread of knowledge about the Holocaust in Italy. Finally, the chapter looks at the site of Auschwitz, marking the Italian memorial presence at this centre and epitome of the Holocaust.

1. Cultural Geopolitics: Israel, America, Europe

ISRAEL

As an event in Jewish history, the Holocaust has always necessarily run on an unevenly parallel path alongside the history of the state of Israel, whose establishment in 1948 and troubled history from then until now has in no small part been determined by the dark shadow cast by the Holocaust. As work by Tom Segev, Idith Zertal and others has shown, the problematic of the Holocaust and what it implied for Jewish-national identity and the new state of Israel was central to its culture and political ideology.[1] But in ways perhaps more surprising, the cultural geopolitics of Israel has consistently had an impact also upon the memorialisation and culture of the Holocaust in other countries. The tricky boundaries between Jewish religion and culture, between Zionist or anti-Zionist positions in the diaspora, and the political and military status of Israel and the Middle East question, are often near the surface of talk about the Holocaust well beyond Israel itself, especially at flashpoint moments of war, crisis and heightened international scrutiny of the region. In Italy, as elsewhere, this intersection of Israel talk with Holocaust talk has been especially pertinent within the Jewish community on the one hand, in its negotiations between Zionism and local identity, and on the other hand within the ideologies and subcultures of major political forces and parties, in particular the Communist PCI after 1967 and the former neo-Fascist AN from the 1990s.

Within Israeli official commemorative culture, an heroic and militarised figure of the Holocaust 'combatant' was celebrated, in particular through the memorialisation of the Warsaw Ghetto resistance at sites such as Kibbutz Lohamei Hagetaot, as a means to counter the widespread myth and stereotype of passive Jews, led to death as lambs to the slaughter.[2] Within the Italian Jewish community, something of this same counterpoint can be found in the 1940s and 1950s, for example in pro-Zionist journals such as the *Rassegna mensile di Israel,* in the form of an optimistic attention to the new state of Israel and a tendency not to dwell on the horror of the genocide. In the opening editorial of the new postwar series of the journal in April 1948, the mourning for the victims of persecution is balanced by a powerful celebration of the new dawn of Israeli nationhood,

> the moment in which a centuries-old dream is realised and on the eastern coast of the Mediterranean, after a millennial eclipse, the Jewish state is reborn. *Rassegna* starts publishing once more in the name of the martyrs, thinkers and pioneers of Israel.[3]

A comparable pattern of playing down the persecution and building optimistic stories about Jewish identity in the early postwar years partly explains the widespread insistence on the part of Italian Jewish survivors and community leaders on the humane altruism of their neighbours—the 'good Italians'—in their heroic sacrifices and risks to save Jewish victims.[4] Guri Schwarz has chronicled and analysed with great acuity the internal tensions within the Italian Jewish community, from the 1940s to the 1960s, with its official body UCII taking up a broadly Zionist position, and other branches and youth sections somewhat less so (including the group that founded CDEC).[5] But if these tensions were played out in the relatively closed-off spaces and institutions of the Jewish community, the Israeli question and its role in the memorialisation of the Holocaust was propelled into a much wider cultural-political sphere through the watershed moment of the Six Day War of 1967.

The events leading up to the war, with a crescendo of anxiety in the Jewish community over the possible destruction of the state of Israel, followed by the extraordinary military victory of the Jewish state and the occupation of large tracts of neighbouring countries' territory, polarised political tensions dictated by Cold War allegiances. After 1967, America was confirmed as the key ally of Israel, and the Soviet Union and with it

Communist Parties the world over as pro-Palestinian. A deep split was opened up between a Jewish community—including some leftist and Communist Jews (such as Umberto Terracini)—largely and emotionally in tune with Israel's heroic victory and survival, and the mainstream of the PCI.[6] At the same time, the ruling Christian Democrats were not, by simple contrast, pro-Israeli: on the contrary, Italian Mediterranean geopolitical interests, and residual postcolonial connections, led to a strengthening of relations with Arab countries in its sphere of interest, such as Libya.

The effects of this polarisation were longstanding and complex, causing inner ructions within the PCI, and creating strange zones of ambivalence in the spectrum of the Communist-led intellectual culture of Italy during the 1970s, including in the sphere of Holocaust culture. So, for example, if the 1970s saw some attention to the phenomenon of the Lager and of Nazi persecution, its specifically Jewish dimension was once again marginalised, for orthodox Communists and also for heterodox Marxists such as Pasolini or Wertmüller. Pasolini in particular in the 1970s, as we saw in Chapter 7, adopted a more generalised, anticolonial *tiersmondisme* and metaphors of Fascism and the new genocide, but his mid-1970s work tends to abandon the specific figure of the 'Jew'. Primo Levi, on the non-Communist liberal left politically speaking, was drawn into ideological squabbles by his 1978 novel about the pleasures of manual labour, *The Wrench* (which is shot through with a vein of Holocaust reflection also), when Marxists accused him of naïve embrace of (capitalist) labour.[7]

Further telling evidence comes in a 1972 article by Natalia Ginzburg in *La stampa*, entitled 'The Jews', written in Ginzburg's signature intimate and lucid style.[8] A response to the massacre of Israeli athletes at the Munich Olympics by the Palestinian terrorist group Black September, Ginzburg's article offers a rare reflection on her own Jewish identity, and on what she calls the 'false' notions her bourgeois upbringing instilled in her, including the insidious idea that the Israelis were somehow superior to the Arabs:

> Sometimes I have thought that the Jews of Israel had rights and priority over others, because they had lived through a genocide [*sterminio*]. This wasn't a monstrous idea, but it was a mistake. [...] After the war we loved and commiserated with the Jews who left for Israel thinking that they had lived through a genocide, that they were homeless and didn't know where to go. We loved in them their memories of suffering, their fragility, their wandering paths and their shoulders weighed down by fears. These are the features we love in mankind. We certainly did not expect to see them turn into a powerful, aggressive, vengeful nation.

Perhaps the most intense case of all was that of the heterodox socialist intellectual Franco Fortini. Born Franco Lattes, from a Jewish father,
Fortini rejected his Jewish heritage in the 1930s, suffered anti-Semitic
prejudice nevertheless, and then political-racial exile in Switzerland in
1944–45.[9] His acid attack on the victors of the 1967 war, *The Dogs of Sinai*,
represented one of the most remarkable ideological-poetical assaults from
the left on the Israeli cause, one explicitly linked to his own ambivalent
relation to his Jewish origins and its disavowed legacy.[10]

The consequences of the PCI's post-1967 anti-Zionism have spun on,
politically and culturally, until the present day. As Israeli governments
moved to the right, starting with the Likud leadership of Menachem
Begin and the Lebanon war of 1982, liberal Jewish intellectuals—including Levi—began to declare distance from, even hostility towards, Israel
whilst defending its right to exist.[11] Related to the Lebanon war, the PLO
terrorist attack on Rome's synagogue of 9 October 1982, in which a two-
year-old boy was killed, prompted an appalled protest at the anti-Israeli
and at times veiled anti-Semitic consensus throughout Italian political and
cultural life.[12]

After the end of the Cold War, the 'new right' of 1990s Italy—in particular Gianfranco Fini's AN but to some extent also Silvio Berlusconi's
Forza Italia (FI)—saw a key strategic advantage in moving closer to Israel.
In an extraordinary operation of political 'cleansing', Fini undertook a
series of diplomatic missions to bind his post-Fascist party and his politics to Israel, to the Jewish community in Italy and to the Holocaust. He
visited Rome's synagogue, the site of Auschwitz, and in November 2003,
accompanied by the charismatic leftist leader of the Italian Jewish community Amos Luzzatto, Fini went to Jerusalem. At Yad Vashem, he made
his boldest break to date with his neo-Fascist heritage, labelling Fascist
anti-Semitism and the Nazi genocide examples of 'absolute evil' and la-
menting the 'apathy, indifference, complicity and cowardice which mean
that many Italians in 1938 did nothing to react to the scurrilous Racial
Laws imposed by Fascism'.[13] In the same speech, Fini defended the Israeli
leader Ariel Sharon and accused anti-Zionists of a form of anti-Semitism,
thus adopting the distinctions of the liberal Jewish intelligentsia as his
own, in a remarkable inversion.

Conversely, whereas elements of the left even after the end of the Cold
War remained deeply hostile to Israel as a militarised occupying power,
there was a loosening of cultural-ideological alignments in this area.
One remarkable cultural manifestation of this loosening was a phase of

importation and lionisation, starting in the late 1980s, by a weakened committed intellectual elite, of a generation of pro-peace, politicised and literarily highly accomplished Israeli writers, whose work was often steeped in the legacy of the Holocaust. Figures such as David Grossman, Amos Oz and Abraham Yehoshua became fundamental literary, moral and historical reference points for an intelligentsia and reading public in Italy looking for some sort of reorientation. Grossman's *See Under: Love*, for example, translated into Italy in 1988 as *Vedi alla voce: amore*, went through five editions with Mondadori publishing house, before being republished in 1990 as an Einaudi paperback to equal success. These writers' success in Italy seemed to coincide, and indeed contribute to, the emergence of new forms of serious, historically alert, contemporary cultural intervention in a postmodern, post-Marxist, indeed postliterary Italy.[14] The new Israeli literature was a model for new forms of 'resistance writing', from within a hostile ideological terrain and with direct links back to the darkest moment of European history. The Israeli writers, tackling the historical and moral legacy of the Holocaust and contemporary political battles, felt like a nostalgic throwback in Italy to the post-war Marxist writer, with her or his Resistance and anti-Fascist certainties and contemporary anticapitalist battles to fight in the new republic.

And yet, cruder political divides remained strong: when Israel was chosen as the official visiting nation at Turin's International Book Fair in 2008, to mark the 60th anniversary of Israel's creation, in a richly anti-Fascist city where many of those recent Israeli authors had been published, a furious debate ensued with calls for a boycott, countered by defences of free speech and of the pro-peace authors who had been invited.[15]

AMERICA

If the transnational lines of connection between Italian Holocaust culture and Israel worked through hard-edged geopolitical as well as cultural-intellectual channels, the case of American connections is of a more directly cultural nature, although all the more pervasive for that. There is a well-established analysis of the late-20th-century explosion of interest in and memorialisation of the Holocaust that sees not only a quantitative leap in attention but also, qualitatively, a recasting of the Holocaust in American colours.[16] Hollywood-style global media events such as *Holocaust* and *Schindler's List*, the establishment of a large number of American Holocaust memorials and museums, foremost among them the

USHMM on the Mall in Washington DC; the shift of the historiographical debate to a new generation of American scholars, as shown by the *cause
célèbre* and controversy surrounding Daniel Goldhagen's *Hitler's Willing
Executioners*;[17] American-led efforts from the 1990s to promote compensa-
tion claims by Holocaust victims and their descendants from banks and
insurance institutions in Europe (and, in the background, the political-
military alliance of America and Israel):[18] these and other factors have led
to a critique of a wholesale 'Americanisation' of Holocaust culture. The
supranational culture of the Holocaust has been, according to this conception, a masked version of a very specific single national Holocaust culture, after all—from America. And although the strongest evidence of this
Americanisation is to be found in a period starting in the 1990s, it is clear
that a vein of American cultural appropriation and mediation had been
present much earlier also: for example, the fame of Anne Frank's *Diary*,
whilst spread significantly through its translation into many languages and
adoption as a text for school students in many nations, was first established in mass public consciousness through its sweetened Broadway stage
and then Hollywood film adaptations of, respectively, 1955 and 1959.

As this chapter argues, however, the national and supranational both
need to be tempered by an acknowledgement of dynamic, local, transnational exchanges that lie beneath and between them. Blanket assumptions about a wholesale and long-term Americanisation of Holocaust
culture do not fully account for instances of fluid contact and exchange
between Italy and America working through two-way processes of appropriation and misappropriation, influence and receptivity.

We can look at three examples of Italian Holocaust work that entered
global Holocaust culture by way of an initial encounter with America, followed by some form of adjusted reentry into the Italian cultural field, in
a three-stage process which is strongly characteristic of the transnational
dynamic under scrutiny here: Wertmüller's *Seven Beauties* (1975); the work
of Primo Levi in the 1980s; and the two key Italian Holocaust films of the
1990s, Rosi's *The Truce* and Benigni's *Life Is Beautiful* (both 1997).

Seven Beauties, already discussed for its remarkable conflation of Italian
stereotypes and Holocaust grotesquerie in Chapter 8, occupies an important niche in the development of the debate in American intellectual culture on Holocaust representation, mass culture and the human instinct
for cruelty and survival. It achieved this in part because of the aura of
the European art movie that accompanied it at the time of its release
in America in 1976. This aura, and the film's Holocaust subject matter,

which was in the process of becoming central to American cultural and intellectual life, combined to lead to its exceptional nomination for four Oscars, including the first-ever nomination of a woman as Best Director for Wertmüller. But, in a pattern closely echoed in American responses to Benigni's film in the late 1990s, a polemical critical debate emerged around the film and about the acceptability of its comic-grotesque mode of representing the concentration camps. In an essay in the *New Yorker*, psychoanalyst, public intellectual and (early) concentration camp inmate Bruno Bettelheim expressed discomfort with the film as an account of the psychological mechanism of adaptation and survival that he witnessed in Buchenwald.[19] Against Bettelheim, Terence Des Pres—also an object of Bettelheim's critique for his book *The Survivor*—defended the function of comedy and the grotesque in the film, setting up a debate between modes of sober realism and witness on the one hand, and formal distortion and comic reimagination of the horrors of the camps on the other.[20] The debate over ethics and psychology was shot through also with an ambivalent cultural transaction between the European Holocaust and America, between Wertmüller's product of European art culture, received in America and assessed as 'correct' or 'incorrect' in its mechanisms for portraying the difficulty and complexity of the Holocaust to American audiences in general, and American-Jewish audiences in particular.

A comparable ambivalence is apparent in the case of Primo Levi in America. Starting in the mid-1980s, Levi's reputation in America underwent a remarkable transformation.[21] Following the publication of the English translation of *The Periodic Table* in 1984, endorsed by Saul Bellow as 'a necessary book', Levi's American and subsequently international reputation rocketed.[22] Levi, however, felt distinctly uncomfortable about aspects of his American reception. He felt mischaracterised as a 'Jewish' writer—not, or not necessarily, in a religious sense, but in the cultural-literary sense associated with figures such as Bellow and his generation of American-Jewish writers whose formation and assumptions Levi did not share. It was all the more galling and telling, then, that when *If Not Now, When?* appeared in 1985, he came under attack from voices within a conservative American-Jewish intellectual elite, such as in the journal *Commentary*, for not embracing fully the 'uniqueness' of the Jewish Holocaust, and for having little sensitivity to Eastern European Ashkenazi culture.[23] In a wilful misprision, Levi was Americanised as a certain kind of 'ideal' figure of the survivor, only to be damned then for not living up to the ideal.

The appropriations and misappropriations of Primo Levi in America did not stop with his flurry of literary fame and controversy in 1984–1986. As Bryan Cheyette has compellingly shown, traces of it are found in other awkward cultural 'translations', academic and popular. Cheyette suggests that Levi's positions on the Holocaust have been repeatedly distorted and falsely fixed in certain representations of them in the academic field of Holocaust studies, largely American-dominated, and he shows how a parallel misappropriation was on display in the uses to which his work *The Truce* was put in Francesco Rosi's film, with John Turturro as the Levi character, a project driven by Rosi, with his own very marked past as an Italian political filmmaker, but also by the film's international production values and the image of Turturro, its Italian-American character actor star. Cheyette criticises both the image of Levi as a character in the film and the insertion of a gesture of forgiveness and redemption offered to a Nazi soldier in one invented scene in Munich.[24]

The faultlines of these transnational misappropriations are interestingly consistent and yet confused: they concern the morally and historiographically loaded distinction between conceptions of the Holocaust as a Jewish phenomenon or as a universal human phenomenon (and the related question of its uniqueness or otherwise). The Levi we saw in Chapter 5—universalist, Resistance-shaped, moral in the 'Actionist' sense, in his understanding of the Holocaust—clashed in America with a Jewish-led conception of the Holocaust and its millennial significance and uniqueness. Levi was, however, genuinely lionised in America and remains a major figure of influence and a constant point of reference in intellectual discourse on the Holocaust, as well as a prominent literary figure.

When the transnational lines were reversed, and the 'Americanised' Levi was reimported—after his death—back into Italy, one key effect was to reinforce a process already under way of reclaiming Levi from his marginalisation in the postwar literary canon. Propelled by a generation of critics in the 1990s led by Marco Belpoliti, Levi was treated with renewed literary seriousness, but not in the terms set by the American response: Levi in Italy was now being reread as a key modern literary voice. At the same time, having been set within the American-Jewish literary frame, others back in Italy were intent on uncovering in Levi a local Jewish dimension to Italian Holocaust culture; thus, to a degree in tension with Belpoliti, critics such as Alberto Cavaglion have built up around Levi and in particular around 'Argon', the first chapter of *The Periodic Table*, a rich Italian-Jewish (not to say Piemontese-Jewish) hinterland, with branches and ramifications back into France, Spain and out to the Risorgimento and the Resistance.[25]

The cases of both Wertmüller and Levi, in their different ways, can be used to situate and explain the high-octane case of transnational exchange between Italy and America represented by Benigni's *Life Is Beautiful*. A dynamic similar to the success of *Seven Beauties* saw *Life Is Beautiful* garner extraordinary success: released in Italy in December 1997, it won prizes and was a major box-office success, fed both by Benigni's considerable fame as a cult comic actor and by the vogue for Holocaust stories of the late 1990s. It was a remarkable critical success also at the 1998 Cannes Film Festival, where it won a Grand Prix de la Jurie. It was released in Europe and the US in late 1998/early 1999, was warmly received and went on to win more than 40 festival and other awards, including the 'Best Jewish Experience' at the Jerusalem Film Festival. Marketed skillfully in the US by its distributors Miramax, it became the most successful subtitled film ever released in America, was nominated for seven Oscars and won three (Best Actor, Best Foreign Film, and Best Original Score). Benigni's extraordinary histrionics at the Oscar ceremony in March 1999 made him front-page news around the world. By October 1999, the film was the most successful Italian film of all time and Colin MacCabe hailed Benigni as 'the supreme European clown of his generation'.[26] Back in Italy, it later broke all records for television audience for a feature film when broadcast on RAI 1 in October 2001. Scheduled against 'Big Brother' on Canale 5, it drew 16 million viewers, or 54 per cent audience share.[27]

Both the film's success and the critical storm it caused ran strongly parallel to the case of *Seven Beauties*. Many were resolutely against the film. In Italy, the leader of the Jewish community, Tullia Zevi, politely wondered whether the film needed to be set anywhere near a concentration camp, since it was more than anything a generic film about family love in hard times, a universal parable about humanity, love and the like.[28] In the US, a number of influential voices came out as viciously hostile: Gerald Peary in the *Boston Phoenix* wrote: 'The Holocaust misrepresentations of *Life Is Beautiful* [are] unforgivably obscene'; Richard Schickel in *Time* in a piece entitled 'Fascist Fable' opined: 'Sentimentality is a kind of fascism too, robbing us of judgment and moral acuity'; David Denby in the *New Yorker* wrote that the film was 'a benign form of Holocaust denial' and alongside his review, Art Spiegelman, author of *Maus*, the widely admired graphic novel about his own father's travails as a Holocaust victim and survivor, drew a vicious whole-page cartoon of a concentration-camp inmate holding an Oscar statue, with the caption taken from the Miramax publicity campaign for the Oscars, 'Be part of history and of the most successful foreign film of all time'.[29]

As with Levi and Wertmüller, although with distinct differences in taste and cultural register,[30] Benigni was caught up in a complex and often contradictory transnational cultural operation: both lionised and damned in his American reception, appropriated and admired for his Europeanness, and also distorted into an American idiom of sentimental storytelling and celebrity, merged with a form of what Gillian Rose has called 'Holocaust piety';[31] and then criticised by an intellectual elite for this transformation, especially the gatekeepers of 'serious' Holocaust knowledge in America.

EUROPE

In talking about *Seven Beauties* and its perception as a cultural phenomenon in America, one factor noted to explain its success and ability to experiment and break taboos was its status as a certain kind of *European* art house film characteristic of the 1960s and 1970s, in particular in its themes, disjointed modes and explicit sexuality. How Italian Holocaust culture taps into and at times merges into a general European Holocaust culture is another key transnational interaction that is worth considering. A European picture of the Holocaust—embracing both a sense of the Holocaust as a moment of European history and its memorialisation as a unified Europe-wide response—is far more than the sum of a series of binary relations between Italy and other single European states (although there would be much to say about, for example, specifically Italian-German or Italian-French transnational lines of Holocaust response). Insofar as this European dimension frequently spills over into myth and metaphor, it echoes in several respects the field discussed in Chapter 7, but also emerges as a more concrete element in the civic and institutional politics of the European Union.

At a low level, there is a transnational, European element identifiable in certain individual career trajectories, in conditions of cultural production and collaboration, and in political-historical self-positioning. A good example of this would be the film career of Gillo Pontecorvo, whose first feature, *Kapò*, marked an important threshold as one of the first in a wave of films in Western Europe to directly represent and narrativise the Jewish genocide.[32] *Kapò* was inspired variously by Pontecorvo and his collaborator Franco Solinas's reading of Primo Levi, by the model of Rossellinian neorealism, as well as by the family history of Pontecorvo, who had been forced into exile in Paris for his Jewish background and had subsequently taken part in the Resistance.[33] *Kapò* was an Italian-French co-production filmed in Yugoslavia, with the on-set consultancy of Edith Bruck, the Italianised Hungarian survivor-writer.[34] It drew on an international cast, largely European, with (and this looks forward to John Turturro's role in *The Truce*) an American star in Susan Strasberg. She was already a key figure in the international culture of Holocaust, having played Anne Frank in the Broadway adaptation of the diary; here, she plays a not-dissimilar role as the piano-playing teenage protagonist Edith. The setting for the initial scenes in the film is in France, not Italy, and the narrative climax of the rebellion against the SS in the camp is led by Russians. For practical (i.e., production), intellectual and historical reasons, then, this film picks up on the transnational nature of the history of deportation, and it paints a generalisable 'European' account of the Holocaust. Pontecorvo made few films over the following 20 years, but it is telling that his four principal features of this period built on the European and transnational dimension of *Kapò*, fitting the film and the Holocaust it pictures into what we might call, borrowing a term from Michael Rothberg, a 'multidirectional' cluster of topics, in which European histories of politics, power, persecution and violent resistance in their many forms are probed, explored and explained.[35] The Holocaust of *Kapò* was followed by the colonial and anticolonial struggle of French Algeria in *Battle of Algiers* (1966), British colonial exploitation of slaves in a Portuguese Caribbean island in *Burn!* or *Queimada* (1969) and terrorism under Franco in *Ogro* (1979). The link is not necessarily visible through specific stylistic or narrative modes, but rather through the auteurist project carried out by Pontecorvo, a form of urgent, transnational political engagement through film. In this perspective, the Holocaust fits as a founding stage in the high ideology of Europe's confrontation with its own history.

Other dimensions of Europeanness as a lens through which the Holocaust can be understood and transmitted are strongly present in the culture of the 21st century, with long hindsight suggesting a macroscopic view of 20th-century history. A European dimension is powerfully present, for example, in the 2006 documentary film *Levi's Journey*, directed by Davide Ferrario and written by Levi critic and cultural commentator Marco Belpoliti.[36] What interests us here is not so much another instance of Levi's filtering influence, but rather the geographical and historical optic the film's operation creates. The film retraces the steps and the map

of Levi's long return journey from Auschwitz to Turin in 1945, narrated
in *The Truce*. In doing so in 2005 Europe, however, it traverses the extraordinary, part grotesque, part tragic, transformed landscapes—and
cultural memories and amnesias—of post-Soviet Eastern Europe (as well
as, briefly, Austria, Germany and Northern Italy). In other words, Levi's
postwar landscape of primeval chaos and return, a suspended 'truce' in
time and space between genocide and 'normality', becomes a template
for a reading of five decades and more of European history, of the Cold
War as a long suspension in history, of the thaw after the Cold War and
new confusions after 11 September 2001 (the film opens with shots of the
World Trade Center attacks).

On an institutional level, something of the dynamic of *Levi's Journey* is
echoed, finally, in collective European efforts to build an official and coordinated supranational structure for the commemoration of the Holocaust.
The most important instance of this was the Task Force for International
Cooperation on Holocaust Education, Remembrance and Research, ini-
tiated in May 1998, leading to the Stockholm forum and declaration on
Holocaust remembrance of January 2000, an initiative later embraced by
the United Nations from 2005.[37] This European-centred set of high, inter-
governmental initiatives cemented at an institutional level the function of
the Holocaust as a negative founding myth of postwar European identity
and polity, working its way through European culture of the period in
what Leonardo Paggi has called the *Europe-mémoire* of a continental civil
war.[38] But if these structures were, in aspiration at least, formally supranational, how they were worked out at local and national levels was closer
to the more fluid transnational dynamics we are tracing here.

2. Translation

Translation—the literal and metaphorical transposition of words, ideas
and images between different countries, cultures and language areas, as
well as the commercial and cultural translation of foreign books, films and
other artefacts—is a pervasive phenomenon in the web of transnational
transmission of knowledge of the Holocaust in the postwar world. This
section explores three instances of importations into Italy of foreign languages and texts as key moments in the formation of the field of Holocaust culture. Many more instances could be adduced: indeed, many of
the migrations described in the previous section were built on only apparently neutral or invisible translation processes (the dubbed print of *Seven*

Beauties distributed in America; the renderings of Levi into English; the multilingual declarations of the Stockholm forum; and so on). Here we will touch first on a peculiar work of partial translation from the 1950s, then on a characteristic translatorly thread in witness literature and finally on a late-20th-century case of lexical borrowing.

MENEGHELLO'S 'TRANSLATION'

As we saw in Chapter 4, the early-to-mid-1950s, although by most accounts a period of 'silence' when the Holocaust was hardly written about and largely unacknowledged, saw several important exceptions to this rule. The years 1954–55 saw the founding of CDEC; Levi's contract with Einaudi; the Carpi exhibition, translations of Anne Frank, Robert Antelme, Lord Russell of Liverpool and Leon Poliakov; influential testimonies in Italian by Piero Caleffi; collective initiatives such as ANED's book *Forgetting Is Wrong* and its sponsoring of the first Italian national monument on a concentration camp site, at Mauthausen again, designed by Mario Labò and Mirko Basaldella.[39] Even before 1954–55, pioneering literary work was being done in Giorgio Bassani's first narratives of Fascist and postwar Jewish Ferrara, such as 'A Plaque in via Mazzini', the extraordinary story of Geo Josz, a survivor of Buchenwald, on his return to Ferrara, first published in 1953.[40]

Also in 1953 came a rather unusual case in the field of historiography, with striking resonance for the question of translation: Luigi Meneghello's three long articles for the Olivetti journal *Comunità*,[41] which set out almost for the first time in Italian—at least since the improvised, 'hot' accounts of the months immediately following the war—a synthesis of the history of the Final Solution.[42]

Meneghello had been working in Reading, UK, since the late 1940s and his contributions to *Comunità*, under the pseudonym Ugo Varnai, came in the form of reviews of work on politics, history and literature coming out in English. He shared *Comunità*'s wider interests in culture, liberal and socialist philosophy and politics, and a moral attention to history. For this piece of work, Meneghello drew extensively on the key findings of the first major history of the genocide to appear in English, and the second major work in Europe following Poliakov's: Gerald Reitlinger's *The Final Solution*.[43] Meneghello/Varnai's articles were an unusual mix of review, summary, selection, translation and reorganisation, to which we might also add visual elaboration, since Meneghello himself sourced from UK press and photographic libraries a series of maps and powerful photographic images to accompany the articles.[44]

The linguistic transmission from English to Italian—by way of Meneghello, living and working in Reading—is itself an important early instance of translation of historiography and the spread of awareness of the Holocaust, often products of accident and circumstance, of transnational accessibility. The availability of both Reitlinger's book in English and of the apparatus of imagery (in correspondence with Meneghello, *Comunità* editor Renzo Zorzi laments that it is nearly impossible to find such images for use in Italy itself),[45] and its malleable adaptation by Meneghello in what is by no means a simple act of translation, speaks volumes about the complexity of such transnational encounters. For Meneghello, this was also self-consciously an act of serious and didactic popularisation, in contrast to the vulgarisations he saw abroad in the contemporary Italian media: and this question of register, of how translation from one language to another is also, by accident or design, a shift in cultural pitch, is a constant dynamic in translation transmissions, as we saw in the case of exported film above. Thus, in describing to Zorzi his plans for his review column in general, Meneghello sees his task in sending news from England as one of a 'middle-brow' service, between scholarship and sensationalism:

> why not aim for popular history [*divulgazione storica*] [...] written with precision and clarity, with no claim to specialist knowledge but also with no concessions to the weakness of certain sectors of the public [...] We should be talking to the averagely educated reader, who does not know a great deal about Italian history but who is not catered for by either specialist reviews or sensationalist magazines' [letter of 28 December 1952].[46]

Further webs of transmission are also in evidence in Meneghello's *Comunità* 'translations': Reitlinger's brief account of the Italian role within the Final Solution, to which Meneghello understandably pays particular attention, is based to a significant degree on Massimo Adolfo Vitale's heroic postwar work of gathering material and evidence within the Jewish community and survivor groups. Vitale's work fed into, as we have seen, the foundation of CDEC and much of the field of archival knowledge of the Holocaust within Italy. There is a circular transmission here: from Vitale to Reitlinger to Meneghello. Further, Reitlinger cites Vitale from sources found in the Paris CDJC, the historic archive founded by Poliakov and others. In fact, *Comunità*'s publishing arm, Edizioni di Comunità, would publish in 1956 a translation of Poliakov's and CDJC's pioneering 1946 work on Jews in Italian-occupied France.[47] Reitlinger also mentions Levi's *If This Is a Man* as a source on two minor points of information on camp conditions; and Meneghello notes (in a letter of 8 February 1954) that he too read Levi, in the 1947 edition of the book. The web of cultural transmission and translation, then, is wide and multilingual, moving between Italian, French and English, at various phases of genesis, publication and translation/summary. And the chain would continue into the 1960s and then the 1990s, first with the publication of a full translation of Reitlinger into Italian by Il Saggiatore in 1962;[48] and finally with the recuperation and republication in book form by Il Mulino in 1994—now that the Shoah had moved to centre stage in the wider culture and Meneghello had become a major Italian novelist in his own right—of the three *Comunità* articles, under the title *Promemoria*.[49]

SELF-TRANSLATION. SECOND LANGUAGES

One of the essential realities, metaphors and linguistic topoi of the aftermath of the Second World War, with the forlorn figure of the Holocaust survivor amongst its darkest incarnations, is the figure of the DP, the displaced person, the refugee wandering homeless or directionless for months or even years around a devastated Europe. For some rare cases (such as Primo Levi's), this was a wandering home; but for many, survival brought with it a permanent sense of displacement, exile and alienation, of the impossibility of return to a 'before'. Emigration, exile or escape—to North or South America, to Israel, from Eastern Europe to Western Europe and so on—forced many survivors, great survivor-writers among them, to reinvent themselves and write after the war in foreign lands and in foreign tongues. Thus, Elie Wiesel began writing in Argentina in one of his native languages, Yiddish, but acquired his essential voice as a writer in French and then as a public figure and writer in America. More devastating and paradoxical were the cases of Jean Améry and Paul Celan, survivors who lost their homes and any possibility of return, but who continued to write in their native German in such a way that acknowledged that their language was no longer their own: they were exiled from and yet bound to their mother tongue. In Celan's case in particular, what this distortion did to his German-language poetry was at the core of his achievement as a poet of the Holocaust (and for both, perhaps, this impossible fate was a prelude to suicide).

Italian Holocaust writing—from historiography to testimony to narrative fiction—has had, as the case of Levi illustrates, a strongly home-bound
dimension. A defining pattern of explanation and storytelling about the
Italian-Jewish experience of arrest and deportation sees rooted local identity and family history, shockingly destroyed by the sudden persecutions of
the Racial Laws and later Nazi occupation, followed, for the survivors at
least, by fragile reentry and reconstruction. Family narratives of this kind
have been prevalent in recent, late or recovered testimonies such as Piera
Sonnino's *This Has Been* and Aldo Zargani's *For Solo Violin.*[50] But there is
a fascinating alternative thread of *Italian* Holocaust literature written by
nonnative speakers of Italian, by writers thrown into exile by the Final Solution or other events, who have adopted Italian and found a voice within
this new language to narrate the Holocaust or their lost homes. These second-language testimonies have a particular role within the national field of
Holocaust writing, allowing the Italian field to tap directly into the central
European cultural ground where the Holocaust was centred, and in doing
so to intermingle distant and local narrative threads.[51]

Four cases of second-language, 'self-translating' Holocaust writers operating in Italian give a sense of the breadth of life histories and modes
of writing the category contains, and the strength of its presence even
within a simultaneously inward-looking and translation-reliant cultural
field such as Italy's.

First, there is the case of an Italianised survivor-historian: Alberto
Nirenstein, born Aron Nirenstajn in Baranow in Poland in 1915, moved
to Palestine in 1936. There, in 1944, he joined the Jewish Brigade, landing
with the Allies at Salerno and fighting up the Italian peninsula. In Florence, Nirenstein met and later married Wanda Lattes, a Florentine-Jewish
woman who fought for the Justice and Freedom Resistance group, and
they settled in Florence after the war. He returned to Stalinist Poland in
the early 1950s, to gather material for a history of the Warsaw and other
Polish ghettoes, only to be de facto imprisoned there for four years, as the
authorities would not let him return to Italy. The work that eventually
resulted was one of the first to depict in full detail, and in Italian, the
horrors and heroism of that legendary moment within the larger history
of the Holocaust, and one of the first to use recovered ghetto diaries,
which Nirenstein had seen first-hand. It was published by Einaudi as *Remember What Amalek Did to You* by 'Alberto Nirenstajn' in 1958, and it
is one of the key entries in the flurry of publications around that year on
the Holocaust. Symptomatic of the moment in which he was writing,

Nirenstein was, however, not subsequently integrated into the Italian historiographical or intellectual field but remained an admired, if marginal figure: nevertheless, his work of self-translation (writing in Italian) and his own documentary work (publishing in Italian the Yiddish documents of the ghetto Resistance) was of enormous cultural significance.

The second translingual figure, Edith Bruck, also moved between Eastern Europe, Palestine/Israel and Italy, but with a very different chronology and set of experiences. And unlike Nirenstein, Bruck has over several decades become a vitally important public figure of the survivor-writer in Italy, perhaps second only to Levi in stature. She was born in a small village in Hungary in 1932. Deported to Auschwitz with other family members in the vast Hungarian round-ups of 1944, she survived to return to Hungary but shortly thereafter moved to Israel, where she settled uncomfortably until, almost by accident, in 1954, she came to Italy on a journey intended to reach Argentina. She adopted Italy as, again, a never-quite-settled new home. She began writing—or rather reconstructing and translating into her new language, Italian, from a draft she had lost back in the 1940s—a first work of testimony, published in 1959 as *Who Loves You Like This*. Over the following 50 years and more, Bruck has constructed an extensive body of narrative, poetry and testimonial writing, always haunted by the trauma of deportation, but also by the alienations of exile in language and the tensions inherent in the very role of the 'witness'. Her Italian, initially rough and newly learned, retained as it became more refined its capacity for raw, acidic bluntness: Italian and Italy are marked as somehow 'outside' the geography of her traumatic past, in some ways a refuge, but also—as language—shot through with risk and violence and human fracture.[52]

This haunting function of past worlds and past languages is a consistent feature of translingual Holocaust writing. Another Hungarian-Jewish writer, who migrated to Italy in the 1950s—without direct experience of the camps, his exile instead a result of the events in Budapest in 1956—is Giorgio Pressburger (coupled in his first books with his twin brother Nicola). The Pressburgers' early work in *Stories of the Eighth District*[53] was set in the Jewish district of Budapest of their childhood, evoking in highly textured and also comic style a world destroyed by the deportations of up to a million Hungarian Jews during 1944. Several of Giorgio Pressburger's later works have addressed directly the thematics of Holocaust writing, of multilingualism and migration and the confusions of identity that result, and of memory: the most recent example came in his extraordinary reworking of Dante, *In the Dark Kingdom*, in which the author is guided by Freud in a journey through the horrors of the 20th century, with the Shoah at its heart.[54] Pressburger is also closely connected, through his work as translator, theatre director and Italian cultural ambassador to Hungary, to transcultural connections between Italian and Hungary and to Mitteleuropean Jewish literary traditions in general. This activity has included translating and promoting the work of Imre Kertesz, the Nobel-prizewinning Hungarian Holocaust survivor-writer; and as in Kertesz's work, and inevitably given his biography, Pressburger's Holocaust evocations frequently compete for attention with the other totalitarian experience of his era, Soviet-bloc Communism.

Finally, at one or more generations' remove from Nirenstein, Bruck or Pressburger, the late-20th-century phenomenon of immigration to Italy has led to often halting steps towards multiculturalism, including a minor explosion of translingual literature; of immigrants writing about immigration and being Italian (and being rejected as such), in Italian. Although often conceptualised through colonial and postcolonial categories, this new wave has thrown into relief earlier examples of Holocaust translingual writing; and, on occasion, it has thrown up new instances of present-day, second-generation translingualism. Examples include Helga Schneider, a German-born writer several of whose books concern her deeply troubled relationship with her estranged mother, a concentration camp guard and into old age a convinced Nazi fanatic.[55] Like Pressburger, however, Schneider was born in the 1930s. To find a writer born in the 1960s who has tackled in Italian, and directly through the problematic of language (first-, second- and third- languages) the profound fractures visited upon the children of survivors—a deep vein of late-century Holocaust writing across many languages—we can turn to Helena Janeczek. Her 1997 narrative, *Lessons of Darkness*, with its circular and spiralling structure, homes in on the site of Auschwitz and the dark, unarticulated heart of her mother's experience of it; the self-conscious construction touches on Polish (a language she never acquired), German (her mother's language and that of the Nazis) and Italian (her chosen medium, and as with Bruck, only apparently detached and pacific).[56]

NONTRANSLATION. 'SHOAH'

Language webs and transnational transmission processes underpin the archival sourcing, publication and translation of single works of historiography (Meneghello); they erupt alongside the motifs of trauma in writers alienated from their own native languages as they struggle to tell their stories (Nirenstein, Bruck and others). Language questions also directly shape conceptions of the Holocaust simply through the movement across cultural and linguistic borders of individual words to name what happened to Europe's Jews and other ethnic groupings under the Nazis. As extant, indigenous words struggle to capture the event, new terms, different kinds of words seem at times to fit the bill better: place names and generic nouns, neologisms and euphemisms, in many instances translated or transliterated from foreign languages. The history of naming the genocide is an extraordinarily complicated and important one. One of the principal historians of the phenomenon, Anna-Vera Sullam Calimani, has traced the emergence of and tensions amongst a panoply of possible terms—Churban, Shoah, the catastrophe or disaster, the *univers concentrationnaire*, deportation, the Lager, genocide, Final Solution, Auschwitz, and Holocaust itself—each with its own origins, etymologies, cultural baggage and histories of usage.[57] The case I wish to concentrate on here— for its particular impact in Italy since the 1990s, and for its illustration of a process of what we might call *nontranslation*, that is the importation and assimilation of foreign terms *qua* foreign—is the case of the Hebrew word *Shoah* (שואה).

A standard word for 'catastrophe' or 'disaster', derived like most modern Hebrew from Biblical Hebrew—but without the sacrificial connotations many have discerned in the Biblical Greek term 'Holocaust'—'Shoah' was in usage in Israel in official documents and public discussion already in the mid-1940s.[58] In the wake of Claude Lanzmann's epoch-making 1985 documentary *Shoah* (starting with its title, a riposte to NBC's television *Holocaust*), the word took on new force as the name of choice for those closest to the events of the Holocaust, the gatekeepers. Steven Spielberg, whose *Schindler's List was* in so many respects the heir to *Holocaust*, nevertheless went on to fund with the film's profits the video testimony project tellingly named the Survivors of the *Shoah* Visual History Foundation (emphasis added). And yet, in English as in most other languages, the term 'Holocaust' remains overwhelmingly dominant.

The Italian case is a striking exception. In Italy, starting in the very late 1990s, 'Shoah' has equalled and overtaken 'Olocausto', becoming widely adopted in the national press as well as in specialist scholarship, as the 'correct', recognised and even official term for the Nazi genocide of the Jews. 'Shoah' was the term was used in the 2000 legislation to establish the 'Day of Memory', where the core aim is 'to remember the *Shoah* (extermination of the Jewish people)'.[59] The term 'Olocausto' is not used. Similarly, in the law to establish a national Holocaust museum in Italy in 2003, as we saw in Chapter 2, the project is named the 'National Museum of the Shoah'. In the print media, the evidence is even stronger: a search of the daily newspaper *La repubblica*'s online archive from 1985 to 2010 shows a dramatic dual shift in the incidence of the two terms. 'Olocausto' grows in usage rapidly, from approximately 50 per year in the late 1980s to anywhere between 200 and 400 per year from 2000 onwards, confirming a general growth in attention. However, even more striking is the parabola of 'Shoah', which moves from near-zero annual uses as late as 1996 (more than 10 years after Lanzmann's film) to around 200–350 per year after 2005, at similar levels to 'Olocausto'. Most telling of all, 'Shoah' actually overtakes 'Olocausto' in 2007, and this pattern is repeated in every subsequent year.

The lexical borrowing of 'Shoah' pulls Italian conceptions of the Holocaust in at least four directions at once. First it reclaims and restates—following decades of early postwar assimilation of the Holocaust to deportation experiences generally, and from there to (often blurred) national narratives of the Resistance or the military or civilian deportees—the Jewish character and substance of the Holocaust. We noted earlier a remarkable wave of cultural philosemitism in Italian culture, starting in the 1980s, and borrowing the Hebrew 'Shoah' undoubtedly feeds into this strain of cultural attention. It also, conversely, risks carving out of the picture other genocides: it is hard to claim that the Rom, Sinti, homosexual, Slav and other victims of Nazi purging—or indeed of Fascist racial violence—are suitably represented by the Hebrew term.

Aside from the Jewish quality imported along with the word, there is also the general fact of its foreignness. A foreign word (although, usefully, 'Shoah' is not difficult to pronounce in Italian) marks something strange, requiring translation and explanation. There is a form of border anxiety at work here: a new word is needed to capture and define something that is perhaps too risky or too uncertain to be easily assimilated. That this should occur in the 1990s, during a period of widespread renewed uncertainly about historical categories and collective memories—a period of divided memory, of collapsed ideology and of frayed or fragmented identity—is no coincidence. Further, a Hebrew word is also a non-Italian word, implying that the genocide was not part of Italian history and can be placidly respected as a catastrophe that was not 'ours'. This 'otherness' was also, in different ways, connoted by the earlier spread of terms such as Lager or Auschwitz, German terms that were, among other things, not

Italian. If to an extent this was fed by a recognisable pattern of national disavowal—the Holocaust as a terrible external event visited upon Italy's Jews, or resisted by Italy's Jews and their 'decent' Italian neighbours— then, paradoxically, the growth in the use of 'Shoah' coincided also with an opposite tendency, to put Italian complicity for the first time at the heart of the Holocaust and the Holocaust at the heart of national narratives of Fascism and the war. These inversions and paradoxical associations—the Shoah as, yes, a specifically Jewish event, but with and through that, as an Italian event also—were best captured in Furio Colombo's emblematic slogan in his campaign for an official Italian Holocaust memorial day: 'the Shoah is, among other things, an Italian crime'.[60] Colombo's point was that there were specific, historical Italian victims and perpetrators of this 'crime', that Jewish history and Italian history intersected, tragically. Colombo's relabelling was a double process, of tightening moral and historical specificity (the Hebrew 'Shoah'), and then recalibrating at the local level to record the national inflection the term and the events took, the Shoah as (also) Italian.

In a comparable manner, the reinsertion of the Holocaust into Resistance historiography, and the recalibration of both in the process, is also facilitated by its distillation out into a separate, foreign term. Alberto Cavaglion, for instance, in his book *The Resistance Explained to My Daughter*, pays careful attention to the Shoah as a fully integral part of his synthesis and explanation of the history and legacy of Resistance.[61]

A similar pattern of association and inversion is discernible in the juxtaposition of 'Shoah' to terms for other genocides and other catastrophic histories. In a period of globalised, mestizo language and culture such as characterised the late 20th century, 'Shoah' takes its place alongside a panoply of other terms in a translingual lexical spectrum of extreme historical events, intermingling with Rwandan tribal massacres, ethnic cleansing, killing fields, desaparecidos, the Gulag, the Ukrainian Holodomor, Armenia.

There is, finally, in the use of 'Shoah' a new inflection to the universal dimension of the Holocaust, one attuned especially to forms of piety or liturgy. Like the Latin mass of the pre-Vatican II Church or Hebrew synagogue prayer outside Israel, foreignness of a certain kind often brings with it a sense of ritual, an aura of piety and sacredness. This can be understood both metaphorically—since many have discerned in the memorialisation of the Holocaust a form of new, transnational civic religion—and indeed literally. One key influence on or symptom of the adoption of the term 'Shoah', in Italy as elsewhere, has been its use in a series of papal pronouncements, especially during the Papacy of John Paul II (1978–2005), on the Holocaust, on the role of Pius XII, and on Church relations with the Jews. Of pivotal importance was the 1998 document *We Remember* (subtitled *A Reflection on the Shoah*), produced by the Catholic Commission for Religious Relations with the Jews, under the Pope's auspices.[62] The document significantly uses the term 'Shoah' throughout and contains key statements of reconciliation and acknowledgement of the gravity of the Holocaust. In a letter prefacing *We Remember*, John Paul II stated 'the Shoah remains an indelible stain on the history of the century'. Both the assertion and the term used were deeply significant.

3. Italy at Auschwitz: Two Memorials

The final thread in the elaborate web of transnational transmission of Holocaust culture that we will explore leads from Italy to the site of what has become the central locus of Holocaust history, collective knowledge and imagination: Auschwitz. The site, museums and monuments at Auschwitz (especially Auschwitz I and II) have a long and unsettling history, which has caused complex tensions and controversies, within Poland and across a large number of other nations and bodies, including flashes of high controversy involving the Vatican (e.g. on the Carmelite convent and cross on the site; or the canonisation of Maximilian Kolbe and Edith Stein).[63] The opening up and restructuring of the camp after 1989 led to renewed elaboration on site of the history of what happened there, with greater attention paid to its Jewish dimension, which had often been neglected during the Warsaw Pact era; but it has also led to the problematic growth in 'Holocaust tourism', here as in other former camps and ghettoes. Within this fraught history, a great deal of intense work of memorialisation and mourning has been carried out, tied to individuals, groups and nations.

Italy's own presence on the site of Auschwitz has had its particular, contingent and difficult history. We can touch on some of its complexities by looking at two specific memorial projects carried out there, quite distinct in origin and purpose, both with strong Italian connections: the international monument to the victims of Auschwitz (1967) and the Italian national memorial pavilion at Auschwitz (1980).

The International Auschwitz Committee (IAC) was formed in 1952, by an internationalist group of mainly Jewish survivors.[64] In 1957, the committee launched a competition to design an official monument to be built at Auschwitz II (Birkenau), where the railway tracks brought victims from all over occupied Europe. Each national member of the IAC set up its own sponsoring group, to raise interest and money by subscription, and was represented on the international committee by prestigious cultural figures including Niels Bohr (Denmark), Pablo Casals (Spain), Dmitri Shostakovich (USSR), François Mauriac (France), and Carlo Levi (Italy). Sculptor Henry Moore presided over the jury, made up of architects, artists, art critics and IAC members. The jury met first at Auschwitz in April 1958, then in Paris later the same year, and subsequently in Rome in 1959. In all 462 designs were submitted, by 685 architects and artists, from 36 countries, in widely varying styles of both sculpture and architecture. Seven were selected for a second stage of review; and subsequently, the three most successful were commissioned, but in a sign of the jury's intense aesthetic and cultural-political challenges, the three groups were invited to revise their work, preferably in collaboration with each other, to come up with one or more final designs. Moore lamented in a public statement at the Paris meeting the near impossibility of creating a

> work of art that can express the emotions engendered by Auschwitz [...]
> a very great sculptor—a new Michelangelo or a new Rodin—might have
> achieved this. The odds against such a design turning up among the many
> maquettes submitted were always enormous. And none did.[65]

The three teams presented four alternative composite projects, using adapted parts of each of the three earlier 'winning' designs. The first of these joint designs was endorsed at the Rome meeting, although with reservations. Several more years of awkward negotiations ensued, with clashes of sensibilities and of personalities (the IAC and the Polish authorities both rejected the jury's final recommended project in 1961), conflict over cost and on political grounds, as the Polish government became ever more closely involved, leading to further revisions and a partial reopening of the competition (although only amongst previously selected winners), further scaling down, reworking and sudden changes, until literally hours before the final unveiling of the monument in 1967. The ceremony took place on 16 May, before a crowd of 200,000, with Polish officials, ex-prisoners and visiting dignitaries from Israel, East Germany and elsewhere (including the Italian foreign minister Amintore Fanfani).

This sketch of the elaborate story of the construction of one of Europe's major monuments to the Holocaust would be of only marginal interest here, were it not for the singular fact that, of the seven projects selected for the second stage in 1958–59, three were by Italian groups (two from Rome, one from Trieste), along with three Polish groups and one West German; and of the three finalists, two were Italian (the two Rome-based groups). The six Italian architects and artists involved in this final competition phase were young and relatively unknown, itself a significant indicator of growing interest beyond first-hand survivors in the memorialisation of the Holocaust, as well as of a varied vitality and international prestige in Italian architecture and design.[66] The first Rome group was made up of the Spanish architect Julio Lafuente and the sculptor brothers Andrea and Pietro Cascella.[67] This group's key contribution was the design of 23 sculptural blocks, in the form of train wagons, bound to each other with sharply sculpted metal hooks, with increasingly abstracted geometry in each stage of revision of the project. The blocks represented the 23 nationalities of the deportees taken from all over Europe to Auschwitz. The other Rome group was four-strong: coordinator Maurizio Vitale, young architects and urban designers Giorgio Simoncini, Tommaso Valle, and sculptor Pericle Fazzini. Their design was for a long path cut into the open ground of the camp terrain, closed in by a wall on one side and by iron railings and the railway track on the other, opening out into a large platform for sculptures and a panorama onto the land in between, including the sites of the crematorium ovens. Key features of this, as of the other Italians and the Polish group (Hansen et al.), were merged in the collaborative final proposal drawn up in 1959. In the long afterlife of the competition, from 1959 to 1967, the principal leaders of the final project were Simoncini and Pietro Cascella, aided by two members of the Hansen group, architect Julien Palka and sculptor Jerzy Jarnuszkiewicz, but multiple elements of the three original groups' work would remain all the way through.[68]

The complex cultural network of collaborations involved in the competition, and the elements that intersected within Italy and the Italian field of Holocaust culture, are well illustrated by events around the May 1959 meeting of the prize jury in Rome, which was followed by an exhibition of the winning projects at the Galleria nazionale d'arte moderna (GNAM, 28 June to 15 July 1959). Moore was unable to attend (or more likely had withdrawn) and the jury was chaired by Italian art historian and critic, as well as former anti-Fascist exile, Lionello Venturi.[69] Also taking a lead role was the Italian architect on the jury, Giuseppe Perugini, who had worked on the monument at the Fosse Ardeatine in Rome in the 1940s. The exhibition showed maquettes and ground plans of the winning designs at various stages of the competition, historical notes and an epigraph from Mauriac, with the original declaration of the project for the monument. The catalogue further documents the local and international associationist network that lay behind the competition.[70] The Italian promotion committee was made up of five high-profile cultural and political figures, each representing a key association:

Piero Caleffi (national president of ANED)
Carlo Levi (member of IAC committee)
Ferruccio Parri (president of INSMLI, the National Institute for the History of Liberation movement in Italy)
Ignazio Silone (president of AILC, the Italian Association for Cultural Freedom)
Elio Toaff (chief rabbi of Rome)

Listed alongside are 11 other members of an Italian Committee for the Monument to the Martyrs of Auschwitz, some present in an individual capacity (e.g. writer Alberto Moravia, Communist senator Umberto Terracini, composer Luigi Dallapiccola), others representing still further national associations, including the Accademia dei Lincei (the highest cultural academy of Italy), Federazione della Stampa (the press association), FIVL (a Catholic partisan grouping), ANFIM, ANPI, UCII, and ANEI. The magazine *L'antifascista* issued a still longer list of the membership of the same committee, adding in a dozen further individuals (among them Primo Levi, Emilio Lussu, Adriano Olivetti, Leo Valiani, Bruno Zevi) and several other associations (such as FIAP, liberal and socialist ex-partisans; ANMIG, an association of war injured; ANPPIA).[71]

The names and acronyms are almost too many to gloss, but the spectrum they represent is worth reflecting on, as it amounts to a snapshot of the state and shape of the field of Holocaust culture, especially official collective Holocaust culture and Holocaust awareness, in late-1950s Italy, meshed in with parallel supranational networks. The sheer number and range of organisations embracing the cause of the Holocaust is eloquent evidence of at least a superficial acknowledgement of the major importance of the Holocaust, and of Auschwitz as its central symbol. We should also note the high profile of the particular writers, artists and intellectuals drawn to the cause: Carlo Levi, Silone and Moravia were nationally and internationally renowned figures of the time; Ferruccio Parri not only was an ex-partisan leader but had also been the first postwar prime minister of Italy. This is, then, a prestigious gathering; but it is not entirely neutrally so. Coalescing around and claiming ownership of the Holocaust in Italy, promoting this heavily Italian-dominated international architectural project, is an anti-Fascist coalition of intellectuals, politicians and Resistance groupings, with a political ecumenism leaning largely towards the non-Communist left. Caleffi, Levi, Parri, Silone and Toaff all fought in the Resistance, but none as Communists: indeed ex-Communist Silone's AILC, a heterodox grouping co-founded with Nicola Chiaromonte in 1956, was sponsored by the international Congress for Cultural Freedom, later revealed to be secretly funded by the CIA as part of a cultural Cold War operation to counter Communist fellow-travellers amongst European intellectuals.[72] There is, further, a numerically minor but crucial presence of Jewish individuals and organisations. Indeed, the key movers—the two associations coordinating donations—were AILC and UCII.

As noted, money was not raised in sufficient quantities initially to fund the monument's construction. In other words, the penetration of this associationist and elite respect for the Holocaust was not necessarily very deep as yet. Press coverage of the meeting and the exhibition in May–July 1959 was widespread, but most often brief and dutiful, based on GNAM press releases to ANSA, which still felt that the term 'Auschwitz' required some glossing: 'Auschwitz (the sadly notorious Nazi Lager where a great many Jews were massacred)'.[73] The press made frequent reference to Mauriac's portentous words on memory and forgetting; and to a rhetoric that betokens awareness but also a sort of formulaic detachment (e.g. 'an abomination that has no precedent in history [...] the most despicable crime that can be imputed to a people and to a civilization'[74]). To underline the point that this is still early in the broad spread of awareness, one of Primo Levi's very first press articles was a piece on this exhibition, 'Monument at Auschwitz', in which he tentatively sets out some of the questions that will preoccupy him as a public witness for nearly the next three decades.[75]

The respectful but relatively restrained popular and press response to the GNAM Auschwitz exhibition, and the elaborate network of organisations that lay behind it, is in contrast to another exhibition that overlapped with it in Rome, opening in July 1959 at the Palazzo delle Esposizioni. This was the Rome stop of the tour of that same touring exhibition about the camps that had begun in Carpi in 1955. The more than 800 photos in this exhibition, including many of the camp liberation photos that were still relatively new to Italian spectators, and its compelling narrative reconstruction of the Italian deportations, from the Racial Laws to the Nuremberg trials, produced (if the press coverage is to be believed) a much more visceral and powerful response. *Italia domani* reproduced over three broadsheet pages some vivid and horrific images; *Corriere d'informazione* published a compelling joint account of the two exhibitions by Arrigo Levi; and *Patria indipedente* interviewed visitors and even museum guards who were all shocked: 'We were boys back then, they said, but then till now, no-one told us anything about it. Why?'[76] The official, public and transnational cultural-political networks at GNAM need to be set alongside a newer process of popular national cultural awareness emerging for many for the first time at the Palazzo delle Esposizioni, the two coming together to capture the complex layering, interweaving national and transnational dynamics, of public Holocaust culture in 1950s Italy.

THE NATIONAL PAVILION

The Italian national pavilion at Auschwitz was opened on 13 April 1980 in Block 21 of Auschwitz I, with the official title 'Memorial in honour of the Italians who fell in the Nazi extermination camps'. In 1979–80, national pavilions were also opened by Austria, France, Hungary and Holland; 1978 had seen the opening of a section dedicated to 'the suffering and martyrdom of the Jews', and 1979 had also seen the extraordinary event of the newly elected Polish Pope, John Paul II, returning to Poland saying mass at Birkenau in front of a crowd of more than one million. This was a period of fervent activity and reconceptualisation of the Auschwitz site.

The Italian project, planned and sponsored by ANED, had been in gestation since the early 1970s and moving forward with uneven progress through gatherings of key collaborators, contacts with the IAC, UCII, local Jewish communities and civic authorities (at one point, the regional government of Tuscany took a lead), and through negotiation with the authorities at Auschwitz and the Polish and Italian governments.[77] As in the case of the international monument, the network of associations and bureaucratic/diplomatic activity draws a map of the constituencies building an image of Italy's intersections with the Holocaust. Overlaying that network, the aesthetics of the memorial and exhibition was determined by a remarkable cluster of artists commissioned to create the work. The design was guided largely (as so often) by the BBPR studio, and in particular by Lodovico Belgiojoso. The carefully calibrated didactic text for display was drawn up by Primo Levi, as we saw in Chapter 5. For ANED, ex-deportee Gianfranco Maris contributed historical material. Luigi Nono provided a musical score to accompany visitors, giving ANED permission to use his 1966 composition *Remember What They Did to You at Auschwitz* (echoing *Remember What Amalek Did to You*). This remarkable composition was itself a fragment growing out of another key work of postwar transnational Holocaust culture: in 1965, Nono had provided Erwin Piscator with the musical intervals for the Berlin production of Peter Weiss's play *Der Ermittlung* (*The Investigation*), a searing documentary dramatisation in 11 'oratorios' of the 1963–1965 Frankfurt Auschwitz trials. The songs of *Remember What They Did to You at Auschwitz* were composed the following year, drawing on and developing Weiss's text and Nono's music.[78] The overall conception of the Italian pavilion was guided by film director (and husband of Edith Bruck) Nelo Risi. Finally, the Sicilian artist Mario (Pupino) Samonà designed the extraordinary, part-abstract, part-figurative spiral strips that draw the visitor through the pavilion in a dramatic swirl representing the storm of history.

As with the international monument again, there were constant problems both with the Polish authorities and within the organising bodies. But the result was a striking, if little visited and poorly maintained, collective product of Italian Holocaust figuration.

The relative neglect of the site was to contribute to a flurry of public controversy nearly 30 years later, in 2008, when a fierce debate erupted in the press and within associationist and intellectual circles about the fate of this 'official' site of Italian national memorialisation at the central site of the Holocaust. The debate, kick-started by a polemical article by leftist historian Giovanni De Luna, focussed on whether it was possible for a national conception and figuration of the Holocaust forged over the 1970s to stand for the collective 'shape' of contemporary ideas of the Holocaust in the new millennium.[79]

Faced with the decay of the monument and the provision of government funds to restore it, De Luna characterised the pavilion as a tired product of the postwar anti-Fascist paradigm of history and memory, as 'almost incomprehensible for today's visitors', especially young visitors, and as neglectful of the Jewish specificity of the Shoah. He called for a root-and-branch remodelling of the block.[80] Responses ensued from several of the most influential historians of Fascism and the Holocaust in contemporary Italy, notably Michele Sarfatti, Sergio Luzzatto, Ernesto Galli della Loggia, Alberto Cavaglion. Furthermore, a group of young art historians and conservationists, based at a Bergamo contemporary historical institute, set up in collaboration with ANED and others a project to conserve the memorial, as a site of historical and cultural importance in its own right. The young activists objected, in favour of conservation, to De Luna's calls for renewal and contemporary reconfiguration, pointing up complex tensions between the categories of Jewish history and memory, and Italian national or anti-Fascist history and memory. Most fiercely of all, they objected to the idea floated of transporting the entire memorial away from Auschwitz and reconstructing it in Milan. There could hardly be a richer example of a reworking in the present, at this site of transnational conflation and national projection, of the tensions of Italy's collective self-positioning within a culture of Holocaust knowledge in the early 21st century, but with a bridge backwards into the history of that culture going back more than 40 years. The project—including work at the site, conferences and the historical reconstruction of the origin and conception of the memorial—is ongoing.[81]

§10 After Such Knowledge

Most of the chapters of Part II have probed the field of Holocaust culture in postwar Italy in transversal, not strictly chronologically bound, ways. This has been part of a deliberate project to mine deeper seams and less visible patterns of response, in this complex engagement with history, than chronology immediately makes apparent. But the field is also, amongst those other patterns, studded with clusters of cultural work tied to specific moments. In acknowledgement of this, Part II is framed by explorations of two such moments: the embryonic early postwar responses (Chapter 4); and, here in the concluding chapter of the book, the remarkable outpouring of interest and cultural engagement with the Holocaust, in Italy as elsewhere, at the turn of the millennium. This was a period of high-profile, 'post-ideological' transformation of the role and value of the Holocaust in Italian culture, a period saturated with senses of 'after-ness',[1] as witnesses grew old and first-hand memories faded, as the entire postwar era increasingly looked in retrospect like a long epilogue to the Second World War, and as the Holocaust came to be seen as the central event of that war and of the dying century.

The chapter looks first at threshold events towards the end of the 1980s that laid down conditions for this late flowering. It then focusses on two specific dates which saw the most marked concentration of attention: the peak of cultural production around 1997, and the first national Holocaust memorial day in Italy in early 2001.

1. 1986–1989

Three events of quite different order and scale marked the late 1980s as a turning point in responses to the Holocaust in the long postwar era.

April 1986 saw the publication of Levi's *The Drowned and the Saved*, a sort of summa of a lifetime's reflections on the Shoah and destined to become a work of striking influence on subsequent accounts of the genocide, cementing Levi's reputation as one of the most admired of Holocaust witnesses anywhere in the world. A year later, April 1987 saw Levi's death, probably by suicide. Reaction to his death was widespread and intense, and in the years following, his profile and reputation in Italy as both witness and writer grew further still, his death only adding new layers of tragic fascination. The ambivalence of the literary elite in Italy over his qualities as a writer began to fade, and waves of both Italian and foreign writers began to take his work very seriously indeed. The broader 'memory culture' surrounding the Holocaust, which had grown markedly in the 1980s, was able to tap into the aura of a figure such as Levi for the rest of the century and beyond. For example, one of the most vivid new Holocaust memoirs to appear in the 21st century was the posthumously published memoir by Piera Sonnino, sole survivor a family of eight deported together to Auschwitz. The title of her work, *This Has Been*, was drawn directly from the poem-epigraph which opened Levi's *If This Is a Man* ('Meditate that this has been', *Opere* I, p. 3).[2] As one critic has described it, this is a generation who tackled the Holocaust with renewed intensity through the 'indispensable legacy' of Primo Levi.[3]

The year after Levi's death, 1988, saw a series of scholarly, public and state-sponsored initiatives to mark the 50th anniversary of the Fascist anti-Semitic Racial Laws in 1938, which led to a step change in the profile given to, and the quality and quantity of research carried out into, Italian Fascist anti-Semitism and its role in the Holocaust broadly understood.[4] High organs of the state—both houses of Parliament—and of the cultural establishment—the Accademia dei Lincei—partook in the anniversary.[5] There was also an important special issue of the journal *Rassegna mensile di Israel*, edited by CDEC historian Michele Sarfatti.[6] From 1988, historiographical and public attention to specifically Italian racism became both widespread and even, as Alberto Cavaglion suggests acidly, 'fashionable'.[7] This in turn would lead to a series of reversals of guiding assumptions about Fascist racial politics held until that moment: central amongst these would be a series of attempts to 'backdate' the origins of Italian anti-Semitism to some point before 1938, whether to the colonial projects of the 1920s and 1930s, or to earlier longstanding Catholic traditions of anti-Semitism, or to the intellectual anti-Semitisms of Mussolini's youth.[8]

A further significant innovation was the first serious research into and recovery of the sites of the network of Fascist concentration camps for Jews in the south of Italy, which had been almost entirely forgotten until the work of Carlo Spartaco Capogreco on Ferramonti di Tarsia in Calabria.[9] This was a pivotal moment in a process which would reverse the overwhelmingly dominant optic of postwar historiography and the shared sense of Fascist past: instead of a totalitarian regime that happened to graft on an alien anti-Semitism in 1938 from which, according to De Felice, the Italian people instinctively took their distance, Fascism for many—especially on the left or former left, including those hostile to De Felice—came to be seen as captured in its very essence in its anti-Semitic phase, in the Racial Laws. From being a footnote in histories of Fascism, 1938 became a central and defining component. (The later 1990s would see a comparable shift of historiographic attention towards Italian colonialism, increasingly seen as a core component of the totalitarian project.[10])

Finally, and at quite another level of global geopolitics, 1989 saw a dramatic caesura in European and world history, with the fall of the Berlin Wall, the collapse of the regimes of Eastern Europe and the end of the Cold War, bringing with it a sunset of grand ideology, and a period of both optimism and uncertainty unseen since the mid-1940s. Of the vast consequences of this moment of rupture, at least two bore directly upon awareness of the Holocaust. First, 1989 led to the horrific genocidal impulses and images (and the vocabulary of 'ethnic cleansing') from the wars of the former Yugoslavia. Alongside Rwanda, Yugoslavia presented a throwback to an era of genocide, and posed dramatic moral and political dilemmas which all but required a turning back to the Holocaust to gauge the present. Secondly, the opening up of Eastern Europe led to a long-delayed, accelerated and distorted recovery of the sites and memories of the camp networks on the ground in Europe. The histories of post-1989 Eastern European engagements with the Holocaust are far too complex to summarise here; but they had at least one striking consequence for countries such as Italy, in the form of the opening up of Holocaust 'tourism'. School trips to concentration camps, and written and visual accounts of the sites of the horror, become ever more common after 1989, feeding a cultural and pedagogical obsession with the legacy of the Final Solution.

1989 and the end of the Cold War also had rapid and profound political consequences in Italy, almost as convulsive as those behind the Iron Curtain.[11] The Christian Democrat, Communist, Socialist and neo-Fascist parties all collapsed in the early 1990s, laying the ground for new parties, such as the separatist, anti-immigrant Northern League and the politico-mediatic phenomenon of Silvio Berlusconi's FI. The new political settlement of the so-called Second Republic was in part built upon a renegotiation of the shared uses to which the past of Fascism, the war and the Resistance had been put. The anti-Fascist consensus of the post-1940s frayed, opening up a period of what Sergio Luzzatto has called 'post-anti-Fascism'.[12] Deeply divisive accounts appeared of the reprisal killings by Resistance partisans in the postwar months, and of repressed local resentments against the partisans for 'causing' as much as 'resisting' Nazi massacres and reprisals.[13] A sense of distance created a strong climate of moral equivalence between the two sides in what Pavone had labelled the civil war of 1943–1945.[14] The reformed neo-Fascist party AN entered government and acquired steadily more respectability; the young men who fought for Salò went from being anathema to being indulged as naive 'boys of Salò', caught only by chance on the wrong side of history. The controversial 1994 Liberation anniversary celebrations—from the 25 April marches in Milan to a broadcast of the American army *Combat Film* (1944) showing the end of the war and Mussolini's execution[15]—were shot through with these division and polemics. Simultaneously, the unblocking of history and memory brought about by the end of the First Republic also opened up new work on and new audiences for the neglected military deportees and victims of Nazi violence as, for example, in Cefalonia, which was widely discussed and narrated in the 1990s.[16]

In this context, the Holocaust took on an astonishing new role as one of the few remaining loci of apparent moral clarity linking history and the present, a pivotal and ubiquitous point of reference in a period of dramatic cultural and geopolitical flux comparable to that of 1945–1948. As a result, it became a site of competition and appropriation in the cultural and political field. Post-1989, to talk about the Holocaust in Italy and to be seen to be sensitive to it, indeed to orient one's core values around it, for post-anti-Fascists and for post-fascists alike, was all but *de rigueur*.

2. 1997

The years following 1989 saw a remarkable outpouring of cultural material of all kinds on the Holocaust, and on the 'stretched' Italian history of the Holocaust—from Fascist Racial Laws to the Republic of Salò—in particular. As Cavaglion writes:

> There is hardly a single Italian province that has not come up with something since 1988, not a single cultural official in the most isolated of towns of the

> Northwest, Northeast, Centre, South or Islands who hasn't gone out on can-
> dlelit searches for the two or three local Jews, who were first registered and
> then forced into hiding in local backstreets.[17]

Cavaglion's polemical tone aside, he picks up on a key feature of this wave: the attention to single cases, to narratives of local experience in this period of Holocaust culture, one influenced by the 1970s academic trends for oral history, life writing and 'history from below';[18] but also the thrust of popularisation and mediatisation of the Holocaust, fed on stories. An emblematic success was Italian-American journalist Alexander Stille's remarkable 1991 book *Uno su mille*, which told the vivid stories of five very different Jewish families and their lives under Fascism.[19]

The wave reached a peak in the late 1990s, and in the year 1997 in particular, when a series of films, books, Holocaust-related public events, memorials and controversies put the Nazi genocide, racism and anti-Semitism at the centre of public, cultural and political discourse.

Roberto Benigni's extraordinary and scandalously successful film *Life Is Beautiful* premièred in December 1997, as we saw. Earlier in the year at Cannes, Francesco Rosi's long-awaited film of Primo Levi's second book, *The Truce*, was shown to a respectful if mixed response. Rosi's film was tied in also to events marking the 10th anniversary of Levi's death. The conjunction of these two films, both in their way focussed on the specifics of an Italian inflexion to the history and experience of the Holocaust, is of cardinal importance in reading the cultural sensitivities of the moment, not least because together they drew on a wide spectrum of secondary filmic and historical practices, tropes and genres in Italian film culture: popular Italian comedy and genre (Benigni); the 'high' tradition of committed Italian filmmaking (Rosi), linked to adaptation of literary texts and the collaboration of writers and historians with directors (Benigni co-wrote with Vincenzo Cerami and historian Marcello Pezzetti and CDEC; Rosi gained Levi's approval shortly before the latter's death); international funding, distribution and marketing, as well as international co-production and its values (linking to the US, through star John Turturro, but also to Eastern Europe, through filming in the Ukraine), and so on. Further films on Holocaust-related topics would flow after 1997, including *Canone inverso* (dir. Ricky Tognazzi, 2000), *The Sky Falls* (dir. Andrea and Antonio Frazzi, 2000), *Unfair Competition* and *Facing Windows*.[20] Benigni, Rosi and the small wave that followed them also tapped into and were conditioned by the wider concurrent trend for mainstream

Holocaust filmmaking, launched by the extraordinary global phenom—enon of *Schindler's List* (1994) and continued in works such as *Jakob the Liar* (dir. Peter Kassovitz, 1999); *Train de vie* (dir. Radu Mihaileanu, 1998) and *The Pianist* (dir. Roman Polanski, 2002).[21] This wave also included the television adaptation of the story of Giorgio Perlasca of 2002, as we saw in Chapter 8.

Books on the Holocaust proliferated also in and around 1997. Associationist, specialist and serious generalist publishing presses were to the fore. ANED was in a phase of intense activism, running local and national conferences, as well as exhibitions and publications. The highly active Turin section of ANED, for example, organised annual conferences, published in a book series by Franco Angeli in Milan: 11 volumes appeared between 1990 and 2000, with two in 1997, on women's deportation and on ANED's work with Primo Levi, again to mark the 10th anniversary of his death.[22] New space opened up in this period for specifically Jewish Holocaust voices. For example, the specialist Florentine Jewish publishing house La Giuntina, which started operating in 1980,[23] was by the mid-1990s producing around half a dozen of its elegantly designed paperbacks per year of new or republished, Italian or translated, works of Holocaust memory and history. During 1995–1997, this included work by Anders Gunther, Israel Gutman, Piero Iotti, Walter Laqueur, Giacoma Limentani, George Mosse, Alexandre Safran, Elie Wiesel; writing variously on Adolf Eichmann, German Jews, the Warsaw Ghetto, Allied silence, children in the camps, local Jewish communities, Jewish education, and so on. This is striking evidence of a rich, multifaceted field of academic study, personal memoir and serious reflection on the Holocaust in Italy, presented here specifically as a Jewish event, sustaining a small but active publishing enterprise.

The wave of testimonies, already gathering strength in the 1980s,[24] continued in the 1990s and included notable examples of late first testimonies: Zargani's *For Solo Violin* or Elisa Springer (another translingual writer; she was born in Austria), whose *Silence of the Living* appeared in 1997.[25] As with Levi in his later years, other long-serving witness-writers show signs of weariness: Edith Bruck, by now author of an extraordinarily rich body of Holocaust literature, published in 1999 a new reflection on her role as a public survivor of the Holocaust. *Signora Auschwitz* (as a schoolchild renames her in one of her many school visits) evokes the devastating psychological lacerations of playing the role of the witness, forced to relive her trauma daily in front of uncomprehending schoolchildren, but aware that the choice not to bear witness, to forget, is not a real choice. Something of this bind had been there in the problem of language intuited in the very first writings on the Holocaust, but now Bruck is stuck as if in another world, with an audience who has not the slightest cultural or historical sense of what it is she has to say, and what it is that tortures her every time she says it. The pervasive spread of Holocaust talk risks becoming inversely proportionate to any understanding of it.

As the list from La Giuntina indicates, this was also a key moment in the field of exchange with work published outside Italy and now translated into Italian. Several strikingly important books appear in Italian for the first time in the period 1995–1997. A fundamental work of testimony—originating in some sense both from within and without Italy and translated for the first time by a small press in 1997, gaining national and international acclaim after 2005—was *Necropolis*, by Boris Pahor. The author was a Triestine, Slovene-Italian writer and camp-survivor, and his book, a searing revisitation of his Lager experiences, was originally published in Slovenian in 1967. Its Italian publication inevitably engaged with the complex fractures of identity and responsibility at Italy's north-eastern border, which we have seen intersecting with the Holocaust in the troubled history of the Risiera di San Sabba and the memorialisation of the foibe and the postwar exodus and ethnic cleansing at these borders (Chapter 5).[26] In historiography, three crucial English-language works were translated at this time, and their impact was made all the more intense by the close clustering of their Italian editions (they were published in English in 1961, 1992, and 1996 respectively). The first was Raul Hilberg's *The Destruction of the European Jews*,[27] certainly the outstanding lacuna amongst translations of the monumental works of historiography on the Holocaust of the postwar era. The second was Christopher Browning's *Ordinary Men*, which probed the question of how a Nazi police battalion was driven to perform the horrific violent murder demanded of them by the Nazi state.[28] The third was Daniel Goldhagen's *Hitler's Willing Executioners*,[29] in many respects a riposte to Browning's work, and a book which was to cause the most vociferous and fierce debate in America and Europe on the history and historiography of the Holocaust since the *Historikerstreit* of the 1980s.

Two of these three books were published by Einaudi, confirming its long-standing position as the dominant publisher in this area.[30] Another significant translation by Einaudi was Annette Wieviorka's *Auschwitz*

Explained to My Daughter, which signalled the emergence of a new pedagogical rhetoric of synthesis, explanation and reflection, distance combined with empathy; this was a book written as if for children but by no
means only for children. This mode of tackling history marks not only a
generational shift but also a new *faux-naif* ('post-ideological') idiom for
repackaging the moral dilemmas the Holocaust presents, with subtle re-
alignment of assumptions and commonplaces.[31]

Against this background of memoirs and historiography, important
works of Holocaust narrative—both conventional novels and hybrids of
fiction, memoir and research—also clustered around 1997. Already the period from the 1980s to the early 1990s had seen a crescendo of echoes and
figures of the Shoah in literary and popular fiction: a pioneer in this regard
was the sophisticated and baroque, late first novel by the Sicilian Gesualdo
Bufalino, *Plague Sower*.[32] Self-consciously drawing on an array of European
literature, above all Thomas Mann's *Magic Mountain*, Bufalino's story of a
postwar sanatorium, of desire, memory, sickness and suicide, is intensely
dependent on the figure of Marta, revealed over the course of the novel
as a Jewish Lager survivor who had also been a Kapo. In the early 1990s
two bestsellers with Holocaust angles appeared: Susanna Tamaro's *For Solo
Voice*, whose title story is a moving monologue by an ageing Shoah survivor; and Paolo Maurensig's Mitteleuropean story of chess and the Shoah
The Lüneberg Variation.[33]

Jumping forward to 1997 itself, we find a remarkable concentration of
novels drawing on the Shoah: Maurensig's second and almost equally successful novel with Holocaust resonances, *Canone inverso*;[34] Lia Levi's saga
of a Jewish family under Fascism, *All The Days of Your Life*, her fourth
novel following her debut *A Baby and Nothing More* in 1994;[35] Rosetta
Loy's *First Words*, her reflection on and research into the author's childhood memories of Jewish families after the Racial Laws; Eraldo Affinati's
Field of Blood, a chronicle of the young author's walk from Venice to Auschwitz, tracing the ground of deportation, steeped in geography and sense
of place but also, like Loy, in a mass of reading;[36] and Helena Janeczek's
Lessons of Darkness, with its second-generation and second-language
memory and trauma. Conversely, the same period saw several works of
intensely narrativised and vivid historiography, drawing on modes of narrative 'fiction': Alessandro Portelli's *The Order Has Been Carried Out*, or
Carla Forti's *The Case of Pardo Roques*, about the murder of a Jewish dig-
nitary and his household in Pisa by the SS in 1944, are powerful examples
of this increasingly hybrid field.[37]

Around the appearance of these works in Italian, we can also locate the translation in 1996 of the Holocaust literary *cause célèbre* and subsequent scandal, Binjamin Wilkomirski's *Fragments*, a disjointed and horrifically powerful memoir of a child's peregrinations through the camps. *Fragments* was feted in Germany and across the world, but gradually uncovered over the course of 1998–99 as a fabrication, almost certainly born of the psychopathological state of its Swiss author, Bruno Grosjean (or Bruno Dössekker). For many, the case was emblematic of a general hyperidentification with the Holocaust survivor and obsession with the Holocaust in general characteristic of this moment.[38] Related to this obsession, almost every work of fiction or historiography in the field at this point shares a relentless fascination with the theme, nature and workings of memory. The 1990s completes a process of transformation that began in the 1950s with the work of Giorgio Bassani: the transformation of Holocaust talk into a fully fledged 'memory culture', where the vocabulary of memory is all but compulsory.

Given the sheer quantity of material on display in the late 1990s, it is perhaps unsurprising that 1997 also saw evidence of a tiring with the heavy obsession with the Holocaust and memory, with its integration in often somewhat loose and undifferentiated ways into the public conversation, as well as increasingly difficult intersections of talk of the Holocaust with the now highly compromised 'moral-political' status of the state of Israel during the era of the 'intifadas'. Internationally, this was reflected in loud polemics such as Norman Finkelstein's *The Holocaust Industry*, with its assault on the international campaigns for financial reparations for the victims from banks and insurance corporations. Something comparable occurred in Italy with the publication in 1999 of the highly tendentious, even anti-Semitic, polemic by Sergio Romano, *Letter to a Jewish Friend*.[39] Romano's book brought in its wake a flurry of controversy and at least one book-length riposte,[40] but its intuition of a sort of 'Holocaust fatigue' and of the legitimacy for a mainstream opinion maker to declare this openly, more or less explicitly to tell 'the Jews' to stop going on about the Holocaust, was telling evidence of the weight and familiarity the theme had acquired; and of the distorting uses to which it could now be put.

3. 2001

Amongst all the myriad activities of the late 1990s was also the beginning of the campaign, sponsored by journalist and politician Furio

Colombo, by ANED and other deportation associations, to establish an official Holocaust memorial day in Italy, a campaign that would bear fruit, alongside the initiatives of the International Task Force and Stockholm agreement of 2000, in the first 'Day of Memory' marked in Italy on 27 January 2001. Of all the public manifestations and official decrees of support, the establishment of this event set the high-water mark of the entry of the Holocaust into national public life in Italy, part of the official calendar of shared national ritual.[41] It is perhaps appropriate, then, to end this book with a study of the first Day of Memory: of the legislation that established it, the events on the day itself and the media response to it.

Law 211 was passed in the Italian Parliament on 20 July 2000, after debate in the Chamber of Deputies on 27–28 March 2000 and in the Senate on 5 April and 5 July 2000.[42] Its signatories were a cross-party group of five deputies, led by Colombo (part of the largest governing party at that time, the DS) and including one member each of FI, AN and the Italian People's Party (PPI). At least two proposals for legislation other than Colombo's were in circulation in 2000, coming from both left and right, indicating political consensus over the planned institution of a memorial day as well as political competition to assume its authorship. The final text, known as the 'Colombo-De Luca' law,[43] read as follows:

> Institution of the 'Day of Memory' in memory of the extermination and persecution of the Jewish people and of Italian political and military deportees in the Nazi camps.
>
> Article 1
> 1. The Italian Republic recognises the day of 27 January, date of the pulling down of the gates of Auschwitz, as the 'Day of Memory', to remember the *Shoah* (extermination of the Jewish people), the racial laws, Italy's persecution of its Jewish citizens, Italians who underwent deportation, imprisonment and death, as well as those, with differing positions and allegiances, who opposed the extermination project and, risking their own lives, saved others and protected the persecuted.
>
> Article 2
> 2. On occasion of the 'Day of Memory' (for which see art. 1) there will be organized ceremonies, initiatives, meetings and shared moments of recounting of events and of reflection, particularly in schools of all categories and levels, on what befell the Jewish people and the Italian military and political deportees in the Nazi camps, so as to preserve for the future of Italy a memory of a tragic, dark period in the history of our country and of Europe, in order that nothing similar might ever happen again.[44]

The law was passed *nem con* in the Chamber of Deputies (although there were some wrangles in the Senate, hence the three-month delay in approval). In this, parliament responded to a powerful plea by Furio Colombo to remember how this very house of parliament had seen the Fascist anti-Semitic Racial Laws enthusiastically and unanimously passed into law on 17 November 1938.

The only signs of formal dissent were four abstentions, all from the centre or centre-right. As this rare (near) unanimity suggests, the text was the product of careful drafting, aiming for a politically neutral pinpointing of the historical and moral necessity of Holocaust commemoration, in Italy and beyond. The compromises, omissions and elisions on display in the text are worth examining, as evidence of the faultlines which underpin this new official memorialisation, several of which pick up on threads of the longer history this book has explored.

First there is the question of Italian responsibility. Despite the openly declared Italian involvement and responsibilities evoked in Article 1 ('the racial laws, Italy's persecution of its Jewish citizens, Italians who underwent deportation, imprisonment and death [...]') several elements of the law work to de-Italianise the events commemorated, starting with the name of the day itself. 'Day of Memory' is decidedly neutral and universalist, in contrast, for example, to the British 'National Holocaust Memorial Day'.[45] The date, 27 January, as noted in Chapter 2, is also distinctly internationalist, rooted in the universal symbolism of Auschwitz, with little that is specifically Italian.[46] A large number of European countries chose the same date, as if to Europeanise the day, although Colombo had preferred 16 October, the date of the round-up of Rome's Jews in 1943.[47] Furthermore, twice in the law, the site of suffering of Holocaust victims is identified simply as 'the Nazi camps', with no reference to Italian collaboration or to camps on Italian territory. Finally, Article 2 lays clear emphasis on memory of victimhood rather than responsibility and, again, adds a European level alongside the Italian, a move which loosens local responsibility ('a tragic, dark period in the history of our country and of Europe').

Secondly, there is the issue of ideological balance. Objectors in the parliamentary debate were keen to set the memory of Holocaust victims alongside the memory of victims of 20th-century Communism; victims of 'all oppressive ideologies [...] before, during and after the 1939–45 war', as one AN deputy phrased it.[48] As we saw in Chapter 2, this impulse for 'balanced' memory would lead in 2005 to the establishment of a rival memory 'Day of Memory' (*Giorno del ricordo*, instead of *Giorno della memoria*), for the victims of Yugoslav Communist violence in the foibe of northeastern Italy. Supporters of the Colombo-De Luca law responded by presenting the Shoah as representative of all ideologically motivated violence, rejecting the idea of memory as a 'zero-sum' game, whereby memory of one event takes away memory from another. Nevertheless, signs of ideological strain remain in the law, in aspects which implicitly de-Fascistise the Holocaust. For example, Article 1 insists in rather a forced and oblique manner that Holocaust resisters came from both Fascist and anti-Fascist sides: 'with differing positions and allegiances'.[49] Indeed, the terms 'Fascism' and 'Fascist' are conspicuous by their complete absence from the text of the law.[50]

Thirdly, in the somewhat repetitious phrasing, we can see reflections of the problem of setting in apt (and politically acceptable) relation the Italian, Jewish and Italian-Jewish experiences of the Holocaust (and Nazi violence generally). Three attempts are made in the short text to find a formula for the victims who are to be commemorated:

> i. in memory of the extermination and persecution of the Jewish people and of Italian political and military deportees in the Nazi camps.
>
> ii. to remember the *Shoah* (extermination of the Jewish people), the racial laws, Italy's persecution of its Jewish citizens, Italians who underwent deportation, imprisonment and death [...]
>
> iii. reflection [...] on what befell the Jewish people and the Italian military and political deportees in the Nazi camps

Uncertainty is evident in several respects here: the 'Jewish people' are set alongside various categories of Italians—and the Jewishness of the event is marked by the use of '*Shoah*'—but there are no Italian Jews at any point (only 'Jewish citizens' in ii., followed by an apparently distinct category, 'Italians'). What happened to Jews and Italians is blurred in i. and merged in the vaguest of formulae in ii ('what befell [...]'). This is symptomatic of an ongoing problem in the conception of the Italian Day of Memory and in its collective memory of the war: how to encompass and order in the general collective memory not only the categories of Jewish, Resistance, military and civilian deportees but also potential present and future victims of war and prejudice to whom this day was flexibly conceived as addressed in part.

Finally, the text of the law raises issues regarding the pedagogical and moral purpose of the memorial day. Article 2 makes clear the pedagogical nature of the day itself, with its emphasis on events in schools.[51] The sense of moral instruction is extended by the emphasis in Article 1 on the counterbalance to the evil of the Holocaust in exemplary figures, those who risked their lives to save others. This intervention of the state as pedagogue and moral instructor is itself not without difficulties; but the law's description of the rituals and events to be enacted on the day at least aspires to be nonprescriptive, informal and 'from below': 'ceremonies, initiatives, meetings and shared moments of recounting of events and of reflection'. The list seems to encourage particularly open and organic forms of collective attention.

27 January fell on a Saturday in 2001 (as it had in 1945). Events of various kinds—exhibitions, readings, concerts, discussions, testimonies, processions, religious ceremonies, film projections—were put on and listed in city and regional sections of the press, in most cities and many smaller towns across Italy. Many of these were public, official or semiofficial and, as prompted by the legislation, to a large degree aimed at schoolchildren. Scheduling commonly spread to include the Friday and the Sunday, in part because of the weekend and in part out of respect for the Jewish Sabbath. The largest national initiative was a public procession in Milan, co-organised by the trade unions.[52] Leading from Piazzale Loreto (site of the public display of Mussolini's body in 1945—raised again in the *Combat Film* controversy of 1994) to the city's central Piazza Duomo, the procession was attended by as many as 20,000 people, studded with dozens of simple black placards, each inscribed with the name of a concentration camp. In Piazza Duomo, the crowd was addressed by ex-deportees (Nedo Fiano, Onorina Brambilla Pesce, Gianfranco Maris), the chief rabbi of Milan Giuseppe Laras, the Jewish community leader Amos Luzzatto, and the charismatic union leader Sergio Cofferati. A separate gathering for students was addressed by radical actor and playwright Dario Fo and Jewish singer/performer Moni Ovadia, among others, at one of more than a hundred gatherings run by the 'Sinistra giovanile' nationwide. There was also an ongoing exhibition at the nearby Palazzo Reale.[53] In Piedmont, film projections and meetings with survivors were organised in towns and cities across the region.[54] In Turin, a concert was held at the Teatro Regio, with a musical performance of 'Songs of the Ghetto' and readings of testimonies gathered in a pioneering 1980s project by ANED and Turinese oral historians.[55] In Rome, the president of the Republic wrote a letter which was read out by Amos Luzzatto at a Friday ceremony at a high school, with ministers and leaders of the centre-left government in attendance

(Tullio De Mauro, Francesco Rutelli, Luciano Violante). Plaques were unveiled to commemorate Rom and child victims. A meeting was held in the recently opened Museum of the Liberation in via Tasso, the infamous location of the Gestapo headquarters in Rome, where the minister of Culture, Giovanna Melandri, opened an exhibition on Jews in Rome, 1938–1944, sponsored by Steven Spielberg's Shoah Foundation. The camp grounds at Fossoli were opened to the public on Sunday. All sporting events over the weekend were preceded by a minute's silence. Dutiful comments by all other major political leaders (including Fini, Prodi and Berlusconi) were reported, although one characteristic of the day seems to have been the relatively secondary public role played by major party and political leaders. Fini, keen to avoid any lapse from his party into old fascist or neofascist habits, commented 'this day is sacrosanct. No political force can be seen to be untouched by it'.[56]

Radio and television news broadcasts reported on the Day of Memory on both 26 and 27 January. RAI 3 scheduled a series of programmes related to the day, including documentaries and a discussion programme. Furio Colombo, Athos De Luca and the RAI president Roberto Zaccaria talked about the significance of the occasion on RAI 2. Of the private channels, Canale 5 contributed with its own discussion programme. The afternoon cultural programme on Radiotre, 'Fahrenheit', also dedicated most of its time to the theme of memory and the Holocaust, with guests including Piero Terracina and Lia Levi.[57] Finally, several publishers launched initiatives: Mursia put up on its website the list of Jewish deportees from Italy and Italian-occupied territory from Liliana Picciotto Fargion's *Book of Memory*. Mondadori released a book for the young by Lia Levi, *What Is Anti-Semitism? Answers Please.*[58]

The events of the day were largely pacific and respectful, marred only by relatively petty controversies. In a building housing the office of a DS deputy near Padua, a door was set on fire; the unfinished scrawl '[?]7 January' led to the assumption that the arson attack was related to the Day of Memory.[59] At the meeting in via Tasso, in Rome, the arrival of the controversial AN politician Maurizio Gasparri caused a flurry of protests from the audience ('have the decency to leave' was one reported cry[60]), before an embarrassed Gasparri was invited to stay by a majority of the survivors present. A brief political spat occurred in Milan, when it was noticed that the banner of the Lombardy Region was missing from the procession: the regional leader, FI politician Roberto Formigoni, immediately expressed regret for what he insisted was a mere administrative oversight.[61] Finally, the ever controversial and contrarian journalist (and former *repubblichino*) Indro Montanelli declared his objection to compulsory festivals and commemorations: 'Memory should be spontaneous'.[62]

The scale of press and other media coverage of the Day of Memory was reasonably substantial without suggesting the scale of a major national event. None of *Corriere della sera*, *La repubblica* and *La stampa* led with the story at any point, but each of them devoted full-page or half-page spreads more than once over the course of the 27 January weekend. If the event did appear on the front page, it was typically in comment pieces, followed up as often on the culture pages as on the news pages. An exception was *Diario*, Enrico Deaglio's strongly committed, independent leftist political-cultural weekly (originally born as a supplement to *L'Unità*), which brought out and kept on sale for a full month an elaborate supplement devoted to the Day of Memory, covering the Holocaust, other genocides, Italian collective memory of Fascism and of the terrorist 'Years of Lead', problems of memory, and more.[63] The weekly *L'espresso* bundled in with its 1 February issues a video of Holocaust testimonies, Ruggiero Gabbai's *Memoria*, and gave over five pages in the 'Culture' section of its 25 January issue.[64]

Coverage reflected the nature and scale of active public participation in the day, which was widespread *in toto* but capillary, made up of a large number of local initiatives with relatively small audiences. This contrasts with vast national gatherings of hundreds of thousands seen for 25 April memorials to the Resistance and the Liberation, for example, or for larger political protest marches, which often focussed on a single city and a single event. The penetration of radio and TV broadcasts was inevitably far greater; although again, within the economy of the television schedule, the most significant coverage of the day was assigned to the culturally 'serious' minority channels, RAI 3 and Radiotre, and to short items on the news. It is thus reasonable to assume that a large proportion of Italians will have been made aware of the day, with a much smaller, but not insignificant, overall number of active participants, especially in schools and associationist circles.

A mix of reportage of events, syntheses of comments from political leaders and cultural authorities, archive images and photojournalism[65] and comment pieces went to make up the context of the press coverage. Comments and responses were shot through with many of the characteristic issues and tensions in Holocaust culture at the turn of the century, born of nearly 60 years of evolving Italian response. As directed by the legislation and by broad consensus, the day's events balanced Jewish memory with global-political messages about 20th- and 21st-century violence.[66] Several speakers and commentators worked to establish links and lessons from the Holocaust to contemporary social and political problems. Sergio Cofferati, in his speech to the Milan procession, spoke of the dangers of xenophobia in contemporary Italy. Tullia Zevi noted the lessons for present-day, multiethnic Italy and beyond, drawing parallels with the Balkan conflicts of the 1990s: 'We must explain the past within the frame of our present. The Jews of then are the Bosnian Muslims of today. There is a powerful analogy; the extermination has not stopped'.[67] The historical elaboration of the memory of the Holocaust moves from the apparent silences and repressions of parts of the postwar era to the present-day 'avalanche' of memory talk and Holocaust talk[68] to its functional and symbolic use for present and future.

There was significant attention paid to Italian 'gentile' rescuers and resisters such as Perlasca and Palatucci, as well as an emphatic trend towards recovering and recording individual testimony, spoken or written, often now recorded by video (as in the documentary offered by *L'espresso*).

Much emphasis was placed on Italian complicity, on Colombo's notion of the Holocaust as 'among other things, also an Italian crime [*un delitto italiano*]'.[69] The most resonant expression of Italian co-responsibility came from President Ciampi's public letter, in which the head of state took the issue to the very heart of Italian national identity and specifically Italian history: 'The racial laws of 1938 marked the *most serious betrayal of the Risorgimento and of the very idea of the Italian nation*, to whose success the Jews had contributed in crucial ways' (emphasis added).[70]

This is a particularly bold and pointed formulation, designed to reclaim an 'anti-Fascist nation' from Galli della Loggia's claim that 1943 marked the 'death of the nation', reassigning the moment of the betrayal or death of the nation to the symbolic act of Fascist moral defection in 1938.

Italy and Italians as perpetrators were balanced with comment on Italy and Italians as victims. This meant pointedly including in Italian memory Italian-Jewish victims, as Michele Sarfatti noted.[71] Two episodes, two Nazi massacres of Italians, recently the object of recovered and divided memory, emerged particularly strongly in the coverage of the Day of Memory: the massacre of up to 10,000 Italian troops of the Acqui division on the Greek island of Cefalonia in late 1943, following their refusal to lay down their arms to the Germans; and the murder of some 500 civilians in the small Tuscan town of Sant'Anna di Stazzema on 12 August 1944.[72]

An interview in *La repubblica* with Elio Toaff, chief rabbi of Rome, is particularly striking in the way it draws lines of connection from the Sant'Anna massacre to the memorialisation of the Holocaust:

> I can say that I got an idea of what the Shoah was [...] the day of the Sant'Anna massacre. I was there with a group of partisans: yes, it was really there that I saw the true face of the Shoah. I saw that face in 508 people— men, women, children and the old—assassinated, piled up in the middle of the square and burned using wood from the church pews. [...] this wasn't only a desire to massacre, to destroy as an end in itself. It was an expression of an inconceivable hatred, of one man against another man.

Toaff merges his own fate as a Jew in hiding, a potential victim of the Final Solution (he also praises a priest who saved him), with innocent Italian victims of Nazi violence, not forgetting also a mention of the partisan Resistance. His brief comments work to perform one of the most crucial and potentially ambiguous tasks of the Day of Memory, to integrate the Holocaust fully into Italian history.

Other tensions running through the first Day of Memory were ideological, a residue of tension between legacies of Nazi and Fascist crimes and Communist crimes. This was intensified in early 2001 by the ongoing preelection campaign, which in May 2001 would result in the reelection of a second FI-AN-Northern League coalition government led by Silvio Berlusconi. Thus discussion of Fascism, the war and Communism at this time meant, variously, the defence of the Italian left, of the legacy of the Resistance and of its founding role in the postwar democratic settlement, as the DS saw through its first parliamentary mandate in government; the legitimisation of AN (and the League, to a degree) as a party of government; and the attempt by Berlusconi to rekindle Cold War fears of the Communist/totalitarian instincts of the left.

Lines of ideologically 'divided memory' were on display in several ways in the days surrounding the Day of Memory in 2001, although the alignments of left and right were by no means clear-cut, suggesting a fractured and dispersed rather than neatly 'divided' memory. Thus, although some on the right pushed general comparisons between the Holocaust and Communist forms of totalitarian violence to make an openly political point,[73] both right and left were receptive to a wide, comparativist perspective on modern genocide. Even commentators from the left such as Adriano Sofri, whilst objecting to facile comparisons of numbers of victims on each side of the ideological divide—what he called 'the spoils system [*lottizzazione*] of tragedies and deaths'—used the objection as the basis of a complex comparative analysis.[74]

Sofri's article 'The Caves of Horror' uses Trieste to tackle this issue, and by extension several of the problems at stake in the Day of Memory, with acuity and also with symptomatic unease. Sofri's piece centres on the geographical proximity of two key symbols of Italy's history of ideologically motivated violence, and by extension the violence of Fascism/Nazism and Stalinism: the Risiera di San Sabba and the foibe. He tackles the irony of their geographical proximity on several levels: first of all, returning to the pedagogical function of collective memory in general and the Day of Memory in particular, he lambasts the arrangement of 'joint' school trips to the area—a Nazi/Fascist atrocity in the morning, a Communist atrocity in the afternoon—and the perversion of the notion of both comparability and memory this entails. He sees the root of such a facile pedagogical project in the long repression of historical memory that has gone on in Italy and the displacements or distortions this has resulted in. This opens out into a sustained discussion of how personal and collective memory make compromises with past histories and loyalties. In Sofri's own case, this means his loyalty to Communism, a cause which he recognises led to the murder of millions, epitomised in the Italian case by the foibe. Sofri's tackling of the thorny issue of the 'memory of those who have been Communists' is distinctly confessional: he reflects on the foibe as a possible inkling of what might have happened in Italy 'if we, the Communists, had won', or if the northeast (as a number of Italian Communists wanted) had seceded from Italy to join the Communist republic. He is also implicitly pleading for a consideration of the moral complexity of choices on a par with recent pleas for the 'boys of Salò', whilst still trying to maintain what he calls his 'alibi' of a moral distinction between Fascism and Communism. Sofri's piece is powerfully representative of the ways in which the trope of divided memory and complex dynamics of debate and dissemination on display in the Day of Memory uncovered issues of affect and subjectivity, of personal memory as identity, as well as issues of public politics, past and present.[75]

Finally, the Day of Memory also elicited widespread comment on the European dimension to the Holocaust itself, in history and in commemoration. Luciano Violante spoke out in support of a day dedicated specifically to the Holocaust (and not to totalitarianism and genocide more broadly) because:

> the civic identity of Western Europe today was built on the struggle against Nazism and Fascism. That is why we are free. It is not that we want to forget other tragedies, but rather to mark out our own identity.[76]

Violante's position was, essentially, a restatement of the early postwar 'anti-Fascist' settlement, in Italy and Europe, one which has shown distinct signs of fraying in the post-1989 era. Michele Sarfatti similarly drew a direct link between the Holocaust and the European Union:

> the killing of millions of Jews was one result of an appalling material attempt to achieve a 'European union', which, in historical terms, is the immediate precedent for the democratic European union that exists today. For this reason, that memory is indispensable for our present and our future. And for this reason, I believe, [Romano] Prodi's first journey, on being nominated President of the European Commission, was to visit Auschwitz.[77]

~

The first Day of Memory coincided with and was symptomatic of a remarkable period of transition in Italian cultural and political history, its sense of nationhood and of its own recent past. The day became a crucible in which the public uses of history and the aftereffects of memory were on vivid display. It demonstrated the very particular status accorded to the Holocaust in the post-1989 polity in Italy: one built on an extraordinarily broad-based consensus and moral respect for the Event (even across a bitterly divided political spectrum, from former Fascists to former Communists, from the president of the Republic to schoolchildren); one also shot through with subtle, indirect tensions and revisionist ideological positioning. In fact, the period of transition begun with end of the Cold War and, in Italy, the collapse of the 'First Republic', was drawing to a dramatic close in January 2001, weeks before Berlusconi's second election victory and only a few months before the events of 11 September 2001 would dramatically alter global geopolitical and cultural alignments, including the shape of the preceding century's history. Future Days of Memory, and the shape of Italy's marking of the event, would inevitably change as a result of this watershed; but the first decade of the 21st century would continue to attend to the lines of cultural continuity and fracture that had bound Italian culture to the Holocaust in such complex and elaborately mediated ways throughout the second half of the 20th century and into the new millennium.

Notes

Chapter 1

1. The problem of the naming of the genocide of Europe's Jews and other Nazi genocides is a fraught one, in any language (Chapter 9, section 2). Every possible term brings with it problems and limitations. I have opted for the most common term in English, 'Holocaust', but also on occasion use 'Shoah'. See Anna-Vera Sullam Calimani, *I nomi dello sterminio* (Turin: Einaudi, 2001).

2. For multinational perspectives, see David S. Wyman and Charles H. Rosenzveig, eds., *The World Reacts to the Holocaust* (Baltimore: Johns Hopkins University Press, 1997); Martin Davies and Claus-Christian Szejnmann, eds., *How the Holocaust Looks Now: International Perspectives* (New York: Palgrave, 2007). Useful national case studies include, on Germany, Mary Fullbrook, *German National Identity After the Holocaust* (Cambridge: Polity Press, 1999); Harold Marcuse, *Legacies of Dachau: The Uses and Abuses of a Concentration Camp, 1933–2001* (Cambridge: Cambridge University Press, 2001); on Israel, Tom Segev, *The Seventh Million: The Israelis and the Holocaust* (New York: Holt, 1991); Idith Zertal, *Israel's Holocaust and the Politics of Nationhood* (Cambridge: Cambridge University Press, 2005); on France, Samuel Moyn, *A Holocaust Controversy. The Treblinka Affair in Postwar France* (Waltham, MA: Brandeis University Press, 2005); Caroline Wiedmer, *The Claims of Memory: Representations of the Holocaust in Contemporary Germany and France* (Ithaca, NY: Cornell University Press, 1999); Joan B. Wolf, *Harnessing the Holocaust: The Politics of Memory in France* (Stanford: Stanford University Press, 2004); on America, Alan Mintz, *Popular Culture and the Shaping of Holocaust Memory in America* (Seattle: Washington University Press, 2001); Peter Novick, *The Holocaust in American Life* (Boston: Houghton Mifflin, 1999); on the Low Countries, Pieter Lagrou, 'Victims of Genocide and National Memory: Belgium, France and the Netherlands 1945–1965', *Past and Present*, 154 (February 1997): 181–222; on Poland, Michael C.

Steinlauf, *Bondage to the Dead: Poland and the Memory of the Holocaust* (Syracuse: Syracuse University Press, 1997); on Britain, Tony Kushner, *The Holocaust and the Liberal Imagination* (Blackwell: Oxford, 1994).

3. Exceptions to this rule include: on Holocaust literature, Risa Sodi, *Narrative and Imperative: The First Fifty Years of Italian Holocaust Writing (1944–1994)* (New York: Peter Lang, 2007); on Holocaust cinema, Millicent Marcus, *Italian Film in the Shadow of Auschwitz* (Toronto: Toronto University Press, 2007) and Emiliano Perra, *Conflicts of Memory: The Reception of Holocaust Films and TV Programmes in Italy, 1945 to the Present* (Oxford: Peter Lang, 2010). Pioneering work on testimonies was done by Anna Bravo and Daniele Jalla, eds., *Una misura onesta. Gli scritti di memoria della deportazione dall'Italia 1944–93* (Milan: Franco Angeli/ANED, 1994), pp. 17–92; and see also Anna Rossi-Doria, *Memoria e storia. Il caso della deportazione* (Rubbettino: Catzanaro, 1998). A recent collective overview is to be found in Marcello Flores et al., eds., *Storia della Shoah in Italia*, vols. I–II (Turin: UTET, 2010), vol. II.

4. See Barbie Zelizer, *Remembering to Forget: Holocaust Memory Through the Camera's Eye* (Chicago: Chicago University Press, 1998). No study exists of the dissemination of this visual material in Italy.

5. Anne Frank's *Diary of a Young Girl* appeared in Dutch in 1947, in English in 1952, in Italian in 1954. It was staged on Broadway in 1955 and released as a Hollywood film in 1959.

6. On *Holocaust* in America and Germany, see, respectively, Jeffrey Shandler, *While America Watches: Televising the Holocaust* (New York: Oxford University Press, 1999); and the special issue of *New German Critique*, 19 (Winter 1980).

7. On the French negationists, see Pierre Vidal-Nacquet, *Assassins of Memory* (New York: Columbia University Press, 1992). On the 'Historikerstreit', see Charles S. Maier, *The Unmasterable Past: History, Holocaust and German National Identity* (Cambridge, MA: Harvard University Press, 1988); Richard Bosworth, *Explaining Auschwitz and Hiroshima: History Writing and the Second World War 1945–1990* (London: Routledge, 1993), pp. 73–93.

8. See Tim Cole, *Selling the Holocaust: From Auschwitz to Schindler: How History Is Bought, Packaged and Sold* (New York: Routledge, 1999), pp. 146–71. Cole counted more than one hundred Holocaust museums and centres in America, as Germany planned its first (p. 147).

9. Arjun Appadurai, *Modernity at Large: Cultural Dimensions of Globalization* (Minneapolis: University of Minnesota Press, 1996). For a reading of the Holocaust as a 'globalized' or 'cosmopolitan' phenomenon, see Daniel Levy and Natan Sznaider, *Holocaust Memory in the Global Age* (Philadelphia: Temple University Press, 2006).

10. For a useful recent overview, see Joshua Zimmerman, ed., *Jews in Italy Under Fascist and Nazi Rule, 1922–1945* (Cambridge: Cambridge University Press, 2005).

11. Perhaps the most influential account of this phenomenon in English is Jonathan Steinberg, *All or Nothing: The Axis and the Holocaust 1941–43* (London: Routledge, 1990).

12. According to Liliana Picciotto Fargion, *Il libro della memoria. Gli ebrei deportati dall'Italia (1943–1945)*, Milan: Mursia, 2002; 1st edition 1991), close to 7,000 Jews were deported from Italy and killed, or killed in Italy directly. A further 800 were deported and survived. The figures omit Jews deported from Italian-occupied territories such as the Dodecanese (more than 1,800), Jews arrested but not deported or killed (and so on).

13. For these figures, which have not been established with anything like the accuracy of the figures for Jewish victims, see the discussion of 'la statistica della deportazione' in Bravo and Jalla, *Misura*, pp. 39–43.

14. This stereotypical myth of national character is most often captured in the phrase '*italiani brava gente*' (good Italians). See David Bidussa, *Il mito del bravo italiano* (Milan: Il Saggiatore, 1994) and Chapter 8 in this volume.

15. Norberto Bobbio, *Trent'anni di storia della cultura a Torino (1920–1950)* (Turin: Cassa di Risparmio, 1977), p. 104.

16. See Manuela Consonni, 'The Impact of the "Eichmann Event" in Italy, 1961', *Journal of Israeli History*, 23.1 (Spring 2004): 91–99.

17. See Ruth Ben-Ghiat, 'The Secret Histories of Roberto Benigni's *Life Is Beautiful*', *Yale Journal of Criticism*, 14.1 (2001): 253–66.

18. There is a vast field of memory and collective memory studies, including vigorous critiques of its own assumptions and terminology. The two most influential works on collective memory are Maurice Halbwachs, *La Mémoire collective* (Paris: Presses universitaires de France, 1950); and Pierre Nora, ed., *Les Lieux de mémoire*, vols. I–III (Paris: Gallimard, 1984–1992). On these and contemporary 'memory culture', see Nancy Wood, *Vectors of Memory: Legacies of Trauma in Postwar Europe* (New York: Berg, 1999); Wulf Kansteiner, 'Finding Meaning in Memory: A Methodological Critique of Collective Memory Studies', *History and Theory*, 41 (May 2002): 179–97. On postmodern fragmentation and mediatisation of memory, see Andreas Huyssen, *Twilight Memories: Marking Time in a Culture of Amnesia* (New York: Routledge, 1995); Susan Rubin Suleiman, *Crises of Memory and the Second World War* (Cambridge, MA: Harvard University Press, 2006). For a formulation of Holocaust representation in terms of 'historical culture' as an alternative vocabulary to memory, see Klas-Göran Karlsson and Ulf Zander, eds., *Echoes of the Holocaust: Historical Cultures in Contemporary Europe* (Lund: Nordic Academic, 2003); and *Holocaust on Post-War Battlefields: Genocide as Historical Culture* (Malmö: Sekel, 2006).

19. For a recent synthesis, see Michele Sarfatti, *La Shoah in Italia. La persecuzione degli ebrei sotto il fascismo* (Turin, Einaudi, 2005); and Zimmerman, *Jews in Italy*.

20. I have attempted a comparative synthesis of Italian and German racial

persecution in the 1930s and 1940s in Robert S. C. Gordon, 'Race', in Richard J. B. Bosworth, ed., *Oxford Handbook of Fascism* (Oxford: Oxford University Press, 2009), pp. 296–316.

21. On this general issue, see Zygmunt Bauman, *Modernity and Holocaust* (Cambridge: Polity, 1989), pp. 83–116; Steven T. Katz, *The Holocaust in Historical Context* (Oxford: Oxford University Press, 1994); Michael Marrus, *The Holocaust in History* (Harmondsworth: Penguin, 1987), pp. 18–25; Alan Rosenbaum, ed., *Is the Holocaust Unique? Perspectives on Comparative Genocide* (Boulder: Westview, 2009).

22. Another sign that the centrality of the 'concentration camp' to definitions of the Holocaust has been influential is found in the important work done, from the 1980s onwards, to recover histories of the network of Fascist internment camps of alien Jews in southern Italy before 1943, such as Ferramonti di Tarsia (see Carlo Spartaco Capogreco, *I campi del duce. L'internamento civile nell'Italia fascista, 1940–1943* (Turin: Einaudi, 2004)). On the figure of the camp as a widely adopted metaphor, see Chapter 7 in this volume.

23. On the vast numbers of DPs and the meagre number of Jewish returnees, and the effects of this on memorialisation, see Pieter Lagrou, 'The Nationalization of Victimhood: Selective Violence and National Grief in Western Europe, 1940–1960', in Richard Bessel and Dirk Schumann, eds., *Life After Death: Approaches to a Cultural and Social History of Europe During the 1940s and 1950s* (Cambridge/Washington, DC: Cambridge University Press/German Historical Institute, 2003), pp. 243–57 [pp. 252–57]. Cf. Silvia Salvatici, *Senza casa e senza paese. Profughi europei nel secondo dopoguerra* (Bologna: Il Mulino, 2008).

24. See Philip Cooke, *The Legacy of the Italian Resistance* (New York: Palgrave, 2011); Stephen Gundle, 'The Civic Religion of the Resistance in Postwar Italy', *Modern Italy*, 55.2 (November 2000): 113–32. On the death of the nation, see Ernesto Galli della Loggia, *La morte della patria* (Bari: Laterza, 1996).

25. This nonindustrial, messy mass murder has emerged with greater clarity since the opening of Soviet archives after 1989, leading to controversial revisionist accounts such as Timothy Snyder, *Bloodlands: Europe Between Hitler and Stalin* (New York: Basic Books, 2010).

26. See Giovanni Contini, *La memoria divisa* (Milan: Rizzoli, 1997); John Foot, *Italy's Divided Memory* (London: Palgrave, 2010); Leonardo Paggi, ed., *Storia e memoria di un massacro ordinario* (Rome: Manifestolibri, 1996).

27. See Alessandro Portelli, *L'ordine è già stato eseguito: Roma, le fosse Ardeatine, la memoria* (Rome: Donzelli, 1999); and Chapter 6 in this volume.

28. For an influential statement of this link, see Bauman.

29. The extent of Mussolini's and Fascism's racism before the 1938 Racial Laws and the reasons for his regime's racist turn at that time continue to be subjects of intense historiographical debate. See Michele Sarfatti, *Gli ebrei nell'Italia fascista. Vicende, identità, persecuzione* (Turin: Einaudi, 2000); Giorgio Fabre, *Mussolini*

razzista. Dal socialismo al fascismo: la formazione di un antisemita (Milan: Garzanti, 2005); Zimmerman, *Jews in Italy.*

30. See, for example, attempts to build a theory of generic Fascism such as the 'palingenetic nationalism' model of Roger Griffin, *The Nature of Fascism* (New York: St Martin's Press, 1991).

31. See Tony Judt, *Postwar: A History of Europe Since 1945* (New York: Penguin, 2005), pp. 803–31; Levy and Sznaider, *Holocaust Memory*, 2006; Lothar Probst, 'Founding Myths in Europe and the Role of the Holocaust', *New German Critique*, 90 (Autumn 2003): 45–58.

Chapter 2

1. Some have queried the location of this photograph (e.g. Lorenzo Grassi, 'Ecco Pio XII a San Giovanni', *Metro*, 29 August 2001).

2. This might be contrasted with the visit of Pope John Paul II to Rome's synagogue on 13 April 1986, which marked a watershed in the troubled history of relations between the Catholic Church and the Jews, not least regarding the Papacy's role at the time of the Holocaust.

3. On Villa Torlonia under Fascism and its later museums and nearby street names, see R. J. B. Bosworth, *Whispering City: Rome and Its Histories* (New Haven: Yale University Press, 2011), pp. 188–93.

4. For a polemical restatement of this fact, see Giorgio Israel, 'Redeemed Intellectuals and Italian Jews', *Telos* 139 (Summer 2007): 85–108 [p. 87].

5. See, for example, Renzo De Felice, *Intervista sul fascismo* (Bari: Laterza, 1975), pp. 22–25. De Felice plays a key role at more than one point in this book: see Chapters 3 and 8.

6. Cf. Michael Burleigh and Wolfgang Wippermann, *The Racial State: Germany 1933–1945* (Cambridge: Cambridge University Press, 1991).

7. See Picciotto Fargion, *Libro della memoria.*

8. Hannah Arendt, *Eichmann in Jerusalem: A Report on the Banality of Evil* (London: Penguin, 1994; 1st edition 1963), p. 170; and cf. similar remarks in Daniel J. Goldhagen, *Hitler's Willing Executioners: Ordinary Germans and the Holocaust* (New York: Vintage Books, 1997), pp. 390, 409.

9. On Italy's tradition of Christian anti-Semitism, see Wiley Feinstein, *The Civilization of the Holocaust in Italy: Poets, Artists, Saints, Anti-Semites* (London: Associated University Presses, 2003); and cf. David Kertzer, *Unholy War: The Vatican's Role in the Rise of Modern Anti-Semitism* (London: Macmillan, 2002).

10. See, for example, Cole.

11. On this and other conceptual problematics of contemporary museums and memorials, and the 'museification' of memory, see the important contributions by James Young, *The Texture of Memory: Holocaust Memorials and Meaning* (New Haven: Yale University Press, 1993); and Huyssen, *Twilight Memories.*

12. See, for example, the catalogue *Dalle leggi antiebraiche all Shoah* (Milan: Skira/CDEC, 2004).

13. See Sullam Calimani.

14. Zevi is the son of the architectural historian Bruno Zevi and of Tullia Zevi, a former president of the Italian Jewish community and a journalist who reported on both the Nuremberg and Eichmann trials. The following account of the details of the museum project draws on contemporary press coverage starting in August 2005 (collated at 'Museo della Shoah, la luce di 7000 nomi', http://www .architettiroma.it/archweb/notizie/07694.aspx; accessed 10 June 2010).

15. For more on this project, see 'Museo virtuale delle intolleranze e degli stermini', http://www.istoreto.it/amis/museo.html (accessed 10 November 2011). See Zevi's own reflections in Luca Zevi, 'Fabio Mauri, metafora del cammino della memoria della Shoah', in Stefania Lucamante et al., eds., *Memoria collettiva e memoria privata: il ricordo della Shoah come politica sociale* (Utrecht: Igitur, 2008), pp. 205–17.

16. See George Steiner's evocation of this trope of naming: 'As in some Borges fable, the only completely decent "review" [of Chaim Kaplan's *Warsaw Diary* and Elie Wiesel's *La Nuit*] would be to re-copy the book, line by line, pausing at the names of the dead and the names of the children as the orthodox scribe pauses, when recopying the Bible, at the hallowed name of God' (Steiner, 'Postscript', in *Language and Silence* (London: Faber and Faber, 1985), p. 193).

17. See Deaglio, *La banalità del bene*; and *Perlasca: Un eroe italiano* (RAI Fiction, 2002). And cf. Perra, *Conflicts*, pp. 223–31 and Chapter 8.

18. Pezzetti was also a consultant on Benigni's *Life Is Beautiful.*

19. For the politics of postwar Italy, see Paul Ginsborg, *A History of Contemporary Italy* (Harmondsworth: Penguin, 1990).

20. See Raoul Pupo and Roberto Spazzali, *Foibe* (Milan: Bruno Mondadori, 2003) and Chapter 10.

21. *Gazzetta Ufficiale*, 96, 26 April 2003.

22. Giorgio Bassani, *Il giardino dei Finzi-Contini* (Turin: Einaudi, 1962).

23. *Gazzetta Ufficiale*, 299, 27 December 2006 (supplemento ordinario n. 244).

24. Michele Sarfatti, 'La Shoah e le case della memoria', *L'Unità*, 17 January 2007; and CDEC, 'La persecuzione degli ebrei in Italia 1938–45', http://www .museoshoah.it (accessed 29 May 2011). There have been financial constraints on elements of the project, including the Milan station.

Chapter 3

1. The term *field* as used here is informed by Pierre Bourdieu's influential, if elusive, concept of 'fields' of cultural production (see, e.g. *The Rules of Art*, Oxford: Polity, 1996). For Bourdieu, a given cultural field is structured by a set of possible positions and strategic orientations across which agents in the field—agents of cultural consumption and production—organise themselves, accruing

authority or cultural capital and commonsense ideas of value (*doxa*) that are at stake in the field. The field of Holocaust culture loosely resembles this model, insofar as it contains agent groups and individuals 'competing' to give shape to definitions and understandings of, and values and meanings drawn from, the Nazi genocide, in the context of both the larger field of Italian culture and the international field of Holocaust culture.

2. Primo Levi, *Se questo è un uomo* (Turin: De Silva, 1947).

3. Serge Barcellini and Annette Wieviorka, *Passant, souviens-toi!* (Paris: Graphein, 1995), pp. 11–29.

4. Ferruccio Maruffi, 'La nascita delle associazioni di ex deportati' in Alberto Cavaglion, ed., *Il ritorno dai Lager* (Milan: Franco Angeli/ANED, 1993), pp. 65–79.

5. A history of ANED remains to be written; see ANED, at http://www.de portati.it/ (accessed 16 November 2010).

6. http://www.deportati.it/Statuto/default.html (accessed 16 November 2010).

7. See Guri Schwarz, *Ritrovare se stessi. Gli ebrei nell'Italia postfascista* (Bari: Laterza, 2004).

8. Renzo De Felice, *Storia degli ebrei italiani sotto il fascismo* (Turin: Einaudi, 1961). On the genesis of the book, see Schwarz, *Ritrovare*, pp. 164–68.

9. See Roberto Bassi, 'Ricordo di Massimo Adolfo Vitale', *Rassegna mensile di Israel*, 45. 1–3 (January–March 1979): 8–21.

10. Picciotto Fargion, *Libro della memoria*. On the history of CDEC, see her 'Eloisa e il CDEC', *Rassegna mensile di Israel*, 47. 1–3 (January–June 1981): 9–44.

11. On the Piccardi scandal, see Renzo De Felice, *Rosso e nero* (Milan: Baldini e Castoldi, 1995), p. 150; and Schwarz, *Ritrovare*, p. 171 (comparing Piccardi to the contemporary revelation of writer Guido Piovene's Fascist and racist past). On the Silone case, see Stanislao Pugliese, *Bitter Spring. A Life of Ignazio Silone* (New York: Farrar, Straus and Giroux, 2009), pp. 295–330.

12. Primo Levi grouped together Langbein (Auschwitz), Kogon (Buchenwald) and Marsalek (Mauthausen) as ex-political-prisoner-historians (*I sommersi e i salvati* [*The Drowned and the Saved*], in Primo Levi, *Opere*, vols. I-II, ed. by Marco Belpoliti, Turin: Einaudi, 1997, II, p. 1024; henceforth *Opere*, II, p. 1024).

13. On Italian Holocaust literature, see Sodi, *Narrative*.

14. On Italian Holocaust cinema, see Marcus, *Italian Film*; Perra, *Conflicts* (also on television); and Giacomo Lichtner, *Film and the Shoah in France and Italy* (London: Vallentine Mitchell, 2008).

15. On the politics of Resistance commemoration in and around 1955, see Cooke, *Legacy*, pp. 60–63.

16. See for the American case Mintz, *Popular Culture*.

17. Perra discusses the embedded transmission of key Holocaust films, using for illustration the case of *Schindler's List*, which was broadcast on Italian television as a mediatised event in its own right and framed by documentary

and discussion programmes, as well as preceding and subsequent print coverage (*Conflicts*, pp. 182–86).

Chapter 4

1. See *Il segno della memoria 1945–1995. BBPR: monumento ai caduti nei campi nazisti* (Milan: Electa, 1995); Foot, *Italy's Divided Memory*, pp. 90–95.

2. On the Carpi/Fossoli projects, see Tristano Matta, *Un percorso della memoria. Guida ai luoghi della violenza nazista in Italia* (Milan: Electa, 1996), pp. 98–109; Giovanni Leoni, '"The First Blow": Projects for the Camp at Fossoli', in Geoffrey Hartman, ed., *Holocaust Remembrance. The Shapes of Memory* (Cambridge, MA: Blackwell, 1994), pp. 204–14.

3. *Segno*, pp. 20–32.

4. Levi, *Opere*, I, pp. 782–83.

5. Liliana Picciotto Fargion, 'Le informazioni sulla "Soluzione finale" circolanti in Italia nel 1942–1943', *Rassegna mensile di Israel*, 55. 2–3 (May–December 1989): 331–36 [p. 336].

6. See, e.g. the extraordinary opening chapters of Judt, *Postwar*.

7. Ginsborg, *History*, pp. 8–120.

8. *Avanti!* 27 May 1945.

9. See Zelizer, esp. pp. 208–10 on 'visual cues'. On Italian press coverage, see Marie-Anne Matard-Bonucci, 'La Libération des camps de concentration et le retour des déportés à travers la presse quotidienne italienne', in Annette Wieviorka and Claude Mouchard, eds., *La Shoah. Témoignages, savoirs, oeuvres* (Orléans: Presses Universitaires de Vincennes, 1999), pp. 101–14; Sarah Fantini, *Notizie dalla Shoah. La stampa italiana nel 1945* (Bologna: Pendragon, 2005).

10. Cesare Merzagora, *I pavidi. Dalla costituzione alla costituente* (Milan: Istituto Editoriale Galileo, 1946), pp. xi–xv [Croce's preface], pp. 43–55.

11. Merzagora, p. xv. See Roberto Finzi, 'Tre scritti postbellici sugli ebrei di Benedetto Croce, Cesare Merzagora, Adolfo Omodeo', *Studi storici*, 47. 1 (January–March 2006): 81–108. There are similar veiled formulations in debates within the Church; see Manuela Consonni, 'The Church and the Memory of the Shoah: The Catholic Press in Italy, 1945–1947', in Eli Lederhendler, ed., *Jews, Catholics and the Burdens of History* (Oxford: Oxford University Press, 2005), pp. 21–34.

12. See Agostino Bistarelli, *La storia del ritorno. I reduci italiani del secondo dopoguerra* (Turin: Bollati Boringhieri, 2007); Cavaglion, *Ritorno*.

13. Lagrou, 'Victims'.

14. See Sandro Antonimi, *DELASEM: storia della più grande organizzazione ebraica di soccorso durante la seconda guerra mondiale* (Genoa: De Ferrari, 2000); Mario Toscano, 'The Abrogation of Racial Laws and the Reintegration of Jews in Italian Society (1943–1948)', in David Bankier, ed., *The Jews Are Coming Back: The Return of the Jews to Their Countries of Origin After WW II* (New York/Jerusalem: Berghahn/Yad Vashem, 2005), pp. 148–68.

15. First published in a celebrated postliberation issue of the Rome journal *Mercurio*, 1. 4 (December 1944): 75–97; in book form (Giacomo Debenedetti, *16 ottobre 1943*, Rome: OET, 1945), with a cover by Alberto Savinio; and in French in Sartre's *Les Temps modernes*, 2.23–4 (August–September 1947), special Italian issue edited by Vittorini.

16. Giacomo Debenedetti, *Otto ebrei* (Rome: Atlantica, 1944).

17. Debenedetti, *16 ottobre 1943. Otto ebrei* (Turin: Einaudi, 2001), p. 58.

18. Debenedetti, *16 ottobre 1943. Otto ebrei*, pp. 77–78.

19. Curzio Malaparte, *Kaputt* (Naples: Casella, 1944).

20. Malaparte was contradictory and slippery in all his ethics and politics, maintaining a deep vein of anti-Semitism. See, e.g. *Mamma marcia* (Florence: Vallecchi, 1959), pp. 266–73 (I am grateful to Simon Levis Sullam for the reference.)

21. Umberto Saba's *Scorciatoie e raccontini* (Milan: Mondadori, 1946).

22. See Paola Frandini, '"Scorciatoie e raccontini" di Umberto Saba tra pensiero ebraico e Shoah', *Strumenti critici*, 1 (January 2009): 25–34; Ettore Janulardo, 'Saba: Scorciatoie dopo Majdanek', *Studi e ricerche di storia contemporanea*, 64 (December 2005): 63–67.

23. Cavaglion, *Ritorno*.

24. Levi, *Opere*, I, p. 1382.

25. Ettore Siegrist, *Dachau. Dimenticare sarebbe una colpa* (Genoa: Sampierdarena/ Stab. grafici Federico Reale, 1945), p. 1.

26. Giancarlo Ottani, *Un popolo piange. La tragedia degli ebrei italiani* (Milan: Spartaco Giovene, 1945); Eucardio Momigliano, *40000 fuori legge* (Rome: Carboni, 1945), also published as *Storia tragica a grottesca del razzismo fascista* (Milan: Mondadori, 1946).

27. Giancarlo Ottani, *I campi della morte* (Milano: Perinetti Casoni, 1945).

28. Momigliano, *Storia*, p. 29.

29. Leonardo De Benedetti and Primo Levi, 'Rapporto sull'organizzazione igienico-sanitaria del campo di concentramento per ebrei di Monowitz (Auschwitz Alta Silesia)', *Minerva medica*, 37/2. 47 (24 November 1946): 535–44; in English as *Auschwitz Report*, ed. by Robert S. C. Gordon (London: Verso, 2006).

30. *Minerva medica* also published 'Presentazione di un giovane deportato castrato nel campo di Auschwitz nel 1943', *Minerva medica*, 36. 32 (18 August 1945): 54; 'Il campo di orrore' (on Belsen) and 'Il centro di sperimentazione umana sul tifo esantematico nel campo di internamento a Buchenwald', *Minerva medica*, 36. 30 (4 August 1945): 44–46; 'L'ospedale del campo VII B per internati italiani in Germania', *Minerva medica*, 37/2. 51 (22 December 1946): 412–20.

31. Figures compiled from Bravo and Jalla, *Misura*, supplemented by CDEC archive. Cf. Annette Wieviorka, *Déportation et génocide* (Paris: Plon, 1992).

32. Aldo Bizzarri, *Proibito vivere*; Anna Seghers, *La settima croce*; and Ernst Wiechert, *La selva dei morti* (all Milan: Mondadori, 1947).

33. Francesco Ulivelli, *Bolzano: anticamera della morte* (Milan: Edizioni Stellissima, 1946), p. 9.

34. Levi, *Opere*, I, p. 60.

35. Gaetano De Martino, *Dal carcere di San Vittore ai "lager"* (Milan: La Prora, 1955; 1st edition Milan: Ed. Alaya, 1945), p. 18.

36. Enzo Rava, *Martirio* (Genoa: Mario Ceva, 1945), pp. 14, 68.

37. See references to Hell in Aldo Pantozzi [8078-126520], *Sotto gli occhi della morte. Da Bolzano a Mauthausen* (Bolzano: Tip. Pio Mariz, 1946), p. 43; Ottani, *Campi*, p. 143.

38. There were exceptions, e.g. the hagiographical accounts of Teresio Olivelli, a Catholic partisan beaten to death at Hersbruck for helping a companion, mentioned by many Mauthausen deportees and subject of a 1947 biography, Alberto Caracciolo, *Teresio Olivelli* (Brescia: La Scuola, 1947).

39. A key text in this regard will be Lidia Beccaria Rolfi and Anna Maria Bruzzone, eds., *Le donne di Ravensbrück. Testimonianze di deportate politiche italiane* (Turin: Einaudi, 1978), a collation of oral histories of women in the camps.

40. See Liana Millu, *Il fumo di Birkenau* (Milan: La Prora, 1947); Frida Misul, *Fra gli artigli del mostro nazista. La più romanzesca delle realtà il più realistico dei romanzi* (Livorno: Stab. poligrafico Belforte, 1946); Luciana Nissim and Pelagia Lewinska, *Donne contro il mostro* (Turin: Vincenzo Ramella Editore, 1946); Giuliana Tedeschi, *Questo povero corpo* (Milan: EdIt, 1946); Alba Valech Capozzi, *A 24029* (Siena: Soc. An. Poligrafica, 1946). Cf. Bravo and Jalla, *Misura*, pp. 58–60.

41. Tedeschi reworked *Questo povero corpo* in *C'è un punto della terra . . .: una donna nel lager di Birkenau* (Florence: La Giuntina, 1988). In 1978–79, Millu published *I ponti di Schwerin* (Poggibonsi: Lalli, 1978), a novel of return, and then a new edition of *Il fumo di Birkenau* (Florence: La Giuntina, 1979).

42. Charles Cohen, *Un quaderno di Buchenwald* (Turin: F. Toso, 1945).

43. Levi, *Opere*, I, pp. 30, 138.

44. Levi, *Opere*, I, p. 119.

45. Enea Fergnani, *Un uomo e tre numeri* (Milan-Rome: Ed. Avanti! 1955; 1st edition Milan: Speroni, 1945), p. 188.

46. Aldo Bizzarri, *Mauthausen città ermetica* (Rome: OET/Edizioni Polilibraria, 1946), pp. 87–88, 110. Cf. Levi's 'Hier ist kein Warum' (*Opere*, I, p. 23).

47. Rava, p. 6.

48. Levi, *Opere*, I, p. 5.

49. Franco Brunello, *Stalag 307* (Vicenza: Edizione del Partito d'azione, 1945; also published in Milan: Casa Editrice La Fiaccola, 1945); Gino Gregori, *Ecce homo Mauthausen* (Milan: Ed. Stucchi, 1946); Egidio Meneghetti, 'L'ebreeta', in *Cante in piassa* (Venice: Neri Pozza, 1955).

50. Paolo Liggeri, *Triangolo rosso* (Milan: La Casa, 1946), pp. 7, 9.

51. Bravo and Jalla, *Misura*.

52. Schwarz, *Ritrovare*.

53. Moyn, *Controversy*, p. 11.

54. Piero Caleffi, *Si fa presto a dire fame* (Milan: Ed. Avanti!, 1954; 6th edition 1958).

55. Bruno Piazza, *Perché gli altri dimenticano* (Milan: Feltrinelli, 1956).

56. Mario Bonfantini, *Un salto nel buio* (Milan: Feltrinelli, 1959); Emilio Jani, *Mi ha salvato la voce* (Milan: Ceschina, 1960).

57. Edith Bruck, *Chi ti ama così* (Milan: Lerici, 1959).

58. Giacomo Debenedetti, *16 ottobre 43* (Milan: Il Saggiatore, 1959).

59. Piero Chiodi, *Banditi*, (Turin: Einaudi, 1961; 1st edition 1946).

60. Robert Antelme, *La specie umana* (Turin: Einaudi, 1954; 1st French edition 1947).

61. David Rubinowicz, *Il diario* (Turin: Einaudi, 1960); Emanuel Ringelblum, *Sepolti a Varsavia* (Milan: Mondadori, 1962).

62. Rudolf Höss, *Comandante ad Auschwitz* (Turin: Einaudi, 1960; 1st German edition 1958).

63. From 1985, Einaudi published it with a preface by Levi (*Opere*, II, pp. 1276–83).

64. Lord Russell of Liverpool, *Il flagello della svastica* (Milan: Feltrinelli, 1955; 1st English edition 1954); cf. Sullam Calimani, p. 53.

65. Léon Poliakov's *Il nazismo e lo sterminio degli ebrei* (Turin: Einaudi, 1955; 1st French edition 1951).

66. Gerald Reitlinger, *La soluzione finale* (Milan: Il Saggiatore, 1962; 1st English edition *The Final Solution*, 1953; see Chapter 9); W. L. Shirer, *Storia del Terzo Reich* (Turin: Einaudi, 1962; 1st English edition 1960).

67. Alberto Nirenstajn, *Ricorda che ti ha fatto Amalek* (Turin: Einaudi, 1958). (See Chapter 9.)

68. Piero Caleffi and Albe Steiner, *Pensaci, uomo!* (Turin: Einaudi, 1960); cf. a similar combination of text and image in Domenico Tarzizzo, ed., *Ideologia della morte. Storia e documenti dei campi di sterminio* (Milan: Il Saggiatore, 1962).

69. De Felice, *Storia*.

70. Edith Bruck, *Andremo in città* (Milan: Lerici, 1962).

71. Natalia Ginzburg, *Lessico famigliare* (Turin: Einaudi, 1963).

72. Giorgio Bassani, *Cinque storie ferraresi* (Turin: Einaudi, 1956); *Gli occhiali d'oro*, (Turin: Einaudi, 1958); *Il giardino dei Finzi-Contini*.

73. On a Manzonian thread in Italian Holocaust writing, see Chapter 7.

74. Ka-Tzetnik 135633, *La casa delle bambole* (Milan: Mondadori, 1959; 1st Hebrew edition, 1953).

75. André Schwarz-Bart, *L'ultimo dei giusti* (Milan: Feltrinelli, 1960; 1st French edition 1959).

76. Marcus, *Italian Film*, pp. 28, 35ff.

77. See Carlo Celli, *Gillo Pontecorvo* (Lanham, MD: Scarecrow Press, 2005), p. 15.

78. Rossellini's film is also an example of reprise or 'republication': it was based on a 1945 short story by Indro Montanelli, which appeared, like Debedenetti's *16 October 1943*, in *Mercurio* (Indro Montanelli, 'Pace all'anima sua', *Mercurio*, 2. 16 (December 1945): 220–23).

79. Perra, *Conflicts*, pp. 74–75; and cf. Chiara Ottaviano, 'Accademia e storia in TV. Una riflessione a partire dalle origini', in Nicola Gallerano, ed., *L'uso pubblico della storia* (Milan: Franco Angeli, 1995), pp. 83–102; Guido Crainz, 'The Representation of Fascism and the Resistance in the Documentaries of Italian State Television', in R.J.B Bosworth and Patrizia Dogliani, eds., *Italian Fascism: History, Memory and Representation* (London: Macmillan, 1999), pp. 123–40.

80. See Consonni, 'Impact'.

81. See, e.g. Giorgio Bocca, 'Eccolo! Sembra un istitutore un po' timido', *Il giorno*, 12 April 1961, with its opening flourish 'I turn, and I see Eichmann'.

82. Gideon Hausner, *Sei milioni di accusatori* (Turin: Einaudi, 1961).

83. Primo Levi et al., 'Tavola rotonda. La questione ebraica'; Gerald Reitlinger, 'Pagavano la propria morte'; and Marco Cesarini, 'La tavola di salvezza degli italiani', *Storia illustrata*, June 1961, pp. 754–84.

84. *L'espresso*, 30 April 1961. Minerbi's book was *La belva in gabbia: Eichmann* (Milan: Longanesi, 1962).

85. Augusto Guerriero, 'Ordine di sterminio', *Storia illustrata*, March 1960; 'Pantera nera', *L'espresso*, 16 April 1960.

86. Bosworth and Dogliani, pp. 7, 25–26. This was also a period of political turbulence triggered by the so-called Tambroni affair, when neo-Fascists entered a government coalition, which then collapsed following violent repression of protests in Genoa in July 1960 (Philip Cooke, *Luglio 1960*, Milan: Teti, 2000).

87. See '"Deportazione e sterminio di ebrei" di Primo Levi, con una nota di Alberto Cavaglion', *Lo straniero*, 11. 85 (July 2007): 5–12. The Milan, Rome and Turin lectures were published, respectively, as *1945–1975: Fascismo, antifascismo, Resistenza, rinnovamento* (Milan: Feltrinelli, 1962); *Lezioni sull'antifascismo* (Rome-Bari: Laterza, 1960); *Trent'anni di storia italiana: 1915–1945. Dall'antifascismo alla Resistenza* (Turin: Einaudi, 1961). In a subsequent cycle, published as *Fascismo e antifascismo 1918–1936* (Milan: Feltrinelli, 1962), short supplementary pieces were included on the Racial Laws (by Achille Ottolenghi, pp. 202–9) and on the camps (by Caleffi, pp. 432–35).

88. Marzia Luppi and Elisabetta Ruffini, eds., *Immagini dal silenzio. La prima mostra nazionale dei Lager nazisti attraverso l'Italia 1955–1960* (Modena: Nuovagrafica, 2005), pp. 38–39.

89. Guido Valabrega, ed., *Gli ebrei in italia durante il fascismo*, vols. I–III (Milan: CDEC, 1961–1963).

90. These pieces fed into Meir Michaelis, *Mussolini and the Jews: German-Italian Relations and the Jewish Question in Italy, 1922–1945* (Oxford: Oxford University Press, 1978).

91. *Rassegna mensile di Israel,* 5 (1960): 228 (Romano on Debenedetti); Dante Lattes, 'Tu quoque Quasimodo?' *Rassegna mensile di Israel,* 1 (1961): 3–5; G. L. Luzzatto, 'Il giardino dei Finzi-Contini', *Rassegna mensile di Israel,* 5 (1962): 239–40.

92. Maurice Pinay, *Complotto contro la chiesa* (Rome: [n. p.], 1962); and Renzo De Felice, 'L'ultima maschera', *Rassegna mensile di Israel,* 1 (1963): 63–68.

93. As noted, 15 books on the Holocaust were published by Einaudi from 1958 to 1963.

Chapter 5

1. On Germany, see Alexander and Margarete Mitscherlisch, *The Inability to Mourn* (New York: Grove Press, 1975; 1st German edition 1967); on Israel, Segev.

2. Novick, pp. 15, 209. The TV miniseries *Holocaust* was in part NBC's response to ABC's groundbreaking 1977 miniseries about slavery, *Roots.*

3. Michael Rothberg, *Multidirectional Memory: Remembering the Holocaust in the Age of Decolonization* (Stanford: Stanford University Press, 2009), pp. 175–98. Much later in the century, Italy's historicisation of its own colonialism, and its racist or genocidal violence, would draw on echoes and analogies with the Holocaust.

4. See Novick, pp. 218–20, 273–78. Wiesel's image and influence was enlarged further in 2006 by the adoption of his book *Night* for Oprah Winfrey's television book club (Dagmar Barnouw, 'True Stories : Oprah, Elie Wiesel, and the Holocaust', *History News Network,* 20 March 2006; http://hnn.us/articles/22099. html, accessed 11 September 2010).

5. Novick, p. 273.

6. Novick, p. 351.

7. Correspondence with Tedeschi in Risa Sodi, 'The Holocaust in Italian Literature', Ph.D. dissertation, Yale University, 1995, p. 267.

8. The exhibition was the Turin staging of the touring exhibition launched in 1955 in Carpi (Chapter 3; cf. Levi, *Opere,* II, pp. 1122–24; Luppi and Ruffini. Levi's article on the Rome exhibition was 'Monumento ad Auschwitz', *La stampa,* 18 July 1959 (*Opere,* I, pp. 1116–19); for Levi on Eichmann, see Levi et al., 'Tavola rotonda'; and Primo Levi, 'Testimonianza per Eichmann', *Il ponte* 4 (1961): 646–50.

9. The fullest bibliography of Levi's occasional interviews and writings is at *Opere,* I, pp. ciii–cxxvi (updates at www.primolevi.it [accessed 1 November 2010]). Selections have appeared in English in Primo Levi, *Voice of Memory: Interviews 1961–87* (Cambridge: Polity, 2000) and *Black Hole of Auschwitz* (Cambridge: Polity, 2005).

10. See Marco Belpoliti, 'Primo Levi traduttore' in Levi, *Opere,* II, pp. 1582–89; Lina Insana, *Arduous Tasks: Primo Levi, Translation, and the Transmission of Holocaust Testimony* (Toronto: University of Toronto Press, 2009).

11. He receives only three mentions in Luisa Mangoni, *Pensare i libri. La casa*

editrice Einaudi dagli anni trenta agli anni sessanta (Turin: Bollati Boringhieri, 1999), *ad indicem*.

12. See Joann Cannon, 'Canon-Formation and Reception in Contemporary Italy: The Case of Primo Levi', *Italica*, 69. 1 (Spring 1992): 30–44. A telling illustration of Levi's shifting canonical status is the work of Alberto Asor Rosa, author and editor of several synoptic histories of Italian literature in this period. His 1985 manual, *Storia della letteratura italiana* (Florence: La Nuova Italia, 1985), gives Levi a brief paragraph only (pp. 625–26). His multivolume *Letteratura italiana* (Turin: Einaudi, 1982–2000) affords him only passing references (the 1991 indices list 10; p. 1063). And yet in the 1996 volumes, *Le opere*, he is fully 'canonized' (Cesare Segre, '*Se questo è un uomo* di Primo Levi', in *Letteratura italiana. Le opere IV. Novecento. II. La ricerca letteraria* (Turin: Einaudi, 1996), pp. 491–508.)

13. 'I had no intention, nor would I have been able, to do the work of a historian' (Preface to *The Drowned and the Saved*, *Opere*, II, p. 1005).

14. Primo Levi, *La ricerca delle radici* (Turin: Einaudi, 1985; *Opere*, II, pp. 1357–1528).

15. Primo Levi, *Conversazioni ed interviste 1963–1987*, ed. by Marco Belpoliti (Turin: Einaudi, 1997), p. 257 (not in Levi, *Voice*).

16. Stuart Woolf, 'Primo Levi's Sense of History', *Journal of Modern Italian Studies*, 3. 3 (Fall 1998): 273–92 [p. 274].

17. Three of Levi's other books also appeared in this series during his lifetime. The first was *The Truce* (1965), with notes by Levi (this was the third book in the entire series); *The Periodic Table*, with preface by Natalia Ginzburg and notes by Levi (1979); and *The Wrench*, edited by G. L. Beccaria (1983).

18. Government decrees in 1960 extended school history teaching to include the war and aftermath, but in practice few teachers reached this point. From 1996, the so-called Berlinguer Decree made 20th-century history compulsory for the last years of *liceo*. See curriculum documents at SISSCO, 'Programmi e curriculi di storia' at http://www.sissco.it/index.php?id=1161 (accessed 14 December 2010). History textbooks of the period mentioned the Holocaust only in passing if at all (see Giovanni Belardelli, 'L'Italia scoprì l'olocausto dopo anni di silenzio', *Corriere della sera*, 12 January 2005). Cf. Enzo Traverso, ed., *Insegnare Auschwitz* (Turin, Bollati Boringhieri, 1995); Milena Santerini, *Antisemitismo senza memoria. Insegnare la Shoah nella società multiculturale* (Rome: Carocci, 2005); 'Scuola e Shoah', at http://archivio.pubblica.istruzione.it/shoah/didattica/index.shtml (accessed 14 December 2010).

19. Edith Bruck, *Signora Auschwitz* (Venice: Marsilio, 1999).

20. Primo Levi, *Se questo è un uomo* (Turin: Einaudi 'Letture per la scuola media', 1973), p. 11. I have translated the headings and comments here but left the bibliographical material in the Italian as presented by Levi, as these details are central to the discussion that follows.

21. See Mangoni and Chapter 3.

22. See *Opere*, I, p. 1194, where Levi notes that he read more foreign work than Italian following his return in 1945.

23. Wiesenthal asked writers and commentators—different groups for different translated editions—to comment on the novella in the first part of the book. The piece by Levi is not in *Opere* but is in the Garzanti edition he cites; and in Simon Wiesenthal, *The Sunflower* (New York: Schocken, 1998), pp. 191–92.

24. See Claudio Novelli, *Il Partito d'Azione e gli italiani. Moralità, politica e cittadinanza nella storia repubblicana* (Milan: La Nuova Italia, 2000); David Ward, *Antifascisms. Cultural Politics in Italy, 1943-46: Benedetto Croce and the Liberals, Carlo Levi and the 'Actionists'* (Madison, NJ: Fairleigh Dickinson University Press, 1996), pp. 124–56. Both Galante Garrone and Antonicelli were associated with the Actionists, as were *Il ponte* and *Il mondo*, where Levi published several early articles and stories.

25. Kushner, pp. 3–5.

26. Hersey and Shirer were journalists, Russell was a war-crimes advisor in the British-occupied zone and Debenedetti gathered evidence directly from the Roman Jewish community.

27. See Annette Wieviorka, *L'Ere du témoin* (Paris: Plon, 1998); Segev, pp. 321–84.

28. On Einaudi and Antelme, see Mangoni, p. 689.

29. *Opere*, I, p. 1160.

30. Simon Wiesenthal, *Gli assassini sono tra noi* (Milan: Garzanti, 1967).

31. The question of forgiveness became an irritant for Levi and a stimulant to some of his most intense late reflections, from his response to Wiesenthal in 1970 to the first question in the 1976 Appendix to *If This Is a Man* (*Opere*, I, p. 174), to his dialogue with Jean Améry (*Drowned*, *Opere*, II, pp. 1091–1108), who had labelled Levi 'the forgiver'.

32. In the Appendix to *If This Is a Man*, three of the seven questions concern Germans and only one Jews.

33. Segev, *passim*. See also Levi on the Warsaw ghetto, *Opere*, II, pp. 1183–86. Levi wrote repeatedly of resistance within the camps and across Eastern Europe, in ways often aligned with the Italian Resistance (e.g. 'La resistenza nel Lager', 1965, *Opere*, I, pp. 1146–51).

34. See *Opere*, II, pp. 1171–72; *Voice*, pp. 259–94.

35. *Se non ora, quando?* (Turin: Einaudi, 1982).

36. Jean Améry, *At The Mind's Limits* (London: Granta, 1999; 1st German edition 1966).

37. Hermann Langbein, *Uomini ad Auschwitz* (Milan: Mursia, 1984; 1st German edition 1972). Levi knew Langbein and wrote a preface for the Italian edition of his book, after trying to persuade Einaudi to publish it (*Opere*, II, pp. 1583–84); and translated its final pages for *The Search for Roots*, where he calls it

'a book I hold dear, which seems to be of fundamental importance, and which I wish I had written myself' (*Opere* II, p. 1519).

38. Gitta Sereny, *Into That Darkness* (London: Deutsch, 1974). Levi mentions Sereny approvingly in several places, e.g. *Opere*, I, p. 1210 (where she is bracketed with Langbein) and at a key point in *Drowned* (*Opere*, II, pp. 1089–90).

39. See Nancy Wood, 'The Victim's Resentments', in Bryan Cheyette and Laura Marcus, eds., *Modernity, Culture and 'the Jew'* (Stanford: Stanford University Press, 1998), pp. 257–67.

40. Levi, *Opere*, II, p. 1519. Another of what he calls the 'deportee-resister-historians' (*Opere*, II, p. 1024), whose work Levi promoted, quoted (*Opere*, I, p. 178–79) and recommended to Einaudi (*Opere*, II, p. 1583) was Eugen Kogon, whose *Der SS-Staat* was first published in 1946. On Kogon, see Donald Bloxham, *Genocide on Trial: War Crimes Trials and the Formation of Holocaust History and Memory* (Oxford: Oxford University Press, 2001), pp. 85–87; Fullbrook, p. 116.

41. The list is numbered for ease of reference in the discussion that follows. For the texts, see the miscellany pages in *Opere, ad indicem*.

42. On Levi and ANED, see Alberto Cavaglion, ed., *Primo Levi per l'ANED, l'ANED per Primo Levi* (Milan: Franco Angeli/ANED, 1997).

43. Sophie Nezri Dufour, *Primo Levi: una memoria ebraica del Novecento* (Florence: La Giuntina, 2002); Paola Valabrega, 'Primo Levi e la tradizione ebraico-orientale', *Studi piemontesi*, 11. 2 (1982): 296–310.

44. Adelphi was especially prominent in this vogue, as was the work of Triestine writer Claudio Magris (*Lontano da dove: Joseph Roth e la tradizione ebraico-orientale* (Turin: Einaudi, 1971); *Danubio* (Milan: Garzanti, 1986)). See Mirna Cicioni, *Primo Levi: Bridges of Knowledge* (Oxford: Berg, 1995), pp. 109–13.

45. Alberto Cavaglion, 'Argon e la cultura ebraica piemontese' *Belfagor*, 43.5 (September 1988): 541–62. Levi helped launch a minor wave of local, Jewish, family-oriented, autobiographical narratives, overshadowed by the Holocaust, e.g. Paolo Levi, *Il filo della memoria* (Milan: Rizzoli, 1984); V. Segre, *Storia di un ebreo fortunato*; Clara Sereni, *Casalinghitudine* (Turin: Einaudi, 1987). Cf. Raniero Speelman et al., eds., *Contemporary Jewish Writers in Italy: A Generational Approach* (Utrecht: Igitur, 2007).

46. On the Risiera camp, see Matta, pp. 125–39.

47. John Foot, *Fratture d'Italia* (Milan: Rizzoli, 2009), pp. 119–98 (not in Foot, *Italy's Divided Memory*); Glenda Sluga, 'The Risiera di San Sabba: Fascism, anti-Fascism and Italian nationalism', *Journal of Modern Italian Studies*, 1. 3 (1996): 401–12. On the Risiera trial, see Mauro Coslovich, 'Il processo della Risiera di san Sabba: una fonte per la storia', in Giovanna D'Amico and Brunello Mantelli, eds., *I campi di sterminio nazisti. Storia, memoria, storiografia* (Milan: Franco Angeli/ANED, 2003), pp. 69–88.

48. Walter Laqueur, *The Terrible Secret* (London: Weidenfeld and Nicolson, 1980).

49. See also Levi's angry articles on the escape of former Nazi SS colonel Herbert Kappler, head of the Gestapo in Rome and responsible for the Fosse Ardeatine massacre, from a military hospital in Rome in 1977 (*Opere*, I, pp. 1219–22).

50. Levi also wrote two other pieces on the series: see *Opere*, I, pp. 1264–71.

51. Ian Thomson, *Primo Levi* (London: Hutchinson, 2002), pp. 333–4.

52. Levi makes the comparison in the *Holocaust* preface, *Opere*, I, p. 1273; see also 'Film e svastiche', *Opere*, I, pp. 1217–18. For a defence of Cavani, see Teresa De Lauretis, 'Cavani's Night-Porter: A Woman's Film?', *Film Quarterly*, 30:2 (Winter 1976–77): 35–38. See also Chapter 7.

53. Bauman; and see Chapter 7.

54. E.g. the 1976 pieces 'Dai lager a Stalin' (*Opere*, I, pp. 1199–1201) and the Appendix to *If This Is a Man* (*Opere*, I, pp. 186–88).

55. Levi, *Voice*, pp. 233–38.

56. Raul Hilberg, *The Destruction of the European Jews* (Chicago: Quadrangle Books, 1961). Hilberg struggled to finding an American publisher for his work. It appeared in Italian only in 1995, with Einaudi.

57. On Hilberg, Poliakov and Reitlinger as early Holocaust historians, see Bloxham, pp. 115, 122, 202.

58. See Sullam Calimani, pp. 77–102 and *passim*.

59. Victor Klemperer's *LTI. Lingua Tertii Imperii* (Berlin: Aufbau, 1947) was another early postwar work which deeply influenced Levi and which he was still citing in *Drowned* (*Opere*, II, pp. 1066–69).

60. Sullam Calimani, pp. 39–41.

61. Levi includes internees and civilian workers as part of Lager history in 'La deportazione degli ebrei' (1967) (*Opere*, I, pp. 1163–66 [p. 1163]), written for ANEI (National Association of Ex-Internees), a parallel association to ANED.

62. Alberto Cavaglion, 'Il termitaio', *Asino d'oro*, 4 (1991); now in Ernesto Ferrero, ed., *Primo Levi: un'antologia della critica* (Turin: Einaudi, 1997), pp. 76–90.

63. Indirect confirmation comes from Giorgio Agamben, *Quel che resta di Auschwitz* (Turin: Bollati Boringhieri, 1998), which makes extensive use of Levi's work but, as Samuel Moyn argues, through the paradigm of Rousset's *univers concentrationnaire* (pp. 160–63).

64. Novelli, pp. 290–91. The post-1989 period of crisis in the Italian Republic saw the reemergence of the moral and political authority of the 'Actionists', embodied by figures such as Norberto Bobbio and Carlo Azeglio Ciampi. In these years also, Holocaust talk became a persistent feature of the Italian cultural and political scene; and both Bobbio and Ciampi made key contributions.

Chapter 6

1. On the Fascist myth of Rome, see e.g. Emilio Gentile, *The Sacralization of Politics in Fascist Italy* (Cambridge, MA: Harvard University Press, 1996).

2. See Peter Bondanella, *The Eternal City: Roman Images in the Modern World* (Chapel Hill: University of North Carolina Press, 1987); Bosworth, *Whispering*.

3. See David Forgacs, *L'industrializzazione della cultura italiana, 1880-2000* (Bologna: Il Mulino, 2002).

4. See Susan Zuccotti, *Under His Very Windows: The Vatican and the Holocaust in Italy* (New Haven: Yale University Press, 2000). The phrase is attributed to the German ambassador to the Vatican during the war, Ernst von Weizsäcker.

5. There is an earlier Italian film on the massacre: *Dieci italiani per un tedesco* (Filippo Walter Ratti, 1962).

6. An array of intellectuals (e.g. Alberto Moravia, Carlo Levi, Giangiacomo Feltrinelli, Bruno Zevi) and foreign correspondents (e.g. from the *New York Times* and London *Times*) were present, and fierce legal and parliamentary debate followed: see Francesca Faccini, '1965: va in scena a Roma il "Vicario"', *L'Unità*, 18 April 2002.

7. See Perra, *Conflicts*, pp. 197–201.

8. Galli della Loggia, *Morte*; and see a sample of the debate in *Liberal*, issues 15 (June 1996) to 17 (August 1996).

9. President and ex-'Actionist' Carlo Azeglio Ciampi pushed against Galli della Loggia's idea in a sustained campaign for a revived, moderate patriotism; see Gaspare Nevola, 'From the "Republic of Parties" to a "Fatherland for Italians": the Italian Political System in Search of a New Principle of Legitimation', *Journal of Modern Italian Studies*, 8. 2 (2003): 249–65.

10. Renzo De Felice, *Mussolini il duce. 1. Gli anni del consenso 1929–36* (Turin: Einaudi, 1974); Philip Cannistraro, *La fabbrica del consenso. Fascismo e mass media* (Bari: Laterza, 1975). And cf. Borden W. Painter, Jr., 'Renzo De Felice and the Historiography of Italian Fascism', *American Historical Review*, 95. 2 (April 1990): 391–405.

11. Variations on this position were embraced well beyond neo-Fascists, e.g. by Ciampi, by the journalist and popular historian Giampaolo Pansa (e.g. *I figli dell'aquila*, Milan: Sperling & Kupfer, 2002), or by the leftist singer-songwriter Francesco De Gregori ('Il cuoco di Salò', *Amore nel pomeriggio*, 2001).

12. This was the trial Debenedetti described in *Eight Jews*. The lynching fits into the wider history of the so-called settling of accounts, the revenge killing of former Fascists in the months after the end of the war, also the subject of intense controversy from the 1990s onwards: see Foot, *Italy's Divided Memory*, pp. 168–81; Sarah Morgan, *Rappresaglie dopo la Resistenza: l'eccidio di Schio tra guerra civile e guerra fredda* (Milan: Bruno Mondadori, 2002).

13. Portelli, *L'ordine*.

14. See Contini; Foot, *Italy's Divided Memory*.

15. Portelli, *L'ordine*, p. 4, and p. 359 on conflicting rulings on via Rasella as a 'legitimate act of war'.

16. Even the term 'wait' was a tricky one, for perceptions of the Resistance

and so of the Holocaust: against what he labelled the 'Resistance vulgate', De Felice had argued since the 1980s that the majority of Italians, far from taking up arms on either side, simply waited out the end of the war (De Felice, *Rosso*, pp. 53ff.; see Chapter 8).

17. As Foot, *Italy's Divided Memory*, pp. 22–29, relates, this included 'massacres' later discovered to have been caused by Allied air raids (e.g. San Miniato).

18. Portelli, *L'ordine*, pp. 287–88.

19. For France, see especially *Le Chagrin et la pitié* (dir. Marcel Ophuls, 1971) and Robert O. Paxton, *La France de Vichy* (Paris: Seuil, 1973).

20. See Katz's own website: http://www.theboot.it/home_2009.htm (accessed 10 October 2010).

21. Robert Katz, *Death in Rome* (New York: Macmillan, 1967), the source for the film *Massacre in Rome*.

22. Robert Katz, *Black Sabbath: A Journey Through a Crime Against Humanity* (New York: Macmillan, 1969). See the hostile review by Lucy Davidowicz in *Jewish Social Studies*, 32.1 (January 1970): 79–82.

23. Katz, 'A Conclusion', in *Black Sabbath*, pp. 316–30.

24. Arendt; and Richard I. Cohen, 'Breaking the Code: Hannah Arendt's *Eichmann in Jerusalem* and the Public Polemic', *Michael*, 13 (1993): 26–86.

25. Rumkowski was central to Levi's influential essay on 'the grey zone' in *The Drowned and the Saved* (*Opere* II, pp. 1037–44).

26. See Furio Colombo, 'Piazza Grande. La memoria della memoria', *Il fatto quotidiano*, 15 May 2010. For more on the memorial day, see Chapter 10.

27. Patrizia Dogliani, 'Constructing Memory and Anti-memory: Representations of Fascism and Its Denial in Republican Italy', in Bosworth and Dogliani, pp. 11–30 [pp. 23–4].

28. Rebecca Clifford, 'The Limits of National Memory: Anti-Fascist, the Holocaust and the Fosse Ardeatine Memorial in 1990s Italy', *FMLS*, 44.2 (April 2008): 128–39.

29. Cooke, *Legacy*.

30. Basaldella also designed in 1955 a monument at Mauthausen in a similar sharp, fragmented style. On the Fosse monument, see Francesca Romana Castelli, 'Un monumento diventato simbolo', *Capitolium*, 6. 21 (March–April 2002): 75–81; Teo Ducci, ed., *In memoria della deportazione. Opere di architetti italiani* (Milan: Mazzotta, 1997); Matta.

31. Michele Battini, *The Missing Italian Nuremberg: Cultural Amnesia and Postwar Politics* (London: Macmillan, 2007).

32. On the Kesselring trial and generally on the 1940s trials and the construction of 'a Nuremberg history of the Holocaust', see Bloxham, *Genocide*, pp. 77–80, 163–69.

33. See contemporary reportage in 'Lynching in Rome', *Life*, 9 October 1944, pp. 35–38.

34. Primo Levi, 'Lettera a Lattanazio', 'I tedeschi e Kappler', *Opere*, I, pp. 1219–22.

35. See John Foot, 'Via Rasella, 1944: Memory, Truth, and History', *Historical Journal*, 43.4 (2000): 1173–81; Clifford, pp. 134–37.

36. Elsa Morante, *La storia* (Turin: Einaudi, 1974).

37. Sodi, *Narrative*, pp. 190–206.

38. Rosetta Loy, *La parola ebreo* (Turin: Einaudi, 1997) and *Concorrenza sleale* (dir. Ettore Scola, 2001). On Loy, see Stefania Lucamante, 'The "Indispensable" Legacy of Primo Levi: From Eraldo Affinati to Rosetta Loy Between History and Fiction', *Quaderni d'italianistica*, 24. 2 (2003): 87–104; on Scola, see Marcus, pp. 111–24.

39. On *vérité* and the Holocaust, see Rothberg, pp. 175–98.

40. On melodrama and Holocaust film, see Marcia Landy, 'Cinematic History, Melodrama and the Holocaust', in Michael Signer, ed., *Humanity at the Limit: the Impact of the Holocaust Experience on Jews and Christians* (Bloomington: Indiana University Press, 2000), pp. 376–90.

41. Jewish participation in Resistance history and testimony has been an important point of contact between national Resistance and Holocaust cultures. Jewish partisans who later became public figures include Vittorio Foa, Carlo Levi, Primo Levi, Enzo Sereni, Emilio Sereni, Umberto Terracini, Leo Valiani. Those who died include the brilliant young intellectual Emanuele Artom, whose Resistance diaries were published by CDEC in 1966 (Emanuele Artom, *Diari: gennaio 1940–febbraio 1944*, Milan: CDEC, 1966).

Chapter 7

1. See Luppi and Ruffini.

2. Levi, *Opere*, I, p. 5.

3. See Ewout van der Knaap, ed., *Uncovering the Holocaust: The International Reception of* Night and Fog (London: Wallflower, 2006). The film was released in Italy in 1959 (Perra, *Conflicts*, p. 63).

4. An interesting Italian parallel was the documentary *All'armi siamo fascisti* (dir. Lino del Fra, 1961), which analysed Fascist racism as class struggle, with minimal reference to Jews or the racial laws (see Franco Fortini, *Tre testi per film* (Milan: Ed. Avanti!, 1963), pp. 5–54). Cf. Giorgio Israel, 'Redeemed Intellectuals and Italian Jews'.

5. Shandler, pp. 179–56.

6. On negationism in Italy, see Luigi Vianelli, 'I negazionisti italiani', *Olokaustos* at: http://www.olokaustos.org/saggi/saggi/negaz-ita/index.htm (accessed 14 December 2010); Francesco Germinario, 'Declinazioni italiane degli assassini della memoria: le vicende della pubblicistica negazionista in Italia', in D'Amico and Mantelli, *I campi di sterminio nazisti*, pp. 247–74. On anti-Semitic incidents in Italy, see Wyman and Rosenzveig, pp. 514–53.

7. See, e.g. Alberto Cavaglion, *Ebrei senza saperlo* (Naples: L'ancora del Mediterraneo, 2002), pp. 31–39, 177–82.

8. Cole.

9. From *The Truce* (Levi, *Opere*, I, p. 226).

10. Martin Crowley, *Robert Antelme: Humanity, Community, Testimony* (Oxford: Legenda, 2003).

11. Elio Vittorini, *Uomini e no* (Milan: Bompiani, 1945); *Conversazione in Sicilia* (Milan: Bompiani, 1945; 1st edition 1941). On Vittorini and Antelme, see Domenico Scarpa, 'Storie di libri necessari. Antelme, Duras, Vittorini' in *Storie avventurose di libri necessari* (Rome: Gaffi, 2010), pp. 165–202.

12. For Levi's 1946 reading of Vittorini, see *Opere*, I, p. 1194. A fourth interlocutor was Rousset (Moyn, pp. 52–56).

13. Later in Natalia Ginzburg, *Le piccole virtù* (Turin: Einaudi, 1962), pp. 69–72.

14. First published in 1954 in *Nuovi argomenti*, in 1964, it became the title piece of Moravia's essay collection *L'uomo come fine e altri saggi* (Milan: Bompiani, 1964). He developed similar positions earlier in 'Sempre amai il calore e la luce', *Mercurio*, 2.9 (May 1945): 93–100.

15. On Fascist book censorship and race, see Giorgio Fabre, *L'elenco: censura fascista, editoria e autori ebrei* (Turin: Zamorani, 1998); Guido Bonsaver, *Censorship and Literature in Fascist Italy* (Toronto: Toronto University Press, 2007).

16. Moravia, *L'uomo*, p. 129.

17. Moravia, *L'uomo*, pp. 129–33.

18. Moravia, *L'uomo*, p. 139, 145.

19. On Christian dimensions of early Holocaust response in Italy, see Perra, *Conflicts*, pp. 27–48; Consonni, 'Church'.

20. *Against Mussolini: Art and the Fall of a Dictator* (London: Estorick Collection, 2010), p. 51. Manzù is one of several Italian artists (including also Guttuso, Carlo Levi, Zoran Music, Corrado Cagli, Aldo Carpi) in the encyclopedic work by Ziva Amishai-Maisels, *Depiction and Interpretation: The Influence of the Holocaust on the Visual Arts* (Oxford: Pergamon Press, 1993).

21. *Against Mussolini*, pp. 39–40.

22. Moyn; cf. Michael André Bernstein's warnings against what he calls 'backshadowing' in *Foregone Conclusions: Against Apocalyptic History* (Berkeley: University of California Press, 1994); and Kushner on the inability of 'liberal universalism' to conceive of the Holocaust at this moment (Kushner, p. 216 and *passim*).

23. For a rare sustained treatment, see Perra, *Conflicts*, pp. 31–39.

24. [Dante Lattes], 'Qualche parola di presentazione', *Rassegna mensile di Israel*, 14. 1 (April 1948): 3–5 [p. 3].

25. Cristina Villa, '. . . e Mnemosine, confusa e smarrita, vaga tra le rovine. Monumenti e luoghi della memoria della deportazione razziale in Italia', in Ste-

fania Lucamante et al., eds., *Memoria collettiva e memoria privata: il ricordo della Shoah come politica sociale* (Utrecht: Igitur, 2008), pp. 181–92; Guri Schwarz, 'L'elaborazione del lutto. La classe dirigente ebraica e la memoria dello sterminio (1944–1948)', in Michele Sarfatti, ed., *Il ritorno alla vita: vicende e diritti degli ebrei in Italia dopo la seconda guerra mondiale* (Florence: Giuntina, 1998), pp. 167–80.

26. The episode was the subject of a film by Carlo Lizzani, *Hotel Meina* (2007).

27. See material reproduced in Luppi and Ruffini.

28. Adele Dei, 'Caproni e Quasimodo', in Franco Musarra et al., eds., *Quasimodo e gli altri* (Leuven/Florence: Leuven University Press/Franco Cesati, 2001), pp. 113–22 [p. 119]. In 1961, Caproni published two diary pieces on the visit, later in *Frammenti di un diario (1948–49)* (Genoa: San Marco dei Giustiniani, 1995).

29. Salvatore Quasimodo, *Il falso e vero verde* (Milan: Mondadori, 1956).

30. The term '*campo*' is also more fluid than it might first appear. Emerging from the landscape vocabulary that proceeds and follows it (the Vistula, the plains), it clearly connotes 'field' as well as 'camp'. The slippage between 'field of death'/'death camp' here was to be echoed in the lexicon of the Cambodian genocide in the late 1970s, where the term 'killing fields' was coined.

31. Sullam Calimani, pp. 71–76.

32. Quasimodo's 'reasons of our fate' (l. 11) perhaps echoes Levi's famous 'moment's intuition' in 'The Canto of Ulysses' chapter of *If This Is a Man*, 'of the reason of our destiny, of our being here [at Auschwitz] today' (*Opere*, I, p. 111).

33. This aspect was far from fully acknowledged in the Polish management of the site of Auschwitz itself in 1948 (Young, pp. 113–33).

34. Lattes, 'Tu quoque Quasimodo?'

35. On Lattes's response to Croce, see Finzi, pp. 84, 87–88, 108.

36. Stefano Pivato, *Bella Ciao: canto e politica nella storia d'Italia* (Bari: Laterza, 2005); Alessandro Portelli, 'The Centre Cannot Hold: Music as Political Communication in Post-War Italy' in Luciano Cheles and Lucio Sponza, eds., *The Art of Persuasion: Political Communication in Italy from 1945 to the 1990s* (Manchester: Manchester University Press, 2001), pp. 258–77.

37. Paolo Jachia, *Francesco Guccini: 40 anni di storie, romanzi, canzoni* (Rome: Editori Riuniti, 2002).

38. Vincenzo Pappalettera, *Tu passerai per il camino* (Milan: Mursia, 1965; 12th ed. 1967). Some accounts have Guccini writing his song in November 1964 (Bravo and Jalla, *Misura*, pp. 163, 439).

39. Bravo and Jalla, *Misura*, pp. 71–72.

40. The song was included on *Folk Beat N.1* but had already been recorded by the group Equipe 84 and was later sung by I Nomadi and Modena City Ramblers, as well as by Guccini himself.

41. Many have noted a relative absence in Dylan of reference to the Holo-

caust, even in his protest period, despite his Jewish background. There are exceptions, however, that might have influenced Guccini (e.g. 'With God on Our Side', on the album *The Times They Are A-Changin'*, 1964, with the lyric 'Though they murdered six million / In the ovens they fried / The Germans now too / Have God on their side)'; and 'Desolation Row' (*Highway 61 Revisited*, 1965). Woody Guthrie, Dylan's folk hero and also an influence on Guccini, wrote a song called 'Ilsa Koch' in 1948 about the infamous torturer at Buchenwald.

42. Toni Morrison, *Beloved* (New York: Plume, 1987). On the unstated Holocaust numbers game in the epigraph, see Novick, p. 194 and n. 100.

43. Further references to the Holocaust in the cantautore tradition are rare, but see Ivan della Mea's 'Chaim' (or 'Se il cielo fosse bianco di carta', on the album *Se qualcuno ti fa morto*, 1972), based on a letter written by a child from the concentration camp at Pustkow (http://www.cantilotta.org/canti_lager/07.htm, accessed 12 September 2010).

44. Bosworth, *Explaining*.

45. John Canaday, *The Nuclear Muse: Literature, Physics, and the First Atomic Bombs* (Madison: University of Wisconsin Press, 2000).

46. C. P. Snow, *The Two Cultures*, ed. by Stefan Collini (Cambridge: Cambridge University Press, 1993).

47. Levi, *Opere*, I, p. 461.

48. Robert Jay Lifton, *The Nazi Doctors: Medical Killing and the Psychology of Genocide* (New York: Basic Books, 1986). Lifton wrote influential works about Hiroshima also, including, with Erik Markusen, *The Genocidal Mentality: Nazi Holocaust and Nuclear Threat* (New York: Basic Books, 1990).

49. See essays such as 'Eclisse dei profeti' (*Opere* II, pp. 853–56); 'Covare il cobra' (*Opere*, II, pp. 990–93); and cf. Nancy Harrowitz, '"Mon maître, mon monstre": Monstrous Science in Primo Levi', in Keala Jewell, ed., *Literary Monsters* (Detroit: Wayne State University Press), pp. 51–64.

50. Pierpaolo Antonello, 'Un inglese in italia: Charles Percy Snow, le sue culture e il dibattito degli anni Sessanta', *Pianeta Galileo* (2009): 515–30.

51. Ernesto De Martino, *La fine del mondo. Contributo all'analisi delle apocalissi culturali* (Turin: Einaudi, 1977), p. 476.

52. Antonello, p. 523.

53. Elsa Morante, *Pro o contro la bomba atomica* (Milan: Adelphi, 1987), p. 99.

54. Giorgio Manganelli, *UFO e altri oggetti non identificati: 1972–1990* (Rome: Quiritta, 2003), p. 69.

55. On the apocalyptic novel, see Florian Mussgnug, 'Finire il mondo. Per un'analisi del romanzo apocalittico italiano degli anni 1970', *Contemporanea*, 1 (2000): 19–32; Bruno Pischedda, *La grande sera del mondo* (Turin: Aragno, 2004).

56. On this trope, see Cheyette and Marcus.

57. See Pier Paolo Pasolini, *Opere*, vols. I–X, ed. by Walter Siti (Milan: Mondadori, 1998–2003): IX.1, pp. 1211–27, 1338–46.

58. Pasolini's location trip became a documentary, *Sopralluoghi in Palestina per il 'Vangelo secondo Matteo'* (1965).

59. Pasolini, IX.1, pp. 1008–9, IX.2, pp. 17–25.

60. Pasolini, V, 751–8.

61. Pasolini, III, pp. 511–17.

62. On this wave, see Saul Friedländer, *Reflections of Nazism: An Essay on Kitsch and Death* (New York: Harper and Row, 1984); on its Italian manifestation, see David Forgacs, 'Days of Sodom: The Fascism-Perversion Equation in Films of 1960s and 1970s', in Bosworth and Dogliani, pp. 216–36; and Forgacs, 'Fascism and Anti-Fascism Reviewed: Generations, History and Film in Italy After 1968', in Helmut Peitsch et al., eds., *European Memories of the War* (Oxford: Berghahn, 1999), pp. 185–99; and cf. on Germany, Dagmar Herzog, '"Pleasure, Sex, and Politics Belong Together": Post-Holocaust Memory and the Sexual Revolution in West Germany', *Critical Inquiry*, 24 (Winter 1998): 393–444.

63. Thematics of the Holocaust and its traumatic memory, played out through family melodrama, already ran through Visconti's *Vaghe stelle dell'Orsa* (1965).

64. The same period saw several conventional film narratives about the Holocaust: for example, Edith Bruck's *Andremo in città* was adapted by Nelo Risi (Bruck's husband) in 1966; a story by the Florentine writer Vasco Pratolini centring on a working class man and his Jewish lover was adapted as *Diario di un italiano* (Sergio Capogna, 1973); and Bassani's *Garden of the Finzi-Continis* was filmed by Vittorio De Sica in 1970, in an internationally feted but bland production (Bassani argued with the director and withdrew his approval). On these, see Marcus, pp. 44–50; Perra, *Conflicts*, pp. 89–97.

65. Michel Foucault, *Discipline and Punish* (Harmondsworth: Penguin, 1978); cf. Irving Goffman's development of the notion of 'total institutions' in his 1961 work *Asylums* (Garden City, NY: Anchor, 1961).

66. Italo Calvino, *La giornata di uno scrutatore* (Turin: Einaudi, 1963); Paolo Volponi, *Memoriale* (Milan: Garzanti, 1962). On such literary analogies, see Alberto Cavaglion, 'Mnemagoghi e memoriosi: materiali per una unità didattica', in Traverso, pp. 114–23 [p. 120].

67. On Basaglia, see Michael Donnelly, *The Politics of Mental Health in Italy* (London: Routledge, 1992); Nancy Scheper-Hughes and Anne M. Lovell, eds., *Psychiatry Inside-Out: Selected Writings of Franco Basaglia* (New York: Columbia University Press, 1987). Basaglia was deeply struck by Levi's *If This Is a Man*, citing it in *Che cos'è la psichiatria?* (Parma: Amministrazione Provinciale di Parma, 1967); cf. Massimo Bucciantini, *Esperimento Auschwitz* (Turin: Einaudi, 2011), pp. 52–98.

68. Angelo Del Boca, *Manicomi come Lager* (Turin: Edizioni dell'Albero, 1966).

69. Giuliana Morandini, *E allora mi hanno rinchiusa: testimonianze dal manicomio femminile* (Milan: Bompiani,1977), p. 14.

70. Leonardo Sciascia, 'Nota', in Alessandro Manzoni, *Storia della colonna infame* (Palermo: Sellerio, 1981), pp. 169–90.

71. Sciascia, p. 176.

72. Charles Rohmer, *L'autre* (Paris: Gallimard, 1951).

73. Sciascia, p. 176.

74. Rohmer, *L'altro* (Turin: Einaudi, 1954); blurb by Elio Vittorini (emphasis indicates the phrase quoted by Sciascia, pp. 176–77).

75. Morante, *Pro e contro*, p. 91, quoted in Antonello, p. 523.

76. Sebastiano Vassalli, 'Se va in onda la destra', *Corriere della Sera*, 30 September 2000. The conceit of the concentration camp as game show was taken up by French novelist Amélie Nothomb, *Acide sulfurique* (Paris: Michel, 2005).

77. Agamben, *Quel*; for a critical response, see Dominic LaCapra, 'Approaching Limit Event: Siting Agamben', in Michael Bernard-Donals and Richard Glejzer, eds., *Witnessing the Disaster: Essays on Representation and the Holocaust* (Madison: University of Wisconsin Press, 2003), pp. 262–304.

78. Giorgio Agamben, *Homo sacer: potere sovrano e nuda vita* (Turin: Einaudi, 1995); *Stati di eccezione. Homo sacer II* (Turin: Bollati Boringhieri, 2003).

79. Another symptomatic work of Italian political philosophy to make comparable analogies from the camps to modern terror and responses to it is Adriana Cavarero, *Horrorism: Naming Contemporary Violence* (New York: Columbia University Press, 2009).

80. See e.g. his play *Dybbuk* (Radio popolare CD, 1995).

81. Marco Rovelli, *Lager italiani* (Milan: Rizzoli, 2006), pp. 7–8 (De Luca), pp. 281–83 (Ovadia), pp. 267–79 (Rovelli's appendix).

Chapter 8

1. Silvana Patriarca, *Italian Vices: Nation and Character from the Risorgimento to the Republic* (Cambridge: Cambridge University Press, 2010).

2. Patriarca, pp. 5–13; cf. Giulio Bollati, *L'italiano. Il carattere nazionale come storia e come invenzione* (Turin: Einaudi, 1983).

3. Levi, *Opere*, II, pp. 1017–44. On the genesis of the essay, dating back to 1975 at least, see pp. 1564–66. On its influence and articulations, see Anna Bravo, 'Sulla "zona grigia"', and Martina Mengoni, 'Variazioni Rumkowski', both at http://www.primolevi.it/Web/Italiano/Contenuti/Auschwitz/105_Sulla_%22zona_grigia%22 (accessed 1 December 2011).

4. Alberto Cavaglion, 'Primo Levi tra i sommersi e i salvati', *Lo straniero*, 7.48 (June 2004): 40–49.

5. See Richard Mitten, *The Politics of Antisemitic Prejudice: The Waldheim Phenomenon in Austria* (Boulder: Westview Press, 1992).

6. Giorgio Bocca, 'La via del perdono passa per Vienna', *La repubblica*, 12 June 1986.

7. Thomson links the episode to Levi's last depression (p. 507).

8. Alessandro Galante Garrone, 'Waldheim il grigio', *La stampa*, 14 June 1986.

9. Quoted in Cavaglion, 'Primo Levi', p. 48. On the Fascist and anti-Semitic pasts of later anti-Fascists, see Mirella Serri, *I Redenti* (Milan: Corbaccio, 2005).

10. See De Felice, *Mussolini il duce. 1.* and *Intervista sul fascismo*. On the impact of the interview, see Manuela Consonni, 'A War of Memories: De Felice and His *Intervista sul Fascismo*', *Journal of Modern Jewish Studies*, 5.1 (March 2006): 43–56; Painter.

11. Jacques Sémelin, *Sans armes face à Hitler. La Résistance civile en Europe (1939–1943)* (Paris: Pavot, 1989).

12. Claudio Pavone, *Una guerra civile: saggio storico sulla moralita nella Resistenza* (Turin: Bollati Boringhieri, 1991); and 'Caratteri e eredità della zona grigia', *Passato e presente*, 16.43 (January–April 1998): 5–12.

13. De Felice, *Rosso*.

14. De Felice, *Rosso*, pp. 55–65.

15. See Raffaele Liucci, *La tentazione della 'casa in collina'. Il disimpegno degli intellettuali nella guerra civile italiana (1943–1945)* (Milan: Unicopli, 1999).

16. De Felice, *Rosso*, p. 161.

17. Pavone, 'Caratteri', p. 5.

18. Edward Banfield, *The Moral Basis of a Backward Society* (New York: Free Press, 1958); Pavone, 'Caratteri', p. 8.

19. Filippo Focardi, 'La memoria della guerra e il mito del "bravo italiano". Origine e affermazione di un autoritratto collettivo', *Italia contemporanea*, 220–21 (2000): 93–99; Filippo Focardi and Lutz Klinkhammer, 'The Question of Fascist Italy's War Crimes: The Construction of a Self-Acquitting Myth (1943–1948)', *Journal of Modern Italian Studies*, 9.3 (2004), pp. 330–48. Already in 1949, Nicola Chiaromonte was commenting sarcastically 'Italy is crowded with *brave persone*' ('Rome Letter', *Partisan Review*, 16. 3, March 1949: 303–13 [p. 303]).

20. Michele Sarfatti, 'Razzisti per ordine superiore', in *Mi ricordo*, special issue of *Diario*, 27 January 2001, pp. 78–81.

21. Filippo Focardi, '"Bravo italiano" e "cattivo tedesco": riflessioni sulla genesi di due immagini incrociate', *Storia e memoria*, 5. 1 (1996): 55–83.

22. Perra, *Conflicts*, pp. 156–58.

23. Perra, *Conflicts*, p. 225.

24. Nicola Caracciolo, *Gli ebrei e l'Italia durante la guerra 1940–45* (Rome: Bonacci, 1986), p. 17.

25. Caracciolo, *Gli ebrei*, pp. 17–20.

26. The passage is worth quoting, since Caracciolo's introduction was not used in the English translation of the book: '[Italian Jews] had nothing in common with the ghetto Jews of central and eastern Europe, who lived in overcrowded neighbourhoods, with their filthy, narrow streets and parchment rolls of Bible verses attached to their doorposts, showing off their black cloaks with their enormous folds ('kaftans'), their broad-brimmed black hats, their rarely

shaven beards and their curls at their temples which had never seen a rasor for reasons of religious duty' (Caracciolo, *Gli ebrei*, p. 20).

27. Renzo De Felice, 'Foreword' in Nicola Caracciolo, *Uncertain Refuge: Italy and the Jews During the Holocaust* (Urbana: University of Illinois Press, 1995), pp. xv–xxiii [bullet points pp. xv–xvii].

28. Bidussa, *Il mito del bravo italiano*; and cf. Claudio Fogu, '*Italiani brava gente*: The Legacy of Fascist Historical Culture on Italian Politics of Memory', in Richard Ned Lebow, Wulf Kansteiner and Claudio Fogu, eds., *The Politics of Memory in Postwar Europe* (Durham: Duke University Press, 2006), pp. 147–76.

29. Respectively, Davide Rodogno, '*Italiani brava gente*? Fascist Italy's Policy Towards the Jews in the Balkans, April 1941–July 1943', *European History Quarterly*, 35. 2 (2005): 213–40; Carlo Spartaco Capogreco, *Ferramonti. La vita e gli uomini del più grande campo d'internamento fascista (1940–1945)* (Florence: La Giuntina, 1987); Angelo Del Boca, *Italiani, brava gente? Un mito duro a morire* (Vicenza: Neri Pozza Editore, 2005).

30. For a recent restatement see Sarfatti, *Shoah*.

31. Deaglio, *La banalità del bene*.

32. Perra, *Conflicts*, pp. 223–30.

33. In the original story (Montanelli, 'Pace')—by another former resister and former Fascist, like Bocca—reportage and fiction are blurred, as the General/Bertoni is executed amongst the 70 killed at Fossoli on 22 June 1944.

34. Patriarca, pp. 217–26.

35. The vision of flawed but decent Italians is a foreign stereotype also. See, e.g. the Italian soldiers (in contrast to the evil Germans) in Louis de Bernières, *Captain Corelli's Mandolin* (London: Secker and Warburg, 1994; film, dir. John Madden, 2001). In historiography too, the good Italian has had strong purchase amongst influential non-Italian historians of the Holocaust, from Poliakov to Arendt to Goldhagen. Jonathan Steinberg compares Fascist and Nazi treatments of Jews and finds that 'German virtues and vices represented the opposite of Italian' (*All or Nothing*, p. 180).

36. Pavone, 'Caratteri', p. 11.

37. Nuto Revelli, *Il disperso di Marburg* (Turin: Einaudi, 1994). Cf. Gianluca Cinelli, *Ermeneutica e scrittura autobiografica: Primo Levi, Nuto Revelli, Rosetta Loy, Mario Rigoni Stern* (Milan: Unicopli, 2008), pp. 89–117.

Chapter 9

1. Segev; Zertal.
2. Segev, pp. 449–55.
3. [Lattes], 'Qualche parola', p. 5.
4. Schwarz, *Ritrovare*, pp. 116–23.
5. Schwarz, *Ritrovare*, pp. 48–100.
6. On Israel and the Italian left, see Maurizio Molinari, *La sinistra e gli ebrei*

in Italia 1967–1993 (Milan: Corbaccio, 1995); Fiamma Nirenstein, *Gli antisemiti progressisti: una forma nuova di un odio antico* (Milan: Rizzoli, 2004).

7. See Gabriella Poli and Giorgio Calcagno, *Echi di una voce perduta: incontri, interviste e conversazioni con Primo Levi* (Milan: Mursia, 1992), pp. 136–47.

8. Natalia Ginzburg, 'Gli ebrei', *La stampa*, 14 September 1972. Cf. Arrigo Levi, 'Una risposta alla Ginzburg', *La stampa*, 15 September 1972.

9. See Franco Fortini, *Sere in Valdossola* (Milan: Mondadori, 1963).

10. Franco Fortini, *I cani del Sinai* (Bari: De Donato, 1967); and see also the edition of 2002 (*I cani del Sinai* (Macerata: Quodlibet, 2002) with Fortini's 'Lettera agli ebrei italiani' as an appendix.

11. See Levi, *Voice*, pp. 259–93.

12. Emiliano Perra, 'La prima guerra del Libano (1982) e la costruzione dell'ebreo come "altro" nel dibattito pubblico italiano', unpublished paper at conference Language, Space and Otherness in Italy Since 1861, British School at Rome, June 2010.

13. 'Il fascismo fu parte del male assoluto', *La repubblica*, 24 November 2003. Cf. the account by Amos Luzzatto, in *Conta e racconta. Memorie di un ebreo di sinistra* (Milan: Mursia, 2008), especially the appendix 'Lettera riservata: Ebrei, sinistra, Fini'.

14. See Pierpaolo Antonello and Florian Mussgnug, eds., *Postmodern* impegno: *Ethics and Commitment in Contemporary Italy* (Oxford: Peter Lang, 2009).

15. The boycott call began within the radical left in Turin but developed internationally and also, with fierce polemic, within the left, after Valentino Parlato, a founder of the radical left newspaper *Il manifesto*, came out against it: Valentino Parlato, 'Un boicottaggio sbagliato', *Il manifesto*, 24 January 2008.

16. See e.g. Novick; Cole; and Hilene Flanzbaum, ed., *The Americanization of the Holocaust* (Baltimore: Johns Hopkins University Press, 1999).

17. Goldhagen; and on the debate that followed, see Robert R. Shandley, ed., *Unwilling Germans? The Goldhagen Debate* (Minneapolis: University of Minnesota Press, 1998).

18. See Novick; and more polemically, Norman Finkelstein, *The Holocaust Industry* (London: Verso, 2000).

19. Bruno Bettelheim, 'Surviving', *New Yorker*, 2 August 1976, pp. 31–52; later in *Surviving and Other Essays* (London: Thames and Hudson, 1979), pp. 274–314.

20. Terence Des Pres, *The Survivor: An Anatomy of Life in the Death Camps* (Oxford: Oxford University Press, 1976); and 'Bleak Comedies', *Harper's*, June 1976, pp. 26–28.

21. Cf. Jonathan Druker and Michael Rothberg, 'A Secular Alternative: Primo Levi's Place in American Holocaust Discourse', *Shofar* 28.1 (Fall 2009): 104–26.

22. Publicity material for Primo Levi, *The Periodic Table* (New York: Schocken, 1984).

23. Primo Levi, *If Not Now, When?* (New York: Summit, 1985). For the assault in *Commentary*, see Fernanda Eberstadt, 'Reading Primo Levi', *Commentary*, October 1985, pp. 41–47; and cf. Thomson, pp. 482–83.

24. See Bryan Cheyette, 'Appropriating Primo Levi', in Robert S. C. Gordon, ed., *Cambridge Companion to Primo Levi* (Cambridge: Cambridge University Press, 2007), pp. 67–85.

25. See Alberto Cavaglion, *Notizie su Argon* (Turin: Instar, 2006).

26. See 'Business Data for Vita è Bella, La', http://us.imdb.com/Business?0118799 (accessed May 2010); and Colin MacCabe, 'Life Is Beautiful/La vita è bella', *Sight and Sound*, February 1999, p. 46.

27. ' "La vita è bella" stravince la serata televisiva', *La repubblica*, 23 October 2001.

28. Tullia Zevi, quoted in 'Congratulazioni da Israele qualche dubbio dalla Zevi', *La repubblica*, 22 March 1999.

29. See respectively Gerald Peary, 'No Laughing Matter', *Boston Phoenix*, 30 October 1998; Richard Schickel, 'Fascist Fable', *Time*, 9 November 1998, pp. 116–17; David Denby, 'Life Is Beautiful', and Art Spiegelman, 'Sketchbook', *New Yorker*, 15 March 1999, pp. 96–99; Cf. Art Spiegelman, *Maus: A Survivor's Tale*, vols. I-II (New York: Penguin, 1987, 1991).

30. On responses to the film as a marker of taste, see Maurizio Viano, '*Life Is Beautiful*: Reception, Allegory, and Holocaust Laughter', *Jewish Social Studies*, 5. 3 (1999): 47–66 [pp. 48–49].

31. Gillian Rose, 'Beginnings of the Day: Fascism and Representation', in *Mourning Becomes the Law: Philosophy and Representation* (Cambridge: Cambridge University Press 1996), pp. 41–62 [pp. 41–48].

32. *Kapò* entered film history, and the debate about Holocaust representation, through a fierce attack on its use of a 'tracking shot' by Jacques Rivette, 'De l'abjection', *Cahiers du cinéma*, 120 (June 1961): 54–55. Cf. Serge Daney, 'The Tracking Shot in *Kapo*' (1992), *Senses of Cinema*, 30 (January–March 2004), at: http://www.sensesofcinema.com/2004/feature-articles/kapo_daney/ (retrieved 4 December 2011).

33. See Celli, pp. 31–46, and *passim*.

34. Bruck fictionalised her on-set experiences with *Kapò* in *Transit* (Milan: Bompiani, 2008).

35. Rothberg.

36. See also Marco Belpoliti and Andrea Cortellessa, *Da una tregua all'altra. Auschwitz-Torino sessant'anni dopo* (Milan: Chiarelettere, 2010).

37. See 'History of the ITF', http://www.holocausttaskforce.org/about-the-itf/history-of-the-itf.html (accessed 15 September 2010).

38. Leonardo Paggi, 'Per una memoria europea dei crimini nazisti', *Passato e presente*, 12.32 (May–August 1994): 105–17 [p. 110].

39. For the translations, see Chapter 5, section 2, and Bibliography. ANED's volume was *L'oblio è colpa* (Milan: ANED, 1954); for the monument, see Ducci.

40. Giorgio Bassani, 'Una lapide in via Mazzini' (1952), in *La passeggiata prima di cena* (Florence: Sansoni, 1953); later in *Cinque storie ferraresi* (Turin: Einaudi, 1956).

41. Ugo Varnai, 'Lo sterminio degli ebrei d'Europa (I–III)', *Comunità*, 7. 22 (December 1953): 16–23; 7. 23 (February 1954): 10–15; 7. 24 (April 1954): 36–39. For a fuller discussion see Robert S. C. Gordon, ' "Fare testo in materia": Ugo Varnai, *Comunità*, and the Holocaust in 1950s Italian Culture', in *Meneghello: Fiction, Scholarship, Passione Civile*, ed. by Daniela La Penna, supplement to *The Italianist*, 32 (2012): 191–206.

42. In 1952 Piero Calamandrei's journal *Il ponte* published four essays by Antonio Spinosa on Fascist persecution of the Jews in Italy (a planned fifth, on 1943–1945, was never published): Antonio Spinosa, 'Le persecuzioni razziali in Italia (I–IV)', *Il ponte*, 7 (1952): 964–78; 8 (1952): 1078–96; 11 (1952): 1604–22; 7 (1953): 950–68. See Schwarz, *Ritrovare*, pp. 161–68.

43. Reitlinger, *Final*.

44. The photographs, some of them shocking images of skeletal bodies, led to threats to sue *Comunità* for indecent publication (Simonetta Fiori, 'Meneghello e l'olocausto', *La repubblica*, 16 September 1994).

45. Correspondence referred to here is held at the Archivio Storico Olivetti in Ivrea, Edizioni di Comunità archive (Carteggio redazionale. Meneghello, Luigi, 1952–1961, cart. 22. 623, faldone n. 39).

46. The postwar years saw a boom in glossy magazines, which often covered trials and scandals linked to recent history: see Valerio Castronovo and Nicola Tranfaglia, *La stampa italiana dalla Resistenza agli anni sessanta* (Rome: Laterza, 1980).

47. Léon Poliakov, *La Condition des juifs en France sous l'occupation italienne* (Paris: Centre de Documentation Juive Contemporaine, 1946); translated as *Gli ebrei sotto l'occupazione italiana* (Milan: Edizioni di Comunità, 1956).

48. Reitlinger, *Soluzione*.

49. Luigi Meneghello, *Promemoria: lo sterminio degli ebrei d'Europa 1939–45* (Bologna: Il Mulino, 1994).

50. Piera Sonnino, *Questo è stato: una famiglia italiana nei lager* (Milan: Il Saggiatore, 2004); Aldo Zargani, *Per violino solo* (Bologna: Il Mulino, 1995).

51. On second-language writing, see Andrea Ciccarelli, 'Frontier, Exile, and Migration in the Contemporary Italian Novel' in Peter Bondanella and Andrea Ciccarelli, eds., *Cambridge Companion to the Italian Novel* (Cambridge: Cambridge University Press, 2003), pp. 197–212.

52. See, for example, the three stories of Edith Bruck, *Due stanze vuote* (Venice: Marsilio, 1974), set in a Hungarian village, a suburb of New York and a boat travelling to Israel. Italy hovers as a fourth perspective from which to explore these other sites of trauma and memory.

53. Giorgio and Nicola Pressburger, *Storie dell'ottavo distretto* (Casale Monferrato: Marietti, 1986).

54. Giorgio Pressburger, *Nel regno oscuro* (Milan: Bompiani, 2008).

55. See, e.g. Helga Schneider, *Lasciami andare, madre* (Milan: Adelphi, 2001).

56. Helena Janeczek, *Lezioni di tenebra* (Milan: Mondadori, 1997).

57. Sullam Calimani, *passim.*

58. Sullam Calimani, pp. 19–24.

59. Legge 211, *Gazzetta Ufficiale*, n.177, 31 July 2000 (emphasis in original). See Chapter 10.

60. See, e.g. Furio Colombo, 'La Shoah, crimine anche italiano', *La repubblica*, 27 January 2001.

61. Alberto Cavaglion, *La resistenza spiegata a mia figlia* (Naples: L'ancora del Mediterraneo, 2005).

62. 'We Remember: A Reflection on the Shoah', http://www.vatican. va/roman_curia/pontifical_councils/chrstuni/documents/rc_pc_chrstuni_ doc_16031998_shoah_en.html (accessed 1 November 2010).

63. Young, pp. 119–54; Cole, pp. 97–120.

64. See Young, pp. 133–41; cf. Giorgio Simoncini, 'Il monumento di Auschwitz Birkenau. Cronologia del concorso e della costruzione', www.giorgiosimoncini.com/pdf/AWZ.Int.Cronologia.pdf (accessed 1 October 2010).

65. Quoted in Young, p. 135.

66. For a general history of Italian architecture of the period, see Terry Kirk, *The Architecture of Modern Italy* Vol. 2: *Visions of Utopia, 1900–Present* (New York: Princeton Architectural Press, 2005).

67. Pietro Cascella, *Opere monumentali* (Milan: Electa, 1993).

68. Simoncini particularly insists on his and Cascella's artistic authorship of the final monument; 'Il monumento di Auschwitz Birkenau. Rassegna di documenti', http://www.giorgiosimoncini.com/rassegna.html, accessed 10 October 2010).

69. Venturi was one of only 12 Italian university professors in the entire country to refuse the oath of allegiance to the regime demanded in 1931.

70. *Monumento internazionale di Auschwitz* (Rome: Galleria nazionale d'arte moderna, 1959).

71. 'Il monumento ai martiri di Auschwitz', *L'antifascista*, June 1959.

72. On the Congress for Cultural Freedom, see Frances Stonor Saunders, *Who Paid the Piper? The CIA and the Cultural Cold War* (London: Granta, 1999); Massimo Teodori, *Benedetti americani. Dall'Alleanza Atlantica alla Guerra contro il terrorismo* (Milan, Mondadori, 2003), pp. 75–110.

73. Typescript of press release, in historical archive of Galleria nazionale d'arte moderna, Rome (fasc. 1, ritagli stampa, X 70).

74. Untitled notice, *La voce repubblicana*, 24 May 1959.

75. Primo Levi, 'Monumento ad Auschwitz', 18 July 1959 (*Opere* I, pp. 1116–19).

76. See, respectively: [S. Su]. 'Tempo di belve', *Italia domani*, 12 July 1959;

Arrigo Levi, 'Un singolare monumento per non far dimenticare. 2 mostre ammonitrici a Roma', *Corriere d'informazione*, 11 July 1959; [I. L.], 'In una vecchia casacca sfilacciata il simbolo del terrore hitleriano', *Patria indipendente*, 6 September 1959.

77. The complicated history of the gestation of the monument is reconstructed in Elisabetta Ruffini and Sandro Scarrocchia, 'Il Blocco 21 di Auschwitz: un cantiere di riflessione e di lavoro', *Studi e ricerche di storia contemporanea*, 69 (June 2008): 9–32. See also the special issue 'La vicenda del Memoriale italiano di Auschwitz', *Studi e ricerche di storia contemporanea*, 74 (February 2011); and Ducci, pp. 56–65.

78. On Nono's work for the monument, see Ruffini and Scarrocchia, and http://www.luiginono.it/it/luigi-nono/opere/ricorda-cosa-ti-hanno-fatto-in-auschwitz (accessed 1 December 2010).

79. Ruffini and Scarrocchia; and Foot, *Italy's Divided Memory*, pp. 93–95.

80. Giovanni De Luna, 'Se questo è un memorial', *La stampa*, 21 January 2008; and Giovanni De Luna, *La repubblica del dolore. Le memorie di un'Italia divisa* (Milan: Feltrinelli, 2011).

81. See 'La vicenda'; Ruffini and Scarrocchia's work is part of this project.

Chapter 10

1. For this and the phrase 'After Such Knowledge' in this chapter's title, see Eva Hoffman, *After Such Knowledge: A Meditation on the Aftermath of the Holocaust* (London: Secker & Warburg, 2004).

2. The story behind the publication of *Questo è stato* meshes with other strands of public Holocaust culture in the 21st century. Written in 1960, the manuscript was sent in 2002 to the campaigning leftist magazine *Diario*, edited by Enrico Deaglio, for a memory project. *Diario* published it in its entirety in their Day of Memory special issue, *Memoria* (January 2003), under the title 'Manoscritto ritrovato. La deportazione della mia famiglia'. The same issue offered a free copy of Deaglio's 1991 book on Giorgio Perlasca, *La banalità del bene*. Publishers Il Saggiatore turned Sonnino's work into a book, with the new title, in 2004.

3. See Lucamante. As we have seen, others such as Pontecorvo or Guccini were already being inspired by reading Levi decades earlier.

4. Something similar had occurred, albeit on a smaller scale and with far less impact, on the 40th anniversary in 1978: for example, *Il ponte* dedicated a special issue to 'La difesa della razza', with contributions from a series of key figures in the history of the journal and in postwar intellectual history (including Norberto Bobbio, Piero Calamandrei, Cesare Cases, Giacomo Debenedetti, Primo Levi, Alberto Moravia): 'La difesa della razza', *Il ponte*, special issue ed. by Ugo Caffaz, 34.11–12 (November–December 1978): 1303–1520. Another contributor, Giuseppe Mayda, published in 1978 a detailed study of Jews under Salò, a

neglected area in previous historiography: *Ebrei sotto Salò: la persecuzione antisemita 1943–1945* (Milan: Feltrinelli, 1978).

5. *La legislazione antiebraica in Italia e in Europa* (Rome: Camera dei deputati, 1989); Mario Toscano, ed., *L'abrogazione delle leggi razziali in Italia, 1943–1987* (Rome: Studi del Senato della Repubblica, 1988); *Conseguenze culturali delle leggi razziali in Italia* (Rome: Accademia dei Lincei, 1989). On 1988, see Enzo Collotti, 'Il razzismo negato', *Italia contemporanea*, 212 (September 1998): 577–87.

6. '1938. Le leggi contro gli ebrei', *Rassegna mensile di Israel*, special issue ed. by Michele Sarfatti, 54. 1–2 (January–August 1988).

7. See Cavaglion, *Ebrei*, pp. 39–54.

8. See several essays in Zimmerman, *Jews in Italy*.

9. Capogreco, *Ferramonti*.

10. On Italian colonialism, see Ruth Ben-Ghiat and Mia Fuller, eds, *Italian Colonialism* (New York: Palgrave, 2005).

11. Paul Ginsborg, *Italy and Its Discontents: Family, Civil Society, State 1980–2001* (London: Allen Lane, 2001).

12. Sergio Luzzatto, *La crisi dell'antifascismo* (Turin: Einaudi, 2004), pp. 10–13.

13. Foot, *Italy's Divided Memory*.

14. Pavone, *Guerra*. De Felice's 1995 interview *Rosso e nero* was one of the intense foci for these debates (Chapter 8).

15. Robert Ventresca, 'Mussolini's Ghost: Italy's Duce in History and Memory', *History and Memory*, 18.1 (Spring–Summer 2006): 86–119.

16. On the military internees, see Ugo Dragoni, *La scelta degli I.M.I. Militari italiani prigionieri in Germania (1943–1945)* (Florence: Le Lettere, 1996); or the autobiographical verse dialogue, based on memories of an internee-father, Franco Marcoaldi, *Benjaminowo. Padre e figlio* (Milan: Bompiani, 2004).

17. Cavaglion, *Ebrei*, p. 54.

18. As noted in Chapter 5, 1996 saw school history teaching transformed by the Berlinguer Decree, which made 20th-century history a compulsory part of the national school curriculum.

19. Alexander Stille, *Uno su mille: cinque famiglie ebraiche durante il fascismo* (Milan: Mondadori, 1991); in English as *Benevolence and Betrayal: Five Italian Jewish Families Under Fascism* (New York : Summit Books, 1991).

20. See Marcus, *Italian Film*; Perra, *Conflicts*, for detailed treatments of the films of this period.

21. See Annette Insdorf, *Indelible Shadows: Film and the Holocaust* (Cambridge: Cambridge University Press, 3rd edition 2003).

22. Bruno Maida, ed., *Un' etica della testimonianza: la memoria della deportazione femminile e Lidia Beccaria Rolfi*, (Milan: Franco Angeli/ANED, 1997); Cavaglion, *Primo Levi per l' ANED*.

23. La Giuntina's first publication in the field was the first Italian edition of

Elie Wiesel's *La Nuit*: Wiesel, *La notte*, tr. by Daniel Vogelmann (Florence: La Giuntina, 1980).

24. Bravo and Jalla, *Misura*, pp. 74–6, 307–9.

25. Elisa Springer, *Il silenzio dei vivi: all'ombra di Auschwitz un racconto di morte e resurrezione* (Venice: Marsilio, 1997).

26. Boris Pahor, *Necropoli* (San Canzian d'Isonzo: Consorzio culturale del Monfalconese, 1997). A 2008 edition of the work was prefaced by Claudio Magris.

27. Raul Hilberg, *La distruzione degli Ebrei d'Europa* (Turin: Einaudi, 1995). On the delay in translating Hilberg, see Collotti, 'Razzismo', p. 585.

28. Christopher R. Browning, *Uomini comuni: polizia tedesca e soluzione finale in Polonia* (Turin: Einaudi, 1995).

29. Daniel Goldhagen, *I volenterosi carnefici di Hitler: i tedeschi comuni e l'Olocausto* (Milano: CDE and subsequently Mondadori, 1997). The Italian edition went through six editions in 1997 alone.

30. 1996–97 also saw the publication by Einaudi of two substantial volumes on the history of Jews in Italy, in the *Annali* supplements to its multivolume *Storia d'Italia* (Turin: Einaudi, 1972–): Corrado Vivanti, ed., *Gli ebrei in Italia*, vols. XI.1 and XI.2 of *Storia d'Italia* (Turin: Einaudi, 1996–97).

31. Annette Wieviorka, *Auschwitz spiegato a mia figlia* (Turin: Einaudi, 1999). A publishing vogue in Italy for books explaining the world 'to children' began with the translation of another French book, Tahar Ben Jelloun's *Il razzismo spiegato a mia figlia* (Milan: Bompiani, 1998; 14 Italian editions in 1998 alone). Similar titles followed on everything from football to God, including Cavaglion, *Resistenza*.

32. Gesualdo Bufalino, *Diceria dell'untore* (Palermo: Sellerio, 1981).

33. Susanna Tamaro, *Per voce sola* (Venice: Marsilio, 1991); Paolo Maurensig, *La variante di Lüneberg* (Milan: Adelphi, 1993).

34. Paolo Maurensig, *Canone inverso* (Milan: Mondadori, 1997).

35. Lia Levi, *Una bambina e basta* (Rome: E/O, 1994); *Tutti i giorni di tua vita* (Milan: Mondadori, 1997).

36. Eraldo Affinati, *Campo del sangue* (Milan: Mondadori, 1997).

37. Carla Forti, *Il caso Pardo Roques: un eccidio del 1944 tra memoria e oblio* (Turin: Einaudi, 1998).

38. Binjamin Wilkomirski, *Frantumi: un'infanzia, 1939–1948* (Milan: CDE, 1996; 1st German edition 1995). See Elena Lappin, 'The Man with Two Heads', *Granta*, 66 (1999): 7–66; Stefan Maechler, *The Wilkomirski Affair* (New York: Schocken, 2000).

39. Sergio Romano, *Lettera a un amico ebreo* (Milan: Longanesi, 1997).

40. Sergio I. Minerbi, *Risposta a Sergio Romano. Ebrei, Shoah e Stato d'Israele* (Florence: La Giuntina, 1998).

41. On national holidays, see Andrea Cossu, 'Memory, Symbolic Conflict and Changes in the National Calendar in the Italian Second Republic', *Modern Italy*, 15. 1 (2010): 3–19.

42. On the law in parliament, see Goffredo De Pasquale, 'Viaggio di una legge', in *Mi ricordo*, pp. 12–18. See also David Bidussa, *Dopo l'ultimo testimone* (Turin: Einaudi, 2009).

43. Sen. Athos De Luca (Greens) had been the law's main sponsor in the Senate.

44. *Gazzetta Ufficiale*, n. 177, 31 July 2000.

45. The phrase 'Day of Remembrance' appears in the Stockholm Declaration. Despite the fixing of the phrase *giorno della memoria* in the legislation, variants appeared in the press coverage around the day itself: apart from '*Giornata della memoria*'(various newspapers) and '*Giorno del ricordo*'(*La stampa*), *La repubblica* used '*Giorno della Shoah*' in its pagehead logo, alongside a Star of David and a menorah. *Corriere della sera*'s logo, by contrast, consisted of two generic pieces of barbed wire.

46. Italy's best-known survivor-writer, Primo Levi, was liberated from Auschwitz on 27 January 1945, as described at the opening of *The Truce*.

47. Compare the French choice of 16 July, the date of the largest Parisian round-up of 1942, when 13,000 Jews were taken.

48. *Mi ricordo*, p. 15.

49. The unspoken references here are probably to Perlasca and Giovanni Palatucci, the former a convinced Fascist, the latter a Catholic police functionary, both of whom saved significant numbers of Jews. Both were named during the debate in Parliament in March 2000.

50. Sarfatti, quoted by De Pasquale in *Mi ricordo*, p. 15.

51. The same emphasis is to be found in the Stockholm Declaration.

52. Gianluca Luzi, 'L'Italia ricorda la Shoah. Ciampi: non torni l'odio', *La repubblica*, 27 January 2001.

53. Margherita Mezan, 'Noi, testimoni della Shoah', *Corriere della sera*, 25 January 2001.

54. E.g. events in Pianezza, Nichelino, Alpignano, Pinerolo, listed in *La repubblica*, 26 January 2001, Turin supplement; in Rivoli and Beiansco, listed in *La repubblica*, 27 January 2001, Turin supplement.

55. Bravo and Jalla, *Vita*.

56. Francesco Grignetti, 'Giornata della memoria, uniti e divisi', *La stampa*, 28 January 2001.

57. Listings, *La repubblica*, 26 January 2001.

58. See Dario Fertilio, 'Lia Levi: "Così insegno ai bambini e non ripetere gli orrori dei padri"', *Corriere della sera*, 27 January 2001.

59. 'Attentato a sede dell'Ulivo', *La repubblica*, 28 January 2001. The Rome edition of *La repubblica* reported on Nazi anti-Semitic graffiti in the capital.

60. Alessandra Longo, 'An divide i sopravvissuti', *La repubblica*, 27 January 2001.

61. Marco Cremonesi, 'Il giorno della memoria, migliaia in piazza per non dimenticare', *Corriere della sera*, 28 January 2001.

62. Reported by Silvio Buzzanca, '"Né oblio né revisionismo" nel giorno della memoria', *La repubblica*, 28 January 2001. A cautionary note against 'compulsory' memory was also sounded by Michele Sarfatti, 'Ecco perché vogliamo ricordare', *La repubblica*, 26 January 2001.

63. See *Mi ricordo, passim*.

64. *L'espresso*, 25 January 2001, pp. 86–91.

65. The majority of photos in the press coverage was drawn from repertory images of deportees, trains, barbed wire, camps, dead bodies and emaciated survivors. A small number of images related to Italian anti-Semitic laws (e.g. *L'espresso*, 25 January, p. 88) and to the Milan procession.

66. On the former, see Cesare Segre, 'Olocausto, il ricordo e il monito', *Corriere della sera*, 28 January 2001; Teofilo, 'Quante Shoah nel calendario degli ebrei', *La stampa* (Turin supplement), 26 January 2001. On the latter, see Ernesto Galli della Loggia, 'L'inutilità dell'orrore', *Corriere della sera*, 27 January 2001; cf. the sheer range of coverage—on Latin America, Vietnam, 1970s terrorism, American racism etc.—in *Mi ricordo*.

67. Alessandra Longo, 'Tullia Zevi e la Shoah tra lacrime e ricordi', *La repubblica*, 28 January 2001.

68. E.g. Elena Loewenthal, 'Strascico di fumo', *La stampa*, 26 January 2001.

69. Furio Colombo, 'La Shoah'; cf. Michele Sarfatti, 'Ecco'.

70. Quoted in Alessandro Capponi, '"Anche gli italiani approfittarono della Shoah"', *Corriere della sera*, 27 January 2001. See Nevola.

71. Sarfatti, 'Ecco'.

72. On Cefalonia, see Marzio Breda, 'Per chi suona il mandolino di Cefalonia', *Corriere della sera*, 25 January 2001, which describes the events and the popular book by Louis de Bernières (and soon-to-be film), *Captain Corelli's Mandolin*. Ciampi would use Cefalonia in ways connected to his Day of Memory letter, to counter the 'death of the nation' idea ('on that day the nation did not die, it was reborn', quoted by Breda). Sant'Anna di Stazzema is discussed because a book appears about it in the days leading up to 27 January: see Cesare Garboli's column in *La stampa*, 25 January 2001; Claudia Fusani, '"Arrivarono i nazisti e sterminarono il paese"', and Orazio La Rocca, '"Ho nel cuore il prete che mi salvò la vita"' (interview with Rabbi Toaff), both in *La repubblica*, 27 January 2001.

73. E.g. Francesco Storace, reported in Grignetti.

74. Adriano Sofri, 'Le caverne dell'orrore', in *Mi ricordo*, pp. 58–62 [p. 60] (also appeared as 'Lager e Foibe, il derby dell'orrore', *La stampa*, 26 January 2001).

75. On the role of the 'Risiera', Trieste and the north-east in Italy's complex divided memory and territory, see Foot, *Fratture*, pp. 119–98 (chapter not included in Foot, *Italy's Divided Memory*); Sluga.

76. Quoted in Grignetti.

77. Sarfatti, 'Ecco'.

Bibliography

1. Archives

Archivio Storico, Galleria nazionale d'arte moderna, Rome (fasc. 1, ritagli stampa, X 70).

Archivio Storico Olivetti, Ivrea, Edizioni di Comunità archive (Carteggio redazionale. Meneghello, Luigi, 1952–1961, cart. 22. 623, faldone n. 39).

Centro di documentazione ebraica contemporanea, Milan.

2. Periodicals

Avanti! (1945–46).

Corriere della sera [*Corriere d'informazione*] (1945–1947; 1961–62; 2001).

Diario (2001–2005).

L'espresso (1960–1962; 2001).

Il ponte (1945–1987).

Minerva medica (1945–46)

Rassegna mensile di Israel (1948–1988).

La repubblica (1984–2010).

La stampa (1959–1963; 1986–87; 2001).

Storia illustrata (1957–1970).

L'Unità (1945–46).

3. Published Sources

'1938. Le leggi contro gli ebrei', *Rassegna mensile di Israel,* special issue edited by Michele Sarfatti, 54. 1–2 (January–August 1988).

1945–1975: Fascismo, antifascismo, Resistenza, rinnovamento (Milan: Feltrinelli, 1962).

Affinati, Eraldo, *Campo del sangue* (Milan: Mondadori, 1997).

Against Mussolini: Art and the Fall of a Dictator (London: Estorick Collection, 2010).

Agamben, Giorgio, *Homo sacer: potere sovrano e nuda vita* (Turin: Einaudi, 1995).

———, *Quel che resta di Auschwitz* (Turin: Bollati Boringhieri, 1998).

———, *Stati di eccezione. Homo sacer II* (Turin: Bollati Boringhieri, 2003).

Améry, Jean, *At The Mind's Limits* (London: Granta, 1999; 1st German ed. 1966).

Amishai-Maisels, Ziva, *Depiction and Interpretation: The Influence of the Holocaust on the Visual Arts* (Oxford: Pergamon Press, 1993).

André Bernstein, Michael, *Foregone Conclusions: Against Apocalyptic History* (Berkeley: University of California Press, 1994).

'ANED', http://www.deportati.it/ (accessed 16 November 2010).

Antelme, Robert, *L'Espèce humaine* (Paris: La Cité universelle, 1947).

———, *La specie umana* (Turin: Einaudi, 1954).

Antonello, Pierpaolo, 'Un inglese in Italia: Charles Percy Snow, le sue culture e il dibattito degli anni Sessanta', *Pianeta Galileo* (2009): 515–30.

———, and Florian Mussgnug, eds., *Postmodern* impegno*: Ethics and Commitment in Contemporary Italy* (Oxford: Peter Lang, 2009).

Antonimi, Sandro, *DELASEM: storia della più grande organizzazione ebraica di soccorso durante la seconda guerra mondiale* (Genoa: De Ferrari, 2000);.

Appadurai, Arjun, *Modernity at Large: Cultural Dimensions of Globalization* (Minneapolis: University of Minnesota Press, 1996).

Arendt, Hannah, *Eichmann in Jerusalem: A Report on the Banailty of Evil* (London: Penguin, 1994; 1st ed. 1963).

Artom, Emanuele, *Diari: gennaio 1940–febbraio 1944* (Milan: CDEC, 1966).

Asor Rosa, Alberto, ed., *Letteratura italiana* (Turin: Einaudi, 1982–2000).

———, *Storia della letteratura italiana* (Florence: La Nuova Italia, 1985).

'Attentato a sede dell'Ulivo', *La repubblica*, 28 January 2001.

Banfield, Edward, *The Moral Basis of a Backward Society* (New York: Free Press, 1958).

Barcellini, Serge, and Annette Wieviorka, *Passant, souviens-toi!* (Paris: Graphein, 1995).

Barnouw, Dagmar, 'True Stories: Oprah, Elie Wiesel, and the Holocaust', *History News Network* (20 March 2006), http://hnn.us/articles/22099.html (accessed 11 September 2010).

Basaglia, Franco, ed., *Che cos'è la psichiatria?* (Parma: Amministrazione Provinciale di Parma, 1967).

Bassani, Giorgio, *La passeggiata prima di cena* (Florence: Sansoni, 1953).

———, *Cinque storie ferraresi* (Turin: Einaudi, 1956).

———, *Gli occhiali d'oro* (Turin: Einaudi, 1958).

———, *Il giardino dei Finzi-Contini* (Turin: Einaudi, 1962).

———, *Il romanzo di Ferrara* (Milan: Mondadori, 1976).

Bassi, Roberto, 'Ricordo di Massimo Aldo Vitale. Dal Comitato ricerche deportati ebrei al Centro di documentazione ebraica contemporanea', *Rassegna mensile di Israel*, 45. 1–3 (January–March 1979): 8–21.

Battini, Michele, *The Missing Italian Nuremberg: Cultural Amnesia and Postwar Politics* (London: Macmillan, 2007).

Bauman, Zygmunt, *Modernity and Holocaust* (Cambridge: Polity, 1989).

Beccaria Rolfi, Lidia, and Bruno Maida, *Il futuro spezzato. I bambini nei lager nazisti* (Florence: La Giuntina, 1997).

Beccaria Rolfi, Lidia, and Anna Maria Bruzzone, eds., *Le donne di Ravensbrück. Testimonianze di deportate politiche italiane* (Turin, Einaudi, 1978).

Belardelli, Giovanni, 'L'Italia scoprì l'olocausto dopo anni di silenzio', *Corriere della sera*, 12 January 2005.

Belpoliti, Marco, 'Primo Levi traduttore' in Levi, *Opere*, II, pp. 1582–89.

———, and Andrea Cortellessa, *Da una tregua all'altra. Auschwitz-Torino sessant'anni dopo* (Milan: Chiarelettere, 2010).

Ben-Ghiat, Ruth, 'The Secret Histories of Roberto Benigni's *Life Is Beautiful*', *Yale Journal of Criticism*, 14.1 (2001): 253–66.

———, and Mia Fuller, eds., *Italian Colonialism* (New York: Palgrave, 2005).

Ben Jelloun, Tahar, *Il razzismo spiegato a mia figlia* (Milan: Bompiani, 1998).

Bettelheim, Bruno, 'Surviving', *New Yorker*, 2 August 1976, pp. 31–52; later in *Surviving and Other Essays* (London: Thames and Hudson, 1979), pp. 274–314.

Bidussa, David, *Il mito del bravo italiano* (Milan: Il Saggiatore, 1994).

———, *Dopo l'ultimo testimone* (Turin: Einaudi, 2009).

Bistarelli, Agostino, *La storia del ritorno. I reduci italiani del secondo dopoguerra* (Turin: Bollati Boringhieri, 2007).

Bizzarri, Aldo, *Mauthausen città ermetica* (Rome: OET/Edizioni Polilibraria, 1946)·

———,*Proibito vivere* (Milan: Mondadori, 1947).

Bloxham, Donald, *Genocide on Trial: War Crimes Trials and the Formation of Holocaust History and Memory* (Oxford: Oxford University Press, 2001).

Bobbio, Norberto, *Trent'anni di storia della cultura a Torino (1920–1950)* (Turin: Cassa di Risparmio, 1977).

Bocca, Giorgio, 'Eccolo! Sembra un istitutore un po' timido', *Il giorno*, 12 April 1961.

———, 'La via del perdono passa per Vienna', *La repubblica*, 12 June 1986.

Bollati, Giulio, *L'italiano. Il carattere nazionale come storia e come invenzione* (Turin: Einaudi, 1983).

Bondanella, Peter, *The Eternal City: Roman Images in the Modern World* (Chapel Hill: University of North Carolina Press, 1987).

Bonfantini, Mario, *Un salto nel buio* (Milan: Feltrinelli, 1959).

Bonsaver, Guido, *Censorship and Literature in Fascist Italy* (Toronto: Toronto University Press, 2007).

Bosworth, Richard J. B., *Explaining Auschwitz and Hiroshima: History Writing and the Second World War 1945–1990* (London: Routledge, 1993).

———, *Whispering City: Rome and Its Histories* (New Haven: Yale University Press, 2011).

———, and Patrizia Dogliani, eds., *Italian Fascism: History, Memory and Representation* (London: Macmillan, 1999).

Bourdieu, Pierre, *The Rules of Art* (Oxford: Polity, 1996).

Bravo, Anna, 'Sulla "zona grigia"', http://www.primolevi.it/Web/Italiano/Conte nuti/Auschwitz/105_Sulla_%22zona_grigia%22 (accessed 1 December 2011).

———, and Daniele Jalla, eds., *La vita offesa. Storia e memoria dei Lager nazisti nei racconti di duecento sopravvissuti* (Milan: Franco Angeli/ANED, 1986).

———, eds., *Una misura onesta. Gli scritti di memoria della deportazione dall'Italia 1944–93* (Milan, Franco Angeli/ANED, 1994).

Breda, Marzio, 'Per chi suona il mandolino di Cefalonia', *Corriere della sera*, 25 January 2001.

Browning, Christopher R., *Uomini comuni: polizia tedesca e soluzione finale in Polonia* (Turin: Einaudi, 1995).

Bruck, Edith, *Chi ti ama cosí* (Milan: Lerici, 1959).

———, *Andremo in città* (Milan: Lerici, 1962).

———, *Due stanze vuote* (Venice: Marsilio, 1974).

———, *Signora Auschwitz* (Venice: Marsilio, 1999).

———, *Transit* (Milan: Bompiani, 2008).

Brunello, Franco, *Stalag 307* (Vicenza: Edizione del Partito d'azione, 1945; also published in Milan: Casa Editrice La Fiaccola, 1945).

Bucciantini, Massimo, *Esperimento Auschwitz* (Turin: Einaudi, 2011).

Bufalino, Gesualdo, *Diceria dell'untore* (Palermo: Sellerio, 1981).

Burleigh, Michael, and Wolfgang Wippermann, *The Racial State: Germany 1933–1945* (Cambridge: Cambridge University Press, 1991).

'Business Data for Vita è Bella, La', http://us.imdb.com/Business?0118799 (accessed May 2010).

Buzzanca, Silvio, '"Né oblio né revisionismo" nel giorno della memoria', *La repubblica*, 28 January 2001.

Caleffi, Piero, *Si fa presto a dire fame* (Milan: Ed. Avanti!, 1954).

———, and Albe Steiner, *Pensaci, uomo!* (Turin: Einaudi, 1960).

Calvino, Italo, *La giornata di uno scrutatore* (Turin: Einaudi, 1963).

'Il campo di orrore', 'Il centro di sperimentazione umana sul tifo esantematico nel campo di internamento a Buchenwald', *Minerva medica*, 36. 30 (4 August 1945): 44–46.

Canaday, John, *The Nuclear Muse: Literature, Physics, and the First Atomic Bombs* (Madison: University of Wisconsin Press, 2000).

Cannistraro, Philip, *La fabbrica del consenso. Fascismo e mass media* (Bari: Laterza, 1975).

Cannon, Joann, 'Canon-Formation and Reception in Contemporary Italy: The Case of Primo Levi', *Italica*, 69. 1 (Spring 1992): 30–44.

'Canti dei Lager', http://www.cantilotta.org/canti_lager/07.htm (accessed 12 September 2010).

Capogreco, Carlo Spartaco, *Ferramonti. La vita e gli uomini del più grande campo d'internamento fascista (1940–1945)* (Florence: La Giuntina, 1987).

————, *I campi del duce. L'internamento civile nell'Italia fascista, 1940–1943* (Turin: Einaudi, 2004).

Capponi, Alessandro, '"Anche gli italiani approfittarono della Shoah"', *Corriere della sera*, 27 January 2001.

Caproni, Giorgio, *Frammenti di un diario (1948–49)* (Genoa: San Marco dei Giustiniani, 1995).

Caracciolo, Alberto, *Teresio Olivelli* (Brescia: La Scuola, 1947).

Caracciolo, Nicola, *Gli ebrei e l'Italia durante la guerra 1940–45* (Rome: Bonacci, 1986), p. 17.

————, *Uncertain Refuge: Italy and the Jews During the Holocaust* (Urbana: University of Illinois Press, 1995).

Cascella, Pietro, *Opere monumentali* (Milan: Electa, 1993).

Cassola, Carlo, *Il taglio nel bosco* (Milan: Fabbri, 1953).

Castronovo, Valerio, and Nicola Tranfaglia, *La stampa italiana dalla Resistenza agli anni sessanta* (Rome: Laterza, 1980).

Cavaglion, Alberto, 'Argon e la cultura ebraica piemontese' *Belfagor*, 43. 5 (September 1988): 541–62.

————, 'Il termitaio', *Asino d'oro*, 4 (1991); later in Ernesto Ferrero, ed., *Primo Levi: un'antologia della critica* (Turin: Einaudi, 1997), pp. 76–90.

————, ed., *Il ritorno dai Lager* (Milan: Franco Angeli/ANED, 1993).

————, 'Mnemagoghi e memoriosi: materiali per una unità didattica', in Traverso, *Insegnare Auschwitz*, 1995, pp. 114–23.

————, ed., *Primo Levi per l' ANED, l' ANED per Primo Levi* (Milan: Franco Angeli/ANED, 1997).

————, *Ebrei senza saperlo* (Naples: L'ancora del Mediterraneo, 2002).

————, 'Primo Levi tra i sommersi e i salvati', *Lo straniero*, 7.48 (June 2004): 40–49.

————, *La resistenza spiegata a mia figlia* (Naples: L'ancora del Mediterraneo, 2005).

————, *Notizie su Argon* (Turin: Instar, 2006).

Cavarero, Adriana, *Horrorism: Naming Contemporary Violence* (New York: Columbia University Press, 2009).

CDEC, 'La persecuzione degli ebrei in Italian, 1938–1945', http://www.museoshoah.it (accessed 4 April 2011).

Celli, Carlo, *Gillo Pontecorvo: From Resistance to Terrorism* (Lanham, MA: Scarecrow Press, 2005).

Cesarini, Marco, 'La tavola di salvezza degli italiani', *Storia illustrata*, June 1961, pp. 762–84.

Cheyette, Bryan, 'Appropriating Primo Levi', in Robert S. C. Gordon, ed., *Cambridge Companion to Primo Levi* (Cambridge: Cambridge University Press, 2007), pp. 67–85.

————, and Laura Marcus, eds., *Modernity, Culture and 'the Jew'* (Stanford: Stanford University Press, 1998).

Chiaromonte, Nicola, 'Rome Letter', *Partisan Review*, 16. 3 (March 1949): 303–13.

Chiodi, Piero, *Banditi* (Turin: Einaudi, 1961; 1st ed. 1946).

Ciccarelli, Andrea, 'Frontier, Exile, and Migration in the Contemporary Italian Novel' in Peter Bondanella and Andrea Ciccarelli, eds., *Cambridge Companion to the Italian Novel* (Cambridge: Cambridge University Press, 2003), pp. 197–212.

Cicioni, Mirna, *Primo Levi: Bridges of Knowledge* (Oxford: Berg, 1995).

Cinelli, Gianluca, *Ermeneutica e scrittura autobiografica: Primo Levi, Nuto Revelli, Rosetta Loy, Mario Rigoni Stern* (Milan: Unicopli, 2008).

Clifford, Rebecca, 'The Limits of National Memory: Anti-Fascist, the Holocaust and the Fosse Ardeatine Memorial in 1990s Italy', *FMLS*, 44.2 (April 2008): 128–39.

Cohen, Charles, *Un quaderno di Buchenwald* (Turin: F. Toso, 1945).

Cohen, Richard I., 'Breaking the Code: Hannah Arendt's *Eichmann in Jerusalem* and the Public Polemic', *Michael*, 13 (1993): 26–86.

Cole, Tim, *Selling the Holocaust: From Auschwitz to Schindler: How History Is Bought, Packaged and Sold* (New York: Routledge, 1999)·

Collotti, Enzo, 'Il razzismo negato', *Italia contemporanea*, 212 (September 1998): 577–87.

Colombo, Furio, 'La Shoah, crimine anche italiano', *La repubblica*, 27 January 2001·

————, 'Piazza Grande. La memoria della memoria', *Il fatto quotidiano*, 15 May 2010.

'Congratulazioni da Israele qualche dubbio dalla Zevi', *La repubblica*, 22 March 1999.

Conseguenze culturali delle leggi razziali in Italia (Rome: Accademia dei Lincei, 1989).

Consonni, Manuela, 'The Impact of the "Eichmann Event" in Italy, 1961', *Journal of Israeli History*, 23.1 (Spring 2004): 91–99.

————, 'The Church and the Memory of the Shoah: The Catholic Press in Italy, 1945–1947', in Eli Lederhendler, ed., *Jews, Catholics and the Burdens of History* (Oxford: Oxford University Press, 2005), pp. 21–34.

————, 'A War of Memories: De Felice and His *Intervista sul Fascismo*', *Journal of Modern Jewish Studies*, 5.1 (March 2006): 43–56.

Contini, Giovanni, *La memoria divisa* (Milan: Rizzoli, 1997).

Cooke, Philip, *Luglio 1960* (Milan: Teti, 2000).

————, *The Legacy of the Italian Resistance* (New York: Palgrave, 2011).

Coslovich, Mauro, 'Il processo della Risiera di san Sabba: una fonte per la storia', in D'Amico and Mantelli, *I campi di sterminio nazisti*, pp. 69–88.

Cossu, Andrea, 'Memory, Symbolic Conflict and Changes in the National Calendar in the Italian Second Republic', *Modern Italy*, 15.1 (2010): 3–19.

Crainz, Guido, 'The Representation of Fascism and the Resistance in the Documentaries of Italian State Television', in Bosworth and Dogliani, *Italian Fascism*, pp. 123–40.

Cremonesi, Marco, 'Il giorno della memoria, migliaia in piazza per non dimenticare', *Corriere della sera*, 28 January 2001.

Crowley, Martin, *Robert Antelme: Humanity, Community, Testimony* (Oxford: Legenda, 2003).

Dall'antifascismo alla Resistenza. Trent'anni di storia italiana (1915–1945) (Turin: Einaudi, 1961).

Dalle leggi antiebraiche all Shoah (Milan: Skira/CDEC, 2004).

D'Amico, Giovanna, and Bruno Mantelli, eds., *I campi di sterminio nazisti. Storia, memoria, storiografia* (Milan: Franco Angeli/ANED, 2003).

Daney, Serge, 'The Tracking Shot in *Kapo*' (1992), *Senses of Cinema*, 30 (January–March 2004), at Serge Daney, 'The Tracking Shot in *Kapo*' (1992), *Senses of Cinema*, 30, January–March 2004, http://www.sensesofcinema.com/2004/feature-articles/kapo_daney/ (accessed 4 December 2011).

Davidowicz, Lucy, review of Katz, *Black Sabbath*, in *Jewish Social Studies*, 32.1 (January 1970): 79–82.

Davies, Martin, and Claus-Christian Szejnmann, eds., *How the Holocaust Looks Now: International Perspectives* (New York: Palgrave, 2007).

De Benedetti, Leonardo, and Primo Levi, 'Rapporto sull'organizzazione igienico-sanitaria del campo di concentramento per ebrei di Monowitz (Auschwitz Alta Silesia)', *Minerva medica*, 37/2. 47 (24 November 1946): 535–44.

———, *Auschwitz Report*, ed. by Robert S. C. Gordon (London: Verso, 2006).

de Bernières, Louis, *Captain Corelli's Mandolin* (London: Secker and Warburg, 1994).

De Felice, Renzo, *Storia degli ebrei italiani sotto il fascismo* (Turin: Einaudi, 1961).

———, 'L'ultima maschera', *Rassegna mensile di Israel*, 1 (1963): 63–68.

———, *Mussolini il duce. 1. Gli anni del consenso 1929–36* (Turin: Einaudi, 1974).

———, *Intervista sul fascismo* (Bari: Laterza, 1975).

———, *Rosso e nero*, ed. by Pasquale Chessa (Milan: Baldini and Castoldi, 1995).

De Filippo, Edoardo, *Napoli milionaria!* (Turin: Einaudi, 1977).

De Lauretis, Teresa, 'Cavani's Night-Porter: A Woman's Film?' *Film Quarterly*, 30:2 (Winter 1976–77): 35–38.

De Luna, Giovanni, 'Se questo è un memorial', *La stampa*, 21 January 2008.

———, *La repubblica del dolore. Le memorie di un'Italia divisa* (Milan: Feltrinelli, 2011).

De Martino, Ernesto, *La fine del mondo. Contributo all'analisi delle apocalissi culturali* (Turin: Einaudi, 1977).

De Martino, Gaetano, *Dal carcere di San Vittore ai 'lager'* (Milan: La Prora, 1955; 1st ed. 1945).

De Pasquale, Goffredo, 'Viaggio di una legge', in *Mi ricordo*.

Deaglio, Enrico, *La banalità del bene: storia di Giorgio Perlasca* (Milan: Feltrinelli, 1991).

Debenedetti, Giacomo, '16 ottobre 1943', *Mercurio*, 1. 4 (December 1944): 75–97; republished as *16 ottobre 1943* (Rome: OET, 1945).

———, *Otto ebrei* (Rome: Atlantica, 1944).

———, *16 ottobre 43* (Milan: Il Saggiatore, 1959).

———, *16 ottobre 1943. Otto ebrei* (Turin: Einaudi, 2001).

Dei, Adele, 'Caproni e Quasimodo', in Franco Musarra et al., eds., *Quasimodo e gli altri* (Leuven/Florence: Leuven University Press/Franco Cesati, 2001), pp. 113–22.

Del Boca, Angelo, *Manicomi come Lager* (Turin: Edizioni dell'Albero, 1966).

———, *Italiani, brava gente? Un mito duro a morire* (Vicenza: Neri Pozza Editore, 2005).

Denby, David, 'Life Is Beautiful', *New Yorker*, 15 March 1999, pp. 96–99.

Des Pres, Terence, 'Bleak Comedies', *Harper's*, June 1976, pp. 26–28.

———, *The Survivor: An Anatomy of Life in the Death Camps* (Oxford: Oxford University Press, 1976).

'La difesa della razza', *Il ponte*, special issue ed. by Ugo Caffaz, 34.11–12 (November–December 1978): 1303–1520.

Dogliani, Patrizia, 'Constructing Memory and Anti-memory: Representations of Fascism and Its Denial in Republican Italy', in Bosworth and Dogliani, *Italian Fascism*, pp. 11–30.

Donnelly, Michael, *The Politics of Mental Health in Italy* (London: Routledge, 1992).

Dragoni, Ugo, *La scelta degli I.M.I. Militari italiani prigionieri in Germania (1943–1945)* (Florence: Le Lettere, 1996).

Druker, Jonathan, and Michael Rothberg, 'A Secular Alternative: Primo Levi's Place in American Holocaust Discourse', *Shofar* 28.1 (Fall 2009): 104–126.

Ducci, Teo, ed., *In memoria della deportazione. Opere di architetti italiani* (Milan: Mazzotta, 1997).

Eberstadt, Fernanda, 'Reading Primo Levi', *Commentary*, October 1985, pp. 41–47.

Ebrei a Torino (Turin: Allemandi, 1984).

Gli ebrei dell'europa orientale dall'utopia alla rivolta (Milan: Edizioni di Comunità, 1986).

Fabre, Giorgio, *L'elenco: censura fascista, editoria e autori ebrei* (Turin: Zamorani, 1998).

———, *Mussolini razzista. Dal socialismo al fascismo: la formazione di un antisemita* (Milan: Garzanti, 2005).

Faccini, Francesca, '1965: va in scena a Roma il "Vicario"', *L'Unità*, 18 April 2002.

Fantini, Sarah, *Notizie dalla Shoah. La stampa italiana nel 1945* (Bologna: Pendragon, 2005).

Fascismo e antifascismo 1918–1936 (Milan: Feltrinelli, 1962).

'Il fascismo fu parte del male assoluto', *La repubblica*, 24 November 2003.

Feinstein, Wiley, *The Civilization of the Holocaust in Italy: Poets, Artists, Saints, Anti-Semites* (London: Associated University Presses, 2003).

Fergnani, Enea, *Un uomo e tre numeri* (Milan-Rome: Ed. Avanti! 1955; 1st ed. 1945).

Fertilio, Dario, 'Lia Levi: "Così insegno ai bambini e non ripetere gli orrori dei padri"', *Corriere della sera*, 27 January 2001.

Finkelstein, Norman, *The Holocaust Industry* (London: Verso, 2000).

Finzi, Roberto, 'Tre scritti postbellici sugli ebrei di Benedetto Croce, Cesare Merzagora, Adolfo Omodeo', *Studi storici*, 47. 1 (January–March 2006): 81–108.

Fiori, Simonetta, 'Meneghello e l'olocausto', *La repubblica*, 16 September 1994.

Flanzbaum, Hilene, ed., *The Americanization of the Holocaust* (Baltimore: Johns Hopkins University Press, 1999).

Flores, Marcello, et al., eds., *Storia della Shoah in Italia*, vols. I–II (Turin: UTET, 2010).

Focardi, Filippo, '"Bravo italiano" e "cattivo tedesco": riflessioni sulla genesi di due immagini incrociate', *Storia e memoria*, 5. 1 (1996): 55–83.

———, 'La memoria della guerra e il mito del "bravo italiano". Origine e affermazione di un autoritratto collettivo', *Italia contemporanea*, 220–21 (2000): 93–99.

———, and Lutz Klinkhammer, 'The Question of Fascist Italy's War Crimes: The Construction of a Self-Acquitting Myth (1943–1948)', *Journal of Modern Italian Studies*, 9.3 (2004): 330–48.

Fogu, Claudio, '*Italiani brava gente*: The Legacy of Fascist Historical Culture on Italian Politics of Memory', in Richard Ned Lebow, Wulf Kansteiner and Claudio Fogu, eds., *The Politics of Memory in Postwar Europe* (Durham: Duke University Press, 2006), pp. 147–76.

Fölkel, Ferruccio, *La risiera di san Sabba* (Milan: Mondadori, 1979).

Fondazione Luigi Nono, 'Ricorda cosa ti hanno fatto in Auschwitz', http://www.luiginono.it/it/luigi-nono/opere/ricorda-cosa-ti-hanno-fatto-in-auschwitz (accessed 1 December 2010).

Foot, John, 'Via Rasella, 1944: Memory, Truth, and History', *Historical Journal*, 43.4 (2000): 1173–81.

———, *Fratture d'Italia* (Milan: Rizzoli, 2009).

———, *Italy's Divided Memory* (London: Palgrave, 2009).

Forgacs, David, 'Days of Sodom: The Fascism-Perversion Equation in Films of 1960s and 1970s', in Bosworth and Dogliani, *Italian Fascism*, 1999, pp. 216–36.

———, 'Fascism and Anti-Fascism Reviewed: Generations, History and Film in Italy After 1968', in Helmut Peitsch et al., eds., *European Memories of the War* (Oxford: Berghahn, 1999), pp. 185–99.

———, *L' industrializzazione della cultura italiana, 1880–2000* (Bologna: Il Mulino, 2002).

Forti, Carla, *Il caso Pardo Roques: un eccidio del 1944 tra memoria e oblio* (Turin: Einaudi, 1998).

Fortini, Franco, *Sere in Valdossola* (Milan: Mondadori, 1963).

———, *Tre testi per film* (Milan: Ed. Avanti!, 1963).

———, *I cani del Sinai* (Bari: De Donato, 1967; 3rd ed. Macerata: Quodlibet, 2002).

Foucault, Michel, *Discipline and Punish* (Harmondsworth: Penguin, 1978).

Frandini, Paola, '"Scorciatoie e raccontini" di Umberto Saba tra pensiero ebraico e Shoah', *Strumenti critici*, 1 (January 2009): 25–34.

Frank, Anna, *Diario* (Turin: Einaudi, 1954; 1st Dutch ed. 1947).

Friedländer, Saul, *Reflections of Nazism: An Essay on Kitsch and Death* (New York: Harper and Row, 1984).

Fullbrook, Mary, *German National Identity After the Holocaust* (Cambridge: Polity Press, 1999).

Fusani, Claudia, '"Arrivarono i nazisti e sterminarono il paese"', *La repubblica*, 27 January 2001.

Galante Garrone, Alessandro, 'Waldheim il grigio', *La stampa*, 14 June 1986.

Galli della Loggia, Ernesto, *La morte della patria* (Bari: Laterza, 1996).

———, 'L'inutilità dell'orrore', *Corriere della sera*, 27 January 2001.

Gazzetta Ufficiale, 177, 31 July 2000.

Gazzetta Ufficiale, 96, 26 April 2003.

Gazzetta Ufficiale, 299, 27 December 2006 (supplemento ordinario n. 244).

Gentile, Emilio, *The Sacralization of Politics in Fascist Italy* (Cambridge, MA: Harvard University Press, 1996).

Germinario, Francesco, 'Declinazioni italiane degli assassini della memoria: le vicende della pubblicistica negazionista in Italia', in D'Amico and Mantelli, *I campi di sterminio nazisti*, pp. 247–74.

Ginsborg, Paul, *A History of Contemporary Italy* (Harmondsworth: Penguin, 1990).

———, *Italy and Its Discontents: Family, Civil Society, State 1980–2001* (London: Allen Lane, 2001).

Ginzburg, Natalia, *Le piccole virtù* (Turin: Einaudi, 1962).

———, *Lessico famigliare* (Turin: Einaudi, 1963).

———, 'Gli ebrei', *La stampa*, 14 September 1972.

Goffman, Irving, *Asylums* (Garden City, NY: Anchor, 1961).

Goldhagen, Daniel J., *Hitler's Willing Executioners: Ordinary Germans and the Holocaust* (New York: Vintage Books, 1997).

————, *I volenterosi carnefici di Hitler: i tedeschi comuni e l'Olocausto* (Milano: CDE and Mondadori, 1997).

Gordon, Robert S. C., 'Holocaust Writing in Context: Italy 1945–47', in Andrew Leak and George Paizis, eds., *The Holocaust and the Text: Speaking the Unspeakable* (London: Macmillan, 1999), pp. 32–50.

————, 'Which Holocaust? Primo Levi and the Field of Holocaust Memory in Post-war Italy', *Italian Studies*, 61. 1. (Spring 2006): 85–113.

————, 'The Holocaust in Italian Collective Memory. "Il giorno della memoria", 27 January 2001', *Modern Italy*, 11. 2. (June 2006): 167–88.

————, 'Postmodernism and the Holocaust in Italy', in Antonello and Mussgnug, pp. 167–87.

————, 'Race', in Richard J. B. Bosworth, ed., *Oxford Handbook of Fascism* (Oxford: Oxford University Pres, 2009), pp. 296–316.

————, '"Fare testo in materia": Ugo Varnai, *Comunità*, and the Holocaust in 1950s Italian Culture', in *Meneghello: Fiction, Scholarship, Passione Civile*, ed. by Daniela La Penna, supplement to *The Italianist* 32 (2012): 191–206.

Grassi, Lorenzo, 'Ecco Pio XII a San Giovanni', *Metro*, 29 August 2001.

Gregori, Gino, *Ecce homo Mauthausen* (Milan: Ed. Stucchi, 1946).

Griffin, Roger, *The Nature of Fascism* (New York: St Martin's Press, 1991).

Grignetti, Francesco, 'Giornata della memoria, uniti e divisi', *La stampa*, 28 January 2001·

Grossman, David, *Vedi alla voce: amore* (Milan: CDE, 1988; 1st Hebrew ed. 1986).

Guerriero, Augusto, 'Ordine di sterminio', *Storia illustrata*, March 1960.

Gundle, Stephen, 'The Civic Religion of the Resistance in Postwar Italy', *Modern Italy*, 55.2 (November 2000): 113–32.

Halbwachs, Maurice, *La Mémoire collective* (Paris: Presses universitaires de France, 1950).

————, *The Collective Memory* (New York: Harper and Row, 1980).

Harrowitz, Nancy, '"Mon maître, mon monstre": Monstrous Science in Primo Levi', in Keala Jewell, ed., *Literary Monsters* (Detroit: Wayne State University Press), pp. 51–64.

Hausner, Gideon, *Sei milioni di accusatori* (Turin: Einaudi, 2009; 1st ed. 1961).

Herman, Marco, *Da Leopoli a Torino* (Cuneo: L'Arciere, 1984).

Hersey, John, *Il muro di Varsavia* (Verona: Mondadori, 1951; 1st English ed. 1948).

Herzog, Dagmar, '"Pleasure, Sex, and Politics Belong Together": Post-Holocaust Memory and the Sexual Revolution in West Germany', *Critical Inquiry*, 24 (Winter 1998): 393–444.

Hilberg, Raul, *The Destruction of the European Jews* (Chicago: Quadrangle Books, 1961).

————, *La distruzione degli Ebrei d'Europa* (Turin: Einaudi, 1995).

'History of the ITF', http://www.Holocausttaskforce.org/about-the-itf/history -of-the-itf.html (accessed 15 September 2010).

Hochhuth, Rolf, *Il vicario* (Milan: Feltrinelli, 1964; 1st German ed. 1963).

Hoffman, Eva, *After Such Knowledge: A Meditation on the Aftermath of the Holocaust* (London: Secker & Warburg, 2004).

Höss, Rudolf, *Comandante ad Auschwitz* (Turin: Einaudi, 1985; 1st Italian ed. 1960).

Huyssen, Andreas, *Twilight Memories: Marking Time in a Culture of Amnesia* (New York: Routledge, 1995).

[I. L.], 'In una vecchia casacca sfilacciata il simbolo del terrore hitleriano.' *Patria indipendente*, 6 September 1959.

Le immagini di Olocausto (Rome: ERI, 1979).

Insana, Lina, *Arduous Tasks: Primo Levi, Translation, and the Transmission of Holocaust Testimony* (Toronto: University of Toronto Press, 2009).

Insdorf, Annette, *Indelible Shadows: Film and the Holocaust* (Cambridge: Cambridge University Press, 3rd ed. 2003).

Israel, Giorgio, 'Redeemed Intellectuals and Italian Jews', *Telos* 139 (Summer 2007): 85–108.

Jachia, Paolo, *Francesco Guccini: 40 anni di storie, romanzi, canzoni* (Rome: Editori Riuniti, 2002).

Janeczek, Helena, *Lezioni di tenebra* (Milan: Mondadori, 1997).

Jani, Emilio, *Mi ha salvato la voce* (Milan: Ceschina, 1960).

Janulardo, Ettore, 'Saba: Scorciatoie dopo Majdanek', *Studi e ricerche di storia contemporanea*, 64 (December 2005): 63–67.

Judt, Tony, *Postwar: A History of Europe Since 1945* (New York: Penguin, 2005).

Kansteiner, Wulf, 'Finding Meaning in Memory: A Methodological Critique of Collective Memory Studies', *History and Theory*, 41 (May 2002): 179–97.

Karlsson, Klas-Göran, and Ulf Zander, eds., *Echoes of the Holocaust: Historical Cultures in Contemporary Europe* (Lund: Nordic Academic, 2003).

———, *Holocaust on Post-War Battlefields: Genocide as Historical Culture* (Malmö: Sekel, 2006).

Katz, Robert, *Death in Rome* (New York: Macmillan, 1967).

———, *Black Sabbath: A Journey Through a Crime Against Humanity* (New York: Macmillan, 1969).

———, 'TheBoot.it', http://www.theboot.it/home_2009.htm (accessed 10 October 2010).

Katz, Steven T., *The Holocaust in Historical Context* (Oxford: Oxford University Press, 1994).

Katzenelson, Yitzhak, *Il canto del popolo ebraico massacrato* (Turin: Amici di Beit Lohamei Haghetaot, 1966).

Ka-Tzetnik 135633, *La casa delle bambole* (Milan: Mondadori, 1959; 1st Hebrew ed. 1953).

Kertzer, David, *Unholy War: The Vatican's Role in the Rise of Modern Anti-Semitism* (London: Macmillan, 2002).

Kirk, Terry, *The Architecture of Modern Italy*, vols. I–II, II: *Visions of Utopia, 1900–Present* (New York: Princeton Architectural Press, 2005).

Klemperer, Victor, *LTI. Lingua Tertii Imperii* (Berlin: Aufbau, 1947).

Kogon, Eugen, *Der SS-Staat* (Berlin: Verlag des Druckhauses Tempelhof, 1947).

König, Joel, *Sfuggito alle reti del nazismo* (Milan: Mursia, 1973).

Kushner, Tony, *The Holocaust and the Liberal Imagination* (Oxford: Blackwell, 1994).

La Rocca, Orazio, '"Ho nel cuore il prete che mi salvò la vita"', *La repubblica*, 27 January 2001.

LaCapra, Dominic, 'Approaching Limit Event: Siting Agamben', in Michael Bernard-Donals and Richard Glejzer, eds., *Witnessing the Disaster: Essays on Representation and the Holocaust* (Madison: University of Wisconsin Press, 2003), pp. 262–304.

Lagrou, Pieter, 'Victims of Genocide and National Memory: Belgium, France and the Netherlands 1945–1965', *Past and Present*, 154 (February 1997): 181–222.

——, 'The Nationalization of Victimhood: Selective Violence and National Grief in Western Europe, 1940–1960', in Richard Bessel and Dirk Schumann, eds., *Life After Death: Approaches to a Cultural and Social History of Europe During the 1940s and 1950s* (Cambridge/Washington, DC: Cambridge University Press/German Historical Institute, 2003), pp. 243–57.

Landy, Marcia, 'Cinematic History, Melodrama and the Holocaust', in Michael Signer, ed., *Humanity at the Limit: The Impact of the Holocaust Experience on Jews and Christians* (Bloomington: Indiana University Press, 2000), pp. 376–90.

Langbein, Hermann, *Menschen in Auschwitz* (Vienna: Europa Verlag, 1972).

——, *Uomini ad Auschwitz* (Milan: Mursia, 1984).

Lappin, Elena, 'The Man with Two Heads', *Granta*, 66 (1999): 7–66.

Laqueur, Walter, *The Terrible Secret* (London: Weidenfeld and Nicolson, 1980).

——, *Il terribile segreto* (Florence: La Giuntina, 1984).

[Lattes, Dante], 'Qualche parola di presentazione', *Rassegna mensile di Israel*, 14. 1 (April 1948): 3–5.

Lattes, Dante, 'Tu quoque Quasimodo?' *Rassegna mensile di Israel*, 1 (1961): 3–5.

La legislazione antiebraica in Italia e in Europa (Rome: Camera dei deputati, 1989).

Leoni, Giovanni, '"The First Blow": Projects for the Camp at Fossoli', in Geoffrey Hartman, ed., *Holocaust Remembrance: The Shapes of Memory* (Cambridge, MA: Blackwell, 1994), pp. 204–14.

Levi, Arrigo, 'Un singolare monumento per non far dimenticare. 2 mostre ammonitrici a Roma', *Corriere d'informazione*, 11 July 1959.

——, 'Una risposta alla Ginzburg', *La stampa*, 15 September 1972.

Levi, Lia, *Una bambina e basta* (Rome: E/O, 1994).

————, *Tutti i giorni di tua vita* (Milan: Mondadori, 1997).

————, *Che cos'è l'antisemitismo? Per favore, rispondete* (Milan: Mondadori, 2001).

Levi, Paolo, *Il filo della memoria* (Milan: Rizzoli, 1984).

Levi, Primo, *Se questo è un uomo* (Turin: De Silva, 1947; 2nd ed. Turin: Einaudi, 1958).

————, *If This Is a Man* (London: Orion, 1959).

————, 'Testimonianza per Eichmann', *Il ponte* 4 (1961): 646–50.

————, *La tregua* (Turin: Einaudi, 1963).

————, *The Truce* (London: Bodley Head, 1965).

————, *La tregua* (Turin: Einaudi 'Letture per la scuola media', 1965).

————, *Se questo è un uomo* (Turin: Einaudi 'Letture per la scuola media', 1973).

————, *Il sistema periodico* (Turin: Einaudi, 1975).

————, *La chiave a stella* (Turin: Einaudi, 1978).

————, *Il sistema periodico* (Turin: Einaudi 'Letture per la scuola media', 1979).

————, *Se non ora, quando?* (Turin: Einaudi, 1982).

————, *La chiave a stella*, ed. by G. L. Beccaria (Turin: Einaudi 'Letture per la scuola media', 1983).

————, *The Periodic Table* (New York: Schocken, 1984).

————, *If Not Now, When?* (New York: Summit, 1985).

————, *La ricerca delle radici* (Turin: Einaudi, 1985).

————, *I sommersi e i salvati* (Turin: Einaudi, 1986).

————, *The Drowned and the Saved* (London: Michael Joseph, 1988).

————, *Conversazioni ed interviste 1963–1987*, ed. by Marco Belpoliti (Turin: Einaudi, 1997).

————, *Opere*, vols. I–II, ed. by Marco Belpoliti (Turin: Einaudi, 1997).

————, *Voice of Memory: Interviews 1961–87*, ed. by Marco Belpoliti and Robert S. C. Gordon (Cambridge: Polity, 2000).

————, *Black Hole of Auschwitz* (Cambridge: Polity, 2005).

————, '"Deportazione e sterminio di ebrei" di Primo Levi, con una nota di Alberto Cavaglion', *Lo straniero*, 11. 85 (July 2007): 5–12.

————, et al., 'Tavola rotonda. La questione ebraica', *Storia illustrata*, June 1961, pp. 754–59.

Levy, Daniel, and Natan Sznaider, *Holocaust Memory in the Global Age* (Philadelphia: Temple University Press, 2006).

Lezioni sull'antifascismo (Rome-Bari: Laterza, 1960).

Liberal, 15–17 (June–August 1996).

Lichtner, Giacomo, *Film and the Shoah in France and Italy* (London: Vallentine Mitchell, 2008).

Lifton, Robert Jay, *The Nazi Doctors: Medical Killing and the Psychology of Genocide* (New York: Basic Books, 1986).

————, and Erik Markusen, *The Genocidal Mentality: Nazi Holocaust and Nuclear Threat* (New York: Basic Books, 1990).

Liggeri, Paolo, *Triangolo rosso* (Milan: La Casa, 1946).

Liucci, Raffaele, *La tentazione della 'casa in collina'. Il disimpegno degli intellet-tuali nella guerra civile italiana (1943–1945)* (Milan: Unicopli, 1999).

Loewenthal, Elena, 'Strascico di fumo', *La stampa*, 26 January 2001.

Longo, Alessandra, 'An divide i sopravvissuti', *La repubblica*, 27 January 2001.

———, 'Tullia Zevi e la Shoah tra lacrime e ricordi', *La repubblica*, 28 January 2001.

Loy, Rosetta, *La parola ebreo* (Turin: Einaudi, 1997).

Lucamante, Stefania, 'The "Indispensable" Legacy of Primo Levi: From Eraldo Affinati to Rosetta Loy Between History and Fiction', *Quaderni d'italianistica*, 24. 2 (2003): 87–104.

———, et al., eds., *Memoria collettiva e memoria privata: il ricordo della Shoah come political sociale* (Utrecht: Igitur, 2008).

Luppi, Marzia, and Elisabetta Ruffini, eds., *Immagini dal silenzio. La prima mostra nazionale dei Lager nazisti attraverso l'Italia 1955–1960* (Modena: Nuovagrafica, 2005).

Luzi, Gianluca, 'L'Italia ricorda la Shoah. Ciampi: non torni l'odio', *La repub-blica*, 27 January 2001.

Luzzatto, Amos, *Conta e racconta. Memorie di un ebreo di sinistra* (Milan: Mursia, 2008).

Luzzatto, G. L., 'Il giardino dei Finzi-Contini', *Rassegna mensile di Israel*, 5 (1962): 239–40.

Luzzatto, Sergio, *La crisi dell'antifascismo* (Turin: Einaudi, 2004).

'Lynching in Rome', *Life*, 9 October 1944, pp. 35–38.

MacCabe, Colin, 'Life Is Beautiful/La vita è bella', *Sight and Sound*, February 1999, p. 46.

Maechler, Stefan, *The Wilkomirski Affair* (New York: Schocken, 2000).

Magris, Claudio, *Lontano da dove: Joseph Roth e la tradizione ebraico-orientale* (Turin: Einaudi, 1971).

———, *Danubio* (Milan: Garzanti, 1986).

Maida, Bruno, ed., *Un' etica della testimonianza: la memoria della deportazione femminile e Lidia Beccaria Rolfi* (Milan: Franco Angeli/ANED, 1997).

Maier, Charles S., *The Unmasterable Past: History, Holocaust and German Na-tional Identity* (Cambridge, MA: Harvard University Press, 1988).

Malaparte, Curzio, *Kaputt* (Naples: Casella, 1944).

———, *Mamma marcia* (Florence: Vallecchi, 1959).

Manganelli, Giorgio, *UFO e altri oggetti non identificati: 1972–1990* (Rome: Quiritta, 2003).

Mangoni, Luisa, *Pensare i libri. La casa editrice Einaudi dagli anni trenta agli anni sessanta* (Turin: Bollati Boringhieri, 1999).

Marcoaldi, Franco, *Benjaminowo. Padre e figlio* (Milan: Bompiani, 2004).

Marcus, Millicent, *Italian Film in the Shadow of Auschwitz* (Toronto: Toronto University Press, 2007).

Marcuse, Harold, *Legacies of Dachau: The Uses and Abuses of a Concentration Camp, 1933–2001* (Cambridge: Cambridge University Press, 2001).

Marrus, Michael, *The Holocaust in History* (Harmondsworth: Penguin, 1987).

Maruffi, Ferruccio, 'La nascita delle associazioni di ex deportati' in Alberto Cavaglion, ed., *Il ritorno dai Lager* (Milan: Franco Angeli/ANED, 1993), pp. 65–79.

Matard-Bonucci, Marie-Anne, 'La Libération des camps de concentration et le retour des déportés à travers la presse quotidienne italienne', in Annette Wieviorka and Claude Mouchard, eds., *La Shoah. Témoignages, savoirs, oeuvres* (Orléans: Presses Universitaires de Vincennes, 1999), pp.101–14.

Matta, Tristano, *Un percorso della memoria. Guida ai luoghi della violenza nazista in Italia* (Milan: Electa, 1996).

Maurensig, Paolo, *La variante di Lüneberg* (Milan: Adelphi, 1993).

———, *Canone inverso* (Milan: Mondadori, 1997).

Mayda, Giuseppe, *Ebrei sotto Salò: la persecuzione antisemita 1943–1945* (Milan: Feltrinelli, 1978).

Memoria, Diario, special issue, 27 January 2003.

[Meneghello, Luigi], see also Varnai, Ugo.

Meneghello, Luigi, *Promemoria: lo sterminio degli ebrei d'Europa 1939–45* (Bologna: Il Mulino, 1994).

Meneghetti, Egidio, 'L'ebreeta', in *Cante in piassa* (Venice: Neri Pozza, 1955).

Mengoni, Martina, 'Variazioni Rumkowski', http://www.primolevi.it/Web/Italiano/Contenuti/Auschwitz/105_Sulla_%22zona_grigia%22 (accessed 1 December 2011).

Merzagora, Cesare, *I pavidi. Dalla costituzione alla costituente* (Milan: Istituto Editoriale Galileo, 1946).

Mezan, Margherita, 'Noi, testimoni della Shoah', *Corriere della sera*, 25 January 2001.

Mi ricordo, Diario, special issue, 27 January 2001.

Michaelis, Meir, *Mussolini and the Jews: German-Italian Relations and the Jewish Question in Italy, 1922–1945* (Oxford: Oxford University Press, 1978).

Millu, Liana, *Il fumo di Birkenau* (Florence: La Giuntina, 1979; 1st ed. 1947).

———, *I ponti di Schwerin* (Poggibonsi: Lalli, 1978).

Minerbi, Sergio, [n. t.], *L'espresso*, 30 April 1961.

———, *La belva in gabbia: Eichmann* (Milan: Longanesi, 1962).

———, *Risposta a Sergio Romano. Ebrei, Shoah e Stato d'Israele* (Florence: La Giuntina, 1998).

Mintz, Alan, *Popular Culture and the Shaping of Holocaust Memory in America* (Seattle: Washington University Press, 2001).

Misul, Frida, *Fra gli artigli del mostro nazista. La più romanzesca delle realtà il più realistico dei romanzi* (Livorno: Stab. poligrafico Belforte, 1946).

Mitscherlisch, Alexander, and Margarete Mitscherlisch, *The Inability to Mourn* (New York: Grove Press, 1975; 1st German ed. 1967).

Mitten, Richard, *The Politics of Antisemitic Prejudice: The Waldheim Phenomenon in Austria* (Boulder: Westview Press, 1992).

Molinari, Maurizio, *La sinistra e gli ebrei in Italia 1967–1993* (Milan: Corbaccio, 1995).

Momigliano, Eucardio, *40000 fuori legge* (Rome: Carboni, 1945), also published as *Storia tragica e grottesca del razzismo fascista* (Milan: Mondadori, 1946).

Montanelli, Indro, 'Pace all'anima sua', *Mercurio*, 2. 16 (December 1945): 220–23.

'Il monumento ai martiri di Auschwitz', *L'antifascista*, June 1959.

Monumento internazionale di Auschwitz (Rome: Galleria nazionale d'arte moderna, 1959).

Morandini, Giuliana, ed., *E allora mi hanno rinchiusa: testimonianze dal manicomio femminile* (Milan: Bompiani, 1977).

Morante, Elsa, *La storia* (Turin: Einaudi, 1974).

———, *Pro o contro la bomba atomica* (Milan: Adelphi, 1987).

Moravia, Alberto, 'Sempre amai il calore e la luce', *Mercurio*, 2.9 (May 1945): 93–100.

———, *L'uomo come fine e altri saggi* (Milan: Bompiani, 1964).

Morgan, Sarah, *Rappresaglie dopo la Resistenza: l'eccidio di Schio tra guerra civile e guerra fredda* (Milan: Bruno Mondadori, 2002).

Morrison, Toni, *Beloved* (New York: Plume, 1987).

Moyn, Samuel, *A Holocaust Controversy: The Treblinka Affair in Postwar France* (Waltham, MA: Brandeis University Press, 2005).

'Museo della Shoah, la luce di 7000 nomi', http://www.architettiroma.it/archweb/notizie/07694.aspx (accessed 10 June 2010).

'Museo virtuale delle intolleranze e degli stermini', http://www.istoreto.it/amis/museo.html (accessed 10 November 2011).

Mussgnug, Florian, 'Finire il mondo. Per un'analisi del romanzo apocalittico italiano degli anni 1970', *Contemporanea*, 1 (2000): 19–32.

Nevola, Gaspare, 'From the "Republic of Parties" to a "Fatherland for Italians": the Italian Political System in Search of a New Principle of Legitimation', *Journal of Modern Italian Studies*, 8. 2 (2003): 249–65.

New German Critique, special issue on *Holocaust*, 19 (Winter 1980).

Nezri Dufour, Sophie, *Primo Levi: una memoria ebraica del Novecento* (Florence: La Giuntina, 2002).

Nirenstajn, Alberto, *Ricorda che ti ha fatto Amalek* (Turin: Einaudi, 1958).

Nirenstein, Fiamma, *Gli antisemiti progressisti: una forma nuova di un odio antico* (Milan: Rizzoli, 2004).

Nissim, Luciana, and Pelagia Lewinska, *Donne contro il mostro* (Turin: Vincenzo Ramella Editore, 1946).

Nora, Pierre, ed., *Les Lieux de mémoire*, vols. I–III (Paris: Gallimard, 1984–1992).

Nothomb, Amélie, *Acide sulfurique* (Paris: Michel, 2005).

Novelli, Claudio, *Il Partito d'Azione e gli italiani. Moralità, politica e cittadinanza nella storia repubblicana* (Milan: La Nuova Italia, 2000).

Novick, Peter, *The Holocaust in American Life* (Boston: Houghton Mifflin, 1999).

L'oblio è colpa (Milan: ANED, 1954).

'L'ospedale del campo VII B per internati italiani in Germania', *Minerva medica*, 37/2. 51 (22 December 1946): 412–20.

Ottani, Giancarlo, *I campi della morte* (Milan: Perinetti Casoni, 1945).

——, *Un popolo piange. La tragedia degli ebrei italiani* (Milan: Spartaco Giovene, 1945).

Ottaviano, Chiara, 'Accademia e storia in TV. Una riflessione a partire dalle origini', in Nicola Gallerano, ed., *L'uso pubblico della storia* (Milan: Franco Angeli, 1995), pp. 83–102.

Paggi, Leonardo, 'Per una memoria europea dei crimini nazisti', *Passato e presente*, 12.32 (May–August 1994): 105–17.

——, ed., *Storia e memoria di un massacro ordinario* (Rome: Manifestolibri, 1996).

Pahor, Boris, *Necropoli* (San Canzian d'Isonzo: Consorzio culturale del Monfalconese, 1997).

Painter, Jr., Borden W., 'Renzo De Felice and the Historiography of Italian Fascism', *American Historical Review*, 95. 2 (April 1990): 391–405.

Pansa, Giampaolo, *I figli dell'aquila* (Milan: Sperling & Kupfer, 2002).

'Pantera nera', *L'espresso*, 16 April 1960.

Pantozzi, Aldo [8078–126520], *Sotto gli occhi della morte. Da Bolzano a Mauthausen* (Bolzano: Tip. Pio Mariz, 1946).

Pappalettera, Vincenzo, *Tu passerai per il camino* (Milan: Mursia, 1965).

Parlato, Valentino, 'Un boicottaggio sbagliato', *Il manifesto*, 24 January 2008.

Pasolini, Pier Paolo, *Opere*, vols. I–X, ed. by Walter Siti (Milan: Mondadori, 1998–2003).

Patriarca, Silvana, *Italian Vices: Nation and Character from the Risorgimento to the Republic* (Cambridge: Cambridge University Press, 2010).

Pavone, Claudio, *Una guerra civile: saggio storico sulla moralita nella Resistenza* (Turin: Bollati Boringhieri, 1991).

——, 'Caratteri e eredità della zona grigia', *Passato e presente*, 16.43 (January–April 1998): 5–12.

Paxton, Robert O., *La France di Vichy* (Paris: Seuil, 1973).

Peary, Gerald, 'No Laughing Matter', *Boston Phoenix*, 30 October 1998.

Perra, Emiliano, *Conflicts of Memory: The Reception of Holocaust Films and TV Programmes in Italy, 1945 to the Present* (Oxford: Peter Lang, 2010).

——, 'La prima guerra del Libano (1982) e la costruzione dell'ebreo come "altro" nel dibattito pubblico italiano', paper given at conference Language, Space and Otherness in Italy Since 1861, British School at Rome, June 2010.

Piazza, Bruno, *Perché gli altri dimenticano* (Milan: Feltrinelli, 1956).

Picciotto Fargion, Liliana, 'Eloisa e il CDEC', *Rassegna mensile di Israel*, 47.1–3 (January–June 1981): 9–44.

———, 'Le informazioni sulla "Soluzione finale" circolanti in Italia nel 1942–1943', *Rassegna mensile di Israel*, 55. 2–3 (May–December 1989): 331–36.

———, *Il libro della memoria. Gli ebrei deportati dall'Italia (1943–1945)* (Milan: Mursia, 2002; 1st ed. 1991)·

Pinay, Maurice, *Complotto contro la chiesa* (Rome: [n. p.], 1962).

Pischedda, Bruno, *La grande sera del mondo* (Turin: Aragno, 2004).

Pivato, Stefano, *Bella Ciao: canto e politica nella storia d'Italia* (Bari: Laterza, 2005).

Poli, Gabriella, and Giorgio Calcagno, *Echi di una voce perduta: incontri, interviste e conversazioni con Primo Levi* (Milan: Mursia, 1992).

Poliakov, Léon, *La Condition des juifs en France sous l'occupation italienne* (Paris: Centre de Documentation Juive Contemporaine, 1946).

———, *Bréviaire de la haine* (Paris: Calmann-Lévy, 1951).

———, *Il nazismo e lo sterminio degli ebrei* (Turin: Einaudi, 1955).

———, *Gli ebrei sotto l'occupazione italiana* (Milan: Edizioni di Comunità, 1956).

———, *Auschwitz* (Rome: Veutro, 1968).

Portelli, Alessandro, *L'ordine è già stato eseguito: Roma, le fosse Ardeatine, la memoria* (Rome: Donzelli, 1999).

———, 'The Centre Cannot Hold: Music as Political Communication in Post-War Italy', in Luciano Cheles and Lucio Sponza, eds. *The Art of Persuasion: Political Communication in Italy from 1945 to the 1990s* (Manchester: Manchester University Press, 2001), pp. 258–77.

'Presentazione di un giovane deportato castrato nel campo di Auschwitz nel 1943', *Minerva medica*, 36. 32 (18 August 1945): 54.

Pressburger, Giorgio, *Nel regno oscuro* (Milan: Bompiani, 2008).

———, and Nicola Pressburger, *Storie dell'ottavo distretto* (Casale Monferrato: Marietti, 1986).

Presser, Jacob, *La notte dei girondini* (Milan: Adelphi, 1976; 1st Dutch ed. 1957).

Probst, Lothar, 'Founding Myths in Europe and the Role of the Holocaust', *New German Critique*, 90 (Autumn 2003): 45–58.

Pugliese, Stanislao, *Bitter Spring: A Life of Ignazio Silone* (New York: Farrar, Straus and Giroux, 2009).

Pupo, Raoul, and Roberto Spazzali, *Foibe* (Milan: Bruno Mondadori, 2003).

Quasimodo, Salvatore, *Il falso e vero verde* (Milan: Mondadori, 1956).

Rava, Enzo, *Martirio* (Genoa: Mario Ceva, 1945).

Reitlinger, Gerald, *The Final Solution: The Attempt to Exterminate the Jews of Europe, 1939–1945* (London: Vallentine Mitchell, 1953).

———, 'Pagavano la propria morte', *Storia illustrata*, June 1961, pp. 762–84.

———, *La soluzione finale* (Milan: Il Saggiatore, 1962).

Revelli, Nuto, *Il disperso di Marburg* (Turin: Einaudi, 1994).

Rigoni Stern, Mario, *Il sergente della neve* (Turin: Einaudi, 1953).

Ringelblum, Emanuel, *Sepolti a Varsavia* (Milan: Mondadori, 1962).

Rivette, Jacques, 'De l'abjection', *Cahiers du cinéma*, 120 (June 1961): 54–55.

Rodogno, Davide, '*Italiani brava gente?* Fascist Italy's Policy Towards the Jews in the Balkans, April 1941–July 1943', *European History Quarterly*, 35. 2 (2005): 213–40.

Rohmer, Charles, *L'altro* (Turin: Einaudi, 1954; 1st French ed. 1951).

Romana Castelli, Francesca, 'Un monumento diventato simbolo', *Capitolium*, 6. 21 (March–April 2002): 75–81.

Romano, Giorgio, *Rassegna mensile di Israel*, 5 (1960): 228.

Romano, Sergio, *Lettera a un amico ebreo* (Milan: Longanesi, 1997).

Rose, Gillian, 'Beginnings of the Day: Fascism and Representation', in *Mourning Becomes the Law: Philosophy and Representation* (Cambridge: Cambridge University Press 1996), pp. 41–62.

Rosenbaum, Alan, ed., *Is the Holocaust Unique? Perspectives on Comparative Genocide* (Boulder: Westview, 2009).

Rossi-Doria, Anna, *Memoria e storia. Il caso della deportazione* (Rubbettino: Catzanaro, 1998).

Rothberg, Michael, *Multidirectional Memory: Remembering the Holocaust in the Age of Decolonization* (Stanford: Stanford University Press, 2009).

Rousset, David, *L'Univers concentrationnaire* (Paris: Editions du Pavois, 1946).

Rovelli, Marco, *Lager italiani* (Milan: Rizzoli, 2006).

Rubin Suleiman, Susan, *Crises of Memory and the Second World War* (Cambridge, MA: Harvard University Press, 2006).

Rubinowicz, David, *Il diario* (Turin: Einaudi, 1960).

Ruffini, Elisabetta, and Sandro Scarrocchia, 'Il Blocco 21 di Auschwitz: un cantiere di riflessione e di lavoro', *Studi e ricerche di storia contemporanea*, 69 (June 2008): 9–32.

Russell, Lord, of Liverpool, *The Scourge of the Swastika* (London: Cassell, 1954).

———, *Il flagello della svastica* (Milan: Feltrinelli, 1955).

Saba, Umberto, *Scorciatoie e raccontini* (Milan: Mondadori, 1946).

Salvatici, Silvia, *Senza casa e senza paese. Profughi europei nel secondo dopoguerra* (Bologna: Il Mulino, 2008).

Santerini, Milena, *Antisemitismo senza memoria. Insegnare la Shoah nella società multiculturale* (Rome: Carocci, 2005).

Sarfatti, Michele, *Gli ebrei nell'Italia fascista. Vicende, identità, persecuzione* (Turin: Einaudi, 2000).

———, 'Ecco perché volgiamo ricordare', *La repubblica*, 26 January 2001.

———, 'Razzisti per ordine superiore', in *Mi ricordo*, 2001, pp. 78–81.

———, *La Shoah in Italia. La persecuzione degli ebrei sotto il fascismo* (Turin, Einaudi, 2005).

———, 'La Shoah e le case della memoria', *L'Unità*, 17 January 2007.

Scarpa, Domenico, 'Storie di libri necessari. Antelme, Duras, Vittorini' in *Storie avventurose di libri necessari* (Rome: Gaffi, 2010), pp. 165–202.

Scheper-Hughes, Nancy, and Anne M. Lovell, eds., *Psychiatry Inside-Out: Selected Writings of Franco Basaglia* (New York: Columbia University Press, 1987).

Schickel, Richard, 'Fascist Fable', *Time*, 9 November 1998, pp. 116–17.

Schneider, Helga, *Lasciami andare, madre* (Milan: Adelphi, 2001).

Schwarz, Guri, 'L'elaborazione del lutto. La classe dirigente ebraica e la memoria dello sterminio (1944–1948)', in Michele Sarfatti, ed., *Il ritorno alla vita: vicende e diritti degli ebrei in Italia dopo la seconda guerra mondiale* (Florence: Giuntina, 1998), pp. 167–80.

———, *Ritrovare se stessi. Gli ebrei nell'Italia postfascista* (Bari: Laterza, 2004).

Schwarz-Bart, André, *L'ultimo dei giusti* (Milan: Feltrinelli, 1960; 1st French ed. 1959).

Sciascia, Leonardo, 'Nota', in Alessandro Manzoni, *Storia della colonna infame* (Palermo: Sellerio, 1981), pp. 169–90.

'Scuola e Shoah', http://archivio.pubblica.istruzione.it/shoah/didattica/index.shtml (accessed 14 December 2010).

Segev, Tom, *The Seventh Million: The Israelis and the Holocaust* (New York: Holt, 1991).

Seghers, Anna, *La settima croce* (Milan: Mondadori, 1947).

Il segno della memoria 1945–1995. BBPR: monumento ai caduti nei campi nazisti (Milan: Electa, 1995).

Segre, Cesare, '*Se questo è un uomo* di Primo Levi' in Alberto Asor Rosa, ed., *Letteratura italiana. Le opere IV. Novecento. II. La ricerca letteraria* (Turin: Einaudi, 1996), pp. 491–508.

———, 'Olocausto, il ricordo e il monito', *Corriere della sera*, 28 January 2001.

Segre, Vittorio, *Storia di un ebreo fortunato* (Milan: Bompiani, 1985).

Sémelin, Jacques, *Sans armes face à Hitler. La Résistance civile en Europe (1939–1943)* (Paris: Pavot, 1989).

Sereni, Clara, *Casalinghitudine* (Turin: Einaudi, 1987).

Sereny, Gitta, *Into That Darkness* (London: Deutsch, 1974).

Serri, Mirella, *I redenti* (Milan: Corbaccio, 2005).

Shandler, Jeffrey, *While America Watches: Televising the Holocaust* (New York: Oxford University Press, 1999).

Shandley, Robert R., ed., *Unwilling Germans? The Goldhagen Debate* (Minneapolis: University of Minnesota Press, 1998).

Shirer, William L., *The Rise and Fall of the Third Reich* (New York: Simon and Schuster, 1960).

———, *Storia del Terzo Reich* (Turin: Einaudi, 1962).

Siegrist, Ettore, *Dachau. Dimenticare sarebbe una colpa* (Genoa: Sampierdarena/ Stab. grafici Federico Reale, 1945).

Simoncini, Giorgio, 'Il monumento di Auschwitz Birkenau. Cronologia del concorso e della costruzione', www.giorgiosimoncini.com/pdf/AWZ.Int. Crono logia.pdf (accessed 1 October 2010).

———, 'Il monumento di Auschwitz Birkenau. Rassegna di documenti', http://www.giorgiosimoncini.com/rassegna.html (accessed 10 October 2010).

SISSCO, 'Programmi e curriculi di storia', http://www.sissco.it/index.php?id =1161 (accessed 14 December 2010).

Sluga, Glenda, 'The Risiera di San Sabba: Fascism, anti-Fascism and Italian nationalism', *Journal of Modern Italian Studies*, 1. 3 (1996): 401–12.

Snow, C. P., *The Two Cultures*, ed. by Stefan Collini (Cambridge: Cambridge University Press, 1993).

Snyder, Timothy, *Bloodlands: Europe Between Hitler and Stalin* (New York: Basic Books, 2010).

Sodi, Risa, 'The Holocaust in Italian Literature', Ph.D. dissertation, Yale University, 1995.

———, *Narrative and Imperative: The First Fifty Years of Italian Holocaust Writing (1944–1994)* (New York: Peter Lang, 2007).

Sofri, Adriano, 'Le caverne dell'orrore', in *Mi ricordo*, pp. 58–62 (also published as 'Lager e *Foibe*, il derby dell'orrore', *La stampa*, 26 January 2001).

Sonnino, Piera, *Questo è stato: una famiglia italiana nei lager* (Milan: Il Saggiatore, 2004).

Speelman, Raniero, et al., eds., *Contemporary Jewish Writers in Italy: A Generational Approach* (Utrecht: Igitur, 2007).

Spiegelman, Art, *Maus: A Survivor's Tale*, vols. I–II (New York: Penguin, 1987, 1991).

———, 'Sketchbook', *New Yorker*, 15 March 1999, pp. 96–99.

Spinosa, Antonio, 'Le persecuzioni razziali in Italia (I–IV)': *Il ponte*, 7 (1952): 964–78; 8 (1952): 1078–96; 11 (1952): 1604–22; 7 (1953): 950–68.

Springer, Elisa, *Il silenzio dei vivi: all'ombra di Auschwitz un racconto di morte e resurrezione* (Venice: Marsilio, 1997).

[S. Su], 'Tempo di belve', *Italia domani*, 12 July 1959.

Steinberg, Jonathan, *All or Nothing: The Axis and the Holocaust 1941–43* (London: Routledge, 1990).

Steiner, George, 'Postscript', in *Language and Silence* (London: Faber and Faber, 1985).

Steinlauf, Michael C., *Bondage to the Dead: Poland and the Memory of the Holocaust* (Syracuse: Syracuse University Press, 1997).

Stille, Alexander, *Benevolence and Betrayal: Five Italian Jewish Families Under Fascism* (New York: Summit Books, 1991).

———, *Uno su mille: cinque famiglie ebraiche durante il fascismo* (Milan: Mondadori, 1991).

Stonor Saunders, Frances, *Who Paid the Piper? The CIA and the Cultural Cold War* (London: Granta, 1999).

Storia vissuta (Milan: Franco Angeli/ANED, 1988).

Sullam Calimani, Anna-Vera, *I nomi dello sterminio* (Turin: Einaudi, 2001).

Svevo, Italo, *La coscienza di Zeno* (Milan: Mondadori, 2010; 1st ed. 1923).

Tamaro, Susanna, *Per voce sola* (Venice: Marsilio, 1991).

Tarzizzo, Domenico, ed., *Ideologia della morte. Storia e documenti dei campi di sterminio* (Milan: Il Saggiatore, 1962).

Tedeschi, Giuliana, *Questo povero corpo* (Milan: EdIt, 1946).

——, *C'è un punto della terra . . . : una donna nel lager di Birkenau* (Florence: La Giuntina, 1988).

Les Tempes modernes, special Italian issue, ed. by Elio Vittorini, 2. 23–4 (August–September 1947).

Teodori, Massimo, *Benedetti americani. Dall'Alleanza Atlantica alla Guerra contro il terrorismo* (Milan, Mondadori, 2003).

Teofilo, 'Quante Shoah nel calendario degli ebrei', *La stampa* (Turin supplement), 26 January 2001.

Thomson, Ian, *Primo Levi* (London: Hutchinson, 2002).

Toscano, Mario, ed., *L'abrogazione delle leggi razziali in Italia, 1943–1987* (Rome: Studi del Senato della Repubblica, 1988).

——, 'The Abrogation of Racial Laws and the Reintegration of Jews in Italian Society (1943–1948)', in David Bankier, ed., *The Jews Are Coming Back: The Return of the Jews to Their Countries of Origin After WW II* (New York/Jerusalem: Berghahn/Yad Vashem, 2005), pp. 148–68.

Traverso, Enzo, ed., *Insegnare Auschwitz* (Turin: Bollati Boringhieri, 1995).

Trent'anni di storia italiana: 1915–1945. Dall'antifascismo alla Resistenza (Turin: Einaudi, 1961).

Ulivelli, Francesco, *Bolzano: anticamera della morte* (Milan: Edizioni Stellissima, 1946).

Valabrega, Guido, ed., *Gli ebrei in italia durante il fascismo*, vols. I–III (Milan: CDEC, 1961–1963).

Valabrega, Paola, 'Primo Levi e la tradizione ebraico-orientale', *Studi piemontesi*, 11. 2 (1982): 296–310.

Valech Capozzi, Alba, *A 24029* (Siena: Soc. An. Poligrafica, 1946).

van der Knaap, Ewout, ed., *Uncovering the Holocaust: The International Reception of* Night and Fog (London: Wallflower, 2006).

Varnai, Ugo [pseud. Luigi Meneghello], 'Lo sterminio degli ebrei d'Europa (I–III)', *Comunità*, 7. 22 (December 1953): 16–23; 7. 23 (February 1954): 10–15; 7. 24 (April 1954): 36–39.

Vassalli, Sebastiano, 'Se va in onda la destra', *Corriere della Sera*, 30 September 2000.

Ventresca, Robert, 'Mussolini's Ghost: Italy's Duce in History and Memory', *History and Memory*, 18.1 (Spring–Summer 2006): 86–119.

Vianelli, Luigi, 'I negazionisti italiani', *Olokaustos,* http://www.olokaustos.org/saggi/saggi/negaz-ita/index.htm (accessed 14 December 2010).

Viano, Maurizio, '*Life Is Beautiful*: Reception, Allegory, and Holocaust Laughter', *Jewish Social Studies,* 5. 3 (1999): 47–66.

'La vicenda del Memoriale italiano di Auschwitz', *Studi e ricerche di storia contemporanea,* special issue, 74 (February 2011).

Vidal-Nacquet, Pierre, *Assassins of Memory* (New York: Columbia University Press, 1992).

Villa, Cristina, '. . . e Mnemosine, confusa e smarrita, vaga tra le rovine. Monumenti e luoghi della memoria della deportazione razziale in Italia', in Lucamante, *Memoria,* pp. 181–92.

'"La vita è bella" stravince la serata televisiva', *La repubblica,* 23 October 2001.

Vittorini, Elio, *Conversazione in Sicilia* (Milan: Bompiani, 1945; 1st ed. 1941).

———, *Uomini e no* (Milan: Bompiani, 1945).

Vivanti, Corrado, ed., *Gli ebrei in Italia,* vols. XI.1–2 of *Storia d'Italia* (Turin: Einaudi, 1996–97).

Volponi, Paolo, *Memoriale* (Milan: Garzanti, 1962).

Ward, David, *Antifascisms. Cultural Politics in Italy, 1943–46: Benedetto Croce and the Liberals, Carlo Levi and the 'Actionists'* (Madison, N.J.: Fairleigh Dickinson University Press, 1996).

'We Remember: A Reflection on the Shoah', http://www.vatican.va/roman_curia/pontifical_councils/chrstuni/documents/rc_pc_chrstuni_doc_16031998_shoah_en.html (accessed 1 November 2010).

Wiechert, Ernst, *La selva dei morti* (Milan: Mondadori, 1947).

Wiedmer, Caroline, *The Claims of Memory: Representations of the Holocaust in Contemporary Germany and France* (Ithaca, NY: Cornell University Press, 1999).

Wiesel, Elie, *La notte* (Florence: La Giuntina, 1980; 1st French ed. 1958).

Wiesenthal, Simon, *Gli assassini sono tra noi* (Milan: Garzanti, 1967).

———, *Il girasole* (Milan: Garzanti, 1970).

———, *The Sunflower* (New York: Schocken, 1998).

Wieviorka, Annette, *Déportation et génocide* (Paris: Plon, 1992).

———, *L'Ere du témoin* (Paris: Plon, 1998).

———, *Auschwitz spiegato a mia figlia* (Turin: Einaudi, 1999).

Wilkomirski, Binjamin, *Frantumi: un'infanzia, 1939–1948* (Milan: CDE, 1996).

Wolf, Joan B., *Harnessing the Holocaust: The Politics of Memory in France* (Stanford: Stanford University Press, 2004).

Wood, Nancy, 'The Victim's Resentments', in Cheyette and Marcus, pp. 257–67.

———, *Vectors of Memory: Legacies of Trauma in Postwar Europe* (New York: Berg, 1999).

Woolf, Stuart, 'Primo Levi's Sense of History', *Journal of Modern Italian Studies,* 3. 3 (Fall 1998): 273–92.

Wyman, David S., and Charles H. Rosenzveig, eds., *The World Reacts to the Holocaust* (Baltimore: Johns Hopkins University Press, 1997).

Young, James, *The Texture of Memory: Holocaust Memorials and Meaning* (New Haven: Yale University Press, 1993).

Zargani, Aldo, *Per violino solo* (Bologna: Il Mulino, 1995).

Zelizer, Barbie, *Remembering to Forget: Holocaust Memory Through the Camera's Eye* (Chicago: Chicago University Press, 1998).

Zertal, Idith, *Israel's Holocaust and the Politics of Nationhood* (Cambridge: Cambridge University Press, 2005).

Zevi, Luca, 'Fabio Mauri, metafora del cammino della memoria della Shoah', in Lucamante, pp. 205-17.

Zimmerman, Joshua, ed., *Jews in Italy Under Fascist and Nazi Rule, 1922–1945* (Cambridge: Cambridge University Press, 2005).

Zuccotti, Susan, *Under His Very Windows: The Vatican and the Holocaust in Italy* (New Haven: Yale University Press, 2000).

4. Audio

De Gregori, Francesco, *Amore nel pomeriggio* (2001).

Dylan, Bob, *The Freewheelin' Bob Dylan* (1963).

———, *The Times They Are A-Changin'* (1964).

———, *Highway 61 Revisited* (1965).

Guccini, Francesco, *Folk Beat N. 1* (1967).

Mea, Ivan, *Se qualcuno ti fa morto* (1972), http://www.cantilotta.org/canti_lager /07.htm (accessed 12 September 2010).

Nono, Luigi, *Ricorda cosa ti hanno fatto in Auschwitz* (1966), http://www.luigi nono.it/it/luigi-nono/opere/ricorda-cosa-ti-hanno-fatto-in-auschwitz (accessed 1 December 2010).

Ovadia, Moni, *Dybbuk* (1995).

5. Cinema

All'armi siamo fascisti (dir. Lino del Fra, 1961).

Andremo in città (dir. Nelo Risi, 1966).

La battaglia d'Algeri (dir. Gillo Pontecorvo, 1966).

La caduta degli dei (dir. Luchino Visconti, 1969).

Canone inverso (dir. Ricky Tognazzi, 2000).

Captain Corelli's Mandolin (dir. John Madden, 2001).

Le Chagrin et la pitié (dir. Marcel Ophuls, 1971).

Il cielo cade (dir. Andrea and Antonio Frazzi, 2000).

Concorrenza sleale (dir. Ettore Scola, 2001).

Diario di un italiano (dir. Sergio Capogna, 1973).

Diary of Anne Frank (dir. George Stevens, 1959).

L'ebreo errante (dir. Goffredo Alessandrini, 1948).
La finestra di fronte (dir. Ferzan Ozpetek, 2003).
Il Generale della Rovere (dir. Roberto Rossellini, 1959).
Il giardino dei Finzi-Contini (dir. Vittorio De Sica, 1970).
Hotel Meina (dir. Carlo Lizzani, 2007).
Italiani brava gente (dir. Giuseppe De Santis, 1964).
Jakob the Liar (dir. Peter Kassovitz, 1999).
Kapò (dir. Gillo Pontecorvo, 1959).
Massacre in Rome (dir. George Pan Cosmatos, 1973).
Memoria (dir. Ruggiero Gabbai, 1997).
La Nuit et le brouillard (dir. Alain Resnais, 1955).
Ogro (dir. Gillo Pontecorvo, 1979).
L'oro di Roma (dir. Carlo Lizzani, 1961).
Pasqualino settebellezze (dir. Lina Wertmüller, 1975).
The Pianist (dir. Roman Polanski, 2002).
Porcile (dir. Pier Paolo Pasolini, 1969).
Il portiere di notte (dir. Liliana Cavani, 1974).
Queimada (dir. Gillo Pontecorvo, 1969).
Salò o le 120 giornate di Sodoma (dir. Pier Paolo Pasolini, 1975).
Schindler's List (dir. Steven Spielberg, 1994).
Shoah (dir. Claude Lanzmann, 1985).
La strada di Levi (dir. Davide Ferrario, 2006).
Train de vie (dir. Radu Mihaileanu, 1998).
La tregua (dir. Francesco Rosi, 1997).
Tutti a casa (dir. Luigi Comencini, 1960).
Vaghe stelle dell'orsa (dir. Luchino Visconti, 1965).
Il vangelo secondo Matteo (dir. Pier Paolo Pasolini, 1964).
La vita è bella (dir. Roberto Benigni, 1997).

6. Television

Combat Film (dir. Roberto Olla and Leonardo Valente, RAI 1, 1994).
Il coraggio e la pietà (dir. Nicola Carracciolo, RAI 2, 1986).
Holocaust (NBC, 1978).
'Omaggio a Giorgio Perlasca', *Mixer* (RAI 1, April 1990).
Perlasca. Un eroe italiano (dir. Alberto Negrin, RAI Fiction, 2002).
Roots (ABC, 1977).
Storia del terzo Reich (dir. Liliana Cavani, RAI 2, 1961–62).
World at War (prod. Jeremy Isaacs et al., Thames Television, 1973–74).

Index